Empires of Love

Empires of Love

EUROPE, ASIA, AND THE MAKING
OF EARLY MODERN IDENTITY

Carmen Nocentelli

*To Diana,
whose spirit of adventure
is a constant source of
inspiration*

Carmen

PENN

UNIVERSITY OF PENNSYLVANIA PRESS   *Philadelphia*

THIS BOOK IS MADE POSSIBLE BY A COLLABORATIVE GRANT
FROM THE ANDREW W. MELLON FOUNDATION.

© 2013 University of Pennsylvania Press

Published by
University of Pennsylvania Press
Philadelphia, Pennsylvania 19104-4112
www.upenn.edu/pennpress

Printed in the United States of America
on acid-free paper

10 9 8 7 6 5 4 3 2 1

Library of Congress Cataloging-in-Publication Data

Nocentelli, Carmen.
    Empires of love : Europe, Asia, and the making of
early modern identity / Carmen Nocentelli. — 1st ed.
        p. cm.
    Includes bibliographical references and index.
    ISBN 978-0-8122-4483-0 (hardcover : alk. paper)
    1. Sex customs—Europe—History—16th century.
2. Sex customs—Europe—History—17th century.
3. Sex customs—South Asia—History—16th century.
4. Sex customs—South Asia—History—17th century.
5. Europeans—Ethnic identity—History—16th
century. 6. Europeans—Ethnic identity—History—
17th century. 7. South Asians—Ethnic identity—
History—16th century. 8. South Asians—Ethnic
identity—History—17th century. 9. Europe—
Colonies—Race relations—History—16th century.
10. Europe—Colonies—Race relations—History—
17th century. I. Title.
HQ18.E8N63 2013
306.77—dc23
                                            2012030906

For Sam

CONTENTS

NOTE ON QUOTATIONS
AND TRANSLATIONS

Foreign language passages in verse are quoted in the original language, followed by an English translation. Passages in prose are quoted in English translation, followed, wherever pertinent, by quotations in the original language. In quoting from print sources, I have expanded abbreviations and distinguished between *u* and *v* but otherwise retained authorial spelling and punctuation. In quoting from manuscript sources, I have amended a few scribal errors and occasionally added punctuation to clarify the meaning.

Unless otherwise noted, all translations are my own, if possible in consultation with published English translations. In a few instances I have silently amended the published translation to supply a more literal reading.

Introduction

Around the year 1625, the birth of a child revealed a secret liaison between John Leachland, an English East India Company factor at Surat, and an Indian woman named Mānyā. When company officials pressured him into leaving her, Leachland refused, wishing "rather to be suspended the Companys service and Wages, then to be constrayned to abandon her Conversacyon."[1] On 20 February 1626, Leachland had his wish, and was suspended. He was not, however, subjected to further discipline: anything more severe than cashiering, it was feared, would simply "have hastened his marrying to her and for consequentlye have forsaken his Country and freinds or, in case of faile therof, to some other desperate undertaking to his aparente Ruine."[2]

Such an outcome East India Company officials were obviously keen on avoiding: at a time when few employees survived their terms of service, Leachland boasted ten years of experience, having arrived in India in 1615 as a purser's mate on the ship *Expedition*. Three years later, he had joined the Ahmedabad factory as a buyer of silks, an occupation for which he seems to have had skill and training.[3] Between 1621 and 1623 he served at Burhānpur, Baroda, Ahmedabad, and Cambay, acquitting himself well enough to have his wages increased.[4] Despite his affective foibles, in short, Leachland remained a man "of fayre demeanor, sufficient Abillities, and cleare of Accounts with the Honorable Company in India"—a combination of qualities that made him especially valuable. No wonder his superiors held out the hope that he might be reclaimed and made "sensible of his owne Errors."[5]

The hoped-for change of heart did not occur, though, for in 1632 John and Mānyā were still together, eking out a precarious existence on the margins of the East India Company community at Surat. Because of a labor shortage following the famine and pestilence of 1630–33, John had been contracted for some convoy work, but had not been fully reinstated.[6] The English traveler Peter Mundy, who accompanied him on a trip to Agra, summed up his story in the following terms: "Mr John Leachland, an Englishman, sometymes the Companies servant, haveing done prime offices, for the love of an Indian Woman refused to returne to his Countrie . . . and soe lives with her in Suratt, by whome hee had sundrie Children; and by reason of the great mortallitie [of 1630–33] hee was imployed in the forementioned service, haveing now noe referrence to them [the Company], but lives of himselfe. The English sometyme resort to his howse to visitt him and to passe away the tyme."[7]

Leachland died in poverty not long after Mundy penned his story, but the legacy of his affections would haunt East India Company officials for years to come. They especially worried about John's half-English daughter, for both her sake and "the honor of our religion and nacion."[8] She had been baptized as Mary Leachland and was being raised as a Christian, but English authorities in India still worried that she might "perish"—as Surat president William Methwold put it in a 1634 letter—in the care of her mother, since the latter was "undoubtedly a most wicked woman."[9] Repeated overtures were made to obtain custody of the child; when it became apparent that Mānyā was unwilling to part from her daughter, the directors in London went so far as to contemplate a plan for Mary's abduction, instructing factors at Surat "to gett possession of the daughter of the said Leachland, which hee had by an Indian, and to send her for England by the next shipps."[10] In response, mother and daughter disappeared, and nothing is known about the pair until 1643, when Mānyā petitioned President Francis Breton for permission to marry her daughter to an Englishman named William Appleton. Although this was "a new thing never before desired or granted," East India Company officials thought well to condescend to the request.[11] As Breton himself explained in a report to London, it was nothing short of a miracle that Mary Leachland still retained her virtue, "though shee wanted not provocations enough from her mother to tempt her to prostitution."[12] Marrying her off had seemed to those concerned the best way to spare the girl from corruption, and keep "her honor and honesty unteinted."[13] By January of the following year,

Mary Leachland and William Appleton had been joined in marriage by the English minister at Surat, where the couple was, by all reports, "poorly yet honestly and decently subsist[ing]."[14]

Spanning two generations, the Leachland story affords a rare glimpse into what Ann Laura Stoler has called "the sexual interface" of Europe's expansion overseas—the often-improvisational system of sexual prescriptions underwriting the practices and discourses of Europe's presence abroad.[15] Admittedly, it is no more than a glimpse. The protagonists never get to speak for themselves, and crucial aspects of their drama remain opaque at best. We never learn, for instance, what made Mānyā "a most wicked woman," or why John's relationship to her was so unpalatable as to warrant his suspension from service. It is true that the early East India Company looked none too kindly on the expenditures and distractions that women could cause: standing orders stipulated that any employee found to have a wife in the East should "uppon knowledge thereof be forthwith dismissed of his place and service and sent home."[16] Yet there is evidence that at least some company employees brought their wives overseas, and that many more established long-term liaisons with local women. Just as Leachland was being cashiered, East India Company factors in Japan were taking wives and mistresses from among the local population without much fuss, stigma, or repercussion.[17] Nor was Japan the only place where this happened. William Hawkins, who led a diplomatic mission to India in 1608, wedded an Armenian Christian from the Mughal court.[18] Gabriel Boughton, the surgeon credited with opening trade with Bengal, wedded "a Mogullana or Morish woman"; and gossip had it that Francis Day, one of the founders of Madras, chose the site because it was near his mistress's home.[19] Against this background, John and Mānyā's relationship stands out only because of the attention—and resistance—that it elicited.

The British official and amateur anthropologist Richard C. Temple, who at the beginning of the twentieth century traced the outline of John and Mānyā's story, chalked up this resistance to the "irregular nature" of the liaison.[20] But the record does not seem to support this hypothesis: as a matter of fact, some of the documents that have come down to us unequivocally identify Mānyā as Leachland's wife, suggesting that at least a few people must have regarded the couple's union as legitimate.[21] If there is one problem the documents hint at with some insistence, it is that East India Company officials saw Mānyā as sexually suspect, if not outright deviant. Not only did they define her as "most wicked," they also indicted her as a prostitute—a term that, as Ruth Karras has argued, denoted just as much a deviant sexuality as a professional occupation. The fact that prostitutes took money for sex, in fact, was often secondary to the fact that they made themselves generally available to men. It was this promiscuity that defined them, marking them off as a category of women whose sexuality was quite literally out of (patriarchal) control.[22]

Mānyā's alleged promiscuity likely informed the efforts made to separate the mother from the daughter, and was certainly a factor in the decision to license Mary's marriage to William Appleton. There is also evidence, however, that issues of sexual propriety were never too far away from issues of racial belonging. The Court of Committees, for one, seems to have kept Mānyā's Indianness firmly in sight: missives from London identify her neither as John's wife nor as Mary's mother, but rather as "an Indian" by whom John Leachland happened to have a daughter. Issues of racial belonging also informed the decisions made by East India Company authorities at Surat—or at least the letters in which they reported on those decisions. It is certainly significant that they regarded John's possible marriage to Mānyā as a renunciation of identity, a "desperate undertaking" that would set him adrift from his country and friends.[23] Even more significant, perhaps, is their belief that Mary's honor could be best safeguarded by being palmed off onto an Englishman, despite the fact that a similar course of action had conspicuously failed to safeguard her mother's reputation. If Francis Breton and his fellow East India Company officers failed to grasp the irony of the situation, it was likely because they saw a fundamental difference between Mānyā and her daughter: the former was an Indian, whereas the latter could claim partial English ancestry. Being married to an Englishman according to the rites and ceremonies of the Anglican Church vivified that heritage, serving simultaneously as a guarantee of sexual probity and a marker of racial identity.

How did perceptions of sexual propriety inflect ascriptions of racial difference during the early modern period? And how did ascriptions of racial difference affect the boundaries of proper sexuality? Taking these questions as a point of departure, *Empires of Love* charts Europe's fascination with the eros of "India"—as the vast coastal stretch from the Gulf of Aden to the South China Sea was then often called—and explores how it shaped the ways Europeans imagined and represented their own sexual and racial identities.[24] It argues that this fascination was not only about policing the contact zone but also, and just as pressingly, about "inventing" European sexuality. Resisting the tendency to view sexual ideologies as if they emerged, fully formed, from within Europe alone, it proposes that the European-Asian encounter deeply inflected the ways in which the West came to define what was acceptable in matters of eros.

In doing so, *Empires of Love* also participates in a broader effort to read race and sexuality together, as overlapping structures of identity rather than as parallel or analogous analytic spheres. Since the early 1990s, when Judith Butler asked how we might go beyond juxtaposing "race," "sexuality," and "sexual difference" to think about their relation to one another, several excellent studies have taken up this challenge.[25] But while scholars have devoted much attention to post-Enlightenment intersections of race and sexuality, we are only beginning to study how eros and ethnos intersected during the sixteenth and seventeenth centuries.[26] Given my training as a literary scholar, *Empires of Love* participates in this endeavor by scrutinizing discursive domains that are particularly amenable to the methods of literary criticism—historical chronicles, epic poetry, travel narratives, and secular drama—but it also complements this focus by reference to illustrations, private correspondence, colonial legislation, and military reports.

Because I understand both race and sexuality as cultural constructs that are always context-bound and historically contingent, I employ these terms without quotation marks, with the obvious caveat that neither one of them should be understood to mean what it generally means today—or, to be more precise, that neither one should be expected to match the nineteenth-century epistemologies that still underwrite current understandings of both categories.[27] Race, for instance, was less a category of biological difference than a broad spectrum of practices and discourses concerned with religious affiliation, cultural habitus, geographic origin, and humoral composition.[28] Likewise, sixteenth- and seventeenth-century understandings of sexuality revolved less around notions of sexual orientation than around an interlocking set of marital injunctions and proscriptions against nonreproductive sex.[29] The marital injunctions combined a reproductive mandate with an effort to regulate spousal intimacies; the proscriptions against nonreproductive sex included not only a rigorous interdiction of sodomy—itself an "utterly confused category" that ran the gamut from zoophilia to interfaith copulation—but also prohibitions against *coitus interruptus* and sexual positions held to inhibit conception.[30]

As unfamiliar as they may appear, such constructions of race and sexuality hardly require us to postulate an absolute discontinuity between past and present. Part of what sustains this project is the belief that the economic, political, and cultural developments associated with early modernity are still very much part of our world, and that this world cannot be adequately apprehended without attending to the recyclings and reinscriptions that brought it into being. As Ania Loomba has noted, race as an identitarian category did not suddenly spring into existence during the eighteenth and nineteenth centuries; instead, modern racial discourses tapped into conceptual repertoires accrued during the course of previous centuries.[31] The same can be said about modern sexuality, which, as David Halperin has argued, resulted from the "historical overlay and accretion" of various earlier categories.[32] Indeed, much of the epistemological arsenal that later periods would bring to bear on definitions of human identity and diversity was developed precisely during the sixteenth and seventeenth centuries, at a time when the experience of overseas expansion catalyzed both a significant transformation in the discourse of race and a substantial shift in the ways that erotic desire could be directed and distributed.

In the domain of race, a veritable explosion in the production and circulation of ethnographic writing culminated in the elaboration of classificatory systems that parceled out humanity on the basis of select physical and psychological traits. In 1566, Jean Bodin's *Methodus ad facilem historiarum cognitionem* distinguished among northern, middle, and southern peoples, attributing to the latter small statures, dark skins, and a marked propensity for sexual excess.[33] In 1650, the German geographer Bernhard Varen included body morphology, social customs, and moral makeup among the characteristics central to the study of human geography; and in 1676, the English scientist and political economist William Petty divided humankind into groups based on physiognomic characteristics, natural manners, and mental capacities.[34] In a related vein, the London physician John Bulwer explored morphological and cultural variance through a world survey of body parts such as heads, breasts, and genitals.[35] Taken collectively, these and other works reveal the tortuous process through which religious and environmental mappings of difference were progressively edged out, identity "implanted" in the body, and intimate corporeal practices invested with special significance.

The intensified scrutiny brought to bear on the private parts and private lives of non-European peoples coincided with a reorganization of erotic life within Europe itself. In both Protestant and Catholic countries, there was a progressive move "away from viewing procreation as the chief justification for marriage and the only justification for sexual intercourse" toward an understanding of marital sex as both an expression of spousal affection and an instrument of domestic harmony.[36] Valerie Traub has dubbed the marital regime that emerged from this shift "domestic heterosexuality," intended as a historical formation that lodged desire at the heart of the family experience. Harnessing the power of eros to the institution of matrimony (and enshrining the former as the latter's raison d'être), domestic heterosexuality encouraged men and women alike to invest more of their emotional energies in their respective spouses, and to express their investment through sex: "Domestic heterosexuality, I suggest, is a form of conjugal relation that *demands* the melding of love and erotic desire. It does not merely privilege emotional connections, a sense of privacy, and the separation of the domestic from the public sphere; it also intensifies the erotic relation between spouses. Under the regime of domestic heterosexuality, erotic desire for a domestic partner, in addition to desire for a reproductive, status-appropriate mate, became a *requirement for* (not just a happy byproduct of) the bonds between husband and wife."[37]

The ascent of domestic heterosexuality worked a momentous change in the way that eroticism could be imagined and represented, both within marriage and outside of it. Against the grain of a tradition regarding passionate sexual love between husband and wife as indecent if not outright illicit (a point to which I will return in Chapter 5), the eroticization of spousal relations eased the polarization between socially productive and socially disruptive sex. The end result was not only a renewed pressure on relations that most obviously threatened the stable transmission of property and lineage (e.g., adultery, fornication, and rape), but also a mounting preoccupation with practices and arrangements viewed as antithetical to the values of domestic heterosexuality (e.g., same-sex eroticism, plural marriage, and concubinage).[38]

Empires of Love contends that these seemingly disparate developments were not just historically coincidental events. Rather, the

progressive crystallization of race as a category of human difference and the emergence of domestic heterosexuality as an organizing
structure of sociosubjective experience formed part of a single shift
rooted in the dynamics of Europe's expansion overseas. Although
their coarticulation never remained constant, race and sexuality
came into existence *in and through* relation to each other, as structures of exclusion and domination that were mutually linked. If this
linkage has thus far remained largely obscure, it is only because
students of early modern race have rarely problematized the erotic
dimensions of racial discourses, whereas students of early modern
sexuality have traditionally privileged the experience of the European metropole over that of its imperial periphery. Yet it is precisely
in the imperial periphery—in those spaces that historians have long
identified as Europe's "laboratories of modernity"—that schemata
of race and sexuality most clearly intersected.[39] It is in these spaces
that some sociosexual practices and arrangements ceased to function as mere confirmations of a shared human weakness and took
on an identitarian valence, becoming markers of an alterity increasingly conceived of as ontological. It is from the perspective that these
spaces can afford, therefore, that intersections of race and sexuality
are most fruitfully investigated.

   As Kobena Mercer and Isaac Julien noted years ago, "historically,
the European construction of sexuality coincides with the epoch of
imperialism, and the two interconnect."[40] In the last few decades,
we have come a long way toward understanding this interconnec-
tion. Empirical studies on French Indochina, the Dutch East Indies,
Spanish Mexico, British India, and other colonial locales have abundantly shown that the regulation of sexual relations was central to
the production and maintenance of racially stratified societies.[41] The
erotic practices and domestic arrangements that obtained in colonial
contexts were largely produced by the hierarchies of imperial rule,
but were in turn productive of relationships that could dramatically
reshape the social structure of European settlements abroad. For this
reason, "who bedded and wedded whom" was something that colonial authorities constantly fretted about.[42]

   Europe's expansion overseas thus had the effect of turning sexuality into an area of great political interest and anxiety, but this
effect was not limited to the colonies alone; one of the most provoca-
tive aspects of recent scholarship on the sexual politics of empire has
been to connect peripheries and metropoles together, thus challenging

the Eurocentric purview (the "tunnel vision," as it has been famously called) of Michel Foucault's *History of Sexuality*.[43] Ann Laura Stoler, Anne McClintock, and Philip Howell—to name just a few—have persuasively argued that the development of sexual discourses within Europe cannot be properly charted without reference to the racialized contexts created by overseas expansion.[44] Indeed, European attempts to regulate sexual relations seem to have routinely exceeded any ossified distinction between metropolis and empire, suggesting instead a complex interplay between the two.

Building on these insights, *Empires of Love* asks how we may begin thinking about early modern race and early modern sexuality in ways that take this interplay into account. The epoch of the Crusades—arguably a foundational moment in the history of Europe's overseas expansion as well as an important step in the emergence of race as a category of identity—saw the rise of ethnoreligious stereotypes that linked Islam to a variety of sexual crimes including male-male sodomy and bestiality.[45] In the *Gesta Dei per Francos*, Guibert of Nogent lamented that Muslims had sexual relations with both women and men; and in the *Historia Orientalis*, Jacques de Vitry accused them of disporting themselves with animals as well.[46] The colonization of parts of Africa, America, and Asia during the sixteenth and seventeenth centuries at once reinforced and transformed these stereotypes, making them applicable on a global scale. It is not only that the reformation of mores perceived as alien or aberrant was a crucial part of Europe's self-appointed mission to refashion the world in its own image.[47] It is also that the establishment of racially mixed colonial societies quickly turned matters of eros into matters of ethnos: sexual practices and erotic proclivities became badges of identity that could evince the truth of one's racial belonging.

Europe's expansion into Asia provides an especially rich terrain for such inquiry. The ancients' knowledge of this part of the world had been relatively vague, yet the vast Asian stretch that many early moderns simply called "India" was not exactly a new world: Greek and Roman writers had handed down a discursive tradition that generally identified the East as a site of wealth and marvels.[48] Travel accounts of the early modern period—from Antonio Pigafetta's *Relazione del primo viaggio attorno al mondo* (ca. 1526) to François Pyrard de Laval's *Voyage* (1619), and Thomas Herbert's *A Relation of Some Yeares Travaile* (1634)—built in part on this tradition but moved in an ethnographic direction.[49] Habits and behaviors became more central, and a new attentiveness to sex began to emerge. Many of the devices that would eventually converge in the construction of "Oriental sexuality" (with its omnipresent tropes of frustration and concupiscence) were elaborated in these texts. More important, these texts erotically cathected a variety of Asian cultural practices, turning them into markers of sexual and racial identity. European representations of *sati* or widow burning are a good case in point: sixteenth- and seventeenth-century writers derived from antiquity the idea that widow burning was invented to protect men from the murderous inclinations of their wives. But whereas classical writers such as Diodorus Siculus had rooted this murderous penchant in the practice of letting youngsters arrange their own marriages—so that mistakes of judgment were common—early modern writers such as Jan Huygen van Linschoten rooted it in the aberrant libido of Asian women.[50]

The often lurid details that Linschoten and other early modern writers left behind colored Europe's understanding of India as a place of sexual license, promiscuity, and deviance. But while it was often understood as a place of debauchery and perversion, India was also the place where colonial authorities (be they Portuguese, Spanish, English, or Dutch) actively promoted the formation of interracial households. In contrast with the Americas, where female immigration from Europe went relatively unimpeded, the flow of European women to Asia was highly restricted throughout much of the early modern period.[51] At the same time, a series of incentives were provided to European males who took native brides. Begun in earnest under Afonso de Albuquerque's governorship of Portuguese India, the *política dos casamentos* (intermarriage policy) was to become a central feature of the European-Asian encounter.[52] Later in the century, Iberian colonists implemented the same policy in the Philippines; and Spanish plans for the colonization of China waxed lyrical on the benefits of marrying Chinese women to Spanish men of all ranks.[53] Consciously following on these precedents after the capture of Jakarta in 1619, Dutch colonial authorities began promoting lawful unions between low-ranking Verenigde Oost-Indische Compagnie (VOC, the Dutch equivalent of the English East India Company) employees and Asian women.[54] In English enclaves as well, intermarriage was far from rare, with formal and informal unions steadily increasing in number throughout the seventeenth century. In 1687, the East India Company decreed formal unions "a matter of such consequence to posterity that we shall be content to encourage it with some expense, and have been thinking for the future to appoint a Pagoda [4 rupees] to be paid to the mother of any child that shall hereafter be born of any such future marriage upon the day the child is Christened."[55]

The point here is not to homogenize Iberian, Dutch, and English tactics of race mixing, ignore the specific circumstances to which they responded, or lump together the results they produced. Instead, it is to recognize that the arguments mobilized in support of these tactics were often very similar if not identical. Regardless of nationality, European authorities seem to have agreed that Asian-born women offered more and demanded less than European-born ones. What is more, they were reputed to be more fertile and to produce healthier children—an especially desirable trait at a time when European outposts overseas were constantly threatened by desertion and disease. Observing that cross-racial unions had already provided the settlement with "many hope-full Children brought up in the Protestant Religion," in 1680 the English East India Company council at Madras suggested that low-ranking employees be encouraged to marry "the weomen of the Country, who are not so expensive [as English ones], and not less modest then our ordinary or common people are."[56] For their part, VOC authorities in Indonesia noted that European-Asian couples in the tropics produced strong and plentiful offspring, whereas European ones proved barren or gave birth to sickly children. "It is known by experience," summarized the Leiden professor Marcus Zuerius van Boxhorn in 1649, "that the children born in India of Dutch father and mother are not vital and die in a short time."[57]

That virtually the same arguments should be made by different imperial establishments at different times and in different geographic locales underscores both the extent to which mimetic rivalries shaped the process of Europe's expansion into Asia—how each imperial power measured its performance against those of its European competitors—and the extent to which *shared* ideologies of gender inflected emerging understandings of racial difference.[58] At a time when men and women belonged less to incommensurable sexes than to a single hierarchical continuum, a man's identity was thought to be more determinative than a woman's; if intermarriage policies could be envisioned as viable tactics of colonization, it was because native women could be imagined as more malleable, and therefore more assimilable, than their male counterparts.

This is not to suggest that intermarriage policies elicited no anxieties or concerns; to the contrary, racial mixing was from the beginning a highly contested terrain, at once an instrument of imperial rule and a vehicle of anti-imperial subversion. For as long as sexual probity could convincingly function as a category of belonging, however, concerns of racial purity were kept at bay by the regulatory power of monogamous, marital, reproductive heterosexuality. Hence the fervor with which European religious authorities in Asia sought to stamp out polygamy and concubinage, the insistence with which the Dutch Verenigde Oost-Indische Compagnie strong-armed its men into marriage, and the zeal with which the East India Company sought to ensure the "Christian and Sober Comportment" of English personnel abroad.[59] In the hybrid environments of contact zone societies, sexual practices and erotic desires clarified affinities and defined racial belonging.

Representations of the cross-racial couple had a particular impact on the way that early modern Europeans came to ascribe race and conceptualize proper sexuality, especially as more and more plots of interracial desire relayed these representations from the imperial outposts in which they were originally produced. Some of these were cautionary tales, depicting the sexual interface of the encounter as a site of mortal danger. Many others were tales of interracial romance—derived in part from Byzantine and medieval antecedents but adapted to the needs and requirements of the times—celebrating the assimilation of Asian women into the fabric of European society. Moving back and forth between colonial periphery and imperial metropole, these narratives functioned as a sort of social conduct literature that helped shape values, attitudes, and policies in a variety of locales. In brief, plots of interracial desire served as "portable machines" of subject formation whose effects reverberated well beyond their contexts of origin.[60]

Because they are dispersed across several genres and national literatures, these works have never been considered together or discussed in the aggregate. Yet many of them—including Luís Vaz de Camões's *Os Lusíadas* (1572), Jan Huygen van Linschoten's *Itinerario* (1596), Bartolomé Leonardo de Argensola's *Conquista de las Islas Malucas* (1609), and Richard Head's *The English Rogue* (1665)—formed a transnational corpus, circulated far outside the boundaries of their countries of origin in a series of translations, borrowings, and adaptations. Whether hailing desire as a venue of assimilation or decrying it as a conduit of degeneration, plots of race mixing marked the boundaries of racial identity while also marking the boundaries of what Europeans took to be licit eroticism. In the process, some practices and desires were marginalized, whereas others were turned into underpinnings of social privilege. In this sense, plots of race mixing discriminated not so much between Asians and Europeans as among the different constituencies that made up each group. The paths they traced marked loci of difference and identity that could be used to distinguish not only between "assimilable" and "unassimilable" Asians but also between "true" and "degenerate" Europeans.

During the second half of the seventeenth century, however, the situation began to change. Eros and ethnos, it seems, were parting ways: race no longer served as a measure of sexual orthodoxy, and sexual behavior was growing increasingly tenuous as a tool for negotiating the boundaries of racial identity. This uncoupling of race and sexuality was perhaps most apparent in the English context. In 1672, John Dryden's *Amboyna* rejected interracial *conubium* (legal marriage) as a utopian pipe dream; meanwhile, East India Company officials in Asia were pleading with London for the importation of English brides.[61] The tone of these pleas, the concerns they expressed, and above all the novel earnestness with which the Company received both suggest a hardening of racial constructs: Indian women no longer constituted viable marriage partners, regardless of whether their sexual morality was questionable or not, and regardless of whether their prospective English husbands were lowly underlings or not.

Empires of Love comprises six chapters arranged in rough chronological order, so as to follow the development of Western dominance in Asia while capturing the discursive convergences brought about by inter-European competition. In the belief that my inquiry could be best pursued from a comparative perspective, I have stretched as far as my linguistic training has allowed, drawing on Dutch, English, French, Italian, Latin, Portuguese, and Spanish materials. If I often refer to these materials collectively as "European," I do not mean by this to imply that they should be taken as representative of all of Europe or that the specificity of their contexts of production and reception should be dismissed or overlooked. Although one of the things that interests me about this project is precisely the way that many of these materials circulated beyond the domains in which they were first produced—and forged, in the process, links and commonalities across linguistic and national boundaries—I have sought to be mindful of the national specificities that inflected the shape of each.

Chapter 1, "Perverse Implantations," sets the stage for the rest of the book by tracing the emergence of an ethnological discourse that tied human morphology to sexual proclivities, and these, in turn, to racial identity. Male genital implements thought to enhance coital pleasure or prevent sodomy—the *palang* of Borneo and Indonesia, the "sagra" of the Philippines, the "buncales" or "yardballs" of Burma and Siam—formed a crucial part of this discourse, literally implanting certain male anatomies with a difference that was at once sexual and racial. By contrast, Asian females were left relatively "unmarked" at the anatomical level: hymenotomy and infibulation, although mentioned starting at least with Pigafetta's *Relazione*, elicited scant attention and virtually no discussion. The resulting asymmetry bolstered gender-specific notions of racial assimilability, underwriting intermarriage as a strategy of colonization and paving the way for most early modern representations of the European-Asian encounter.

Chapter 2, "The Erotic Politics of *Os Lusíadas*," focuses on Camões's epic celebration of Vasco da Gama's "discovery" of India, situating the poem's climactic segment at the Isle of Love within the historical context of the Portuguese *política dos casamentos*. On their return voyage, da Gama and his crew stumble across an enchanted island peopled with enamored nymphs. The orgiastic revel that ensues has long been a source of critical embarrassment, if for no other reason than it is precisely the kind of situation epic heroes are supposed to eschew. Nevertheless, the encounter between sailors and nymphs is critical to the poem's ideological economy: if the power play that opens the episode naturalizes violence as a fundamental component of eroticism, the nuptials that follow seek to channel desire away from perversion. Using an array of sixteenth-century sources (including Afonso de Albuquerque's letters and João de Barros's famous *Décadas da Ásia*), this chapter shows how *Os Lusíadas* enshrines conubium as both a tool of colonial interpellation and an instrument for "reordering" wayward desires.

Chapter 3, "Discipline and Love: Linschoten and the *Estado da Índia*," furthers the argument set forth in Chapter 2 by way of Jan Huygen van Linschoten's *Itinerario*. Written in Dutch but quickly translated into a variety of languages, this influential travelogue deflated Camões's optimistic vision by underscoring the often lethal effects (for immigrant settlers) of interracial conubium. For Linschoten, the política dos casamentos is a battleground, and European males are losing: when they are not murdered by adulterous wives, or consumed by their partners' insatiable lust, they are "Orientalized" beyond recognition, thereby disappearing as Europeans. Nonetheless, the *Itinerario* hardly advocates an absolute division between Europeans and Asians; rather, it argues for an education of desire that might redirect women's unruly eroticism toward the preservation of the colonial state. Reviewing (and eventually rejecting) disciplinary techniques ranging from surveillance and seclusion to Chinese foot binding and Indian widow burning, Linschoten's text alights on marital love as an ideal instrument for molding pliant colonial subjectivities.

If Chapter 3 considers the reformation of Indian women, Chapter 4, "Polygamy and the Arts of Reduction," deals with the erotic profligacy of both native and European males in Asia. I pay particular attention to representations of Asian polygyny contained in Bartolomé Leonardo de Argensola's *Conquista de las Islas Malucas* and François Pyrard de Laval's *Voyage*, but contextualize these representations by reference to European debates on the relative advantages of monogamy and non-monogamy as well as colonial efforts against polygamy and concubinage. In the early decades of the seventeenth century, I maintain, the *zenana*, the *hougong*, and the *keputren*—that is, the Indian, Chinese, and Indonesian equivalents of the Middle Eastern harem—found themselves unwittingly recruited in the construction of a new ideology of marriage. What made Asian polygyny so salient was neither its scandalousness nor the alleged penchant of immigrant settlers for indulging in it, but rather the fact that the practice could be regarded as perfectly licit under both natural and divine laws. In this manner, the polygynous Eastern household became part of an increasingly secular debate on the virtues and advantages of monogamy, securing for the latter a crucial role in the construction of Western identity.

Chapter 5, "The Ideology of Interracial Romance," uses John Fletcher's *The Island Princess* to explore the early modern vogue for narratives of cross-racial desire. Recent scholarship has brought the play's engagement with the dynamics of European expansion fully into focus. Reworking Iberian sources, the play adapted the medieval topos of the "enamored Moslem princess" to seventeenth-century exigencies, turning the title character's conversion to Christianity into a vantage point from which England could imagine its success in the Spice Islands of Southeast Asia.[62] What has escaped attention, I argue, is the way that *The Island Princess* aligns God with eros, making religious conversion virtually undistinguishable from an erotic refashioning. By proposing a vision of overseas expansion that is simultaneously a specific vision of conubium—one that can provide fulfillment not just in spite of but because of the inherent inequality between partners—Fletcher's play underscores the ideological overlap between merchant imperialism and domestic heterosexuality.

Chapter 6, "English Whiteness and the End of Romance," focuses on Richard Head's *The English Rogue*—a picaresque work that enjoyed great success both within and without England—as well as John Dryden's *Amboyna* (1673), a tragedy penned on the eve of the third Anglo-Dutch War. Set in "India" and produced not long after the acquisition of Bombay in 1661, these seemingly disparate works suggest that, by the last quarter of the seventeenth century, eros and ethnos had begun to go separate ways, putting under increasing pressure the coarticulation of race and sexuality proposed by Camões, Linschoten, and Fletcher. In *The English Rogue*, the title character achieves material comfort and social respectability by marrying an affluent "Indian-Black," yet construes this act as an erotic renunciation—or better yet, a transaction in which erotic desire is tendered in exchange for economic security.[63] For its part, *Amboyna* embraces the topoi of interracial romance only to disallow them at the end of the play; in a scathing critique of empire as venereal contamination, Dryden's tragedy sacrifices the fantasy of cross-racial requitedness on the altar of sexual (and racial) purity.

Where earlier writers had yoked erotic deviance and racial otherness, John Dryden and Richard Head unyoked them. In their works, sexual propriety no longer serves as a criterion of racial belonging, and racial belonging no longer functions as a yardstick of sexual propriety. If the shift paved the way for the emergence of sexual "races" characterized not by geographic origin but by sexual habits and erotic proclivities, it also made for a more rigid understanding of human difference. Deprived of the power of eros, European imperialism lost all confidence in its power to seduce, transform, and assimilate without losing itself in the process. Yet with that loss came something that did not quite exist before: a sense of identity defined both against the epidermal darkness of natives and the moral blackness of European rivals.

CHAPTER I

Perverse Implantations

Antonio Pigafetta's *Relazione del primo viaggio attorno al mondo* (An account of the first voyage around the world, ca. 1526) is relatively well known as an eyewitness narrative of Magellan's historic voyage of circumnavigation. As the first ethnographic report on the newly discovered Philippines, it is also the earliest European description of what has come to be known as palang piercing. In the Iban language of Borneo, "palang" means crossbar; palang piercing is the name now commonly associated with the practice of perforating the glans of the penis via the insertion of a crossbar device, which is then left in place.[1]

In certain parts of Asia, palang piercing boasts a long history, going back at least a millennium and a half. The *Kāma Sūtra*, which is generally dated to the sixth century, records its currency in "southern countries," details the piercing procedure, and describes the kinds of implements that could be threaded through the piercing: "The artificial aids used . . . may be round, ring-shaped, curved, in the shape of a lotus bud, irregular like bamboo bark, resembling a heron's bone or elephant's trunk, octagonal, square, [or] horn-shaped. They can be made hard or flexible."[2]

In the West, the palang (also known as ampallang) is far more recent. In the United States, its introduction seems to date to the 1970s, when it entered the BDSM (bondage/domination, dominance/ submission, sadism/masochism) scene along with other forms of genital modification. While still a marginal practice of body marking, palang piercing has lately achieved mainstream visibility: the piercing procedure is performed at most piercing-and-tattoo businesses around my campus.

Long before becoming a piercing parlor staple, however, the palang played an important role in early modern ethnography, featuring conspicuously in the works of humanists, travelers, missionaries, and colonial administrators. Nor was it alone: throughout the sixteenth century and for much of the seventeenth, European writers often associated (and sometimes confused) palang piercing with another form of genital modification thought to be just as "foul and diabolical."[3] This was reputedly original to continental Southeast Asia, and required the insertion of round hollow bells under the skin of the penis. The English merchant and adventurer Ralph Fitch, who traveled through the kingdom of Pegu (southern Burma) around 1586, noted that some of these inserts were called "Selwy" because they rang "but litle."[4] According to the Flemish merchant Jacques de Coutre (1575–1640), Peguans and Siamese knew them as "buncales"; early modern Europeans generally referred to them as "bells" or "yardballs."[5]

In this chapter, I explore Europe's fascination with palangs and bells. Drawing from a wide range of sources in a variety of languages—from Niccolò de' Conti and Poggio Bracciolini's *India Recognita* (1492) to João de Barros's *Décadas da Ásia* (1552–1615), Jan Huygen van Linschoten's *Itinerario* (1596), and Thomas Herbert's *A Relation of Some Yeares Travaile* (1634)—I trace the contours of a transnational discourse that joined evolving constructions of racial difference to emerging constructions of sexual identity. Never innocent digressions or mere expressions of jocularity, early modern representations of palangs and bells imprinted with alterity bodies and minds that might otherwise have been construed as not very different from European ones. Increasingly invested with metaphoric significance, Asian practices of genital modification came to be seen as stigmata of identity: the implantations they left behind revealed a peculiar nature that was both racially alien and sexually perverse. A single process of *incorporation* thus produced subjects that were simultaneously racialized and eroticized.

PERVERSE IMPLANTATIONS I: THE PALANG

In an entry for April 1521, Pigafetta wrote that on Cebu, a chief port in the Visayan Islands (Philippines), all males had pierced genitals:

> Big and small have the head of their members pierced from side to side with a rod of gold or tin, as thick as a goose quill. At each end of this rod some have what resembles a star with pointy ends; others [have]

what resembles the head of a cart nail. I often asked many, both young and old, to see [their members], because I could not believe it.

> Grandi e picoli hanno passato il suo membro circa de la testa de l'una parte a l'altra con uno fero de oro overo de stanio, grosso como una penna de oca, e in uno capo e l'altro del medesimo fero alguni hanno como una stella con ponte sovra li capi, altri como una testa de chiodo da caro. Asaissime volte lo volsi vedere da molti, cosí vechi como ioveni, perché non lo potteva credere.[6]

Although scholars have often assimilated it to the realm of the marvelous—along with Pigafetta's Patagonian giants, wind-caused pregnancies, and perambulating leaves—this meticulous depiction of Visayan privities inaugurates a gesture that would soon become a *topos obligé* of early modern ethnology.[7] It is at this point that the ethnographer becomes voyeur, inviting readers to share not only in the repeated scrutiny of these ornamented genitalia but also in the scopophilic contemplation of Visayan intercourse:

> They say that this is the wish of their wives, and that if they did otherwise they would not have intercourse with them. When they want to lie with their women, the latter take [the member] still soft and begin little by little to put inside first the one star on top and then the other. Once it is inside, [the member] stiffens and remains there until it becomes soft [again], for otherwise they would not be able to pull it out. These peoples do this because they are of a weak nature. They have as many wives as they want, but only a principal one. . . . The women loved us much more than the [men of the country]. All of them, from the age of six onward have their natures gradually opened by reason of their men's [enlarged] members.

> Loro diceno che le sue moglie voleno cussí e, se fossero de altra sorte, non uzariano con elli. Quando questi voleno uzare con le femine, loro medisime lo pigliano non in ordine e cominciano pian piano a metersi dentro primo quella stella de sovra e poi l'altra. Quando è dentro diventa in ordine e cusí sempre sta dentro finché diventa molle, perché altramenti non lo porianno cavare fuora. Questi populi uzanno questo perché sonno de debille natura. Hanno quante moglie voleno, ma una principalle. . . . Le donne amavano asai piú noi che questi. A tucti, da sei anni in su, a poco a poco li apreno la natura per cagion de quelli sui membri. (241)

The passage locates palang piercing firmly at the center of aberrant practices that confounded and denaturalized accepted erotic scripts. Since at least classical antiquity, sexual intercourse was conceptualized as an activity based on a rigid dichotomy between active and passive, penetrator and penetrated, masculine and feminine.[8] As described in the *Relazione*, Visayan coitus effectively undermined this dichotomy: while intromission without erection scrambled the linear narrative (arousal-penetration-climax-resolution) that structured dominant understandings of sexual intercourse, the agency of women (and the relative passivity of men) blurred the line between penetrator and penetrated, thereby disturbing notions of sex/gender difference that reserved the "active" role for adult males. Although still recognizable as a legitimate sexual act—that is, one that was heterosexual, marital, and potentially reproductive—Visayan coitus mixed dominance with submission, confused prescribed gender roles, and disrupted accepted scripts of sexual intercourse. From this perspective, the palang served quite literally as an index of perversion (from the Latin *pervertere*, meaning "to turn about" or "turn the wrong way"). Wherever it appeared, even that most orderly form of human sexuality, the decorous, reproductive embrace between husband and wife, turned indecent and disorderly. It is therefore hardly coincidental that Pigafetta should alight on a language of order-disorder—"still soft" ("non in ordine"), "stiffens" ("diventa in ordine")—to describe the appearance and behavior of the palang-equipped penis during coitus. The presence of this language creates a normative baseline against which the coital dynamics described in the *Relazione* are assessed, and implicitly registers the anxiety generated by the mismatch between the two.

The close of Pigafetta's description provides native disorder with a specific etiology: at its root, we are told, lies a peculiarly "weak nature" ("debille natura"). An erudite reading of this phrase would point us in the direction of Aristotle, Augustine, and Aquinas. "These peoples" ("questi populi") would refer to the entire population, and "weak nature"—construed as an essential or permanent characteristic—would indicate a weakness of the will known ever since antiquity as *akrasia* or incontinence.[9] Yet the *Relazione* is quick to remind us that, in sixteenth-century Italian, "nature" was also a common euphemism for genitals. In fact, the noun is used precisely in this sense just a few lines later, when we learn that Visayan women "have their natures gradually opened" ("a poco a poco li apreno la natura") to suit the oversize members of their countrymen. Read in this light, "weak nature" would indicate less a moral incapacity than a physiological deficiency, and "these people" would refer more restrictively to native males. This allows Pigafetta to turn ethnographic description into an ethnological argument in the service of European prowess and superiority: as he makes sure to point out, Visayan women enjoyed the company of Magellan's crewmen much more than they enjoyed the company of their countrymen.

If Pigafetta's double entendre reminds us that in early modern Europe notions of "nature" were never too far apart from the image of "Nature" as the goddess of procreative sex, it also alerts us to the existence of an inextricable link between culture and biology.[10] With both meanings of "nature" simultaneously at play, Visayan "weakness" is configured as a physiological and psychocultural disposition that could prove refractory to religious conversion as well as to physical coercion.[11] "Since arriving among these people, the Spaniards have had special care to abolish this abominable and bestial custom, confiscating many of these [genital implements] and flogging those who use them," wrote a sixteenth-century reporter, "and yet in spite of this [the natives] keep on using them, and it is very common for them to keep the pin or nail that goes . . . through their virile member constantly stuck in place."[12]

By the mid-seventeenth century, palang piercing had become somewhat of an ethnographic commonplace. In part, this was simply the result of the *Relazione*'s wide circulation: first published in epitomized form as *Le voyage et navigation faict par les Espaignolz es Isles de Mollucques*, the account appeared in Italian in 1536 and again in 1550, this time as part of Giovan Battista Ramusio's *Delle navigationi et viaggi*; abridged and translated, it was then included in Richard Eden's *Decades of the newe worlde* (1555) and *History of Travayle* (1577), eventually finding its way into Samuel Purchas's *Pilgrimes* (1625).[13] By and large, though, the notoriety of palang piercing in early modern Europe was the combined effect of texts ranging from Andrés de Urdaneta's "Relación del viaje de . . . García de Loaisa à las islas de la Especería" (ca. 1535) to Francesco Carletti's *Ragionamenti del mio viaggio attorno al mondo* (ca. 1606; pub. 1701). While often covering much of the same ground as the *Relazione*, these sources made clear that practices of genital piercing were not circumscribed to Cebu and neighboring Mactan, but rather distributed throughout the Philippines and beyond. The Suffolk gentleman Francis Pretty, who visited the region with Thomas Cavendish in 1588, saw palangs on Capul Island, even obtaining a specimen "from a sonne of one of the kings which was of the age of 10 yeeres, [and] did weare the same in his privie member."[14] The Portuguese factor Gabriel Rebelo observed similar piercings in the Moluccas, the Spanish chronicler Gonzalo Fernández de Oviedo located them in

Sulawesi, and the Jesuit missionary Francisco Ignacio Alcina reported them in use among Cambodians, Malays, and Bengalis.[15]

As the palang's geographical scope dilated, so did the amount of detail made available to European readerships. In the *Historia general y natural de las Indias* (1535–50), Fernández de Oviedo characterized the implement as a "little tube" through which metal ticklers could be threaded as occasion demanded. For his part, Friar Juan de Medina described it as a "brass bolt" that held in place a device "resembling a St. Catherine's Wheel with the points blunted."[16] According to Antonio de Morga and Francisco Ignacio Alcina, the spur-like implement was worn just above the glans, and was known among locals as a "sagra" or "sacra."[17] An especially detailed account of the piercing can be found in the Boxer Codex, a lavishly illustrated manuscript datable to the last decade of the sixteenth century. Presumably compiled for Philippine governor Gómez Pérez Dasmariñas, or for his son and successor, Don Luis, this ethnological compendium surveyed the entire stretch between Borneo and Japan, passing through China and the Philippines.[18]Although the manuscript contains little that was new or original —much of the Philippine material, for instance, has been traced to earlier sources such as Miguel de Loarca's *Tratado de las yslas Filipinas* (1582) and Juan de Plasencia's *Costumbre de los Tagalos* (1589)—several passages suggest that the writer "was either a keener observer or had spent more time with the [native] people than his contemporaries."[19] The close of the section entitled "Constumbres y usos, serimonias y ritos de Bisayas" (Customs, traditions, ceremonies, and rites of the Visayas) is one of those passages: it details what a "sacra" looked like, describes how it was used, and complements this description with a life-size illustration of the device, drawn in the folio's margin and illuminated in costly gold leaf (Figure 1):

> The men place and commonly carry on their genital members certain wheels or rings with round spurs—similar in shape to the one [drawn] in the page's margin—that are made of lead or brass and sometimes of gold. The round part of the wheel or ring has two holes, one on top and the other at the bottom, in which they lodge [the ends of] a small pin or nail, of the same metal as the ring, with which they pierce the lower part of the prepuce, so that the wheel or ring is worn on the genital member just as a ring is worn on the finger. Thus they have intercourse with women, and spend a whole day or night tied to one another in the same way that dogs remain [tied together] when completing a similar act. From this they derive great delight,

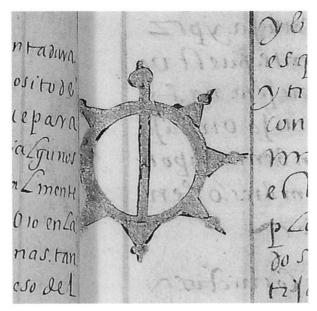

Figure 1. A *sagra*, as depicted in the Boxer Codex, Boxer MSS II. Courtesy of the Lilly Library, Indiana University, Bloomington, IN.

especially the women. . . . Some of these wheels or rings are quite large; there are more than thirty types of them, each with its special name. The general name of all in their language is *sacra*.

Los hombres se ponen en el miembro genital y traen de hordinario en el unas rrodajas o sortijas con unas puntas alarredonda que salen de lass mismas rrodajas o sortijas como de la fforma de esta que esta en el margen, las quales hazen de plomo o de estano y algunas ay de oro. Tienen echos dos agujeros en la parte que haze el rredondo la sortija o rrodaja uno por la parte de arriba y otro por la parte de abajo por donde entra o meten un pernete o clavo del mismo metal que es la sortija que atraviesa el miembro del hombre por el nacimiento del prepucio, y asi queda la rrodaja o sortija puesta en el mismo miembro genital de la misma manera como quando se pone una sortija en el dedo y asi tienen acceso con las mugeres y estan todo un dia o una noche pegados y asidos el uno con el otro de la manera que quedan los perros quando acavan de hazer semejante acto, sintiendo en esto gran delectacion mayormente las mugeres. . . . [A]y algunas de estas rrodajas o sortijas que son muy grandes tienen mas de treynta suertes dellas y de cada suerte tienen su nombre diferente y el general de todas es en su lengua *sacra*.[20]

Although written in different languages and ostensibly derived from different sources, virtually every single one of these works follows Pigafetta in depicting genital piercing as something desired—or better yet, positively *demanded*—by women. And while some commentators noted that the latter could be severely wounded during intercourse, most of them were adamant that unpierced males were ridiculed and rejected. Juan de Medina, for instance, claimed that Filipino women "would suffer no man to approach them without a sagra."[21] Such was the pressure that women exercised, echoed the Spanish Jesuit Francisco Ignacio Alcina, that many Filipino males felt compelled to undergo the piercing procedure, no matter how much pain and danger it involved.

From a European perspective, this meant not only placing women in the unusual position of controlling their partners' sexual organs but also granting their pleasures and desires an unprecedented weight in the establishment of societal practice. This is not to suggest that the sexual gratification of women had no space in the practices and ideologies of early modern Europe: in the sixteenth century, the French surgeon Ambroise Paré and the Italian anatomist Realdo Colombo openly enjoined husbands to attend to their wives' coital satisfaction; in 1636, the English physician John Sadler advised men to fondle the "secret parts and dugs" of their female partners, so that the latter may "take fire and be inflamed in venery."[22] But these injunctions always sprang from the belief that a woman's orgasm was either necessary or at least adjuvant to conception; they hardly testify to a positive valuation of female pleasures and desires.[23] As a matter of fact, most early moderns viewed these pleasures and desires with deep suspicion, in the conviction that their unchecked expression would undermine the proper power relationships between men and women, and threaten the rational principles on which civilized society was founded. Hence the scandal with which Europeans in the Philippines regarded the behavior of native women— their apparent unconcern for virginity, the ease with which they walked away from unhappy marriages, and especially their fondness for male piercings.[24] Asymmetries of power that most early modern Europeans would have taken for granted were seemingly reversed, traditional gender hierarchies inevitably perverted. Indeed, at a time when the analogy of the body politic routinely assimilated the well-run state to the human body, the common metaphorical rendering of the palang-wielding glans as a head "pierced from side to side" boded none too well for the orderliness or rationality of Filipino society.[25]

It is far from a coincidence, in this respect, that early modern sources implicitly associate palang piercing with ventrodorsal coitus: of all "deviant" forms of heterosexual congress known in Europe, the approach *more canino*—that is, in the manner of dogs—was held to be especially disorderly and irrational. What made it so troubling was the suspicion that it might afford special pleasure, coupled with the apprehension that it might collapse the boundary between humankind and animal kind.[26] By placing humans in the position of dogs, ventrodorsal coitus was inevitably linked to bestiality, "the most grievous" of sins, as Thomas Aquinas would have it, and a capital crime punishable by burning at the stake.[27] From Pigafetta's *Relazione* through Medina's *Historia*, European accounts of palang piercing seem to be minutely calculated to conjure the specter of bestiality. Not only does the palang function as a canine *os penis* (the penile bone that makes intromission impossible with a full erection), it also serves as an engorged knot or *bulbus glandis* (a penile structure that swells after intromission), locking partners together "as if they were dogs."[28]

There can be no doubt that these animalized bodies and sexualities often served purposes of ideological expediency: wherever they appear, palangs are never too far away from depictions of Asian savagery and irrationality. In the *Relazione*, for example, Pigafetta's account of the palang sits at the center of an interlude placed strategically between the triumphant beginning of the Spaniards' visit and its disastrous end. The early part of April 1521 was a period of astounding success for Magellan. Having easily obtained an oath of fealty from the rajah of Cebu, Humabon, he devoted himself to the task of conversion, often delivering sermons in person. Within a short while, pagan idols were destroyed, crosses planted, and Christian altars erected; on Thursday, 14 April, Humabon himself was formally christened. The solemn ceremony opened the door to mass conversion, and within a week the island's whole population had been baptized. By the beginning of May, however, the tide had turned: Magellan himself lay dead and unburied at Mactan Island, his punitive expedition against Rajah Lapu-Lapu having gone spectacularly awry. Much of the crew had struggled back to Cebu only to fall into an ambush and be captured or killed at Humabon's orders.[29] Since Pigafetta's *Relazione* glosses over the less idyllic aspects of the Spaniards' visit—barely a mention is made, for instance, of Magellan's unprovoked sacking and burning of Bulaia on Mactan Island—and elides all evidence of their unsavory conduct on Cebu, Humabon's turnabout has no intelligible motive.[30] The islanders' strange customs fill this narrative gap, rhetorically setting the stage for the rajah's final "treachery" and all-too-likely apostasy. In the process, the palang is made to mark the space of Filipino otherness even in the absence of native hostility and resistance.

Similar textual strategies can be traced in a number of other sources; in Richard Eden's *Decades of the newe worlde*, for instance, the practice of "wear[ing] rynges of golde abowt theyr privie members" is attributed exclusively to the inhabitants of Mactan Island, thereby strengthening the locale's association with savagery and revolt. For the Augustinian missionary Juan de Medina, sagras served as both a synecdoche of Filipino lasciviousness and a metaphor for the archipelago's Islamic penchants. Even Francis Pretty, who depicted his stay at Capul Island in rather positive terms—the natives having just pledged their aid against the Spaniards—viewed genital piercing as a marker of radical alterity: his description of the palang ends with the claim that the islanders "wholly worship[ed] the devill."[31]

Yet we should not reduce Europe's fascination with the palang to a mere rhetorical extension of specific political interests, a way of justifying imperial expansion. Rather, the discursive currency of palang piercing needs to be understood as the result of a conceptual shift that framed anew the question of human diversity. Before the early modern period, Europeans conceptualized identity primarily (albeit not exclusively) in terms of religious affiliation; in the early modern period, physical and psychological traits increasingly supplemented religion as a central category of identity formation. This is not to say that religious modalities of identity-making were any less *racial* than later ones: as Geraldine Heng has noted, theocentric perspectives can be quite effective at biologizing and essentializing human difference.[32] Nor is this to suggest that religious modalities of identity formation were in any way uniform, stable, or exclusive. Rather, it is simply to observe that, during the early modern period, religious modalities of identity-making came progressively under stress. Just as the Reformation fractured the unity of Christendom, waves of mass conversions—from the forced conversions of Jews and Muslims in fifteenth-century Iberia through the religious apostolates of Dominicans, Augustinians, Jesuits, and Franciscans in Asia, Africa, and America during the sixteenth century and beyond—brought into the Christian fold large groups of neophytes whose allegiances and beliefs were regarded at best with suspicion.[33] As a result, new categories were increasingly called upon to supplement religion as indexes of identity:

while purity-of-blood ideologies sought to redefine what it meant to be Christian, the resurgence of classical geohumoralism (which posited an essential connection among individuals, nations, and climates) linked morphophysiology to geography and even diet.[34]

The process of overseas expansion added yet another strand to this complex formation: building in part on preexisting stereotypes, it elaborated a discourse that latched onto eros as a category of human experience that could be invoked to delimit the boundaries of identity. From Pigafetta's *Relazione* onward, Asian practices of male genital modification formed an integral part of this discourse, serving as markers of a racial difference that was effectively construed in erotic terms. Unencumbered by theocentric frameworks, unmoored from the semiotics of blood, and untouched by the resurgence of geohumoralism, palangs became simultaneously the sign, the effect, and the perpetuating instrument of a peculiar eroticism. This peculiar eroticism, in turn, was construed as an inherent psychocultural trait that manifested itself through an aberrant genital morphology. In short, to the extent that they could be understood as phenotypic characteristics directly related to moral and rational capacities, genital piercings were also understood as marking the boundaries of an identity that was distinctly racial.

PERVERSE IMPLANTATIONS II: THE PENIS BELLS OF BURMA AND SIAM

The palang is by no means the only "exotic" sexual custom broached in the *Relazione*. Writing about Java, an island he never visited but about which he presumably heard while on Timor, Pigafetta noted that local rituals of courtship required men to insert small ringing bells between the glans and the foreskin:

> The young men of Java, when they are in love, tie certain little bells between the member and the foreskin, then go below their lovers' windows and, under pretense of urinating, shake their members and make their bells ring. When their beloved hear that sound, they immediately come down and oblige their desires, always with those bells on, because they greatly enjoy hearing the bells ring from inside them.

> Li ioveni de Iava, quando sono inamorati in qualche gentildonna, se ligano certi sonagli con fillo tra il membro e la pelessina e vanno soto le fenestre de le sue inamorate e, facendo mostra de orinare e squasando lo membro, sonano con quelli sonagli e, fin tanto le sue inamorate odeno lo sono, subito quele veneno iú e fanno suo volere,

> sempre con queli sonagliti, perché loro donne se piglianno gran
> spasso a sentirsi sonare de dentro. (339)

It is unclear whether Pigafetta gathered this information during the trip, as the account suggests, or derived it from earlier reports.[35] Tomé Pires's *Suma Oriental* (1512–15), for one, had discussed similar bells several years before: "All the lords of Pegu, and the other people according to their wealth, have the custom of wearing little round bells in their privy parts," wrote the Portuguese apothecary, adding that Malay women seemed exceedingly fond of the instruments' "sweet harmony."[36] Writing from Malacca, where he was stationed, Pires might well have drawn from direct experience; but he might himself have known of the bells from the account of one Niccolò de' Conti, a fifteenth-century merchant whose travel narrative had widely circulated in manuscript and repeatedly appeared in print.

How this travel narrative had come into being is in itself an interesting story: during the many years he had spent wandering in Asia, Conti had converted to Islam; on his return to Italy, he sought to be reconciled with the church; and legend has it that the story of his travels was exacted as a penance for his apostasy.[37] Collected by the pope's secretary, Poggio Bracciolini, and redacted in elegant Latin around 1447, the story of Conti's travels enjoyed instant success, as can be garnered by the large number of manuscript copies still extant.[38] A first print edition of the account appeared at Milan in 1492, under the title *India Recognita* (The Indies rediscovered); this was soon followed by translations into Portuguese (1502), Spanish (1503), Italian (1550), and English (1579). From the late fifteenth century through the late sixteenth, Conti's travelogue remained a crucial source of information on India, being eventually replaced only when more accurate reports became widely available.[39]

The attentiveness of *India Recognita* to erotic matters and sociosexual practices has often been remarked upon.[40] Even within this generally frank context, however, Conti's experience in Burma easily takes pride of place for its unusual candor:

> In this city [of Ava, Upper Burma] there are several shops of ridiculous and lascivious things . . . [and] in these shops only women sell things we call bells, which are made of gold or silver. Men visit these stores before taking a wife (for otherwise they would not be able to marry). Here the skin of their member is cut in places and between the skin and the flesh are inserted as many as twelve bells or more, each as big as a small nut. . . . This they do to satisfy the lasciviousness of women, because these piercings and swelling of the member give women great pleasure.

Hac in sola civitate plurimas tabernas rei . . . ridiculae lascivaeque
esse affirmat. Vendi in his a solis feminis ea quae nos sonalia affirma-
mus, aurea & argentea. Ad has virum antequam uxorem capiat (aliter
enim reicitur a coniugio) proficisci. Reiecta atque eleuata paululum
membri virilis cute, trudi inter pellem et carnem ex his sonaliis quae
in modum parvulae avelanae sunt usque ad xii et amplius. . . . Hoc ad
explendam mulierum libidinem faciunt. His enim tanquam intermo-
diis membrique tumore feminas summa voluptate affici.[41]

Yet when local women derided "the smallness of his member" ("par-
vitate priapi") and encouraged him to obviate the shortcoming by the
aid of a few bells, Conti emphatically declined, refusing to purchase
"the pleasure of others" ("aliis voluptati") at the price of his own pain
(sig. A5v).

While belittling genital modification practices as both ridiculous
and lascivious, the passage also construes Conti's experience as a scene
of temptation—at least for a moment, the European traveler hovers on
the threshold of a different world where new pleasures, intensities, and
attachments might become possible. Read in this light, Conti's refusal
to undergo the knife serves as an index of his moral fiber—his unmodi-
fied genitals a standing monument to cultural steadfastness and erotic
restraint. The bells of Burma thus have a specific function: by con-
juring and dispelling the specter of genital cutting, they allow both
Bracciolini and Conti to pass under silence the circumcision that would
have likely marked the latter's entry into the Islamic fold—a genital
modification that called into question his identity as a Christian. While
this narrative sleight of hand undeniably served Conti's desire to be
readmitted into the Roman Catholic Church, its conditions of possibility depended on a larger shift in the ways Europeans were beginning
to bound and ascribe identity. Circumcision, or the lack thereof, had
long served as a powerful sign of racial belonging; especially in plural societies, this meant that male genitalia could be effectively relied
on to "tell the truth" even where language, phenotype, and dress did
not. In *India Recognita*, the bells of Burma clearly retain this revela-
tory power, but the truth they reveal is no longer that of a belonging
rooted in belief; instead, it is a truth that lodges identity in the alleged
peculiarities of native eroticism.[42] An age-old metonymy linking penile
modifications and religious membership was thus overlaid with a synecdoche that invested genital morphology with an overtly sexual significance, inaugurating thereby a long tradition that would eventually
produce Europe's nineteenth-century fascination with the "Hottentot apron" (an overdevelopment of the nymphae associated with both

racial inferiority and erotic aberrancy).[43] This was, of course, no sim-
ple process of overwriting; rather, during the period that we call early
modern, various systems of signification remained simultaneously at
play, often in mutually sustaining relations, but occasionally complicat-
ing and even undercutting one another.

Either alone or in association with the palang, the penis bells of
Burma and Siam enjoyed a veritable vogue during the sixteenth and
seventeenth centuries, both as an ethnographic topos and a collec-
tor's item, drawing Europe into an already flourishing trade in erotic
paraphernalia.[44] The Englishman Ralph Fitch, whose description of
Burma appeared in both Richard Hakluyt's and Samuel Purchas's collections, brought "divers of these bels" back into England; the Dutch
traveler Jan Huygen van Linschoten gave them away to friends; the
Florentine slave trader Francesco Carletti bought a few from Siamese
mariners; the East India Company factor Edmund Saris received a
freshly dislodged one as a gift; and London physician John Bulwer
was so proud of the one he owned that he had it immortalized in
print (Figure 2).[45] Spotted here and there across not only Burma and
Siam but also India, Malaysia, Indonesia, and the Philippines, they
were described or discussed in a multitude of travelogues and com-
pendia, from Duarte Barbosa's *Livro* (ca. 1518), Garcia de Resende's
Miscellanea (1545), and Gasparo Balbi's *Viaggio dell'Indie orientali* (1590) to Roelof Roelofszoon's "Kort ende waerachtigh verhael" (ca. 1604), Pierre d'Avity's *Les Estats, empires, et principautez du monde* (1613), and Thomas Herbert's *A Relation of Some
Yeares Travaile* (1634). They even made a cameo appearance in *Os
Lusíadas*, Camões's epic celebration of da Gama's journey to India;
by 1707, they occupied a racy spread in Pieter van der Aa's *Naaukeurige versameling der gedenk-waardigste zee en land-reysen na
Oost en West-Indiën* (Figure 3). European readers thus learned that
the bells could be as small as chickpeas or as large as chicken eggs; that
they could be made of various materials, silver and gold being generally reserved for the elites; that they were hollow, with a pebble or "an
Adders tongue" inside; that they could be inserted and removed easily;
that up to three (or four, or five, or twelve) could be worn at any given
time; that women far preferred men who had them over those who did
not; and that they could be given out as a sign of preferment.[46] "The
king [of Pegu] sometimes taketh his out, and giveth them to his noblemen as a great gift," reported Ralph Fitch in this regard. "And because
he hath used them, they esteeme them greatly."[47]

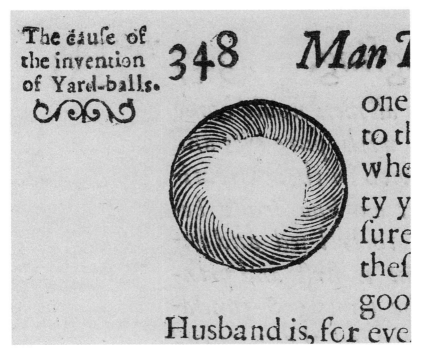

The cause of the invention of Yard-balls. 348 Man ... one to t... wh... ty y... fure thef goo Husband is, for eve...

Figure 2. A "yardball" of continental Southeast Asia, as reproduced in the 1654 edition of Bulwer's *Anthropometamorphosis* (published as *A view of the people of the whole world, or, A short survey of their policies, dispositions, naturall deportments, complexions, ancient and moderne customes, manners, habits & fashions*). Courtesy of the Huntington Library, San Marino, CA.

In the process, what Conti, Pires, and Pigafetta had described as a frivolous but relatively innocuous custom acquired new meanings. In 1563, the Portuguese historian João de Barros linked it to a creation myth according to which the people of Burma and Siam descended from the coupling of a Chinese woman and a dog:

> [The people of Pegu, in southern Burma] say that the Siamese descend from them, which is likely to be true since they are the only nations to observe the abominable custom of the bells. We can therefore accept as true the story according to which the people of that land descend from the copulation of a woman and a dog: for in the act of copulation they seek to imitate dogs and must therefore descend from a dog.
>
> The story of their origin is the following: a Chinese junk was shipwrecked on the coast of the kingdom of Pegu (which was then

Figure 3. The penis bells of Pegu, as represented in volume 19 of Pieter van der Aa's *Naaukeurige versameling der gedenk-waardigste zee en land-reysen na Oost en West-Indiën* (Leiden, 1706–8). Courtesy of the John Carter Brown Library at Brown University, Providence, RI.

uninhabited) and only a woman and a dog survived. They mated and the woman bore children with whom she later [paired off and] had children. This is how the land was populated, and not to degenerate from their father, they invented the bells. Later on, their population rose steadily and some of them migrated to Siam. Therefore, the people there have the same custom. Since in both of these countries the women are more attractive than the men, they say that the former take after their first mother, and the latter after the father.

E ainda dizem êles que os siames procedem da sua linhagem; e será assi, porque esta torpeza dos cascavéis em tôdas aquelas partes não se acha em outro povo. Donde se pode crer ser verdade o que êles contam—que aquela terra se povoou do ajuntamento de um cão e ũa mulher; pois que no auto do ajuntamento dêles querem imitar os cães, porque quem o imita, dêle deve proceder.

E a história desta sua gèração é que, vindo ter à costa daquele reino Pegu, que então eram terras êrmas, um junco da China, com tormenta se perdeu, de que sòmente escapou ũa mulher e um cão, com o qual ela teve cópula, de que houve filhos, que depois os houveram dela, com que a terra se veo a multiplicar, e por não degenerarem do pai, inventaram os cascavéis; e daqui, depois que a gente foi muita, se passou a Sião,

donde os daquele reino têem o mesmo costume; e porque em ambas estas partes as mulheres têem melhor parecer que os homens, dizem elas
que as fêmeas saem à primeira mãe, e os machos ao pai.[48]

The specter of bestiality we have seen conjured in palang piercing
returns, here, in a grotesquely literalized form. For Barros, the penis
bells of Burma and Siam do not merely express a peculiar eroticism.
Rather, they constitute a central feature of native identity, securing
lines of descent that are marked by radical otherness. Generated in
breach of both natural and divine laws, Siamese and Peguans are
construed as literal monsters—unnatural mixtures of species meant
to be kept apart.[49] At first blush, Barros's genealogy may seem to
find roots in a long-standing tradition identifying Asia as a land
of strange births, curious customs, and marvelous creatures. Like
the one-legged Monosceli or dog-headed Cynocephali catalogued by
Pliny, Siamese and Peguans are distinguished by anatomical peculiarities that are passed on from father to son. In this sense, they are
just another monstrous race, one of the many held to inhabit the
margins of the known world. But where Pliny had traced the origin
of these monstrous races back to the playfulness of nature, Barros's
teratogenesis is firmly rooted in bestiality and incest. In this sense,
Barros's account aligns Asian bell wearers less with Pliny's fabulous
races than with those half-human, half-animal creatures famously
featured in Geronimo Cardano's De Varietate Rerum (1556) and
Ambroise Paré's Des monstres et prodiges (1573). For both Paré and
Cardano, sexual congress between humans and animals engendered
offspring with animal traits, as in the case of the dog-child who
resembled his mother from the waist up but whose "lower parts"
were "similar in form and shape to the animal that was the father."[50]
Yet here again the parallel only goes so far, for the people of Burma
and Siam have no such animal traits. All that is left of their canine
ancestry is a peculiar manner of sexual congress deliberately modeled after the mating of dogs, the purpose of which is to prevent
them from "degenerating" from their father. The sexual heterodoxy
of Burmese and Siamese is hence revealed as a bestial taint passed
down from generation to generation; at the same time, this taint
is transposed from the physical to the psychic domain, producing
effects less in morphology than in behavior.

But Barros does not stop here. In the Décadas da Ásia, the
bells' monstrous etiology is supplemented by yet another genealogical myth—one in which King Solomon, the "unspeakable sin" of

sodomy, and the gold of Ophir are meshed together in a single narrative of erotic aberration and enforced redemption:

> Others say that this land [of Pegu] and that of Arakan [in western Burma] were peopled by criminal exiles, and that the bells served as remedy against the unspeakable sin against nature. And some Jews of that region, who know the language and can read their writing, say that such exiles were sent by King Solomon of Judea, at the time that his ships sailed those parts in search of gold, that they took from Ophir. This they think was in the isle of Sumatra, which at the time must have been attached to this land.

> Outros dizem que esta terra e a de Arracão foi povoada de degradados, e que o uso dos cascavéis foi remédio contra aquêle nefando pecado contra natura. E ainda alguns judeus daquela região, que sabem a língua e entendem a escritura dêles, dizem que êstes degradados eram enviados por el-Rei Salamão, de Judéa, no tempo que as suas naus navegavam àquelas partes, em busca de ouro, que levavam de Ofir, que êles têem ser na Ilha Samatra, que naquele tempo haviam ser terra contínua a esta. (130)

Once more, Barros invokes tradition, linking the genital inserts of Burma and Siam to a scriptural past in which, as the Bible tells us, Jewish fleets "brought gold from Ophir; and from there they brought great cargoes of almugwood and precious stones" (1 Kings 10:11). The otherness of Southeast Asia is thus made doubly familiar: not only are the people of Burma revealed to be of Jewish ancestry, but their strange sexual practices turn out to be a preventive against the all-too-well-known sin of sodomy.

To many of Barros's readers, this myth of origin might also have seemed familiar for featuring "degredados" or criminal exiles as settlers—for the forced expatriation of convicts had been part and parcel of Portugal's colonial expansion since the very beginning. At least 455 convicts were exiled to Ceuta between 1415 and 1456; prisoners sentenced "for shameful crimes" ("por culpas e por feitos vergonhosos") accompanied Vasco da Gama to India (and appeared as characters in Camões's epic celebration of that voyage); degredados served in Asia under Afonso de Albuquerque, occasionally gaining pardons for their good services; and in Brazil, at least four hundred of the original one thousand settlers of Bahia were exiled convicts.[51]

Banishment to overseas outposts was generally reserved for serious offenses—including bigamy, witchcraft, and murder—as well as for unpardonable ones such as heresy, sodomy, counterfeiting, and treason.[52] In theory, punishment for unpardonable crimes was death by burning; in practice, though, capital punishment was more often threatened than executed. This seems to have been especially the case for sodomy, for while the Crown retained the legal possibility of applying the death penalty, convicted sodomists were frequently sentenced either to exile or to the royal galleys.[53] Read in this light, the scriptural past in which King Solomon's ships sailed the Indian Ocean is but a refraction of Portugal's sixteenth-century present: relatively recent tactics of forced colonization are revealed as mirrors of ancient Jewish policies similarly invested in policing unpardonable acts and desires. In short, while Barros's biblical etiology of the penis bells may tell us little or nothing about Burma and Pegu, it has much to tell us about Portugal's tactics of colonial expansion—and their profound investment in reproductive sex.

The central decades of the sixteenth century thus mark a turning point in what was already an established discursive tradition. In Barros's *Décadas*, as well as in António Galvão's roughly coeval *Tratado dos descobrimentos* (1563), the penis bells of Burma and Siam are construed, for the first time, as a disciplinary technique in the service of erotic normativity. By the end of the century, this etiology had become axiomatic. As Linschoten claimed in 1596, the practice of inserting ringing bells under the skin of the penis had been introduced because Burmese and Siamese men were "great Sodomites."[54] They were so "addicted to that villany," noted Ralph Fitch, that in times past all those parts "were very scarse of people."[55] For this reason, echoed the English traveler Thomas Herbert, a powerful "Queene Rectrix" had ordered "that all male children at their births, should have a round bell of Gold (in it an Adders tongue dryed) put through their fore-skin and the flesh."[56] No longer described as instruments of sexual gratification, the penis bells of Burma and Siam became state-sponsored interventions: they inscribed on the body the presence of a new power that was no longer based on the sovereign right to kill, but rather on the responsibility to manage life.[57] As such, the penis bells of Burma and Siam became susceptible of novel and even positive evaluations. "This invention [of the bells]," wrote John Bulwer in the first edition of his *ever-growing Anthropometamorphosis: Man Transform'd; or, The Artificial Changeling*, "since [it is] not for an ornament or delight, but accommodated to the restraint of wicked Sodomy . . . is not to be condemned, but were good if severely imposed upon the *Persians* and other Nations of the *Levant*, among whom there are infinite swarms of *Catamites* or *Sodomitical Boyes* who make an unrighteous use of their *Rectum Intestinum*, to the foule shame and dishonour of their bodies."[58]

Bulwer does not mention the palang, but his evaluation of the penis bells could have been easily extended to cover it—for sodomy had already emerged as a primary cause of both practices. "This custome [of piercing the penis]," Francis Pretty had written in his account of Thomas Cavendish's voyage around the world, "was granted at the request of the women of the countrey, who finding their men to be given to the fowle sinne of Sodomie, desired some remedie against that mischiefe."[59] Similar claims were advanced by the Spanish Jesuit Francisco Ignacio Alcina, a contemporary of Bulwer's who spent thirty-six years as a missionary in the Philippines. Discussing the use of genital piercings among the Visayas, Alcina noted that these piercings could serve not only as a means of enhancing women's pleasure but also "for the prevention of the unspeakable sin." It was for this latter purpose that a wise Cambodian queen had mandated the use of palang-like implements among her subjects, he explained. And although genital piercings should still be considered inventions of the devil, "for no one else could be responsible for something so foul," the queen's laudable intent made Cambodian palangs somewhat more excusable than non-Cambodian ones .[60]

To an extent, Pretty's and Alcina's etiologies follow established tradition, assigning women a determinant role in the introduction of palang piercing. Their accounts cast Asian practices of genital modification much in the same light as Pigafetta and others had done before them: that is, as emblems of difference measuring the chasm between Europeans and Asians. In construing the palang less as an instrument of pleasure than as a disciplinary apparatus, however, Pretty and Alcina also put the inherited tradition to new use. Far from merely illustrating the variability of human customs, the aberrant lechery of Asian women, or the insufficiency (physical or psychological as it might be) of Asian males, palang piercing testified to a heteronorm that held sway all over the world. Practices of genital modification thus came to play a twofold function, serving as both markers of difference and indexes of allegedly universal norms. As tropes of otherness, they acted as prurient repositories for bodies and behaviors that Europe was edging out as unacceptable. As disciplinary techniques from faraway countries, they helped fantasize heterosexual coupling as a universal norm of political governance and sociocultural reproduction.

SODOMITICAL RACES

By the seventeenth century, there was broad consensus in Europe that Asian practices of genital modification should be interpreted as an-tisodomy techniques. Yet no one seems to have been clear as to how they worked. According to some writers, they served primarily as a pedagogical prop, "so that if [the children] demand why[,] tis an-swered them for deterring them the hatefull sinne of Sodomy."[61] Ac-cording to others, they functioned as chastity devices, whether be-cause they made the penis swell to such a size as to make it "incapable of that vice" or because they prevented a full erection.[62] Either way, no one seems to have doubted, or at least not out loud, that they were effective: according to early commentators, wherever palangs and bells flourished, sodomy was rare. While observing that all Indians were much inclined to licentiousness, for instance, Niccolò de' Conti also pointed out that they did not engage in practices such as male-to-male sex.[63] Writing about the palang-friendly Moluccans, an anony-mous Portuguese noted: "There is one virtuous thing among them: they do not indulge in the abominable sin. Some are said to commit it, but generally all of them frown upon it and punish it with death."[64] As for the rarity of sodomy in the Philippines, missionaries and colonial administrators insisted that even the word had been unknown until the arrival of the Spaniards and (especially) the Chinese.[65]

Given these premises, one might logically expect to find male genital modifications at the center of discourses that highlighted the *absence* of sodomy from certain parts of Asia. But this is not what happened. Instead, the very technologies that should have guaranteed some peo-ples' reputation for erotic licitness became morphological markings on which sexual stereotypes were built. Sodomy became a racial trait—a habit assumed to be so pervasive among some Southeast Asian popu-lations as to require no exception, proof, or explanation. This drift is already apparent in the Burma section of Jan Huygen van Linschoten's *Itinerario* (a text I discuss at some length in Chapter 3). Like many other late sixteenth-century writers, Linschoten characterizes Burmese sodomy as a custom of yesteryear, writing that the wearing of bells "was ordained . . . because the Peguans [in time past] were great Sod-omites, [and using this custome of belles], it would be a meane to let them from the same."[66] Yet the plate that accompanies the text, etched by Joannes van Doetecum after a sketch presumably drawn from life, suggests something quite different. Of the many ethnic types portrayed

Figure 4. A man from Pegu, as portrayed in Linschoten's *Itinerario*. Courtesy of the John Carter Brown Library at Brown University, Providence, RI.

in the *Itinerario*, the man from Pegu is among the few male figures missing a female companion, and the only one to be shown seated rather than standing. And where the Moluccan next to him holds a sword in his hand and a shield on his arm, the Peguan seems all about amorous languor: he holds a flower in his left hand, while with his right hand he clasps a lotiform fan (an implement otherwise reserved exclusively for women). He sits cross-legged on a plump, tasseled cushion, in a posture that at once conceals his buttocks and makes a spectacle of their hidden presence (Figure 4).[67] In short, the composition's every detail seems calculated not only to bear out Linschoten's claim that the Peguans were once "great Sodomites" but also to insinuate that sodomy continued to characterize them across the chasm of time. In this sense, the figure of the Peguan does not merely transcend Linschoten's (rather laconic) treatment of Burmese sodomy; it effectively contradicts the claim that it was a thing of the past. The Peguans are sodomites, the plate seems to say, regardless of whether they currently engage in sodomitical practices or not. Far from being just a "category of forbidden acts," as Michel Foucault famously proposed in his *History of Sexuality*, sodomy appears in the *Itinerario* as a category of identity, an innate trait that could be made to reveal itself even in the absence of illicit behavior.[68] Thus, while sodomy continued to be construed as universally available—a set of "unspeakable" acts to which everyone was at least potentially liable—it also came to be increasingly thought of as inhering in distinct individuals and groups. It is telling that in 1644, when the prominent Dutch official Joost Schouten was accused of sodomy, he made no attempt to deny or contest the charges; in his confession, he simply declared to have picked up the practice during his stay among the Siamese.[69]

The minoritizing drift adumbrated in both Linschoten's *Itinerario* and Schouten's confession comes to narrative fruition in the Siamese portion of Richard Head's *The English Rogue: Described, In the Life of Meriton Latroon, a Witty Extravagant* (a text I return to in Chapter 6). As it might be expected from this sexually explicit work, the chapter in which Latroon visits Siam first foregrounds the claim that in times past the country was "much given to *Sodomy*," then details the measures taken in response. Siamese women wore scanty clothing, "the more to allure the men from that detestable and unnatural act of *Sodomy*."[70] As for the men, they spent their youth with a bell of gold "put through the prepuce and flesh" until the time that the urge for coitus made them seek its removal: "When the desire of copulation stimulates any of them, he presents himself to some expert Midwives; who advise him to drink *Opium*, or some such somniferous potion; which having done in their presence, he falls asleep; during which interval, they remove the bell, and apply to the orifice from whence it was taken, an unguent, which affords a speedy cure: then is he free to make use of such as his fancy leads him to" (sig. Ggg2v).

By the time that *The English Rogue* was first published, in 1665, much of this was an ethnographic commonplace. As a matter of fact, most of what Head has to say about Siam derives, often verbatim, from

Thomas Herbert's *A Relation of Some Yeares Travaile*, itself largely a compilation of earlier materials. In Head's rendition, however, what begins as a recitation of antisodomy measures ends up as a spectacular demonstration of their ineffectiveness. During the course of his sojourn in Siam, Latroon meets a *talapoin* or Buddhist monk, who points him to a secluded spot where three young women are lounging. Here again, Head is taking his cue from *A Relation of Some Yeares Travaile*: the episode is closely modeled after Herbert's account of his own encounter with a Persian dervish. But where Herbert had feared the dervish's "villainy" and prudently declined the invitation, Latroon cannot resist the lure presented by the three young women.[71] The irrepressible sexual adventurer that he is, he eagerly sits among them, and before too long he is deep in dalliance with the one he thinks prettiest. Just as he is on the verge of consummating, the talapoin grabs him from behind and attempts to sodomize him: "This *Satyr-Goat-Devil* (I cannot invent a name bad enough to call him by) presently falls down upon us; and taking me thus unawares, lying on my belly, I was no able to help my self, that he had like to have performed his business; and questionless he had effected it, but that the two Maidens standing by (no wayes ashamed at this most shameful sight) assisted me, pulling him off" (sigs. Ggg3v–Ggg4r). What follows represents one of the narrative's most disturbing moments. Having shaken off the talapoin, Latroon immobilizes him and ties him down. Then he takes out his knife and proceeds to castrate him: "I presently started up, & seized him; and tripping up his heels I laid him on his back: having so done, I bound him; then taking out my knife, I could not find in my heart to spare him one inch; and that he might not have any witnesses lest of what was done, I took away his testicles too" (sig. Ggg4r).

The pun on the etymology of "testicles" as "little witnesses" is no doubt intended here. While the dubious bit of humor does little or nothing to camouflage the gratuitous violence of the scene, it creates a peculiarly intimate bond between readers and narrator. Invited to partake in the Latinate joke, audiences are also implicitly invited to share in the text's racism and homophobia—that is, to recognize themselves as part of a community formed at the expense of outsiders unlikely to catch the drollery of the situation. If in this particular case the list of outsiders can be stretched to include English readers unattuned to Latin etymologies, its most obvious members are Siamese and sodomites. Drawing a sharp dividing line between English and Siamese, men who like women and men who like other men (men "inclining to Sodomy," as the narrator puts it in a later edition of the text), the emasculation of the Buddhist monk erases from Head's narrative the last vestiges of their propinquity.[72] While this erasure has the effect of insulating Latroon, at least momentarily, from the sodomitic "contagion" that claimed Joost Schouten, it also testifies to the centrality of European expansion to the emergence of sexuality as a category of identity.

RACE AND THE "NATURE" OF WOMEN

Pigafetta's careful description of male genitalia ends with a brief remark on the genitals of Cebuan females. All the girls on the island, we are told, "from the age of six onward have their natures gradually opened by reason of their men's [enlarged] members" ("da sei anni in su, a poco a poco li apreno la natura per cagion de quelli sui membri").[73] Several decades later, Antonio de Morga pointed in the same direction when he noted that in the Philippines there were men whose profession it was "to take maidens' virginity."[74] Recent scholarship suggests that these might have been hymenotomy rituals "parallel . . . to the attachment of the *sagra* device to the penises of young boys."[75]

Strikingly similar practices of female genital modification were reported in use in both Burma and Siam. The Venetian jeweler Gasparo Balbi, whose firsthand account of Pegu was abstracted in Purchas's *Pilgrimes*, echoed in Adam Olearius and Johann Albrecht von Mandelslo's *Morgenländische Reyse-Beschreibung* (1658), and reproduced in Johann Theodor de Bry and Johann Israel de Bry's *Indiae Orientalis* (1598–1628), wrote that "in that Kingdom [of Pegu] there are no virgins, as all the women since childhood put in their place of generation a certain mixture that they also put in the opening of their ears, for the purpose to make them wide." As for Siam, Thomas Herbert's *A Relation of Some Yeares Travaile*—which appeared in no less than seven English, French, and Dutch editions during the author's lifetime— noted that Siamese virgins were as rare as "a blacke Swanne: in regard at very greene yeares, they give the too forward maydens a virulent potion, which being drunk, by its efficacious power distends their *muliebra* to such a capacitie, that bels and all may find too easie entrance."[76]

The *Itinerario* provided a variation by referencing infibulation. After mentioning that Burmese men wore bells "upon their yarde," Linschoten went on to describe how in Pegu "some . . . doe sowe up the privie member of their female children as soone as they are borne, leaving them but a little hole to avoid their water; and when she marrieth the husband cutteth it open, [and maketh it] as great or as little as hee will" (1: 100). Lest readers find the story too fanciful, Linschoten hastened to add that the information had come to him from multiple independent sources, including Peguan ones. As if that were not enough, he himself had been a witness, having seen "one of those women in Goa whom the Surgeon of [my Mayster] the Archbishops house did cut open" (1: 100). As late as 1665, we find the story echoed in *The English Rogue*, according to which the girls of Siam had "their *Pudenda* . . . sowed up, and only a small *foramen* or passage left, as an *aqueduct*" (sig. Ggg2v). But whereas Linschoten had read infibulation as a chastity technique, Head apparently held the surgical closure of the vulva to be no obstacle to female promiscuity. His narrative accommodates both Linschoten and Herbert—reconciling infibulation with hymenotomy without any trouble: "About eight or nine . . . [the girls are] unstitcht; and it is as great a rarity, to finde a pure Virgin here at ten years old, as to finde a Maid at sixteen, in most places of *France*, or its neighbouring Countreys. And that these young leacherous Fry may be capable of that employment they are destinated unto, they have potions given them to drink, which have the efficacious power as to distend their *muliebra* to such a capacity, as that (if their bells were not withdrawn) their males would finde too easie an entrance" (sigs. Ggg2v–Ggg3r).

Despite their relative scantiness, these references demonstrate a keen awareness—if not on the part of all European travelers, then at least on the part of some of them—that some Asian societies engaged in practices of female genital modification. Nevertheless, while palangs, sagras, and buncales were endlessly described, dissected, and commodified for European consumption, no parallel discourse accreted around reports of hymenotomy and infibulation. Indeed, to the extent that these practices appear at all in early modern ethnographies, they do so only as a kind of *pendant* to male genital modifications. Like Pigafetta before them, Balbi and Herbert posited hymenotomy as the logical consequence of male genital augmentation. For his part, Linschoten placed his brief remarks on infibulation immediately after his description of the penis bells, as if to suggest that the former had its point of origin in the latter. Thus, wherever they are present, Asian practices of female genital modification are never more than a flourish in a discourse that is essentially concerned with male genitalia.

This is not to suggest that women played no role in this discourse. It was, after all, their libido that always lay at the root of the practice, whether this was decried as an aberration or excused in the name of sexual normativity. Where palangs and bells were construed as state interventions, it was always a queen—never a king—who stood behind them. Women sold the necessary implements; and women were reportedly in charge of the surgical procedure. In short, as Europeans saw it, Asian practices of male genital modification were creatures of the female imagination. "And that this was a woman's invention," wrote Carletti in his discussion of the penis bells, "is abundantly proven by the fact that women are the ones who excel at placing and adjusting the aforementioned bells."[77]

But while the imagination, skills, and preferences of women were understood as central, it was nevertheless on the bodies of men that discourses of Asian aberrancy routinely focused. Whenever they were object of sustained attention, the bodies of women were instead regularly praised for their form, texture, and proportion—in other words, for their adherence to Europeans standards of beauty and desirability. As a result, while the racial and sexual identities of Asian males came to be imagined as a set of alterities that were literally implanted in their flesh, the racial and sexual identities of Asian females remained somewhat unmoored from physical morphology, and therefore conceivable as neutral or malleable.[78] This peculiarity suggests that in Asia, no less than in the Americas, European ideologies of gender had a significant impact on the way that race was bounded and ascribed.[79] In the early colonial or incipiently colonial conditions that are the focus of this study, the doubly othered status of Asian women translated, paradoxically, into enhanced social mobility. To put it in the terms favored by many early modern writers, Asian women were eminently "convertible"—a belief that, as I show in the following chapters, played an important part not only in the dynamics of the European-Asian encounter but also in the way that these dynamics were represented.

CHAPTER 2

The Erotic Politics
of *Os Lusíadas*

In the summer of 1499, Vasco da Gama and his crew returned to Portugal after a two-year voyage that had taken them to India and back. In many ways, the expedition had been a failure: one ship was lost and over two thirds of the crew lay dead, no trade agreements had been concluded, and the explorers had committed so many blunders that, by report, "the whole land [of India] wished [them] ill."[1] But the small cargo of Eastern spices the survivors brought with them was the first to have ever come via the Cape of Good Hope. Da Gama was given a hero's welcome, a title of nobility, and a generous pension. Meanwhile, King Dom Manuel took for himself the title of "Lord of the Conquest, Navigation, and Commerce of Ethiopia, Arabia, Persia, and India," embarking on a ruthless, unrelenting campaign of infiltration and domination.[2]

Within two decades, the Portuguese had fortified their positions at Cochin and Cannanore; destroyed a joint Egyptian-Gujarati fleet off Diu; captured Goa, Malacca, and Hormuz; and taken most of the city-states on the East African coast. Although the area of land acquired in each case was extremely small, the importance of these conquests was immense. Collectively, they had given the Portuguese almost complete control over the Indian Ocean, and provided them with much new knowledge in the process. By 1508, the soldier-cosmographer Duarte Pacheco Pereira could extol the magnitude of these achievements by comparison with those of the past. For while the Romans and the Macedonians had surely known something of the world beyond the Mediterranean, still "the best part . . . of so many regions and provinces has been reserved for us, and we are the ones who have taken its maidenhead."[3]

In this formulation, the difference between Portugal and its imperial predecessors could be conceptualized as a sexual matter: the present was to the past as deflowering to foreplay. It is hardly a coincidence that Luís de Camões's *Os Lusíadas*—a poem written expressly to celebrate Portugal's expansion into Asia—quite literally climaxes at the Isle of Love.[4] The episode is well known: on the return portion of their trip, da Gama and his men stumble across an enchanted island that Venus has populated with enamored Nereids. This is an erotically charged *locus amoenus* where vines cling amorously to trees, pomegranates suggestively expose their flesh, and lemons protrude from the branches like pubescent breasts (9.56).[5] Against this luscious background, beautiful sea nymphs roam the meadows, play rustic instruments, or bathe in crystal waters.

The scene, as Américo da Costa Ramalho has noted, is an ekphrastic rendering of *poesia* painting, a sixteenth-century pictorial genre inspired by the fables, myths, and legends related by Ovid, Virgil, and Apuleius.[6] Indeed, the poem explicitly identifies the enchanted island as a painted artifact, an intentionally voyeuristic space inviting readers and explorers alike to partake of its proffered delights:

Que as Ninfas do Oceano tão fermosas,
Tétis e a Ilha angélica pintada,
Outra cousa não é que as deleitosas
Honras que a vida fazem sublimada.
(9.89)

For the ocean nymphs in all their beauty, / Tethys, and the magic painted island, / Are nothing more than those delightful / Honours which make our lives sublime.

The sailors' enjoyment of this space, however, is not supposed to be merely voyeuristic: Venus has in fact designed the island as a sensuous paradise where the Portuguese might fulfill their every desire. To ensure the desired outcome, she has recycled an old Virgilian trick, dispatching Cupid to enflame the Nereids' hearts. For good measure, she has also enlisted the Titan goddess Fame to sing the praises of the Portuguese, and personally taken the time to coach the nymphs on the finer points of lovemaking. Given these punctilious preparations, one would expect the nymphs to be almost beside themselves with excitement. This is hardly the case: although wounded by Cupid's arrows, exposed to Fame's propaganda, and tutored by Venus herself, the Nereids flee as soon as the sailors approach. The encounter turns quickly into a hunt, with the nymphs running and the Portuguese chasing greedily after them:

> Outros, por outra parte, vão topar
> Com as Deusas despidas que se lavam;
> Elas começam súbito a gritar,
> Como que assalto tal não esperavam;
> Ũas, fingindo menos estimar
> A vergonha que a força, se lançavam
> Nuas por entre o mato, aos olhos dando
> O que às mãos cobiçosas vão negando;
>
> Outra, como acudindo mais depressa
> À vergonha da Deusa caçadora,
> Esconde o corpo na água; outra se apressa
> Por tomar os vestidos, que tem fora.
> Tal dos mancebos há que se arremessa
> Vestido assi e calçado (que, co a mora
> De se despir, há medo que inda tarde),
> A matar na água o fogo que nele arde.
> (9.72–73)

> Others, elsewhere, stumbled upon / The unclothed nymphs who were bathing; / These suddenly began to scream / As if surprised by the assault; / Some pretending to be troubled less / By shame than by violence, scampered / Naked into the bush, letting them see / Just where their itching hands would like to be. // One, resorting faster to the famed / Modesty of Diana the Huntress / Hid herself in the lake, as another / Dashed for her tunic on the bank. / But at this, a sailor flung himself / Fully clothed and shod as he was (not / Bothering to undress for hurry's sake) / To quench his ardour right there in the lake.

The nymphs have ample reason to flee. Intimations of sexual violence are so deeply embedded in the island's description as to be almost an integral part of its landscape. Not nightingales but Philomels sing from the branches. Actæons—not deer—mirror themselves in the lake.[7] Breezes and flowers call to mind Zephyrus's defilement of Flora, and laurel trees evoke Apollo's assault on Daphne. Almost every detail, in short, seems to be there just to prefigure future ravishments. The sailors' attitude, moreover, is decidedly aggressive. Although they have come ashore to hunt for "caça agreste" (woodland game) (9.66), da Gama and his men immediately transfer their predatory appetite onto the nymphs, seeing them as a "caça estranha" (strange game) that is both gentler and easier to catch (9.69).[8]

Reading the eventual capture as sexual violence, however, would mean taking theater for reality. For while the dynamics of the encounter between Portuguese and nymphs clearly rest on the iconography of rape, the poem also insists that this is not rape, but erotic power play. After all, these nymphs are not chaste votaresses of Diana's. They demand nothing better—or so we are told—than being captured and subdued. Their flight is a game, their fear an act meant to amplify the pleasures of lovemaking. Their screams, torn garments, and disheveled hair are all performative cues, part of an elaborate staging in which the Portuguese are both intended audience and unwitting participants. The end result is a mass tumble from which we seem to be visually excluded only so that we might better become agents in its reproduction:

> Oh, que famintos beijos na floresta!
> E que mimoso choro que soava!
> Que afagos tão suaves! Que ira honesta,
> Que em risinhos alegres se tornava!
> O que mais passam na menhã e na sesta,
> Que Vénus com prazeres inflamava,
> Milhor é exprimentá-lo que julgá-lo,
> Mas julgue-o quem não pode exprimentá-lo.
> (9.83)

> What ravenous kisses filled the wood! / What little moans and tender weeping! / What sweet caresses! What virtuous anger, / Yielding to happy, compliant laughter! / What further happened that morn and noon / As Venus fanned the flames of love, / Better to relish than disparage it; / Let those begrudge who cannot manage it.

And as if to underline that the game has been consensual all along, the consummation is followed by a wedding ceremony: each sailor gets a nymph, and da Gama marries no less than the sea goddess Tethys. This, in turn, provides the occasion for an epic catalogue of heroes largely derived from João de Barros's *Décadas da Ásia* and Fernão Lopes de Castanheda's *História do descobrimento e conquista da Índia pelos Portugueses.*[9] The episode eventually ends on a mountain summit, where a transparent globe with the power to represent all times and places offers a proleptic survey of Portugal's worldwide empire.

Spanning two cantos and forming almost one-fifth of the entire poem, the Isle of Love represents one of the longest and best-known parts of *Os Lusíadas.* Nevertheless, the episode's frank eroticism has historically proven disconcerting to critics.[10] Voltaire, for one, compared the island to a brothel; and even the sympathetic Maurice Bowra felt compelled to admit that, if taken literally, the encounter between sailors and nymphs is as "unsuitable for heroes" as "improper for men."[11] As a result, many have taken refuge in interpretations that mute or suppress the most overtly sexual dimensions of the episode. Vítor Manuel de Aguiar e Silva, for instance, warns us that reading the nymphs as anything other than a poetic function might prevent "any acceptable exegesis" of the text.[12] In a related vein, Landeg White exhorts us to resist the island's erotic charms, lest they seduce us away from the episode's *true* purpose—that is, to present "a complete portrait not only of the solar system and of the true dimensions and riches of the planet . . . but of the relationship between the physical and the intellectual, the sensual and the philosophical, the imaginative and the moral, the 'Roman' and the Christian visions of the world."[13] If we are to understand the episode correctly, in other words, we need to look *past* the encounter between sailors and nymphs, and *toward* the epistemological revelations of canto 10. As the lowest step in a ladder of ascent moving from appetite to knowledge, eros is acknowledged just to be dismissed: it serves a function only insofar as it can be sublimated and left behind.[14]

David Quint has partly countered this dismissal by focusing on the relationship between the Isle of Love interlude and the episode of the would-be lover-rapist Adamastor, the earthborn Titan who appears when da Gama's fleet approaches the Cape of Good Hope. As Camões recounts it, the story of Adamastor's transformation into the Cape's landmass is inextricably linked to his unconsummated desire for Thetis, a sea nymph whose name is virtually indistinguishable from that of da Gama's goddess wife. The relationship between the Titan's erotic disgruntlement and the sexual exploits of the Isle of Love is thereby configured as "one of inversion: the Portuguese get the girls, and consummate fame and power, while the enemy monster is consumed with frustration."[15] This near-chiastic pattern has the advantage of highlighting the importance of eros within the narrative economy of the *Lusíadas*. Its drawback, though, is that it subordinates the encounters of the Isle of Love to the confrontation with Adamastor. In Quint's reading, the nymphs figure as "willing native girls in a thin mythological disguise," and their sexual submission serves as a graphic representation of power asymmetries that truly obtain only in the political world—that is, in the male world of da Gama and Adamastor.[16] While the salience of eros in the poem is recognized, its relevance to the discourse of early modern imperialism is occluded.

This is the case even among those critics who have linked the episode most explicitly to the process of Portugal's imperial expansion. According to René Garay, for one, the encounter between sailors and nymphs "illustrates not only the conquest and conversion of the new peoples, but also the Portuguese mastery of the oceans leading to the coveted Eastern realms."[17] Reduced to a trope, the erotic dimension of the episode is once again severed from the poem's imperial subject matter—making it virtually impossible to postulate a meaningful relation between the two. Yet there can be no doubt about this relation. Without the island there would be no epic catalogue of imperial heroes, and no vision of Portugal's future successes in Asia. Without the encounter between sailors and nymphs, in short, there would be no properly imperial dimension to the poem. Seen in this light, the consummations at the Isle of Love are neither a "domestic" interlude in an otherwise "political" text nor a mere metaphor for struggles and negotiations taking place at other societal levels. Rather, they bespeak the importance of eros in both the semantics and the pragmatics of Europe's imperial expansion. The point here is not only that this expansion was often envisioned as a release of male sexual energy, but also that colonial regimes latched onto the production and management of differentiated sexualities as a means for securing authority. As Ann Laura Stoler has argued, the "regulation of sexual relations was central to the development of particular kinds of colonial settlements and to the allocation of economic activity within them. Who bedded and wedded whom in the colonies of France, England, Holland and Iberia was never left to chance."[18] In such circumstances, erotic attachments and domestic arrangements were also quite obviously matters of state—"political and economic affairs that acted to sharpen or mute the categories of ruler and ruled."[19]

In this chapter, I chart the literary and historical contexts of the Isle of Love episode, locating the first in the reception of Rome's imperial tradition, the second in the legacy of colonial practices dating back to the first half of the sixteenth century. My basic argument is that the encounter between sailors and nymphs imaginatively engages with what we have come to know as the política dos casamentos or intermarriage policy, a tactic of racial mixing that characterized Portugal's expansion into Asia long before being adopted by the English and the Dutch. In this way, Camões's poem also elaborates an erotics of marriage that delicately registers the cleavages and contradictions of the imperial enterprise, thus helping us trace at least some of the ways in which the history of sexuality is intimately connected to the history of European imperialism.

OF SABINES AND INDIANS

Almost from the beginning, Portugal's Eastern ventures were ideologically construed as an extension of the centuries-long crusade known as the Iberian Reconquest. This perceived continuity facilitated the implementation of warfare tactics putatively developed during the Middle Ages. First among these were conquest marriages, by which captive Muslim women could be baptized and married to their Christian captors.[20] Fátima, the small village north of Lisbon catapulted to international fame in 1917 by sightings of the Virgin Mary, stands as a testament to the popularity of this medieval topos. The name of this site is in fact linked to the Reconquest legend of a Muslim princess who, following capture by Gonçalo Hermigues, Count of Ourém, abandoned Islam and became his wife. Her baptismal name was Oureana, but her birth name had been Fátima, after the daughter of the prophet Muhammed. When she died, a few years after marriage, her burial place became known as Fátima—a permanent reminder of her forcible incorporation into the Christian camp.[21]

Although we do not know how many of these Muslim-Christian unions actually took place, the widespread popularity of conquest marriage narratives testifies to their ideological saliency throughout the Reconquest period and beyond. In these tales, intermarriage is construed as the total victory of a virile Christendom over an effeminized Islam, with the knight or hero generally insisting on conversion and even refraining from kissing the woman on the mouth until she has become a Christian. And to better drive home the point that in these cases carnal consummation satisfies both physical and spiritual desire, the sacraments of baptism and marriage are generally conferred together, with the bride taking as her name some variant of the groom's.[22] This renaming procedure symbolically confers on the husband both marital and paternal rights, in a Pygmalion-like fantasy of cultural omnipotence that affords Christian men the satisfaction of generating their partners and possessing them too.

When the Portuguese went to Asia, conquest marriages became part and parcel of contact-zone reality. "We took here some Moorish women, white and good-looking," reported Portuguese governor Afonso de Albuquerque in 1510, shortly after the conquest of Goa. "Several of [our] men, well-born and gentlemanlike, asked them in marriage, in order to settle in this land . . . and so I had them married according to the orders received from Your Highness, and to each of them I gave a horse, house, land, and cattle."[23] Indeed, during the early phase of expansion, Portuguese authorities in Asia not only condoned but actively encouraged the formation of interracial households. Female immigration from Europe was severely restricted, and financial incentives were provided to cross-racial couples willing to tie the knot. In 1511, for instance, Portuguese grooms pocketed grants between 16,000 and 24,000 reais; Indian brides received up to 800 reais, twice as much as the going reward for a Muslim's head.[24] By the following year, the intermarriage scheme was in full swing, with European immigrants marrying and settling down at a brisk pace. For Governor Afonso de Albuquerque, in particular, the future of the empire rested on the shoulders of these domestic pioneers, who were known as "married men" or *casados*. "The business of the casados is making great progress . . . at Cannanore and Cochin there are about one hundred of them, and almost two hundred in Goa," he wrote in a 1512 dispatch to the king, expressing the belief that these unions would soon pave the way for the territorial dispossession of the natives: "If [our] people continue to marry and settle down at the present rate, I believe it will be necessary for Your Highness to evict the natives of the island [of Goa] and give land and farms to the casados."[25] And "if your Highness could see how great an inclination and desire people have to marry in Goa, you would be amazed," Albuquerque gloated in the same letter. "There seems to be something divine about the strong wish that Portuguese men have to marry and settle in Goa. . . . I believe that Our Lord has ordained this, inclining their hearts toward something hidden from us, but of great service to him."[26]

In truth, there was nothing mysterious or divine about the rank and file's willingness to settle in Asia. Most of these settlers were illiterate pages, assorted wastrels, and exiled convicts. Many could not return; others had nothing to return to. For men like these, the *política dos casamentos* unlocked opportunities of unprecedented proportions. Casados were exempt from both military duty and municipal taxes, enjoyed preferment in local administrations, could not be jailed for any civil offense, and had license to engage in private trade—an activity from which single men were barred.[27] Through marriage, moreover, casados also acquired rights over their wives' labor and property, and often gained access to native economic networks.

The expense and dangers of the six- to eight-month voyage from Portugal to India surely played a role in the implementation of the política dos casamentos: recruiting wives locally was both cheaper and more convenient than importing them from Europe.[28] Yet calculations of convenience were never innocent of ideological charge. Deep beneath the relative success of the intermarriage scheme, in fact, lay the notion of the female body as racially pliable material. Through marriage, native women were thought to "absorb" the status of their husbands, and it was assumed that mixed-race children would automatically identify as Portuguese. This idea found comfort in medical theories according to which men alone gave soul and form to the fetus: children would resemble their fathers more than their mothers because male stock was more determinative than female stock. Coupled with the belief that more "civilized" seed was stronger than its "uncivilized" counterpart, medical discourse enabled a eugenic construction of racial mixing as a gradual Europeanization of native stock.[29]

The point is implicitly made in the 1579 "Sumario de las cosas que perteneçen a la provincia de la Yndia Oriental y al govierno della" [Compendium related to the Province of the East Indies and its governance], where the Jesuit Alessandro Valignano subdivided "those born in India" into four groups: native Indians; mestiços, "born of Portuguese father and native mother"; castiços, "born of Portuguese father and mestiço mother"; and Portuguese, "born of Portuguese father and mother."[30] Significantly, Valignano's compendium provides no specific nomenclature for those born of Portuguese father and castiço mother, thereby suggesting that these were not clearly distinguishable from Portuguese born of pure Portuguese parentage (of whom there were likely very few). Even more significantly, Valignano's description of "those born in India" is arranged less as a taxonomy than as a eugenic ladder, progressively moving from "pure" Indians to "pure" Portuguese: provided that Indo-Portuguese offspring kept intermarrying exclusively with Portuguese, this process of assimilation could be completed in as little as three generations.[31]

In this perspective, socially sanctioned practices of racial mixing served as the cornerstone of power structures on which the colonial project as a whole depended: they advanced colonial penetration, promoted religious conversion, and ensured acculturation to European practices and values.[32] The history of Rome offered good precedent to this effect, a fact Camões and his contemporaries—attuned as they were to the homologies between the story of the Roman Empire and that of Portugal's overseas expansion—could not possibly miss. For even Rome, as the historian Jõao de Barros noted in his *Décadas da Ásia*, was born from the violent conscription of alien women: "Every nation began humbly—from people we would consider scum. For if [we] look at the origins of Rome . . . queen of the Roman Empire . . . [we] find that it was a company of shepherds, or (better yet) a band of criminals; and that the Sabine maidens, whom they took for wives, if they were whiter by reason of the climate, they were not of nobler blood than [the women] of India, nor did they have better knowledge of God . . . nor were their nuptials consensual, as the matrimonial act requires; rather, they were the result of violence with a mass rape in view."[33] As Barros saw it, the intermarriage scheme deployed in Asia simply revived time-honored tactics of state formation and empire building. It mattered little that the brides were lowborn and oftentimes Christian in name only. Nor did it matter that these marriages were nonconsensual, in violation of both societal values and the law. Political necessity justified the practice, and the example of Rome vouched for its effectiveness.

Following the lead of Barros, whose *Décadas da Ásia* were a major source for *Os Lusíadas*, Camões's Isle of Love recast the intermarriage scheme into a novel Sabine myth. This is made evident not only by the episode's reliance on the iconography of rape but also by the presence of "palavras formais e estipulantes" (formal vows and covenants) binding nymphs and sailors in a marriage contract (9.84). In Camões's formulation, however, what Barros had envisioned as a mere co-optation of reproductive labor becomes a specific structure of desire deeply rooted in the reception of Ovid.

As critics have long noted, no other part of *Os Lusíadas* is as indebted to Ovid as the Isle of Love episode.[34] References to *The Metamorphoses*, in particular, are too ubiquitous to count and too obvious to miss: Actaeon and Diana (9.26), Venus and Adonis (9.60), Apollo and Daphne (9.57), Byblis and Myrrha (9.34)—these are just few of the many tendrils tying the Isle of Love to Ovid's *Metamorphoses*. The nymphs' seductive poses, as well, find precedent in Ovid's many bathing scenes; and Lionardo Ribeiro's pleas to the wayward nymph Ephyre recall Apollo's speech to Daphne in *Metamorphoses* 1. More important, the rape iconography deployed in the Isle of Love episode seems directly borrowed from the heroic rapes—plots in which the rapist is a god or a hero—contained in the *Metamorphoses*.[35] These mythological ravishments exposed power at its rawest and roughest, as if to flaunt its ability to violate, terrorize, and dispossess; at the same time, they legitimized it by reencoding violence as an act of love that brought order and fertility to the universe. This simultaneity of effect was achieved through a series of manipulations and emendations that aestheticized the action while muting the victim's fear and pain: sexual intercourse was expunged from view, and force might be suggested but not displayed. The idyllic mood of the setting—often a springtime landscape of great pastoral beauty—further facilitated a pleasurable fruition of the scene, effectively naturalizing violence as a fundamental component of desire.

Yet a significant part of the inspiration behind the Isle of Love episode comes less from *The Metamorphoses* than from Ovid's *Ars Amatoria*, echoes of which are easily discernible in much of the episode.[36] In this mock-didactic poem, Ovid had propounded the thesis that "no" means "yes"—thereby paving the way for Camões's figuration of rape as erotic power play. He had also unabashedly traced the origins of the Roman Empire back to the lustful desires of the city's early settlers.

Although it is not Rome's originary rape—that dubious distinction, as Mary Beard reminds us, lies even further back, with Mars's rape of the Vestal Rhea Silvia—the rape of the Sabine women marks a foundational moment in the mythic history of the city and its empire. As a direct or indirect result of the rape, the Romans would build their first temple, celebrate their first triumph, and establish their first colonies, transcending their humble beginnings and experiencing a sizeable increase in both size and might.[37] As narrated by Ovid's contemporary Livy, to whom we owe what is often considered the "official" version of the story, the rape of the Sabine women was an act of political necessity. Needing reproductive labor to assure their fledgling city of a future, the Romans had initially sought partners through peaceful negotiations with their neighbors. Only after these conventional venues were exhausted did they resort to unconventional means, organizing a solemn celebration and inviting the neighboring Sabine tribe to attend. At a prearranged signal, while the guests' attention was riveted on the spectacle, the Romans rushed in and snatched away the maidens. The outraged Sabine men of course sought revenge, and a series of wars ensued. Eventually, the Sabine women (by then Roman wives and mothers) brokered a peace between the two camps, and the Sabine men became citizens of Rome.[38]

If Livy presented the rape of the Sabine women as a classical case in which the means (rape) justifies the end (expansion), Ovid ironically suggested that the means might very well be an end in and of itself. Indeed, in Ovid's *Ars Amatoria*—as in Camões's encounter between sailors and nymphs—there is no hint of political necessity. Violence arises neither from the political urgency of procreation nor from the exigencies of state formation, but rather from the pull of desire and the pleasures that such desire promises and affords. In other words, Ovid's account of the Sabine myth emphasized precisely those things that Livy was so careful to write out. "Romulus, thou only didst know how to bestow bounty on thy warriors," the poet proclaimed, "so thou but bestow such bounty upon me, I will be a warrior."[39] Reframing the Sabine myth in terms less of collective need than of individual appetite, Ovid bound the dynamics of empire building to the erotic potentialities of violence. The end result is a specific configuration of desire that confuses Cupid with Mars, electing eros as the emblem of a voracious *libido dominandi* that vanquishes in the bedroom just as roundly as on the battlefield.[40]

It is precisely this figuration of the Sabine myth that Camões appropriates in the Isle of Love episode. Like Ovid's early Romans, da Gama and his men partake of a libidinal expansionism that is enacted both sexually and militarily. Better yet, their very desires— as the obviously performative dimension of the episode suggests— are deeply shaped by the asymmetries of power generated by imperial expansion. The encounter between sailors and nymphs stages a power exchange in which the former learn to wield power, and the latter to submit to it.[41] Once normalized by marriage, such exchange embeds the moment of conquest in the most intimate of domestic rituals: violence comes to function as a necessary component of conjugal desire, and this desire, in turn, produces and maintains the rule of empire. The erotics that shape the Isle of Love episode are thus not only reproductive but also productive—in the sense that they are crucial to the production of Portugal's imperial identity. Hence the episode's reliance on the iconography of sexual violence; by enacting an Ovidian script of eroto-military aggression, the encounters of the Isle of Love metamorphose eros into epos, transforming a bunch of sailors into a mighty band of conquerors. In this manner, the poem covers up the epic inadequacy of its immediate subject matter—a reconnoitering voyage in which, as Richard Helgerson has remarked, arms "are often mentioned [and] occasionally shown off" but hardly ever used in battle.[42]

We are then in a better position to appreciate the strategic placement of the episode within the overall structure of the *Lusíadas*. Poised as the narrative bridge between da Gama's uneventful voyage and the military exploits of later decades, the island provides a crucial link between past and future. It is simultaneously an accomplished enterprise, and a call to action; a reward, and an invitation to venture east. Incidentally, this seems to be what Venus had in mind from the beginning, or at least from the moment she conceived of the island as the cradle of a progeny that might serve as proof of eros's potency:

> Quero que haja no Reino neptunino,
> Onde eu nasci, progénie forte e bela,
> E tome exemplo o mundo vil, malino,
> Que contra tua potência se revela,
> Por que entendam que muro adamantino
> Nem triste hipocrisia val contra ela;
> Mal haverá na terra quem se guarde,
> Se teu fogo imortal nas águas arde.
> (9.42)

> I wish to populate Neptune's realm / Where I was born, with a strong and beautiful progeny, / And let the base and wicked world / Which challenges your powers, take note, / That neither walls of adamantine / Nor hypocrisy can avail against it; / For who will find on land any quarter / If your fires rage unquenched in the water?

Despite its reproductive suggestions, here the term "progeny" does not refer to the offspring that nymphs and sailors might engender together.[43] Rather, it identifies the Portuguese themselves—and more specifically those Portuguese whose attitudes and desires have been properly molded by the imperial experience. As the poem makes clear, the enchanted island will continue to beckon for generations to come: all worthy conquerors will get to taste of its delights. Or to put it another way, for as long as there is an Isle of Love, there will also be worthy Portuguese conquerors.

Capitalizing on Ovid's equation of love and war, Camões's island enshrines imperial violence both at the heart of the *Lusíadas* and at the center of domestic heterosexuality—an ideology that made erotic desire a requirement for marriage.[44] To the extent that Camões's eroticization of violence has become an integral part of normative heterosexuality—the stuff of MGM movie classics (the staircase scene in *Gone with the Wind* being perhaps the most notorious example), pulp romances, and confessional columns—we have grown oblivious to the historical specificities that helped bring it into being. This may well be the reason why the encounter between sailors and nymphs is generally passed over in silence: its erotic dynamics are so recognizable that they have become invisible.

Yet a closer reading of the Isle of Love episode suggests that these familiar dynamics can be made unfamiliar again. It is not only that the episode insists on the social and rhetorical constructedness of eros, or that it reminds us that structures of desire have eminently political uses. It is also that its performative dimension exposes sexual normativity as radically contingent. As a "scene" of power exchange—that is, a staging in which one's dominance is necessarily predicated on another's deliberate will to submit—the Isle of Love betrays the vulnerable instability of both sexual and imperial mastery. It is to that vulnerability that I now turn, to trace the ways in which *Os Lusíadas* might be seen to explore the cleavages and contradictions of its own ideological enterprise.

AMOR NEFANDO

It has become almost a critical commonplace that the *Lusíadas* construes Portugal's imperial expansion as part and parcel of a larger campaign waged by Love itself. At the most literal level, this is certainly true: after all, if Venus can so easily recruit Cupid into her scheme, it is precisely because she finds him already engaged in a campaign meant to correct mankind's amatory errors. As the god sees it, the problem is not so much that human beings don't love enough, as that they are in love with the wrong things—or, as the poem puts it, that they love "cousas que nos foram dadas, / Não pera ser amadas, mas usadas" (things meant to be used rather than loved; 9.25). In theory, Cupid's military campaign should engender a love capable of restoring the world's desires to their proper objects. In practice, though, the expedition ends up creating just as many problems as it solves. While Cupid takes care of the nymphs, the "tiros . . . desordenados" (disorderly shots) fired by his troops bring into being all sorts of "amores . . . desconcertados" (ill-assorted passions), engendering loves so wicked as to be utterly unspeakable:

Destes tiros assi desordenados,
Que estes moços mal destros vão tirando,
Nascem amores mil desconcertados
Entre o povo ferido miserando;
E também nos heróis de altos estados
Exemplos mil se vêem de amor nefando,
Qual o das moças Bíbli e Cinireia,
Um mancebo de Assíria, um de Judeia.
(9.34)

From these disorderly shots / Fired by such inexpert cherubs, / Were
born among their wounded victims / A thousand ill-assorted passions. / And even among the noblest were seen / Countless cases of
unspeakable love, / Such as happened to Byblis and Myrrha, / To one
Assyrian youth, and to a Judean one.

Although the stanza clearly equates "amor nefando" (unspeakable
love) with incest (Biblys and Myrrha) and possibly incestuous rape
and adultery (the Judean youth mentioned in the last line is presumably Amnon, who raped his sister Tamar; the Assyrian youth is usually identified as Seleucus, who married his stepmother, Stratonice),
the early modern currency of "unspeakable" as a quasi-legal term for
sodomy defied easy circumscription, as the seventeenth-century edi-
tor and commentator Manuel de Faria e Sousa acknowledged when he
noted: "In this context, the term *unspeakable* certainly suggests more
than I believe the poet to mean; and it is in truth possible to think that
he means it."[45] Indeed, while Camões's gloss explicitly cites Byblis
and Myrrha—who, as Ovid recounts, fell respectively for brother and
father—the resonances of "unspeakable" invite connotations that
would have ranged from zoophilia and interfaith sex to masturbation and anal intercourse. It is no surprise that the unspeakable passions of Byblis and Myrrha find an intratextual echo in the "unspeakable love" attributed to Semiramis, whom the *Lusíadas* accuses not
only of incest with her son but also of bestiality with her horse (7.53).
The specter of bestiality, in turn, haunts the poem's deployment of
"unspeakable" in the geographical survey of canto 10—this time a
reference to the alleged sodomitic propensities of Burmese males:

Olha o Reino Arracão; olha o assento
De Pegu, que já monstros povoaram,
—Monstros filhos do feio ajuntamento
De ũa mulher e um cão, que sós se acharam;
Aqui soante arame no instrumento
Da gèração costumam, o que usaram

Por manha da rainha que, inventando
Tal uso, deitou fora o error nefando.
(10.122)

See the Arakan kingdom and the throne / Of Pegu, once peopled by
monsters / —Children of the horrible coupling / Of a solitary woman
and a dog: / Today men wear on their genitals / Tiny tinkling bells,
a custom / Invented very subtly by their queen / To put pay to the
unspeakable crime.

Here again, *Os Lusíadas* takes its cue from Barros's *Décadas*, compressing in a single stanza many of the tropes discussed in Chapter 1.
Rehearsing the bells' bestial ancestry as well as their relation to sodomy, Camões's ethnological tour de force evinces the extent not only
to which practices of genital modification informed Europe's representations of Asia but also to which tropes of Asian "deviance" came
to delimit the boundaries of licit eroticism.

Unspeakable love thus covers a whole range of socially disorderly
behaviors, which are seemingly connected to one another only by
their Eastern setting and the amount of erotic agency they assign to
women. The relevance of the Eastern setting is perhaps most obvious in the case of the Burmese, whose erotic peculiarities take pride
of place in the geographic survey of canto 10. But a similar case can
also be made with Semiramis, especially since the poem identifies the
infamous Babylonian queen as one of the ancient conquerors of India.
Perhaps less explicitly, an Eastern setting appears also in the stories
of Byblis and Myrrha: for the former was from Anatolia (in modern-
day Turkey), while the latter lived in Panchaia, a legendary island in
the Indian Ocean.

Taken collectively, these unspeakable loves point not only to a
long-standing tradition identifying the East as a site of sexual excess
but also to the disruptive potential of women's erotic agency. While
the power exchange at the Isle of Love ostensibly binds erotic agency
to masculinity, unspeakable structures of desire expose the vulnerability of that bind: Byblis actively pursues her brother; Myrrha tricks
her unwary father into intercourse. In Burma, it is women rather than
men who seemingly call the shots in sexual matters. As for Semiramis, the poem's insistence on her erotic hippophilia triggers an eques-
trian fantasy epitomizing the scandal of female dominance: she is,
quite literally, a woman on top.

If we look at the Isle of Love episode within this larger context,
it becomes obvious that Cupid's expansionist enterprise is far from

being coterminous with the erotic exploits of the Portuguese. Cupid's campaign mobilizes a polymorphous desire that takes various shapes, makes use of diverse objects, and seeks satisfaction in many different ways. The Isle of Love, by contrast, is shown to channel desire into a conjugal erotic especially suited to the political requirements of imperial rule in Asia. At the same time, because these different structures of desire share the same genealogy—that is, because they all result from Cupid's military campaign—the encounter between sailors and nymphs represents only one of many possible outcomes that have been simultaneously mobilized. To put it another way, the unspeakable loves that lap the shore at the Isle of Love are all erotic potentials that the island itself has temporarily foreclosed.

On close inspection, in fact, even those features that more precisely seem to identify and delimit the range of unspeakable desire—that is, patterns of female agency set against the backdrop of more or less "Oriental" locales—are revealed to be just as integral to the construction of the Isle of Love episode as to the poem's account of unspeakable love. As willing participants in a scene of power exchange, the nymphs have no less erotic agency than the incestuous Mhyrra or the hippophilic Semiramis. And because it is clearly a Dionysian space conjured into existence by a goddess of Asian origin, the Isle of Love itself is no less Oriental than Byblis's Anatolia or Myrrha's Panchaia. To the extent that the Isle of Love episode can be said to engage directly with the política dos casamentos, in short, the picture that emerges from it is a far cry from Albuquerque's view of racial mixing. Like Albuquerque, Camões implicates desire in a preternatural plan. But whereas for Albuquerque this preternatural plan rested firmly in the hands of God, for Camões it derives from a pagan goddess with a dubious genealogy and a penchant for extramarital affairs.

We can then characterize the relation between the normalized erotics of the Isle of Love and the unspeakable erotics found elsewhere in the poem as one of vexed mutuality: within the fabric of the *Lusíadas*, the former could not exist without the latter. Without bestiality, incest, and sodomy, there would be no play of dominance and submission at the Isle of Love. If a boundary can be said to keep these different structures of desire apart, it is a boundary that can be sustained only through an immense effort. The poem makes this point quite forcefully when it underscores the laborious genesis of the island: Venus conjures the setting, Cupid enflames the nymphs, and Fame sings the praises of the Portuguese. The boundary between productive love and socially disruptive lust is sustained through the combined energies of three mythological figures—not to mention the combined energies of the nymphs and the sailors.

By recognizing the fundamental continuity between the normative and the nonnormative, the West and the East, the productive and the disruptive, the poem acknowledges not only the constructedness of desire, but also an urgent need for its management and control. For if the normative and the nonnormative are fundamentally similar, how can we possibly guard against sliding from one into the other? In this sense, Camões's poem partakes of a larger colonial discourse that was keenly invested in the proper disposition of bodies, pleasures, and affects. Not that this is surprising: the *Lusíadas* might have become Portugal's national epic, but it is, first and foremost, an artifact of the contact zone. Born of the nearly seventeen years Camões spent in Asia as a soldier and a minor colonial official, it is both riven by the anxieties and contradictions of the imperial enterprise and informed by the knowledge and discourses generated by the cross-cultural encounter.

EROS AND THE CONTACT ZONE

Having begun at stanza 18 of the ninth canto, the Isle of Love episode closes at stanza 143 of the tenth, where the Portuguese weigh anchor and sail for Europe, leaving the "painted island" behind. They do so, however, only after taking aboard "a companhia desejada / Das Ninfas, que hão-de ter eternamente" (the delectable company / Of the nymphs, bound to them eternally; 10.143). In the following stanza, the Portuguese enter the Tagus River and arrive at Lisbon, symbolically offering India to king and country. It is presumably in the blank space between the two stanzas that we are somehow supposed to shake off allegory and return to history. For not doing so, as Anna Klobucka has observed, would mean facing the embarrassment of an encounter between the nymphs and the sailors' wives, whose tearful farewell we have witnessed in the fourth canto (4.91–93).[46] We are thus left to wonder why the Nereids did not simply remain on the island, to be recycled by lesser imperial epigones—as the poem seems to imply when it forecasts that future worthy conquerors will stumble across the same island and enjoy the same rewards: "Estes e outros barões . . . / . . . / Virão lograr os gostos *desta* ilha / . . . / E acharão *estas* Ninfas e *estas* mesas, / Que glórias e honras são de árduas empresas" (These and other heroes . . . / Will taste *this* island's pleasures

/ . . . / Will find *these* lovely nymphs and *these* tables / Which are the glorious rewards for tasks accomplished; 10.73, my emphases). Even this solution, though, turns out in retrospect to be unsatisfactory. It is not only that proper nuptials have bound sailors and nymphs together with "formal vows and covenants" (9.84); the canto also emphasizes that the nymphs' active presence is essential to the production of Portugal's imperial identity. And yet if the *Lusíadas* cannot allow the nymphs to stay behind on the island, neither can it give them a place in Portugal. Its only option, it seems, is to return them to the watery expanse between Portugal and India—and to consign them to the unwritten corners between history and allegory.

The nymphs' uncertain fate reflects a fundamental dilemma of the política dos casamentos as a technology of race predicated on simultaneous processes of assimilation and distinction.[47] Construed as a unidirectional conduit of assimilation, the intermarriage scheme articulated a fantasy of incorporation that did not disrupt, but actively upheld, the distinction between colonizers and colonized. According to Barros, Afonso de Albuquerque envisioned racial mixing in Asia as a way of extirpating "the vine stock of bad blood" planted there by the Muslims. In time, this would be replaced by "Catholic vine stock" that would "bear fruit in honor of God . . . [and] in His name conquer all those Eastern parts."[48] By encouraging the formation of families patterned after European models, colonial authorities in Asia hoped to replicate in unfamiliar terrains the sociocultural dynamics of sixteenth-century Portugal, with their attendant values of personal honor and public morality.

Yet many doubted that this would be the case, especially since so many of the settlers were but "the scum of the [Portuguese] kingdom."[49] Hijacking Albuquerque's viticultural conceit, detractors of the intermarriage scheme cautioned that the Indian vineyard would end up producing just wild grapes, partly because it was grafted onto Muslim vines, and partly because the grafts themselves came but from "the lowliest plants of the kingdom."[50] Even Albuquerque, for all his support of the política dos casamentos, seems to have been sensitive to its "corrupting" potential: while encouraging his soldiers to marry, he insisted that brides be chosen from among Muslim and upper-caste Hindu women, who were "white and chaste." Being "black and corrupted," low-caste women were explicitly excluded.[51]

In practice, most marriages fell short of this ideal, as few of the women conscripted in the scheme would likely have been light-skinned

Muslims or upper-caste Hindus.[52] "The men who are marrying are not the kind that Your Highness would wish [to see marry]," wrote António Real in a 1512 letter to the king, openly questioning the social extraction of both brides and grooms. "The only ones who have married so far are men of low birth and dubious worth who have married their slaves in order to get the dowries and enjoy the privileges and honors that Your Highness bestows." Nothing good could come from these unions, he concluded, noting that many of the newlyweds ended up defecting and "tak[ing] refuge among the Moors."[53]

Real had personal axes to grind, since Albuquerque had just confiscated two of his female slaves in order to give them away in marriage.[54] Yet his complaint registers more than ad hominem grudges, voicing widespread anxieties about the consequences and implications of the intermarriage scheme. In the letter, these anxieties are clearly emblematized by the apostate Portuguese "tak[ing] refuge among the Moors"—a figure in which the specter of reverse acculturation combines with the horrors of apostasy and defection.[55] Possibly in response to negative reports, in 1513 the Crown had the intermarriage scheme temporarily suspended; in 1514, it withdrew financial support, ordering Albuquerque to stop paying dowries. Interracial unions nevertheless continued apace, especially where propertied women could be made available. In 1514, for instance, Albuquerque had several Indian widows of "reasonable means" remarried, ostensibly to prevent them from falling into prostitution, but more likely as a way of keeping the política dos casamentos going.[56]

At the root of the disagreements over the intermarriage scheme were competing visions over what constituted a critical mass of European settlers, and whether their quality should matter more than their quantity.[57] The ways such disagreements were articulated, however, also suggest that early modern notions of racial membership were based just as much on perceptions of moral propriety as on indices of somatic and religious difference. It is instructive to return to Albuquerque's dichotomy between "white and chaste" Indians versus "black and corrupted" ones: by conjoining phenotype with sexual behavior, this formulation underscores the importance of eros in the making and unmaking of racial distinction. With the política dos casamentos sexual matters decisively entered the colonial fray, being increasingly relied on as a way of distinguishing not only between assimilable and unassimilable natives but also between "true" and "degenerate" Europeans. As a result, conflicts over the moral and

social significance of erotic acts and sociosexual arrangements profoundly charged the politics of identity-making that characterized
Portugal's imperial enterprise.

Although ostensibly written out of the encounter between sailors
and nymphs, these conflicts obliquely inflect the Isle of Love episode.
As the conqueror of Hormuz, Goa, and Malacca, and one of the main
architects of Portugal's colonial enterprise, Afonso de Albuquerque
could not fail to make a conspicuous appearance in the heroic catalogue of canto 10. But of the stanzas devoted to him, only five celebrate his political and military exploits. The other five focus on the
death of Rui Dias, a Portuguese *fidalgo* Albuquerque had ignominiously executed for sleeping with an Indian woman.

It is unclear who this woman was, and whether the sex was consensual. According to Barros, whose *Décadas da Ásia* provide one of
the most detailed accounts of the episode, she was one of Albuquerque's own slaves, "whom he called daughters, and gave away in marriage."[58] All we know for sure is that the execution took place in the
trying summer of 1510, as an embattled Albuquerque lay at anchor
near Goa "with his forces prostrated by sickness and his supplies
of food very much reduced," and that the harshness of the sentence
prompted vehement protests from some of the captains.[59] For its part,
the *Lusíadas* exonerates Rui Dias from any crime, making it abundantly clear that his execution should be regarded as an act of unwarranted brutality. As Camões points out, the fidalgo had committed
neither "abominoso incesto" (abominable incest) nor "violento estupro" (violent rape) nor "adultério desonesto" (dishonest adultery)—
in short, nothing that could qualify as unspeakable love (10.47). In
addition, the woman involved was not a "virgem pura" (pure virgin)
but a mere slave (10.47). And to better drive home the point that she
was hardly worth the fuss, Camões describes her as "lasciva e escura"
(swarthy and lascivious; 10.47)—a definition uncannily echoing the
terms of Albuquerque's own proscription against low-caste Indian
women.

By underscoring the would-be bride's racial and sexual abjection,
Camões's critique implicitly acknowledges the conflicts and contradictions generated by the política dos casamentos. To the extent that
these conflicts and contradictions are tucked away in the epic catalogue of canto 10, however, *Os Lusíadas* avoids bringing its critique
to the heart of the Isle of Love episode. Sidestepping the thorny legacy of Portugal's colonial erotics, the poem effectively safeguards the

ideological integrity of the encounter between sailors and nymphs. The "painted island" is thus preserved as an idealized domain both within and without history— a place where love and empire perfectly coincide. Indeed, this is exactly the vision that early modern plots of interracial romance, from Camões forward, routinely propose: island worlds where the violence of conquest subtends and underwrites the licit pleasures of the conjugal bed.

CHAPTER 3

Discipline and Love

Linschoten and the Estado da Índia

The years that followed the publication of Camões's *Os Lusíadas* were dense with important events for Portugal and its seaborne empire. In 1578, King Sebastian I was killed at Ksar el Kebir in Morocco; in 1580, Spanish troops under the command of the Duke of Alva crossed into Portugal; and in 1581, Philip II of Spain entered Lisbon as Philip I of Portugal. In the meantime, a young Dutchman named Jan Huygen van Linschoten embarked on a voyage that would last almost thirteen years and take him, among other places, to Spain, Portugal, India, and the Azores. It is unlikely that Linschoten had read or even heard of the *Lusíadas* before his departure, but it is fair to assume that Camões's epic would have fascinated him just as much as the "Histories, and straunge adventures" of which he was admittedly fond since childhood.[1]

Having left the Netherlands in 1576, Linschoten moved to Spain and then to Portugal. In 1584, he reached India in the retinue of João Vicente da Fonseca, newly appointed to the archbishopric of Goa. Although he never rose far above the status of a modest clerk, the young Dutchman distinguished himself enough to gain the trust of the archbishop, laying the foundation of a promising career. In 1587, however, Fonseca's sudden demise shattered Linschoten's every hope for preferment. Suddenly, India had lost much of its attractiveness, and Holland beckoned: "God had opened mine eies," Linschoten was to write in later years, "and by my Lords death made me more cleare of Sight, & to call my native soile unto remembrance" (2: 217). Having set sail for Europe early in 1589, Linschoten reached his home town of Enkhuizen, after many misadventures, in September 1592. Here he renounced Catholicism, joined the Dutch Reformed Church, and came under the wing of renowned town surgeon Bernardus Paludanus (Berent ten Broecke). Like Linschoten, Paludanus was a former Catholic who had traveled extensively, gathering a substantial collection of curiosities along the way. Together, the two began to set in writing the observations and information Linschoten had amassed during his stay abroad. The finished product of this collaboration, entitled *Itinerario, voyage ofte schipvaert van Jan Huygen van Linschoten naer Oost ofte Portugaels Indiën* (Itinerary, voyage, or ship's passage by Jan Huygen van Linschoten to the East or Portuguese Indies) was a work of monumental proportions comprising three distinct parts: the *Itinerario* proper, which covered just about every aspect of Portuguese India that was conceivable at the time, from peoples and customs to religions and commodities; the *Beschrijvinghe van de gantsche Custe van Guinea* (Description of the whole coast of Guinea), a general survey of the coasts of Africa and America largely derived from Duarte Lopes, Filippo Pigafetta, Peter Martyr, Gonzalo Fernández de Oviedo, and Jean de Léry; and the *Reysgeschrift van de Navigatiën der Portugaloysers in Oriënten* (Travel document of the navigations of the Portuguese to the Orient), which described the routes used by Portuguese mariners in the East. The *Reysgeschrift* was the first part of the *Itinerario* to appear in print, having been prepared in great haste to accompany Cornelis van Houtman on his first voyage to the East Indies; the complete work was published by Cornelis Claeszoon in 1596.

Embellished by maps, botanical illustrations, and ethnographic plates allegedly "drawn from life" (1: 183), the *Itinerario* was an instant best seller.[2] A second Dutch edition appeared in short order, and by 1598 the work had been translated into English and German. Two Latin editions followed in 1599, and two separate French translations were published in 1610 and 1619. With several Dutch reprints issued between 1604 and 1644, the *Itinerario* was perhaps the most widely circulated early modern source on the East Indies, remaining a virtually undisputed authority well into the eighteenth century. In England, the indefatigable Richard Hakluyt referred to the *Itinerario* twice in the recommendations he made to the founders of the English East India Company in October 1599 and January 1601. A report on the trading ports east of the Cape of Good Hope identified Linschoten's account as one of its main sources; and in 1613, Captain

John Saris, the first Englishman to sail to Japan, noted in his journal: "Wee found Jan Huyghen van Linschotens booke very true, for thereby we directed our selves from our setting forth from Firando."[3]

The rapid dissemination of the *Itinerario* dealt a severe blow to the Portuguese, whose "trading advantage," as Karel Steenbrink has noted, was mostly "due to the fact that their knowledge of this area was much more extensive than other Europeans'."[4] Up to this point, the Portuguese had done their best to keep this knowledge to themselves. By providing reliable and up-to-date information, the *Itinerario* removed the veil of mystery in which Asia had been shrouded, and exposed the continent to Europe's scrutinizing gaze. In addition, Linschoten told his readers that the Portuguese were no longer the unassailable power everyone thought them to be. He described the poor discipline and inexperience that reigned aboard Portuguese vessels, drew attention to the corruption that existed at all levels of government, and denounced the general lack of interest in "the common profit or the service of the king" (1: 203). In short, he portrayed a colonial system that was not only unable to sustain further expansion, but also showed the first signs of contraction: "There is no more [countries] in India won or new found out, but rather heere and there some places lost, for [the Portuguese] have enough to doe, to hold that they have alreadie, [and to defende it from invasion]" (1: 203–4).

Linschoten was not the first, nor was he alone, in decrying the decline of the Estado da Índia (as Portugal's far-flung possessions in Asia were then called). The *Itinerario* in fact reflects a vision that can also be found in many other contemporary sources, such as the histories of Fernão Lopes de Castanheda or João de Barros, the writings of missionaries and merchants, and even political exposés addressed to colonial authorities. Indeed, the last part of the sixteenth century appears to be characterized, if not by an actual decadence, at least by the acute and generalized perception of a crisis.[5] The Florentine humanist Filippo Sassetti—who resided on the Malabar Coast roughly at the same time as Linschoten—likened Portuguese enclaves in India to so many "crumbs left on the tablecloth after a meal," writing: "Every year there come from Portugal between 2500 and 3000 men and boys, as wretched as they can be. A quarter, a third, and sometimes a half of them [die on the way and] are cast into the sea. Those who make it on land alive meet up with death or knavery, and for the most part they come to a bad end, except for a few nobles or others who, either with the help of their relatives or by their own ability, manage to better their positions."[6] Sassetti's bleak assessment finds ample corroboration in the writings of Diogo do Couto and Francisco Rodrigues de Silveira, both of whom served in India during the last two decades of the sixteenth century. In his 1612 *Soldado Prático* (The experienced soldier), Couto expresses the deepest contempt for his countrymen, writing that the fencing schools of Goa had turned into brothels and dancing studios, and complaining that it was becoming harder and harder to find a Portuguese soldier worthy of the name.[7]

Couto does not expound on the causes of this change, but Silveira's *Reformação da milícia e governo do Estado da Índia Oriental* (Reform of the military and governance of the state of East India) does: because the viceroys routinely embezzled funds and left the troops unpaid, soldiers often dodged service or refused to fight. Even when this was not the case, many of the recruits who made it to India disappeared anyway, dying of disease and malnutrition, taking up service with Indian rulers, or intermarrying and blending into the local peasantry. In the meantime, royal administrators pocketed their pay, and requested new levies of men to be sent from Portugal.[8]

While Linschoten's *Itinerario* presents a vision of Portuguese Asia that is, in many respects, quite similar to Sassetti's, Couto's, and Silveira's, in other respects it is as unique as Linschoten's subject position. In the second half of the sixteenth century, most of the laymen who left Europe for India did so either to trade, like Sassetti, or to fight, like Couto and Silveira. Linschoten, however, was neither a merchant nor a soldier. Moreover, neither Sassetti's letters nor Couto's and Silveira's exposés had been intended for general consumption, whereas the *Itinerario* was developed with a large public audience in mind.[9] In this light, the passages in which Linschoten draws attention to the many Asian regions "as yet . . . not discovered, nor by the Inhabitants themselves [well] knowne" (1: 111), can easily be read as an open invitation suggesting, as Pieter Anton Tiele has proposed, "that an energetic rival would have every chance to supplant" the Portuguese.[10] Other passages of the *Itinerario* seem to address a specific invitation to Linschoten's countrymen, hinting that the Dutch Republic might be ideally placed to supplant the Habsburg Crown. Speaking of the Azores, for instance, Linschoten notes that the islands of this archipelago—Portuguese possessions logistically crucial to ocean voyaging—were "also called the Flemish Islands, that is of the Neatherlanders, because the first that inhabited . . . [them] were Neatherlanders" (2:

276). In addition, the islanders were "greatly affected to the Neather-landers" (2: 290), and thus potentially amenable to a Dutch takeover.

As a result, during the heyday of Dutch imperialism Linschoten was hailed in several quarters as a national hero, a colonial trail-blazer conciously paving the way for his countrymen to follow. It is certainly not a coincidence that the Linschoten-Vereeniging (Lin-schoten Society), a publishing concern founded in 1908 on the model of the British Hakluyt Society, was named after him. Yet we should be wary of reducing the *Itinerario* to any narrow ideological framework or nationalist agenda. In the first place, the incessant religious dis-sensions, central power vacuums, and frequent territorial shifts that beset the young Dutch republic hindered the emergence of any defined sense of nationhood.[11] In addition, the anti-Spanish and anti-Catholic sentiments that had sustained the Dutch struggle for independence put former Catholics like Linschoten—who had left for Spain right at the time when Holland was experiencing its most significant Calvinist upsurge—in a peculiarly ambiguous position.[12] It is telling that even after joining the Dutch Reformed Church, Linschoten chose to self-identify not as a citizen of Calvinist Enkhuizen but rather as a citizen of predominantly Catholic Haarlem.[13]

These complexities are well reflected in the *Itinerario*. On the one hand, the text relies heavily on Spanish and Portuguese sources, dem-onstrates concerns that were shared by many Iberians, and evinces deep respect for the Habsburg Crown. On the other hand, the publica-tion was dedicated to the Dutch States General, which were staunchly Protestant and vehemently anti-Spanish. What is more, much of the *Itinerario* seems inspired by a Reformed ethic anchored in social dis-cipline and individual self-denial. The end result is a palimpsest that reflects on Portugal's imperial decline while also advancing an idyo-sincratic plan of politico-erotic reform. Taking as his point of depar-ture the politics of racial mixing extolled by Barros and Camões, Lin-schoten roots the problems of the Estado da Índia in the unruliness of its women's libido. This peculiarly misogynistic etiology of Portugal's imperial decline does not, however, translate into a rejection of racial mixing as a strategy of colonial rule. Instead, the *Itinerario* locates in domestic heterosexuality a crucial instrument of social, personal, and economic discipline—that is, as a vehicle of internalization capable of producing pliant colonized subjectivities.

HYBRIDITY AND DECADENCE

Chroniclers, merchants, and missionaries concerned with the decadence of the Estado da Índia found in the "decline literature" of antiquity a ready mold in which to cast their observations. The enervating power of the "Orient" was already a trope in the Hellenistic and Roman republican periods; from 33 B.C. onward, Octavian's propaganda campaign against Antony and Cleopatra exploited and further consolidated the existing prejudice, crystallizing once and for all the stereotype of a lascivious and emasculating East.[14] By the end of the first century A.D., the contraposition between effeminate East and masculine West was so familiar that the poet Statius could put the trope to new use, and turn imperviousness to Oriental pleasure into an index of moral fiber.[15] Building on this tradition, sixteenth-century commentators routinely blamed Portugal's imperial problems on the corrupting influences of the Asian environment. The "constant commerce with nations who have no knowledge of the true God," remarked the Jesuit Giovanni Pietro Maffei in his *Historiarum Indicarum libri XVI* (Sixteen books of Indian histories), "has made it easier for Europeans to learn each day some part of Asian lechery than to teach the natives any part of Christian sanctity and severity. To this corruption of mores must be added the nature of the land . . . [which], unless great diligence is used, extinguishes all martial vigor with the sweetness of leisure and the lure of pleasure."[16]

Like Maffei's *Historiarum Indicarum*, the *Itinerario* connects the ailments of the Estado da Índia with the progressive entanglement of European settlers in Indian life. It tells how the Portuguese have taken up the custom of the country, wearing lightweight and colorful garments "so fine that you may see al their body through it" (1: 206), surrounding themselves with droves of slaves (1: 193), adopting local diet and table manners—including the contemptible habit of eating everything "with their handes" (1: 207)—and incorporating Indian practices into virtually every aspect of their daily lives.

Among the most pervasive of these practices was what some nineteenth-century writers called "palanquining"—that is, using palanquin carriages as a means of transportation (Figure 5). As described in Francesco Carletti's *Ragionamenti del mio viaggio attorno al mondo* (Chronicles of my voyage around the world), palanquins were portable litters in which passengers sat "with the thighs and legs extended, as if on a bed, with cushions at the back and rugs beneath."[17] The

Figure 5. Linschoten's *Itinerario*. Woman carried in a palanquin. Courtesy of the John Carter Brown Library at Brown University, Providence, RI.

Itinerario provides no gloss on the term, but palanquins feature conspicuously both in the text and in the accompanying engravings: at once vehicles and items of display, they were as popular with European immigrants as with Asian natives, and formed an integral part of both Christian and non-Christian ceremonials. In other words, they were a contact zone fixture, with men palanquining just as often as horseback riding, and women being routinely "carried in a Pallamkin covered with a mat or [other] cloth, so that they [could] not be seene" (1: 205).

To be properly appreciated, Linschoten's interest in the palanquin needs to placed in the context of the larger discourse that had accreted around portable litters since the early sixteenth century. As an object—one made of this or that material, more or less ornate, carried by two or more bearers—the palanquin had been known in Europe for a long time, having been mentioned by Franciscan friar Giovanni de' Marignolli as early as the fourteenth century. As a word, however, it came to be known only in the sixteenth century, when the noun *palanquim*—a coinage obtained by tacking a characteristic Portuguese nasal onto the East Indian vernacular *pālankī*—was imported from the contact zone.[18] The diffusion of this noun from about 1515 onward indicates a level of contact between colonizers and colonized sufficient for part of the latter's vernacular to make its way into the former's active vocabulary. In this sense, the Portuguese *palanquim* is quite literally a creation of the contact zone, where both object and word became emblems of hybridity's dangers.

Virtually from the beginning of the European-Asian encounter, cultural prejudice had turned the portable litter into an epitome of softness and effeminacy, intended as Asian traits always implicitly opposed to the vigor and masculinity of the European conquerors. In spite of this, palanquins spread quickly and widely among immigrant settlers, soon inviting serious scrutiny on the part of colonial authorities. In 1591, a viceregal proclamation restricted this means of transportation to people over sixty, establishing stiff penalties for those who contravened: the vehicle and its belonging would be forfeited, a fine exacted, and "the *boys* or *mouços* who carry such *palanquys*" condemned to the royal galleys.[19] A few years later, an ecclesiastical council declared the covered palanquin "prejudicial to the morality of the state," threatened excommunication on the clergy who used it, and urged the viceroy to prohibit it altogether.[20] Both of these proscriptions seem to have fallen on deaf ears, though, for when the Roman aristocrat Pietro della Valle (1586–1652) visited the Malabar coast in 1623, he complained that although in the territories of Portuguese India men were forbidden "to travel in palanquin, *as in good sooth too effeminate a proceeding*," the prohibition was consistently ignored.[21]

The tenor of these comments, along with the authorities' repeated attempts to curtail use of the palanquin among Estado da Índia residents, suggests the extent to which portable litters came to function both as synecdoches of contact zone hybridity and as metaphors for the vulnerable instability of Western cultural identity.[22] In the *Itinerario* plate depicting how Portuguese men "cause themselves to be carried in Palamkins" (1: 205), for instance, Asian artifacts do not merely appear side by side with European ones; they compete with and even predominate over them (Figure 6). Placed squarely at the center of the composition, and defining its principal axes, palanquin and parasol enclose and almost compress the figure of the reclining Portuguese, forcing it into a semifetal position. Within this grand but confining setting, the figure's sword and hat—European articles denoting racial and social standing—feel strikingly out of place. Instead of covering the man's head, the broad-brimmed hat sits idly in his lap, while

Figure 6. Linschoten's *Itinerario*. A Portuguese man carried by two *boys* or palanquin-bearers. Shaded by a parasol and surrounded by a numerous retinue of servants and slaves, the Portuguese holds in his hands, as social and racial markers, a sword and a hat. The juxtaposition of these Western accessories with palanquin and parasol indexes the hybridity of contact zone cultures. Courtesy of the John Carter Brown Library at Brown University, Providence, RI.

the unsheathed sword rests awkwardly against his chest. The overall effect is one of European retrenchment and enervation in the face of a strong and expansive Asian environment.

The fact that palanquins could be easily covered, thereby hiding their passengers from view, was yet another source of concern. By allowing passengers to see without being seen, palanquins resisted the gaze of colonial authorities and inverted prescribed asymmetries of power. No early modern document puts it quite in these terms; yet the insistence with which Linschoten's contemporaries associated palanquins with illicit sex suggests a deep anxiety about their relative opacity. Francesco Carletti, for example, described the palanquin as a "good mean" ("buono mezzano")[23] for women to go about unseen and unrecognized, especially when they wanted "to go in search of men" (182). Carletti's characterization of the palanquin as a "mean" or sexual go-between may be especially blunt, but it is typical of early modern discourses concerned with the hybridity and

fluidity of contact zone societies. At a a time when statutory identity and geographical fixity were often thought of as prerequisites of
social and political order, the reciprocal and largely unpredictable
exchanges between colonizers and colonized easily fit a conceptual
mold of erotic promiscuity. Hence the close and frequent association between palanquins and illicit sex. As instruments of mobility,
palanquins facilitated the circulation of people as well as the propa-
gation of suspect practices, values, and affects; as sites of opacity,
they emblematized the autonomy of this circulation as well as the
unpredictability of its outcomes.

DEGENERACY AND MISCEGENATION

While linking the decline of the Estado da Índia to the blurring of
cultural and racial distinctions that obtained in the contact zone, the
Itinerario locates the initial moment of such blurring in the sexual
traffic between European men and Asian women. Keeping erotic desires in check seems to have been a major problem for the Europeans in India, so much so that the apostolate of Francis Xavier and
other Jesuits was partly devoted, as Ines G. Županov has observed,
to the mission "of bringing back to the righteous path those Europeans whose souls and bodies were imperiled by the Oriental environment."[24] Amost every aspect of life in Asia seemed to conspire against
moral purity and erotic restraint: writing from Japan in 1580, the
Jesuit Alessandro Valignano blamed the climate, the spicy diet, the
"dishonest clothes," and the lax morality of native women for the loss
of European virtue in the East.[25]

In a different vein but much to the same effect, Francesco Carletti devoted a long section of his *Ragionamenti* to the charms of
women in Portuguese Goa. Indeed, he confessed, there was no way
for him to explain "how amorous, courteous, attractive, and clean"
these women were "except by saying that in every way they lead all
the women who have ever been or are endowed with similar graces,
if not everywhere in the world, at least among those women whom
I have seen and experienced in circumnavigating the whole world"
(180). Thus Carletti's description of Goan women turns the world
into an erotic *Wunderkammer*, where women of different nations and
races are randomly juxtaposed, displaced from their proper contexts,
and ranked according to the aesthetic and libidinal pleasure they can
afford the spectator. In the following paragraphs, Carletti invites

readers to share in this voyeuristic exercise, dressing and undressing women in gauzes so fine and transparent that "one could say that they are naked from the waist up, and one sees all of the shoulders, the breasts, and the arms through the transparent bodice—and from the waist down one sees little less, as they display the outlines of the entire body" (181).

Passages of the *Itinerario* present the same voyeuristic tendency, penetrating the walls of women's secluded quarters to offer titillating vignettes of barely clothed flesh. Within their houses, Linschoten writes, women "goe bare headed with a wastcoate . . . that from their shoulders covereth [their] navels, and is so fine that you may see al their body through it, and downewardes they have nothing but a painted cloth wrapped thrée or foure times about [their] bodies" (1: 206). But desire and appreciation are never too far away from revulsion and derision; a paragraph that opens by extolling the cleanliness and attractiveness of Indian women ends by disparaging their toilet practices and ridiculing their chewing of betel:

> The women are by nature very cleanelie and neat . . . yet they have a manner everie day to wash [themselves] all the body [over], from head to foote, and some times twyse [a day] . . . and as often as they ease themselves or make water, or [else] use the companie of their husbands, everie time they doe wash [themselves], were it a hundreth times a day and night: they are no great workers, but much delighted in swéet hearbs, and in perfumes and frankincense, and to rub their bodies and their foreheads with swéet sanders and such like woods . . . also the whole day long they [doe nothing, but sit and] chawe leaves [or hearbes], called Bettele, with chalke and a [certaine] fruit called Arrequa. . . . [T]hese 3 thinges they sit all the whole day chawing [in their mouthes], like oxen or kyne chawing the cud. (1: 212–13)

The power of these female bodies to charm and seduce is acknowledged and then progressively obscured by the accumulation of suspect habits and inclinations. Even practices of personal hygiene take on negative connotations: far from serving as indexes of civility, they evince idleness and debauchery.

"The women are very luxurious and unchaste," claims another passage of the *Itinerario*, "for there are verie few among them, although they bee married, but they have besides their husbands one or two of those that are called souldiers, with whome they take their pleasures" (1: 209). The Portuguese in India have tried to curb women's inordinate appetites by keeping them indoors—rarely allowing them outside, and then only if chaperoned and escorted. Even within the home, men keep their womenfolk in separate quarters, for they are extremely jealous and "suffer no man to dwell within their houses, where the women and daughters bee, howe néere kinsman [soever] he be unto them" (1: 209). And because Iberian law makes the murder of an adulteress a negligible offense, Linschoten adds, the mere suspicion of infidelity can carry the penalty of death: "There are likewise many women brought to their ends by [meanes of] their husbandes, and slaine when soever they take them in adulterie, or that they doe but once suspect them, [if they doe presently] they cut their throats, and bring three or foure witnesses to testifie that strange men entred into their houses . . . [and had their pleasures] of their wives, or in other sort as they will devise it, whereby they are presently discharged [of the crime]" (1: 211–12).

It soon becomes apparent, however, that none of these measures has produced the desired results. Instead of preventing adultery, female claustration has raised the incidence of incest, so that it is often the case "that the uncles sonne hath laine by his aunt, and the brother by the brothers wife, and the brother with his sister" (1: 209). And instead of hindering sexual expression, the constant threat of being killed has made both "Indian and Portingall women" all the more callous (2: 69). Bold and relentless in their illicit pursuits, "they use al the slights and practises [they can devise]" to escape surveillance and fulfill their desires (1: 209). And when the occasion calls for it, they do not hesitate to feed their husbands datura—a stupefying drug often associated with criminal activity—"so that in [their] presence they may doe what they will" (1: 210).[26]

It should be noted that Linschoten makes no distinction between "Indian" and "Portuguese" women, implying not only that conversion to Christianity has failed to curtail "Indian" lechery, but also that "Portuguese" women have found it easy to adopt these lecherous manners. A deep asymmetry is thereby revealed: the natives cannot be shorn of their innate ways by contact with European immigrants, yet the latter seem perfectly receptive to native mores and values. As a group, the Portuguese residents of India are slowly but inexorably being obliterated, almost swallowed and absorbed into that Asian landscape to which—as conquerors and missionaries—they had presumedly been called upon to give shape:

> The Portingales in India, are many of them married with the natu-
> rall borne women of the countrie, and the children procéeding of

them are called Mesticos, that is, half countrimen. These Mesticos
are commonlie of yelowish colour, notwithstanding there are manie
women among them, that are faire and well formed. The children of
the Portingales, both boyes and gyrls, [which are] borne in India, are
called Castisos, and are in all things like [unto] the Portingales, onely
somewhat differing in colour, for they draw towards a yealow colour:
the children of those Castisos are yealow, and altogether [like the]
Mesticos, and the children of Mesticos are of colour and fashion like
the naturall borne Countrimen . . . so that the posteritie of the Portingales, both men and women being in the third degrée, doe séeme to
be naturall Indians, both in colour and fashion. (1: 183–84)

Neatly inverting Valignano's idea of a movement going from Indian
to Portuguese in three generations, the passage conveys the sense of
a precipitous racial descent: instead of assimilating the natives to
European customs and values, immigrant settlers are quickly turning into "naturall Indians, both in colour and fashion" (1: 184). What
is most remarkable about this portrayal is not so much the notion
that through intermarriage the Portuguese are incorporated into the
local population and eventually erased as the idea that such erasure
could occur even in the absence of any racial mingling.[27] The castiços,
who are born of Portuguese parents in India, "draw towards a yealow
colour," and their children are indistinguishable from the mestiços,
even though not a single drop of native blood may run through their
veins.[28] In twinning the intimately linked fears of degeneracy and miscegenation, the *Itinerario* anticipates central features of later eugenics
discourse, according to which acquired cultural characteristics were
as inheritable as physical ones.[29]

The social and cultural dynamics observed by Linschoten in late
sixteenth-century India were largely the result of the intermarriage
policy known as the política dos casamentos. Central to this policy, as
I argue in Chapter 2, was the idea that racial mixing could function as
an instrument of colonization, easing native assimilation to European
customs and values. In keeping with this idea, Portuguese legislation
generally held that religion should be the sole criterion for citizenship,
and that no distinction should be made on the basis of ethnicity or
skin color.[30] But there was a wide gap between theory and practice:
recent Portuguese immigrants were routinely preferred, while mestiços and castiços got snubbed and passed over. By and large, castiços were thought of as ill behaved and untrustworthy. Mestiços
fared even worse, to the point of being intermittently barred from
Crown service.[31] So widespread was the prejudice that, by the latter

part of the sixteenth century, many religious orders refused to admit Eurasians into their ranks. "As far as those born in India are concerned . . . we should admit very few," wrote Valignano in 1579, "for, having been conceived in . . . a bad climate and debauchedly brought up, they are hardly capable of mortification and religious perfection." Even those of allegedly pure European ancestry, he warned, should be admitted only with the utmost caution, for although born of Portuguese parents "they generally . . . turn out weak and contemptible."[32] Thus, the law's insistence that all Christians (or, more precisely, all Catholics) should be considered Portuguese citizens radically destabilized what it meant to be Portuguese. In the process, tactics meant to bolster European dominance and colonial control metamorphosed into vehicles of European degeneracy and colonial dissolution.

In the *Itinerario*, the dangerous effects of contact zone hybridity find a corporeal equivalent in the "bloody flixe" (dysentery), a primary cause of mortality among colonists. The reason why so many of the European settlers contract dysentery, Linschoten explains, is that they "use much company of women, because ye land is naturall to provoke them therunto . . . for although men were of iron or stéele, the unchaste [life] of [a] woman, with her unsatiable lustes were able to grinde him to powder, and swéep him away like dust" (1: 236–37). The association between sex and dysentery is, as Ivo Kamps has pointed out, a "disturbingly appropriate" one, for it precisely mirrors the moral situation of the Estado da Índia.[33] While the disease can be seen as a strong metaphorical illustration of the socially and psychologically destabilizing effects of uncontrolled sexual appetites, the diarrhea which is symptomatic of it ominously forecasts the liquefaction of the Portuguese body politic. By associating dysenteric bodies and cultural hybridity, personal conduct and race survival, eroticism and imperial rule, the *Itinerario* highlights the destructiveness of sexual self-indulgence to individuals and collectivities alike.

In this perspective, Linschoten's *Itinerario* is not only about the failures of Portugal's Estado da Índia. It is also, and just as insistently, about the definition of a "proper" sexuality keyed to the exigencies of imperial rule. For if the text explicitly disparages Asian and Eurasian women for their debauched idleness, it hardly exempts European indolence from critique. And while Linschoten harps consistently on the unruly libido of Asian and Eurasian women, he also makes clear that European settlers can be just as libidinous and unruly. Portuguese and mestiço weddings, for instance, are ostentatious but brief affairs that often end with bride and groom rushing to consummate "[at ye least] two hours before Sunne setting, not having the patience to stay so long as [we do] in these countries" (1: 198).

Nowhere are the effects of European unruliness more graphically illustrated than in the cautionary tale of Flemish diamond polisher Frans Coningh (Francis King in the English translation), his mestiço wife, and her Portuguese lover. We first encounter the young Flemish jeweler as an apprentice merchant in Syria, where he immediately proves to be less adept at trading than at squandering the funds entrusted to him. Hoping to recoup his losses, he moves farther and farther away from Europe and deeper into Portuguese Asia. "Being young and without government" and "seeing himselfe so far distant" from his family, he once again throws thrift, prudence, and responsibility to the wind, "taking no other care, but onlie to [be merrie and] make good cheare so long, till in the end the whole stock was almost clean [spent and] consumed" (2: 205–6). Unable to repay his debts and unwilling to face the consequences of his prodigality, he resolves not to return home. While understandable—early modern Netherlanders seem to have deemed insolvency an especially heinous crime—this decision marks Coningh's ultimate fall from grace. He settles in Goa and marries a young mestiça, "fair and comelie of bodie and limme, but in villanie, the worst that walked uppon the earth" (2: 207). The lurid tale that follows brims with twists, turns, and secret plots: although barely twelve, Coningh's bride promptly takes her husband's best friend as a lover—her precocious depravity precisely mirroring that of a teenage brother who had been executed "for sodome or buggery" some time before (2: 215). When at last Coningh begins to suspect her infidelity, he is drugged with datura and murdered in his sleep (Figure 7).

Linschoten explains that he has set the story "downe at large, that hereby men may the better perceyve the boldnesse and [filthie] lecherous mindes of the Indian women, which are commonly all of one nature and disposition" (2: 204). Yet the pedagogical thrust of the exemplum seems concerned less with the lechery of Indian women than with establishing a causal connection between Coningh's misfortunes and his moral shortcomings. Well before being betrayed by his wife and the man he considers his best friend, Coningh is betrayed by his own lack of "government" (2: 205), his inability to perceive the limits of liberty and resist the temptations of pleasure. While idleness, dissipation, and lewdness—the low instincts of the

Figure 7. The murder of Frans Coningh, as depicted in Johann Theodor and Johann Israel de Bry's *Tertia Pars Indiae Orientalis* (1601). In the upper left corner, Coningh's wife helps her lover into the house. In the lower right corner, the fateful couple flees the scene with Coningh's valuables. Courtesy of the Newberry Library, Chicago, IL.

body—were regarded in Europe as serious threats to the well-being of the body politic, they were even more dangerous in the periphery, where increased distance from the source of authority allowed European travelers and colonists the possibility of "forgetting themselves," neglecting their social and familial obligations, or even "betraying" their "true" cultural identity. Only a constant vigilance could protect Europeans against the dangers of foreign enticement.

DOCILE BODIES, DISCIPLINED SELVES: CHANZU AND SATI

Although Linschoten never ventured farther east than India, he included in his *Itinerario* information on Sumatra, Java, the Moluccas, China, and Japan. In the three chapters devoted to China, which are mostly derived from Juan González de Mendoza's *Historia de las cosas mas notables, ritos y costumbres del gran reyno de la China*

(1585), Linschoten enthusiastically describes an industrious and orderly nation rivaling, if not besting, the most advanced European societies. Education is so highly valued that no man is "estéemed or accounted of, for his birth, family or riches, but onely for his learning and knowledge" (1: 133); idleness is unknown, and no one is allowed to "travaile through the Country to begge" (1: 135); "printing, painting, and gun-powder, with the furniture thereto belonging, have béene used in China many hundreth yeares past, and very common, so that it is with them out of memorie when they first begun" (1: 142). In their mores and customs, in short, the Chinese rival and even surpass the most advanced of European societies.

Interestingly enough, the first chapter of this panegyric ends with a brief description of Chinese women: "The women goe verie richly apparelled . . . and estéeme it for a great beautifying [unto them] to have small féete, to the which end they use to binde their féete so fast when they are young, that they cannot grow to the full, whereby they can hardly goe, but in a manner halfe lame. Which custome the men have brought up, to let them from much going, for that they are verie jealous, and unmeasurable leacherous and unchast, yet is it estéemed a beautifying and comlinesse for the women" (1: 136–37). Here the *Itinerario* espouses a view already expressed by Mendoza, according to whom the practice of *chanzu* (foot binding) had been devised by men to keep their womenfolk chaste. Far from inspiring revulsion, the custom of compressing women's feet so that they could only hobble about with difficulty evoked almost unanimous admiration among early modern commentators: indeed, given Europe's traditional association between women's mobility and unruly sexuality, foot binding was regarded as one of China's strong points. In 1659, the Dominican friar Domingo Fernández Navarrete went so far as to propose that other countries would be well advised to do the same, writing, "The custom of swathing women's feet is very good for keeping females at home. It were no small benefit to them and their menfolk if it were also practised everywhere else too, not only in China."[34] In the specific case of the *Itinerario*, Chinese practices of foot binding appear as techniques of governance that mark the country as "civilized." Chanzu in fact ensures female chastity without spectacular violence or even the threat of punishment; instead, it "corrects" women's desires by disciplining their bodies, and subjects both to the demands of the patriarchal state.

If the *Itinerario* places the Chinese clearly at the top of the civil hierarchy of Asia, Indian Brahmans—"the honestest and most estéemed nation amonge [all] the Indian heathens" (1: 247)—do not lag far behind: skillful and sharp-witted, they hold the most prestigious offices and enjoy such high regard that "the King doth nothing without their counsell and consent" (1: 247). They also serve as priests in Hindu temples and are venerated by the common people as prophets. At this point, in a manner that is consistent with most contemporary European accounts about India, Linchoten relates in some detail the ceremony that takes place when a Brahman dies: friends and relatives build a pyre and lay the corpse on it, singing songs of praise. Meanwhile, the widow distributes her worldly possessions among her fiends, and is exhorted to join her husband in death. She then throws herself willingly into the fire, where she is quickly consumed (Figure 8): "Then cometh his Wife with Musike and [many of] her néerest friends, all singing certain prayses in commendation of her husbands life, putting her in comfort, and encouraging her to follow her husband, and goe with him into the other world. Then she taketh [al] her Jewels, and parteth them among her frends, and so with a chéerefull countenance, she leapeth into the fire, and is presently covered with wood and oyle: so she is quickly dead, and with her husbands bodie burned to ashes" (1: 249).

At first glance, Linschoten's description of sati—as *sahagamana* (Sanskrit for "keeping company") or widow sacrifice has come to be known in English since the eighteenth century—seems to ascribe to Brahman women a singular wifely devotion. In fact, most sixteenth- and seventeenth-century commentators extolled sati in order to admonish, implicitly or explicitly, their readerships. The mid-sixteenth-century "Tratado de las yslas de los Malucos" (*A Treatise on the Moluccas*), for instance, mentions sati as one of the reasons why Asian women "are very praiseworthy and exemplary."[35] Initially, Linschoten appears to agree with the author of the "Tratado," implicitly proposing widow burning as a striking counterpoint to the unbridled sexuality of the wives of the Portuguese. Soon, however, his account of sati takes an unexpected turn. Apparently in the attempt to explain the historical origin of the practice, the *Itinerario* evokes a distant past in which women's anarchic body natural had threatened the survival of the body politic: "The [first] cause . . . why the women are burnt with their husbandes, was (as the Indians themselves do say), that in time past, the women (as they are very leacherous and inconstant both by nature, and complexion) dyd poyson many of their husbands, when they thought good . . . thereby to have the better means

Figure 8. Linschoten's *Itinerario*. Widow-burning. Courtesy of the John Carter Brown Library at Brown University, Providence, RI.

to fulfill their lusts. Which the King perceiving . . . [he] ordayned, that when the dead bodies of men were buried, they shold also burne their wives with them, thereby to put them in feare, and so make them abstaine from poysoning of their husbands" (1: 250–51). The seemingly innocent parenthetical interpolation "as the Indians themselves do say" buttresses the power of classical tradition with Linschoten's own authority as an ethnographic observer, precipitating Brahman wives into a distant past in which they too were as lustful, deceitful, and murderous as their counterparts in Portuguese settlements.[36] Linschoten's history of widow burning creates in this manner a version of the Indian past that precisely mirrors the present of the Estado da Índia. Far from demonstrating an uncommon wifely devotion, sati reveals itself as an Indian version of chanzu: a creation of the state meant to curb internal disorder.

I have dwelled on Linschoten's treatment of Chinese foot binding and Indian widow burning to illustrate how the *Itinerario* construes both practices as progressive training techniques capable of producing not just docile bodies but also disciplined selves: women who can embrace loss of mobility, physical pain, or a horrifying death as defining aspects of their lives and places in society. In this respect,

Chinese chanzu and Indian sati are training procedures that supersede repression: they construct subjectivities that may discover anew the meaning of authority in their immanent freedom. External compulsion disappears, remaining visible in discourse only as a vestige of the past, an original law that no longer needs to be enforced. Contestable as it may be, this model allows us to identify the intimate connection between the excessive, anarchic sexuality of the women of Portuguese India and the normalized, productive conjugal sexuality of Chinese and Brahman women. These mutually constituted polarities are essentially effects of the same discourse, and define the limits within which Europe came not only to imagine and represent Asia but to imagine and represent itself in relation to Asia.

DOCILE BODIES, DISCIPLINED SELVES: THE "QUEENE OF ORMUS" ROMANCE

As I have shown in previous sections of this chapter, the *Itinerario* goes to great lengths to underscore both the dangers of female sexuality and the strategies that Estado da Índia colonists have deployed to contain them. Yet even the most cursory of comparisons makes abundantly clear that these strategies fall considerably short of Chinese chanzu or Indian sati. The Portuguese may try to assert their mastery by segregating women indoors, but female claustration has only compounded adultery with incest. Every year jealous husbands may dispatch their wives, but not even the fear of death can deter adulteresses from taking "their filthie pleasures" (1: 212). Quite to the contrary, Linschoten writes, women "flatly [affirme], that there can be no better death, than to die in that manner, saying that so they are sacrificed for love, which they thinke to be a great honour [unto them]" (1: 212).

This is not the context to assess either the veracity of this affirmation or the possibility that Indian widows may have actually faced sahagamana cheerfully. It will suffice, for the moment, to indicate that the two statements are intimately connected: the enshrinement of sati from "law" into custom is made possible, in fact, by the alleged propensity of Indian women to sacrifice themselves for love—or, to put it in Carletti's terms, to be prone to a love so great as to be "more bestial than human" (182). In this perspective, sati is not an act of violence but an act of will—Brahman women "choose" to die on their husbands' pyres just as the wives of the Portuguese "choose" to sacrifice themselves for adulterous love. The substantial difference between the two lies in the *kind* of will that propels the action: in the case of the Brahman women, it is a will that has been educated and directed toward the security of the state.

It is precisely in the alleged propensity of Indian women to love beyond the limits of self-interest and self-preservation that the *Itinerario* locates a terrain favorable to the requirements of empire. In the process, the *Itinerario* also suggests that European colonists may find in domestic heterosexuality a unique discursive instrument to represent the East and their place in it. During the course of his stay, recounts Linschoten, there arrived in Goa the "Queene of Ormus," a "faire white woman" who had converted to Christianity and come to India to be baptized. Muslim by birth, she had married a gentleman named António d'Azevedo (Antonio Dazevedo Coutinho in the *Itinerario*), later captain of the Portuguese fortress at Hormuz. The conversion of elite figures was a prized objective of missionary activity, so the baptism of a "queen" would have received ample publicity throughout India and beyond.[37] In the hands of Linschoten, however, this missionary achievement (of which the Augustinian friars in Hormuz seem to have been quite proud) becomes a full-fledged romance that is worth quoting at some length:

> At the same time the Queene of Ormus came to Goa, being of Mahomets religion, as all her auncesters had beene before her, and as then were contributarie to the Portingall. She caused her selfe to be christened, and was with great solemnitie brought into the Towne, where the Viceroy was her Godfather, and named her Donna Philippa, after the King of Spaines name, being a faire white woman, very tall [and comely]. . . . She had married with a Portingall Gentleman called Antonio Dazevedo Coutinho, to whome the king in regarde of his mariage gave the Captaineshippe of Ormus, which is worth above two hundred thousande duckets. . . . This Gentleman after hee had beene maried to the Queene about halfe a yeare, living very friendly and lovingly with her, hee caused a shippe to bee made, therewith to saile to Ormus, there to take order for the rentes and revenewes belonging to the Queene his wife: but his departure was so grievous unto her, that she desired him to take her with him, saying, that without him she could not live: but because he thought it not as then convenient, hee desired her to be content, promising to returne againe with all the speede he might. Whereuppon hee went to Bardes . . . about three myles off: and while hee continued there, staying for winde and weather, the Queene (as it is saide) tooke so great greefe for his departure, that she dyed, the same day that her husbande set saile and put to sea, to the great admiration of all the Countrey, and no lesse sorrowe, because shee was the first Queene in

those countries that had been christened, forsaking her kingdome and
high estate, rather to die a Christian, and married with a meane Gentleman, then to live like a Queene under the lawe of Mahomet, and so
was buried with great honor according to her estate. (2: 187–88)

Several things should be noted here. First, if Donna Philippa's death
for love aligns her with the other women of the *Itinerario*, it also sets
her apart as an exceptionally devout wife: separated from her husband, she seems to have no choice but to wither and die. Second, her
love for a "meane" Portuguese gentleman stands at the center of a cir-
cuitous route through which the forcible nature of European expansion in Asia is elided and colonial relations are naturalized. By granting Dazevedo the captainship of Hormuz "in regarde of his mariage"
(that is, as if it were a dowry), King Philip of Spain assumes the role of
the bride's father. The construction of this fictive genealogy—by virtue of which the "Queene of Ormus" is set apart from her people and
cut loose from her origins—is then completed through the Mediterranean institution of *compadrazgo* or godparenthood, a system of ritual
kinship that established alliances reputedly as strong as blood ties.
The operation works on two levels: on one hand, it turns the "Queene
of Ormus" into an honorary European; on the other, it legitimizes
both Western patriarchy and Portugal's rule in Asia. This strategy
allows Linschoten to present the Portuguese occupation of Hormuz—
brought to its knees only after intense and bloody confrontations—as
a peaceful acquisition. Native resistance to European infiltration is
blotted from view, and colonial conquest recast as a private transaction between the bride's (god)father and her prospective husband.[38]

The powerful nexus between marriage and baptism that subtends
Linschoten's narrative bespeaks the relevance of both in the *Itinerario*'s project of sociopsychological engineering. A rejection of Islam or
Hinduism was only part of the picture; true conversion also required
the repudiation of native mores and values that Europeans regarded as
abusive and irrational. The growing dissatisfaction with earlier models of conversion—that is, those derived from the experience of the
Reconquest and its forced mass baptisms—can be traced with ease in
Jesuit correspondence from the mid-sixteenth century forward. In a
1550 letter written from Quilon (Kerala State, India), the Jesuit Nicola Lancillotto complained that many Indians had become Christians
only in name. "Since the people of this land are very wretched, poor
and faint-hearted," he wrote, "some got baptized out of fear, others for secular interests, and others still for filthy and awful reasons

unfit to be mentioned."[39] While registering the power struggle among different colonial authorities regarding the administration of natives' souls and bodies, the complaint also evinces a novel preoccupation with social and cultural practices. In the words of another Jesuit, one of the main problems faced by missionaries in Portuguese Asia was that Christians behaved exactly as non-Christians, and that there was little or no difference between the two groups, "neither in [their] eating and drinking, nor in [their] keeping company."[40]

Marriage came thus to function as a key discriminant in religious and civil taxonomies that distinguished not only between Christians and non-Christians but also between "redeemable" (assimilable) and "unredeemable" (unassimilable) natives. Among Christians, marriage renewed the covenant between Christ and the church, aligning social practice with spiritual ethos. Among non-Christians, the presence of "true" marriages—monogamous, patrilinear, patriarchal family alliances based on exogamy and marital fidelity—was considered an important prerequisite for religious and cultural grafting. Colonial authorities especially insisted that monogamy was a matter of natural law: "Even the mating of birds," wrote the Jesuit Diogo Gonçalves in the early seventeenth century, "is performed between *one* female and *one* male."[41] That both Hindus and Muslims practiced polygamy merely demonstrated how far the peoples of India had drifted from both God and Nature.

We can now begin to understand the complex implications of the "Queene of Ormus" episode. In Linschoten's version of the story, baptism marks the queen's entrance into the Christian fold, but her most significant transformation is effected by marriage. Indeed, baptism comes to sanction a preexisting situation, the transformation of the "Queene of Ormus" into the wife of a "meane [Portuguese] Gentleman" (2: 188). No longer a queen either in name or in practice, Donna Philippa relinquishes her public role and withdraws into the private sphere, seemingly content to do nothing more than living "friendly and lovingly" with her husband (1: 187). From now on, Dazevedo will be the one to act and speak for her or, as Linschoten puts it, "to take order for the rentes and revenewes" on her behalf (1: 187).

Hence the *Itinerario* turns marital love into a uniquely European disciplinary technique, one that precedes and in a sense replaces conversion to Christianity as an instrument in the formation of colonized subjectivities that will embrace Europe's dominance as natural and proper. By encoding domestic heterosexuality as an adequate compensation for powerlessness and objectification, the "Queene of Ormus" romance legitimizes Western rule over a submissive and feminized Asia while offering symbolic compensation for the political and economic disruption resulting from it. In doing so, it also speaks to prospective European colonists as well as their wives, sisters, and daughters, instructing the latter in their true mission within patriarchy and depicting for the former the possible rewards that some—those endowed with the necessary self-restraint and the appropriate moral qualities—may derive from the Orient.

CHAPTER 4

Polygamy and the Arts
of Reduction

In 1606, an army under Philippine governor Don Pedro Bravo de Acuña landed on the island of Ternate, overcame native resistance, and took possession of the island in the name of King Philip III of Spain. In the capitulation that followed, the Ternatens acknowledged Habsburg overlordship, pledging to abide by the terms of the Iberian monopoly on the spice trade, give Christian missionaries free rein, and refrain from associating with the English and the Dutch. For their part, the victors immediately set out to transform the island's social and political landscape: abandoned Portuguese churches were restored, an Iberian settlement established, and the local mosque turned into a convent. The island's vanquished ruler, Said al-din Berkat Syah (r. 1584–1606), was deported to the Philippines along with his family and entourage.

Achieved after decades of ineffectual attempts and at "remarkably little cost" for the attackers, the capture of Ternate marked the beginning of the first and only period of Spanish influence in the Moluccas.[1] The site of lucrative clove plantations, these tiny Indonesian islands stood at the center of a vicious struggle that for much of the early modern period pitted Europe's leading powers against one another. An early dispute between Portugal and Spain, each of which claimed that the Moluccas lay on its side of the Tordesillas Line, had been settled in 1529 in favor of the former. But the Portuguese did not enjoy their possession for long. In 1575, a native insurgence ousted them from their fortified settlement on Ternate, forcing them to repair to nearby Tidore Island.[2] This was the situation in 1579, when Francis

Drake called at the Moluccas during his famous voyage of circumnavigation, and in 1599, when a Dutch expedition under the command of Jacob Corneliszoon van Neck and Wijbrand van Warwijck reached the archipelago and left a few factors behind.[3] By the early years of the seventeenth century, inter-European rivalries in the archipelago had spiraled into open conflict. In the spring of 1605, under the attentive eye of English East India Company merchants, a Dutch-Ternaten fleet led by Cornelis Sebastiaanszoon attacked Tidore and forced it to surrender, effectively shutting the Portuguese out of the region.

News of Tidore's fall lashed the Habsburg government into action: the loss of the island had to be avenged and Protestant expansionism forestalled, two goals that meshed neatly with Spain's smoldering hopes of gaining the Moluccas for itself. Acuña's victory turned these hopes into reality. In the wake of the 1606 campaign, the islands ceased to be a dependency of Portugal, their administration being quickly reformed along lines more in keeping with Spanish precepts of empire. The flow of spice was also reorganized to accommodate Spanish commercial interests.[4] "At present the Portuguese no longer have any cloves at their disposal," noted the French traveler François Pyrard in 1611, "which annoys them much, and they have a plea about it against the Spaniards in the Council of the King of Spain" ("auiourd'huy les Portugais n'ont plus de girofle en leur disposition, ce qui les fasche fort, & plaident là aussi au Conseil du Roy d'Espagne contre les Espagnols").[5]

As it happened, the supreme governing body of Spain's colonial possessions was then presided over by Pedro Fernández de Castro, Count of Lemos, probably better known among literary scholars as Miguel de Cervantes's patron. It was probably at the count's request that Bartolomé Leonardo de Argensola, an Aragonese priest who had achieved some notoriety as a poet, began to set down in writing an account of the campaign, whose organization Fernández de Castro had spearheaded and whose success he evidently regarded as a main achievement of his administration. The finished product, entitled *Conquista de las Islas Malucas* (The conquest of the Molucca Islands), appeared at Madrid in 1609. Despite its title, this was no mere account of Acuña's victory. Rather, it was a synthesis of totalizing ambitions—a veritable summa of geographic, historical, and ethnographic information drawn from a vast array of sources including Barros's *Décadas da Ásia*, Maffei's *Historiarum Indicarum*, and Linschoten's *Itinerario*. Its avowed purpose was to celebrate Spain's imperial mission; its effect was to inaugurate an image of Asia that would prove both durable and pervasive.

Modern criticism has treated Argensola as the poor stepchild of a rich and compelling literary age, thus foreclosing any serious consideration of the popularity he enjoyed during the early modern period. Yet evidence of the high regard in which this poet and historian was held is both quantitatively and qualitatively impressive: Miguel de Cervantes, for one, praised him for his "wit, elegance, style, and inventiveness," while Lope de Vega singled him out as the best writer of the age.[6] By and large, the *Conquista* shared in this prestige, earning John Locke's admiration and providing for a number of translations, borrowings, and adaptations. Excerpts from the work found their way into *Purchas his Pilgrimes* (1625), ensconced themselves inside French and Dutch translations of Cervantes's *Novelas Ejemplares*, and provided material for the stages of England, France, and Spain. An integral French translation made its appearance at Amsterdam in 1706; English editions were printed in 1708 and 1711; and a German translation was published in 1710. Thanks to this wide circulation, Argensola's *Conquista* actively participated in, and contributed to, a transnational discourse that shaped Europe's view of Asia throughout the seventeenth century and beyond.

Among the most cherished topoi of this discourse was polygamy— a term that, while technically comprising polygyny, polyandry, and group marriage, was generally synonymous with polygyny. This encompassed various situations in which a man, having become "one flesh" with one woman (Genesis 2:24), proceeded to do the same with other women, be that by having more than one wife, by marrying again after the death of the first wife, or by marrying a woman he had already known carnally. More commonly, polygamy was glossed as "having several wives at the same time" ("plures simul habere uxores")—a formulation referring *stricto sensu* to plural marriage but covering *lato sensu* all forms of sexual commerce that involved more than one woman on an ongoing basis (including marriage-cum-concubinage and plural concubinage).[7]

That many societies practiced polygamy was hardly newsworthy. It was in the early modern period, however, that having several wives at the same time became inextricably associated with alterity—a sign of racial difference rather than a privilege accorded to elite males in stratified societies the world over. Argensola's account marks a significant moment in this transformation: within the *Conquista*, plural marriage is not merely an aspect of Moluccan society but its most representative feature, its shortcomings defining the limitation of a native worldview portrayed as antithetical to Spanish values. In this manner, the *Conquista* not only worked out conventions for understanding and representing Asian polygamy but also played an important part in making monogamy a foundational institution—if not *the* foundational institution—of true civility.

Imperial exigencies no doubt played a role in this transformation: construed as a marker of cultural and moral backwardness, plural marriage could help justify the political and economic subordination of whole peoples and countries. In this perspective, Argensola's account of Moluccan polygamy can be understood as part of a broader Orientalist discourse that underpinned the dynamics of European imperialism. Yet as scholars in the wake of Edward Said's *Orientalism* have pointed out, expansionist agendas cannot fully account for the increased salience of polygamy in early modern writing, if for no other reason than this salience does not always map onto obvious geopolitical concerns.[8] As a matter of fact, early modern Europeans seem to have been just as interested in the polygamous practices of countries they had successfully infiltrated (such as the Moluccas or certain parts of India) as in those of countries where they were barely tolerated (such as Siam or the Maldive archipelago). And where Argensola's *Conquista de las Islas Malucas* clearly reflects Habsburg ambitions of universal monarchy, works such as Francesco Carletti's *Ragionamenti* and François Pyrard's *Voyage*—both roughly contemporary with the *Conquista* and similarly concerned with polygamy— are far less obviously imperial in inspiration. Even where geopolitical concerns were the same, moreover, early modern representations of plural marriage were by no means monolithic: they were heterogeneous and even fractious, inflected as they were by their producers' different backgrounds, experiences, and positions.[9]

Nonetheless, during the early decades of the seventeenth century European accounts of polygamy began to converge on a number of points. First, they understood polygamy as expressing the peculiar character of a whole society, even where, as in the Moluccas, its practice was limited to the elites.[10] In consequence, having several wives at the same time ceased to function as a sign of social status, and began serving as a racial marker. Second, although they saw monogamy as indissolubly linked to Christianity—one could hardly be a "true" Christian without also being monogamous—these accounts rarely explained polygamy in terms of religious belief. Even where religion was explicitly mentioned, it was rarely identified as a *cause* of polygamy; lust, not faith, was the spring from which nonmonogamous arrangements were thought to issue. As a result, polygamy became a symptom of an aberrant libido that could potentially operate as a principle of human classification. Finally, most of these accounts presented polygamy not just as *different from* monogamy, but as *antithetical to* it: thus the polygamous Asian household served as a foil for the European family, providing tropes over and against which its evolving ideals could take substance and shape. In this sense, early modern representations of nonmonogamy assisted in the construction of domestic heterosexuality—and helped enshrine its ideology as a *conditio sine qua non* of European identity.

As a historically specific configuration founded on gender hierarchy and patriarchal authority, domestic heterosexuality is a far cry from modern-day companionate marriage, which is generally predicated on a mix of eroticism and friendship between relatively autonomous social equals. Yet to the extent that both domestic heterosexuality and companionate marriage are rooted in erotic desire—that is, to the extent that erotic desire *still* functions as the primary means by which the family experience is made meaningful—it is easy to underestimate the difficulties that beset the harnessing of eros to matrimony. As Catherine Belsey has noted, the very idea of marrying for love was a paradox. Desire was infected with error, poisoned with jealousy, deaf to reason and authority; it knew no bounds and respected no law but its own. As such, desire militated against stability and made but a poor foundation on which to build a family.[11] For eroticism to be institutionalized within marriage, it was paramount that desire itself be domesticated and cleansed of its most troublesome aspects. In response to this need, eroticism split and polarized: "love" and "lust" emerged out of an originally undifferentiated eros as a way of containing the contradictions implicit in the new ideology of marriage.[12] This is precisely where nonmonogamy came in: as the antithesis of the European family, the polygamous household functioned as an apophatic description of domestic heterosexuality, defining its scope and ideals in terms not so much of what it was as of what it was not.

In this chapter, I take up Argensola's *Conquista* and (to a more limited extent) Pyrard's *Voyage* to show how early modern representations of Asian polygamy answered the many uncertainties attending the early modern institutionalization of heterosexual desire. My purpose is twofold: on the one hand, I suggest that polygamy served to minimize and obscure Europe's internal challenges to domestic heterosexuality, and that in so doing it became an index of racial difference. On the other hand, I highlight the extent to which the experience of overseas expansion participated in the construction of Europe's sexual ideologies. To this end, I first survey the circumstances that brought polygamy into the limelight, showing how the sixteenth and seventeenth centuries witnessed a novel marginalization of the nonmonogamous household. In the second section, I chart the slow and uneven emergence of a new understanding of polygamy that drastically reduced the social, political, and affective possibilities of the practice: using Pigafetta's *Relazione* as a point of departure, I illustrate how having several wives at the same time went from being a marker of wealth and esteem to being a symptom of erotic aberrancy. In the third and final section, I focus on Argensola's *Conquista* and Pyrard's *Voyage*, pointing to the ways that their representations of Asian polygamy participated in the construction of domestic heterosexuality.

MONOGAMY: EUROPEAN DEBATES AND CONTACT ZONE CONCERNS

Europe, we are often told, has been monogamous since the beginning of its recorded history. Roman society was monogamous, and the Christian Church has always been opposed to polygamy in any shape or form.[13] Yet de facto polygamy was widespread in Roman society both before and after Christianity became the official religion of the empire, most commonly in the form of unrestricted sexual access to one's slaves, but sometimes also in the form of parallel cohabitation alongside de jure marriage.[14] And although monogamous marriages were almost certainly the norm, polygamy was not unknown among the late Roman emperors. Indeed, no explicit prohibition against plural marriage seems to have existed until the sixth century, when the Code of Justinian declared it unlawful to "have two wives at once."[15] Not that this new prohibition hit everywhere the mark, especially where the elites were concerned: both Charlemagne (742–814) and Emperor Frederick Barbarossa (1152–90) had more than one wife in marriages that seem to have been at least tolerated by religious authorities.[16]

The church itself was less than straightforward in its opposition to polygamy. For Augustine of Hippo (354–430), having more than one wife was neither immoral nor illicit. "There are sins against nature and sins against custom and sins against the laws," he wrote in *Contra Faustum Manichaeum* (Reply to Faustus the Manichean). "In which, then, of these senses did Jacob sin in having a plurality of wives? As regards nature, he used the women not for sensual gratification, but for the procreation of children. For custom, this was the common practice at that time in those countries. And for the laws, no prohibition existed."[17] Even Thomas Aquinas, although by no means a supporter of polygamy, thought that plural marriage might be permissible under some circumstances.[18] Pope Gregory II (715–31) probably felt the same way, for in 726 he decreed that a man whose wife could not discharge her conjugal duties might legitimately take a second spouse, provided he continue to look after the first one.[19] The fourteenth-century Gerard Odonis, a Franciscan friar who taught moral theology at the University of Paris, considered polygamy a good alternative to divorce.[20] And as late as the 1530s, the Catholic theologian Tommaso de Vio (more commonly known as Cardinal Cajetan) held that plural marriage was against neither natural law nor Christian doctrine.[21]

If polygamy was forbidden by God, some asked, then why did biblical patriarchs have more than one wife? If the primary end of marriage was reproduction, would not polygamy secure this end more efficiently than monogamy? If marriage was a remedy against concupiscence, would not polygamy afford this remedy to women who might, otherwise, be deprived of it? And if marriage was meant for help and companionship, would not polygamy provide *more* of both? These were not mere quibbles, nor ad hoc arguments devised to ease the minds of a few potentates caught in unhappy unions (even though these few potentates may well have had a stake in the debate). Rather, they were moral, ethical, and political quandaries that revealed deep uncertainties about the nature and purposes of marriage. That having several wives at the same time should have preoccupied early moderns so intensely does not simply suggest that there were doubts regarding the value of (male) monogamy.[22] It also implies that polygamy could lay claim "to the credentials of a proper marriage"[23]

The Reformation undoubtedly had something to do with these uncertainties. Scriptural devotion had given new prominence to polygamy, threatening to turn biblical examples into legal precedent susceptible of practical application. No one could deny that plural marriage had an illustrious history in the Judeo-Christian tradition: among patriarchs and Old Testament worthies, Abraham had Sarah and Hagar (Gen. 16) plus an indeterminate number of concubines (Gen. 25); Jacob had Leah and Rachel (Gen. 29); and Solomon had "seven hundred wives . . . and three hundred concubines" (1 Kings 11.3).[24] To these positive examples was often added the consideration that, as John Milton noted in *De Doctrina Christiana*, there is no open interdiction of polygamy anywhere in the Bible.[25] This was the conclusion reached by Martin Luther in 1524, when he declared plural marriage not to be "against Holy Scripture"; and by Philip Melanchthon in 1531, when he appealed to the authority of the Bible to argue that polygamy was "not against divine law."[26] In a controversial dialogue published the year of the Council of Trent (and translated into English in 1657), the Capuchin-turned-Protestant Bernardino Ochino added new fuel to the fire by noting that plural marriage was once used in Europe "as a good thing, and very profitable to Man-kind."[27] Nor did these positive evaluations of polygamy remain just a matter of theory: during the well-known Anabaptist experiment in the German city of Münster, plural marriage was made not just licit but mandatory. Even after Münster's bloody end, a number of religious groups continued to allow the practice: a polygamous community was established in Westphalia in 1567, and in the Netherlands another such community seems to have been active until the 1580s.[28]

As important as the Reformation was, it was not the only force propelling polygamy into the limelight. An incipient interest in demography, coupled with the perception of a population crisis within Europe, played a crucial part. The Swiss physician Paracelsus (1493–1541), for one, recommended plural marriage as a way of balancing uneven sex ratios: "God has always created more women than men," he wrote, echoing the widespread belief that females vastly outnumbered males. And because unattached women were at the root of every social evil, Paracelsus concluded, men should be allowed to have as many wives as "may be required to take care of the surplus."[29] According to other commentators, polygamy was simply better than monogamy when it came to God's command to increase and multiply. The Dominican Giordano Bruno, for example, thought that men should not be forced to "waste" their seed on women already pregnant, but allowed to have as many wives as they could "feed and impregnate."[30] Where there were only one husband

and one wife, echoed fellow Dominican Tommaso Campanella, marital intercourse without hope of procreation was common: the wife might turn out to be sterile, or might be unable to conceive by her husband, or might be unable to conceive because already pregnant. Where there were one husband and several wives, by contrast, a man never had to be sexually idle or find himself in the position of "blossom[ing] without giving fruit."[31]

Opponents of plural marriage were fond of pointing out that in practice polygamous arrangements were rarely more fruitful than monogamous ones. As the Jesuit-trained Giovanni Botero noted in his 1589 *Della ragion di stato* (The Reason of State), plural wives often hindered each other's pregnancies out of jealousy, or sought to injure the children who were already born. As if that were not enough, polygamous husbands took little or no interest in their offspring's education, or lacked the means to secure their well-being. For these reasons, Botero concluded, Christendom was far more populous than Ottoman Turkey, and the monogamous nations of the north more thickly inhabited than the polygamous nations of the south. "Some people have thought they had provided well by *Poligamy*, allowing one man to have many Wives," reiterated the French diplomat Philippe de Béthune in 1632. "Yet experience hath taught us, that whether that a man being imployed in many places, cannot commonly get Children which live long; or not able to extend the care of a Father to so many Children through necessity, or otherwise they cannot ataine to ripe age; the Countrey which make use of Poligamie, finde not themselves better peopled then others."[32]

As may be inferred from the tenor of Botero's and Béthune's comments, early modern debates on the relative merits of monogamy and nonmonogamy rarely occurred without reference to the world outside Europe. In point of fact, most of these debates keenly reflect the increasingly global scope of early modern politics. Many eyed with alarm Islam's allowances for plural marriage, claiming that it gave Muslims a reproductive advantage; and some went so far as to suggest that European nations might be well advised to follow suit.[33] "Thanks to plural marriage, our Muslim enemies increase in number, whereas we [Christians] dwindle," noted Campanella in the early seventeenth century, as he cast fretful eyes south and east toward Africa and Asia. "And this custom [of plural marriage] is followed by the king of the Turks, by the king of the Fezites, and by most Eastern princes, [both] Muslim and pagan."[34]

The cross-cultural encounters that accompanied the process of Europe's expansion overseas further exacerbated these political concerns: from Mexico and Brazil to India, China, and the Moluccas, polygamy seemed to be everywhere. It was partially in reaction to this perception that European authorities proceeded to marginalize and criminalize polygamy. In 1537, a papal bull made single marriage a prerequisite for baptism, thereby strengthening the nexus between monogamy and Christianity.[35] Polygamous converts could only retain the wife from the first valid marriage (that is, a marriage for which no canonical impediments existed). All other spouses had to be dismissed.[36] Within Europe, prohibitions on nonmonogamy became more insistent and severe. Bigamy—the term under which the West has historically subsumed its own polygamous practices—became a criminal offense in the Holy Roman Empire in 1532 and was declared a capital crime in England in 1603. For convicted bigamists, the penalties became harsher: in Spain, verbal condemnations were replaced by beatings, galley service, and exile; in France, temporary confinement and public humiliation gave way to banishment, galley service, or execution.[37] Meanwhile, the Roman Catholic Church issued its clearest and strongest pronouncement against plural marriage. In 1563, the Council of Trent declared the practice unlawful and proclaimed anathema against anyone who thought otherwise. The same council also condemned concubinage, especially reprimanding "married men . . . [who] have the audacity at times to maintain and keep [concubines] at their own homes even with their own wives."[38]

Part of the impetus behind these legal developments came from the practical difficulties encountered by Christian missionaries overseas. Another part came from the perceived dangers of colonial environments that seemed to encourage nonmonogamy: while colonial authorities sought to reduce polygamous converts to one wife, European settlers abroad were surrounding themselves with droves of concubines. Their scandalous behavior belied Christian claims to moral superiority, and eroded the boundaries between natives and Europeans. "I say this of the Portuguese [in Asia], who have adopted the vices and customs of the land without reserve," reported a Jesuit missionary in 1550. "There are innumerable married settlers who have four, eight, or ten female slaves and sleep with all of them. . . . This is carried to such excess that there was one man in Malacca who had twenty-four women of various races, all of whom were his slaves, and all of whom he enjoyed."[39] Efforts against concubinage thus became indissolubly linked to the battle against polygamy, to the point that it is often difficult to tell where the first ended and the second one began. In 1567, Portuguese authorities in India issued a ban on polygamy and concubinage, regardless of religion. Men who had more than one wife were required to dismiss all but the first; those who kept multiple concubines were expected to marry one and forsake all others.[40] Four years later, the Crown ordered an inquiry into all captains, officials, and other "people of quality" living openly in concubinage.[41] In 1606, the Fifth Church Council of Goa came up with new strictures against suspected concubinaries, barring bachelors and widowers from keeping female servants under the age of fifty.[42]

Portuguese authorities were not alone in their efforts to enforce monogamy. Spanish officials in the Philippines also sought to stamp out polygamy and concubinage, even as they admitted that the problem might never be eradicated.[43] In 1620, shortly after the conquest of Batavia (modern-day Jakarta, Indonesia), a VOC edict outlawed concubinage among Dutch settlers, citing among other things "deplorable and well-known cases" of jealous concubines trying to murder one another by poison.[44] Eighteen months later, a new edict extended the prohibition to employees of all ranks, and further criminalized concubinage by equating it with adultery and incest.[45] Titled "Renovatie en ampliatie van . . . ordonnantien en plakaten betreffende concubinage, overspel en bloedschande" (Renovation and expansion of . . . ordinances and edicts concerning concubinage, adultery, and incest), the new piece of legislation connected marriage to the preservation of the colonial state, and emphasized the importance of monogamy to the conservation of Dutch purity. Concubinaries were accused not just of debauching themselves, but also of besetting their communities with "unrest, partiality, dissension, murder [and] slaughter."[46] Through their "lack of self-restraint," moreover, concubinaries betrayed the colony's Christian values and allowed for the mixing of "Christians, Moors [and] Heathens."[47] In doing so, they effectively undermined the foundations on which Dutch identity rested.

Central to the "Renovatie" was the threat of severe penalties. "Newe lawes . . . weare heere published with great solemnitye," wrote East India Company merchants Thomas Mills and John Milward in a 1622 letter from Pulicat, where the Dutch had an important base, "the tener of which contayned that noe merchantt, souldier or else under [the] authoretye [of the VOC] should hence forward after the publication thereof keepe any woman exceptt hee absolutte marry her."[48] A first offense would carry a hefty fine of 50 reals; a second one would draw a fine of 100 reals; a third would bring the death penalty by means of "a greatte blowe to the loss of [one's] head." This severity, Mills and Milward continued, "hath caused such a feare ammongst them, that licke beasts as they are, each thatt keeptt a blacke base whore have marryed them, and in [just] one daye weare heere marryed 38 persons."[49]

The doggedness with which Portuguese and Dutch authorities in Asia combated polygamy and concubinage evinces the centrality of marital monogamy in the colonial ideologies of early modern Europe. Within settlements characterized by great linguistic, ethnic, and religious diversity, the marital couple was not only a synecdoche for the colonial body politic; it was also a means through which racial affinities could be clarified and fixed. Construed as peculiarly "Oriental" practices, polygamy and concubinage were decried as both alien to Europe and inimical to Christianity. To the extent that they were obviously practiced among Christian European immigrants, their presence was usually explained as a contamination—a form of degeneracy affecting only a small part, and definitely not the best one, of the settler population. Meanwhile, monogamy was enshrined as a structure of prestige that might naturalize the colonial state while also domesticating its heterogeneity. In this manner, nonpolygamy became an integral part of European identity—a way of marking the settlers' social (and sexual) distance from the native population.

POLYGAMY: TRAVEL LITERATURE AND MISSIONARY ACCOUNTS

Information on the polygamous practices of Asia had filtered into Europe for centuries, peppering a whole range of classical and medieval texts from Cicero's *Tusculanae disputationes* and Strabo's *Geographika* to *The Book of Sir John Mandeville*. By and large, however, these reports amounted to little more than incidental references, oftentimes comprising just a few words. The enterprise of expansion built exponentially on this existing tradition. As new data accumulated, the very meaning of polygamy shifted: what was primarily a marker of wealth turned into a sexualized index of racial difference.

On 8 November 1521, Antonio Pigafetta and his companions reached the island of Tidore in the Moluccas. Here they were warmly received by King Al-Mansur, who was evidently eager to secure allies against neighboring Ternate.[50] In the days that followed, Al-Mansur pledged allegiance to the Spanish Crown, even decreeing that "henceforth his island would no longer be called Tidore but Castile, for the great love he bore our King his lord" ("da qui in avanti sua isola non se chiameria piú Tadore ma Castiglia, per l'amore grande portava al nostro re suo signore").[51] In a brief but vivid sketch, Pigafetta described Al-Mansur as "a Moor approximately forty-five years old, well-proportioned, royal in bearing and skilled in astrology" ("moro e forsi de quarantacinque anni, ben facto, con una presentia realle e grandissimo astrologo"; 280–81). He dutifully described the king's rich clothing, and detailed his family relations to other Moluccan kings. But what seems to have struck Pigafetta the most was the number of women allegedly at Al-Mansur's disposal: "The King of Tidore had a large house outside the city where he kept two hundred of his chief women along with a like number to serve them," he wrote. "No one is allowed to see them without the King's permission, and whoever is caught by day or night in the vicinity of the King's house is killed" ("Il Re di Tadore aveva una casa grande fuora de la cità, dove estavano ducento sue donne de le piú principali con altretante le servivano. . . . Niuno senza lisentia del re le può vedere e, se alguno è trovato o di giorno o de nocte apresso la caza del re, è amazato"; 286). Such an imaginative provocation could hardly be resisted. Penetrating the walls of this forbidden enclosure, Pigafetta regaled readers with a glimpse of its interior: "The king eats alone or with his principal wife in an elevated place . . . from where he can see all the other [women] sitting around him; and the one he likes the best is ordered to his bed for the night. When he is done eating, the women eat together if he orders them to do so; otherwise, each one goes to eat in her chamber" ("Quando lo re mangia, sta solo overo con la suo moglie principalle in uno luoco alto . . . ove pò vedere tucte le altre che li sedenno atorno e, a quella che piú li piace, li comanda vada dormire seco quela nocte. Finito lo mangiare, se lui comanda che queste mangiano insieme, lo fanno; si non ognuna va mangiare nella sua camera"; 286).

Insisting on the prohibition only to violate it, Pigafetta's account inaugurates a standard feature of what scholars have called "harem discourse"—a system of statements on female claustration that was both enabled and inflected by the permeability of allegedly impermeable boundaries.[52] As a forbidden space, barred to most men and charged with erotic significance, Tidore's royal *keputren* (the Indonesian equivalent of the harem) is rendered as an epistemological object that is only voyeuristically knowable and imaginatively reproducible. In this sense, the *Relazione* already anticipates later accounts of the polygamous household. Yet Pigafetta's representation of the keputren also lacks those features of luxurious indolence, moral degradation, and endemic strife that would become characteristic of harem discourse from the seventeenth century onward. There is none of the lustful languor ascribed by Pyrard to the polygamous Maldivians, of the aberrancy evoked in Carletti's *Ragionamenti*, or of the promiscuity showcased in Argensola's *Conquista*. Perhaps even more important, there is none of the opacity that later works often associated with the women's quarter—an opacity that, as Inderpal Grewal has suggested, turned the harem into a "metaphoric opposite" of the panopticon.[53] Quite to the contrary, Pigafetta's royal enclosure is a utopian space of absolute transparency where vision is coterminous with power. From his central position, Al-Mansur can survey all his wives and concubines without difficulty. His unobstructed gaze symbolizes his total control, so that the whole passage can be said to hinge on visibility as a governing technology of power. This visibility, in turn, is accompanied by principles of order: within the controlled space of the keputren, the very rhythm of daily life seems to be minutely keyed to the king's will—even the modality of the women's repast depends on him, and so does their rotation to his bed. All in all, the passage seems to be precisely calibrated to impress upon readers both the wealth of Tidore and the power of its king. Pigafetta had good reasons for wanting to create such an impression: after all, reaching the Moluccas had been the main goal of Magellan's voyage. By underscoring the wealth of Tidore and the power of Al-Mansur (who was now reportedly a vassal of the king of Spain), Pigafetta drove home the full extent of the expedition's success.

Principles of order and visibility continued to organize European representations of Asian polygamy throughout the rest of the sixteenth century and into the early years of the seventeenth. Take, for instance, the plate depicting the keputren of Tuban (eastern Java)—an image that routinely accompanied accounts of Van Neck and Van Warwijck's 1598–1600 voyage to the East Indies (Figure 9).[54] Behind an artificially shaded pond thick with waterfowl (marked with the letter A) stand the enclosure for the king's four wives (marked with the letter B) and the apartments reserved for his three hundred concubines (marked with the letters C, D, and E). Reproducing at the visual level Pigafetta's rhetorical move, the engraver has gone to great

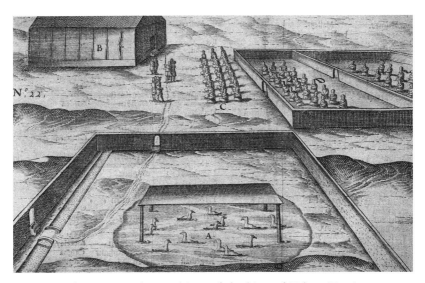

Figure 9. The wives and concubines of the king of Tuban (Java), as reproduced in the 1619 *Historiale beschrijvinghe, inhoudende een waerachtich
verhael vande reyse ghedaen met acht schepen van Amsterdam.* Courtesy
of the James Ford Bell Library, University of Minnesota, Minneapolis, MN.

lengths to make the wives' enclosure relatively permeable. Next to the
letter B, two narrow openings cut the wall across, revealing the shape
of an outstretched arm that seems to invite readers to peer in. To the
right, the concubines' enclosure is deprived of both roof and walls, so
as to make it utterly transparent. Here again, there is little that could
be said to anticipate later depictions of the harem. As a matter of fact,
the engraving's most striking feature is its painstaking orderliness,
which is especially noticeable in the rank-and-file arrangement of the
concubines. Far from functioning as an index of disorder, the royal
keputren serves as a testimony of Tuban's wealth and power. Wives
and concubines are just some of its king's many possessions—along
with his waterfowl (conspicuously present in the engraving), horses,
dogs, and elephants (omitted from the engraving but included in the
account).

But as the seventeenth century progressed, the sedate and orderly
space of Tuban's keputren gave way to places of "lascivious sensual-
ity, wanton and reckless festivity, superfluous pomp, [and] inflated
pride."[55] In the process, polygamy itself changed, becoming a byword
of disorder. "Every man [in China] . . . may keepe as many Wives as

hee will," wrote the Spanish Jesuit Diego de Pantoja in a widely circulated and much-reproduced letter from Peking, "which is the cause
of many tumults, quarrels, and disorders in their houses among their
wives, and among the Sonnes of divers Mothers."[56] As the Spanish
Jesuit saw it, these quarrels and disorders provided a tremendous
opportunity for the spreading of Christianity: no prospective convert
could fail to appreciate the superiority of a creed that did "not permit
any more but one lawfull Wife onely."[57]

Unfortunately for European missionaries, things did not quite turn
out the way Pantoja envisioned. Instead of encouraging Christian conversion and European acculturation, polygamy proved a formidable
impediment to both. It hindered the work of missionaries in the Philippines, and was reputedly responsible for the collapse of the Jesuit
mission in Tonquin (northern Vietnam).[58] For their part, missionaries in the Moluccas routinely bemoaned the islanders' resistance to
the dictates of Christian marriage, and their penchant for taking new
wives as soon as they grew weary of the old ones.[59] The most obstinate were the ruling elites: in a letter from Ternate, the Jesuit Francis
Xavier complained that lust, not religious conviction, stood in the
way of the king's conversion. If the latter could not be prevailed on
to become Christian, he explained, it was not so much because he
was a devout Muslim as because he loathed the prospect of giving
up his "carnal vices."[60] Similar complaints came from the Jesuits at
the Mughal court, as well as from many missionaries to China.[61] By
1669, the Benedictine Clemente Tosi could use polygamy to characterize most, if not all, of Asia: "No abuse is as widespread in those
parts of the Orient . . . as this one," he generalized with confidence.
"There is not a house of the well-to-do . . . or a palace of reigning
princes that is not defiled by herds of lewd females. Nor is there a vice
more difficult to uproot from the minds of these soft and effeminate
men than polygamy."[62]

An almost endless combination of social customs, religious allowances, economic factors, and political rationales stood behind the
highly differentiated family arrangements that Europeans subsumed
under the umbrella of polygamy, but certainly a major motive for these
arrangements was the desire, on the part of ruling elites, to promote
expansion, gain vassals or allies, and stabilize their power. Thus, when
the sultan of Aceh (northern Sumatra) sought to forge an alliance with
the English, he entreated James I to send "two white women" for him
to marry. "For (said hee) if I beget one of them with child, and it

proove a sonne, I will make him king of Priaman, Passaman, and of the coast from whence you fetch your pepper; so that yee shall not need to come any more to mee, but to your owne English king for these commodities."[63] As the language of this proposal suggests, wives and concubines could serve as diplomatic agents, their offspring cementing alliances of both political and economic import. Early modern writers were clearly aware of this. In his account of Moluccan polygamy, Pigafetta observed that many families contributed one or more daughters to the king's harem. The author of the "Tratado de las yslas de los Malucos" (identified by some as António Galvão, who was captain of the Portuguese fortress on Ternate in the late 1530s) confirmed this report, adding that some women were designated for that purpose "while still in their mothers' wombs."[64] For his part, a member of the first Jesuit mission to Akbar's court noted that Muslim rulers used polygamy "to ratify peace" as well as "create friendly relationships with . . . vassal princes or neighboring monarchs."[65]

As time went by, however, these sociopolitical rationales were silenced or ignored, and polygamy reduced to being just the symptom of an exorbitant libido.[66] This seems to have been the conclusion drawn not just by missionaries but by lay commentators as well. "And surely if there were men of Learning . . . to instruct them, a number of [Javanese] would be drawn to the true Fayth of Christ, and also would be brought to civilitie," wrote Edmund Scott, an English East India Company merchant stationed at Bantam (northern Java) in the early years of the seventeenth century, "for many which I have reasoned with concerning the lawes of Christians, have liked all well, excepting onely their pluralitie of Women, for *they are all very lasciviously given* both men and women."[67] Ventriloquizing what was an already-conventional missionary discourse, Scott's report walks the tightrope between Christian universalism and a stiffening sense of racial difference: because of their receptiveness to European values, Scott's interlocutors are potentially capable of both civility and salvation. It is their innate lasciviousness that stands in the way, and prevents them from ever achieving this potential. Measuring the chasm between English and Javanese, Scott construes nonmonogamy as the tangible sign of an otherwise untangible essence, which he then uses to separate and distinguish among human groups.

Scott's account of the East Indies represents an especially clear example of how early modern Europeans used nonmonogamy as a racial discriminant, but is by no means the only one. Jean Bodin's

1573 *Les Six livres de la République* (The Six Books of the Common-wealth), for one, had already used the presence of polygamous customs among Africans, Persians, Peruvians, West Indians, and Moluccans to illustrate the chasm between peoples of the South and peoples of the North, "for that [those of the North] are more chast and abstinent, and those of the South much given to lust."[68] As a symptom of innate aberrancy that was implicitly or explicitly opposed to European ideals of erotic self-mastery, polygamy came to inflect early modern discourses of civility, informing human taxonomies that would deny some peoples the faculty of *recta ratio* and the capacit for self-government.

ARGENSOLA, PYRARD, AND THE ARTS OF REDUCTION

As a piece of official historiography written by a priest, Argensola's *Conquista de las Islas Malucas* combines Habsburg dreams of universal monarchy with the militancy of Counter-Reformation Catholicism, construing Spain's acquisitions in the Moluccas as part of a global struggle that was at once political and religious. The point is made forcefully in the book's opening paragraph, which locates the significance of Acuña's victory not so much in the economic advantages that the Habsburg Crown might derive from the region, as in the spiritual benefits that would accrue from fighting Islam while also curtailing Protestant advances into Asia:

> I write of the reduction of the Moluccas to the obedience of Philip III, King of Spain, and of their kings to their former subjection, acknowledged by their predecessors and reintroduced by Don Pedro de Acuña, governor of the Philippines and admiral of the Spanish fleet. A victory worthy of the foresight of such a godly monarch, the application of the good ministers of his Supreme Council, and the valor of our nation, not so much because of those provinces' rare fertility, as because it deprived the northern fleets of an important reason for sailing our seas, preventing them from debauching with [their] heresy the faith of the newly converted East Indians and of the colonists who trade among them.

> Yo Escrivo la Reduccion de la Islas Malucas, à la obediencia de Felipe III Rey de España, y la de los Reyes dellas, al vasallage antiguo, que reconocieron sus predecessores, introduzido de nuevo por Don Pedro de Acuña, Governador de las Filipinas, y General de la armada Española. Vitoria digna de la providencia de tan pio Monarca, del cuydado de los Ministros graves de su Consejo supremo, y del valor de nuestra nacion; no tanto por la rara fertilidad de aquella Provincias,

como por aver quitado con ella à las armadas Setentrionales, una
gran causa de navegar nuestros mares, por que no inficionen con
heregia, la pureza de la Fê reciente de los Indios Assiaticos, y de los
habitadores de nuestras Colonias, que tratan con ellos.[69]

The impersonality of the passage is noteworthy. Although explicitly mentioned, neither Philip III nor Pedro de Acuña—nor, for that
matter, Spain as a whole—emerges as protagonist of the narrative.
Rather, as the syntax of the passage indicates, the subject matter of
the *Conquista* is an abstract teleological process: the "reduction"
("Reduccion") of the Moluccas to Iberian domination.

The Spanish *Diccionario de Autoridades* (1737) glosses Argensola's "reduction" as a synonym for military conquest. Yet in the
Latinate usage deployed above, "reduction" also indicates the act of
bringing something back, restoring it to its original place or position
(from *Redūcere*, to bring back). In this sense, "reduction" bespeaks
the relevance of the Reconquest as an ideological and diegetic model
for Argensola's *Conquista*. As Anthony Pagden has observed, the narrative of Iberia's deliverance from its Muslim "invaders" was predicated on the "absurd claim that the Christian rulers of the north had
prior political and property rights" over the southern portion of the
Iberian Peninsula.[70] Likewise, the *Conquista* capitalized on Portugal's colonial precedents in the Moluccas to advance claims of prior
Spanish possession. By positing a spurious continuity between Spanish present and Portuguese past, the text sought not only to transform
an act of foreign invasion into a war of liberation but also to smooth
over the fact that the 1606 conquest was no return to the *status quo
ante*. Far from turning the clock back to the days of Portugal's ascen-
dancy, in fact, Acuña's campaign heralded the advent of a colonial
regime that was markedly Spanish in character.

In a way, the very salience Argensola assigns to "reduction" is
emblematic of this new colonial regime, for the term would not have
failed to evoke those Spanish experiments of resettlement, conversion,
and acculturation commonly known as "reductions" or "reduccio-
nes." The fundamental principle behind these colonial experiments
was one of simplification: from Paraguay to the Philippines, originally
distinct groups were merged, native worldviews reassembled according to European logics, new orders fashioned out of ancient social
dynamics that colonial authorities disparaged as chaos.[71] Read in this
light, "reduction" also points toward a numerical diminishing, a less-
ening of complexity, and a decrease of mobility. It thereby testifies to

the renewed vigor that *reductio ad unum*—the principle according to which the world's plurality could be traced back to its fundamental oneness—enjoyed during the early modern period.

Fully partaking of this ideology, Argensola's *Conquista* depicts the progress of Iberian imperialism in Asia as a process of political and moral reduction: a movement from variety to uniformity, from dissonance to harmony, from dispersal to concentration. Where Habsburg Spain is an orderly hierarchy organically fused by a singleness of purpose, its enemies are disorderly assemblages riddled with hostility and discord. In the case of the Moluccas, this was already an established topos, the archipelago's internecine struggles having become standard fare among European writers since at least the mid-sixteenth century. The Moluccans "are always waging war, they enjoy it. . . . They kill and capture each other: fathers do so to sons, brothers to brothers," wrote the author of the "Tratado de las yslas de los Malucos," whose sixteenth-century account of Moluccan life was one of Argensola's main sources.[72] "There is no country in the world . . . more unstable, fraudulent, and perfidious" than the Moluccas, echoed Giovanni Botero in his *Relationi Universali* (1593–96).[73]

At first blush, Argensola simply seems to follow in the footsteps of these earlier writers. Like them, he laments the constant warfare and frequent "suspicions, frauds, and lies" ("rezelos, fraudes, y mentiras"; 11) that beset Maluccan society. Yet in identifying polygamy as both a component and a cause of all this strife, the *Conquista* departs in radical ways from earlier European accounts. Although similarly negative in their assessments of Moluccan society, neither Botero nor the author of the "Tratado" had complained much about the islanders' sexual mores. Indeed, while remarking that the elites had large retinues of wives and concubines, the latter had also waxed admiringly on the Moluccans' propriety in sexual matters: adultery was punished, virginity prized, sodomy rare, and prostitution unknown. By contrast, Argensola presented polygamy as an emblem of the variety, dissonance, and dispersal to which Spanish processes of "reduction" stood opposed.

Behind the relevance that the *Conquista* assigns to nonmonogamy stood a humanist tradition that saw the family as a miniature model of both church and state, the harmony of the domestic unit serving as the foundation for the unity of the polity as a whole.[74] The bond between husband and wife was especially important, since it naturalized the relationship between monarchs and subjects while also reiterating the rapport between Christ and the church. As the melding of two bodies in "one flesh," moreover, the marital couple served as a crucial synecdoche for reductio ad unum as a political principle underwriting the Habsburg bid for universal monarchy. Understood as sanctioning the legal and ontological incorporation of the wife into the husband, the "one flesh" metaphor replicated and legitimized the "reduction" of colonial communities to political obeisance and economic subjection. It is hardly a coincidence that monogamization, whether in the form of anti-polygamy legislation, the criminalization of concubinage, or a combination of the two, was such a conspicuous part of Iberian policies in both Asia and America.[75] Foisting Christian marriage on native communities meant not only altering their social organization, reshaping their economies, and marginalizing their values, but also, and perhaps more critically, embedding the principle of their subjection into the most elemental structures of community formation.

It is precisely the idea of marriage as a synecdoche for political reductio ad unum that Argensola invokes in the *Conquista*, where polygamy—both literal and metaphorical—is taken as a sure indicator of civil inadequacy and social disorder. The Protestant Dutch, for example, are depicted as spiritual polygamists who have repudiated Christ's true "bride" to espouse a plurality of heretical sects. And because these polygamous arrangements made social cohesion impossible, Dutch society would inevitably collapse. "When the father is a Calvinist, the mother is a Huguenot, the son a Lutheran, the servant a Husite, and the daughter a Protestant," Argensola wrote in the *Conquista*. "Such a fragmentation, unworthy [even] of beasts, means that . . . these people cannot unite in true peace. . . . And let no one believe, that because they don't fight among themselves, love is the reason for it. The ground of their false tranquility should be called idleness, not peace" ("Quando el padre es Calvinista, suele ser la madre Huganota, el hijo Luterano, y el criado Husita, y la hija Protestante. . . . Desta division, indigna de fieras, resulta . . . no poder estas gentes unirse entre si a verdadera paz. . . . Y nadie crea, que aunque no guerrean unos contra otros, es amor la causa. Ocio se ha de llamar y no paz, el fundamento de su falsa quietud"; 233).

While disparaging the Dutch for their spiritual polygamy, the *Conquista* reserves its harshest critique for the Moluccans: "Their laws are barbarous. They place no limit to the number they can marry" ("Sus leyes son barbaras. No ponen numero a los matrimonios"; 11).

While the two statements are only paratactically related, their juxtaposition suggests a precise logical relation: plural marriage provides the measure of Moluccan barbarism. This suggestion is fully borne out by various inset stories set at the court of Ternate. Interspersed within the *grand récit* of Spain's imperial progress, these extended anecdotes offered a voyeuristic escape from the constraints of historical decorum; at the same time, they exposed the polygamous household as a hotbed of deceit, adultery, incest, and murder—and underscored its psychosexual and sociopolitical inadequacies. "The love of a husband for several wives," noted Giovanni Botero in his *Ragion di Stato*, could never be "so warm and undivided as for one wife."[76] The *Conquista* amply elaborated on this premise, suggesting that polygamous men lost all chance at emotional attachment the moment they exercised their inflated sexual rights. The sweet rewards of monogamous marriage, with its attendant notions of emotional intimacy and erotic fulfillment, would forever be precluded to them.[77] And because having access to multiple women fostered lechery instead of curbing it, polygamous men were more likely than monogamous ones to commit adultery, indulge in incest, or follow "unnatural" lusts. From this perspective, polygamy was fundamentally opposed to marriage, which guaranteed social order through the containment of sexual expression.

As for the wives, neither looks nor smarts could spare them from the pangs of jealousy, preserve them from humiliation, or save their minds and souls from corruption. Even Celicaya, King Said's favorite wife, failed to escape this destiny. In the beginning of the marriage, Said had devoted himself to his new bride with transport and passion. Yet, "divided among so many women," even this transport and passion "had not the usual power over him, and allowed for other diversions" ("divididos con tantas mugeres, no causavan en su animo la sugecion que suelen, y le daban lugar à otras diversiones"; 308). The intricate plot that follows highlights the disastrous consequences of these polygamous premises. When Said seduced the wife of his cousin Amuxa, the latter evened the score by seducing Celicaya—who, for her part, "justified herself by alleging the wrong the king had done her by looking at another woman" ("se defendia con la ofensa que el Rey le avia hecho en mirar a la otra"; 309). Unwilling to displease his wife, and unable to confront his powerful cousin, Said opted for murder: he lured Amuxa to a secluded spot and ordered his guards to dispatch him. The intended victim nevertheless escaped, and the scandal that ensued from the attempted murder put Said's rule in serious jeopardy. Eventually, a reconciliation was brokered: Amuxa returned to Said's favor, and both men to that of their respective wives, with no further notice seemingly taken of the whole affair.

Inviting readers to measure the chasm between Moluccan barbarism and Iberian civility, Argensola's depiction of the polygamous household indicted plural marriage as a social structure incapable of regulating desire, inculcating hierarchies, aiding political stability, and maintaining family cohesion. Perhaps more important, this depiction countered common European fantasies of the polygamous household as a haven of male hegemony. "Their Polygamy hath this convenience in it, that there is not Woman, but uses all Industry and Artifice imaginable to gain her husbands affection, and defeat her Rivals," wrote Johann Albrecht von Mandelslo in his account of Mughal India. "All the caresses, all the kindnesses she can think of, she makes use of to ingratiate her self. There is no Drug eminent for its venereal Vertues, but she will find out some means or other to give him, to excite him into Voluptuousness; and she thinks no complyance too great, to purchase his more frequent enjoyments."[78] In Mandelslo's masculinist utopia, the asymmetries of polygamy enable an economy of supply and demand that is radically skewed in favor of the husband: cognizant of their own replaceability, wives have no choice but to compete for attention and approval. Working against this grain, the *Conquista* suggests that polygamy might actually work *against* male hegemony. Instead of vying for Said's attentions, Celicaya imitates him—and in doing so undermines the foundations of his power as both a husband and a ruler. And because Celicaya's adulterous liasion with Amuxa also conjures the specter of polyandry, Argensola's anecdote counterbalances the utopian vision of female replaceability implicit in many European accounts of polygamy with a dystopian vision of male replaceability. Far from being an erotic paradise, the polygamous household is at best a sexual purgatory, and at worst a hell of political misrule.

If Argensola suggested that having several wives at the same time made men replaceable, some of his contemporaries went even further, proposing that polygamy could make men altogether unnecessary. For these writers, polygamy was less an economy of male scarcity and female competition than an economy of female self-sufficiency—one in which other intimacies and pleasures thrived side by side, if not in competition with, those that a husband could share with his wives.

Take the case of François Pyrard's *Voyage*. The survivor of an ill-fated French expedition dispatched to the East Indies in 1601, Pyrard spent about five years as an unwilling guest in the Maldives, an island chain off the coast of southwestern India. The story of his adventures, published in 1611, reissued in 1615, and much augmented in 1619, provides a rich account of the islands' history, language, and customs. By and large, Pyrard's *Voyage* describes Maldivian society in terms of its similarity to French society. But the similarities cease abruptly when it comes to Maldivian sexuality: "[In the Maldives] there is nothing but adultery, incest, and sodomy" ("ce n'est rien qu'adulteres qu'incestes, que sodomie"; 1: 215), the text observes. And because the heat of the climate and the manners of the country sap vigor and strength from the body, the men's greatest desire "is to find, if they can, some recipe to satisfy their wives, and get themselves greater strength to practice their lechery. . . . They talk of this continually, even in the presence of their wives, of whom they have as many as three, as I have said, which is the reason why they are unable to satisfy each" ("c'est de recouvrer s'ils pouvoient quelque recepte, pour mieux contenter leurs femmes, & les rendre plus forts à exercer leur paillardise. . . . Aussi parlent-ils continuellement de cela, & sont fort dissolus en paroles, & ne bougent presque tousiours d'auprés de leurs femmes, dont ils ont pluralité, jusques à trois comme j'ay dit, qui est ce qui les empesche de satisfaire à chacune d'elles"; 1: 216).

Elsewhere in the account, Pyrard reveals that Maldivian men might have additional reasons to look for sexual stimulants: for if Asian women in general "are naturally much inclined to every kind of ordinary lewdness" ("sont fort enclines naturellement à toute sorte de lubricité & paillardise ordinaire"), Maldivian women are so extraordinarily lewd "that they have no other talk or occupation" ("qu'elles n'ont jamais autres discours ny occupation"; 1: 325). From this voraciousness comes a peculiar "sin" ("peché") called *pouy tallan*, in which women "make use of a local fruit they call *Quela* and we *Banana*, which is as long as a palm and as thick as the arm of a ten-year-old child" ("se servant d'un certain fruict du pays qu'ils nomment *Quela* & nous *Banane*, dont il y en a tel long comme un pan & gros comme le bras d'un enfant de dix ans"; 1: 324). Two women were caught in the act during the time of Pyrard's stay in the Maldives, prompting a massive investigation and a spectacular trial. In the end, about thirty women were publicly punished, "with a warning that, if they returned to these practices, they would be drowned" ("avec menace que si elles y retournoient, elles seroient noyees"; 1:327).

The threat, it seems, proved ineffective, with some of the same women being arrested again shortly thereafter. And because none of these repeat offenders were actually drowned, "but only beaten with those whips that are called *gleau*" ("mais seulement battuës de ces cuirs qu'ils appellent *gleau*"; 1: 327) readers are left to imagine pouy tallan as a permanent feature of sexual life in the Maldives. By foregrounding women's voraciousness and underscoring the independence of their pleasure from male genitalia, Pyrard's account gives voice to the specters that haunted domestic heterosexuality—"not only fears about male subordination to female sexual demands, but also anxieties about the expendability of the penis."[79] Displacing these specters onto the polygamous Asian household, the *Voyage* could deflect them away both from Europe and from monogamy.

Despite their obvious differences, Argensola's *Conquista* and Pyrard's *Voyage* testify to a new understanding of polygamy, slowly accreted during the course of the sixteenth century to become visible in the early years of the seventeenth. Both construe polygamy as a sign of erotic aberrancy, thereby making it incompatible with marriage proper; both depict the polygamous household as a source of sociopolitical instability, thereby making it antithetical to the well-ordered polity. Finally, they both associate nonmonogamy with the East, as if this were the only place where nonmonogamous relationships could obtain. In doing so, Argensola and Pyrard turned polygamy into a symptomatology of Eastern inferiority. As time went on, and other writers followed in their path, Europe conveniently forgot its own polygamous history, and embraced monogamy as a timeless component of its own identity.

CHAPTER 5

The Ideology of Interracial Romance

On 29 October 1617, a civic pageant titled *The Tryumphs of Honor and Industry* was performed in London to celebrate the installation of George Bowles as the city's lord mayor. It was the third in a series of spectacles devised by Thomas Middleton for the Society of Grocers, a guild whose business in "rich Aromatick Commodities" was intimately linked to the still-uncertain fortunes of England's expansion overseas.[1] After an opening show of dancing Indians bagging pepper and planting spice trees, there followed an emblematic arrangement composed of India, Traffic, and Industry—the latter holding in her hand a golden ball surmounted by a Cupid. "Behold this Ball of Gold, upon which stands / A golden Cupid wrought with curious hands," Industry proclaimed in her address. "The mighty power of Industry it showes, / That gets both wealth, and love."[2]

Considered by itself, Industry's "Ball of Gold" bears distinct reference to the Hesperidian fruit of classical mythology, a recurring trope for the precious goods that early modern Europeans were busy trading and plundering across the globe.[3] The golden Cupid that stands atop the pome, however, also links Industry's ball to a *globus cruciger*, the cross-surmounted orb that had been an emblem of temporal power since the time of Constantine the Great. Conjoining golden apple and royal orb, Industry's ball of gold aligns the interests of the merchant classes with those of the monarchy, equating profits with national concerns. Yet even as this orb derives its suggestive power from the symbolic valence of the globus cruciger, it also differs from it in profound ways: it is not a cross, but an emblem of erotic desire, that surmounts it. It is not from God, but rather from Cupid, that Industry derives its authority and legitimacy. Seen in this light, Industry's "Ball of Gold" resembles less a globus cruciger than a cosmogonic eros—a force bringing order and harmony to the world—which was typically represented as Cupid astride a globe.[4] At the crossroads of trade, love, and empire, Industry's ball of gold eroticizes Europe's economic and geopolitical onslaught on the rest of the world, portraying it as a quest for sexual and sentimental rewards.

Love and empire accompanied each other from the beginning of Europe's expansion overseas, giving rise, as Roland Greene has argued, to a "reciprocal protocol of representation" that invested each realm with the force and import of the other.[5] At first, this protocol of representation clustered around Petrarchan tropes of unrequitedness. But as time went by, conjugal fulfillment replaced unrequitedness as a thematic principle capable of organizing both the dynamics of imperial expansion and the phenomenology of erotic experience. It became possible to conceive of empire as a marriage between European metropole and non-European periphery—as Camões did in the Isle of Love episode, or as VOC shareholders implied when they noted that the king of Spain regarded his possessions in America "as his lawful wife, of whom he is exceedingly jealous and firmly resolved to maintain inviolate."[6] By the same token, it became customary to speak of marriage as if it were a mercantile-imperial venture: "Who so ever marries a wife may well be called a *Merchant venturer*," noted the soldier-writer Barnabe Riche in 1613, "for he makes a great adventure that adventures his credit, his reputation, his estate, his quiet, his libertye, yea many men by marriage do not onely adventure there bodyes but many times their soules."[7]

Nowhere is the ideological conjuncture of love and empire more noticeable than in the period's penchant for cross-racial couples—as evinced from the union of Vasco da Gama and Tethys in Camões's *Os Lusíadas*, or from the marriage between Antonio Dazevedo Coutinho and the "Queene of Ormus" in Linschoten's *Itinerario*. Indeed, between the late sixteenth century and the mid-seventeenth, interracial desire became something of a fixture both on the stage and on the page, oftentimes at the center of stories casting expansion in overtly erotic terms. While the specific details of these stories vary greatly, their basic outlines are fairly consistent. In a setting more or less remote, a European man and a non-European woman meet and fall in love; the latter willingly renounces her background in order to embrace his; and the tale ends with the happy pair either betrothed or married. A long list of early modern couples can be found cast in similar narratives. Taking into account only plots that are explicitly set in the East, such a list would have to include at least Rodrigo Gallinato and the Cambodian Tipolda in Andrés de Claramonte's *El Nuevo Rey Gallinato* (ca. 1600), Robert Shirley and Teresia Khan in Anthony Nixon's *The Three English Brothers* (1607) and the collaborative play *The Travailes of the Three English Brothers* (1607), Juan Serrano and the queen of Cebu in François Loubayssin de Lamarque's *Historia tragicomica de Don Henrique de Castro* (1617), a "Portuguese gentleman" and Idalcan's sister in Jean Mocquet's *Voyages en Afrique, Asie, Indes orientales et occidentales* (1617), Armusia and Quisara in John Fletcher's *The Island Princess* (1621), and Ruy Diaz de Acuña and Quisaira in Melchor Fernández de León's *Conquista de las Malucas* (ca. 1679).

Perhaps the most obvious point one could make about these interracial plots is that a profoundly evocative power resides in the border crossings they depict. Happily resolving cultural differences, social tensions, and religious conflicts, they enact a compelling "ideal of cultural harmony through romance."[8] Yet it is just as obvious that this ideal is systematically realized through border crossings of a gendered kind: somehow, it is always the native woman who enters the world of the European man, never the other way around. While seemingly articulating a vision of mutuality and reciprocity, then, these narratives fantasized the application of Western entrepreneurship onto a feminized and receptive East. As tales of love, they proposed Europe's overseas expansion as a self-evident good. As tales of marriage, they hid coercion under a veneer of contractual consent. And because marriage was a contractual relation that was deemed to be naturally unequal—after all, the husband was supposed to govern, the wife to obey—these narratives also legitimized the political and economic subordination of countries from which enormous profits could be extracted in the form of commodities, labor, and consumer markets.[9] From this perspective, interracial romances were tales of empire, the main purpose of which was to celebrate expansion and mystify inequalities via a rhetoric of exchange and reciprocity. It is unsurprising that so many of them, even those not purporting to be histories, were highly topical. Whether written in a celebratory or compensatory mode, interracial romances voiced the hopes and aspirations of specific merchant capitalist groups: penetrating Cambodia, trading with Persia and with India, securing the Philippines, or scoring a victory in the race for the spice-producing Moluccas.

For interracial romances to work in this manner, a specific vision of conubium needed to be made available. Marriage had to be reconfigured as a privatized relationship, oriented toward the lovers' fulfillment and disconnected from (the bride's) kin and community, whose needs and desires were in fact often at odds with those of European capitalism. This required not only institutionalizing desire as a foundation of family life but also obscuring the link between marriage and property. Domestic heterosexuality, I submit allowed precisely for this reconfiguration: its emphasis on erotic desire placed individual wishes above those of the community, and muted the interdependence of marriage and economics. Although they remained effectively central to most marriage decisions, property concerns were pushed into the background, coming to be conceived more as an expression of the bond between husband and wife than as its raison d'être. Charged with this new ideological burden, desire itself became "industrious"—its wayward power transformed into a form of labor that should be "won" or profitably exchanged.[10] From this perspective, interracial romances were tales of domestic heterosexuality, the main purpose of which was to celebrate eros and smooth over the many anxieties that accompanied the institutionalization of desire within marriage.

All of this is not to suggest that Europe's expansion overseas was the sole catalyst in the ideological shift that harnessed eros to conubium. As Valerie Traub has noted, domestic heterosexuality "was the result of a variety of discourses and cumulative changes that occurred unevenly" between the sixteenth and eighteenth centuries.[11] Yet the frequency with which early modern texts construe marriage-minded desire as an engine of empire implies a deep connection between the dawn of modern imperialism and the emergence of a new sexual regime centered on spousal eroticism. Indeed, if we accept the contention that this new sexual regime emerged in response to the social, economic, and political dislocations of incipient capitalism, it is perhaps not too far off the mark to suggest that Europeans arrived at domestic heterosexuality as a means of underwriting, at least in part, the hopes and uncertainties of the expansionist enterprise.[12] To put it in Louis Althusser's terms, domestic heterosexuality acted as a powerful means of interpellation, constituting subjects (and relations among subjects) suitable to the requirements of early modern imperialism.[13] The vision of conubium that resulted—a bridge across the chasm of competing interests, a mutual bond uncontaminated by selfish ambitions or illegitimate desires—became in turn the yardstick against which all sexual unions and all erotic subjectivities would be measured, both in Europe and outside of it. It is this vision that Argensola likely had in mind when he decried the political and social pitfalls of polygamy; and it is this same vision that shaped Linschoten's critique of Portugal's Estado da Índia.

Within this larger context, plots of interracial romance played a crucial role. As racial representations, they exerted pressure on the ways that identities could be bounded and ascribed; as sexual representations, they celebrated certain erotic scripts and marginalized others. Reflecting and reformulating the experience of the contact zone for home consumption, they taught European men and women what and how to desire—that is, how to perform and distribute affect in ways that were both gender specific and racially appropriate. It is not that Europeans consciously learned these lessons, or that it became impossible for them to ignore or discard the message. Although interracial romances certainly provided templates of behavior, their primary effect was to delimit the range of acts, desires, and affects that could be legitimately available within Europe. In the process, these plots of love and empire also assayed the ambiguities and paradoxes of domestic heterosexuality: its positive requirement for female erotic agency, but at the same time its need to subsume this agency under that of the husband; its drive for mutuality, and at the same time its concern that this mutuality might translate into male erotic dependency (and abjection).[14]

In this chapter, I explore the entwining of mercantile imperialism and domestic heterosexuality by way of John Fletcher's *The Island Princess*, perhaps the most successful interracial romance of the early modern period. Derived from an inset tale in Argensola's *Conquista*, Fletcher's tragicomedy was penned between 1619 and 1621, performed at court in the winter of 1621, and published as part of Beaumont's and Fletcher's *Comedies and Tragedies* (1647) after the closing of the theaters by the Puritans. Revived with much applause during the Restoration, it was repeatedly adapted and eventually transformed into an opera that was regularly produced, often several times a year, well into the eighteenth century.[15] In short, the fortunes of the play coincided almost exactly with the establishment and consolidation of what has come to be known as the first British Empire.

Several recent studies have brought *The Island Princess*'s engagement with England's overseas expansion fully into focus. Ania Loomba, for instance, sees Fletcher's tragicomedy as a "fantasy of colonial and sexual possession" hinging on the title character's eventual conversion to Christianity, while Shankar Raman suggests that the hero's eventual success should be viewed as an attempt to envision England's presence in the Iberian-controlled Moluccas.[16] For his part, Michael Neill underscores the relevance of mounting Anglo-Dutch rivalries in the neighboring Banda Islands, pointing out that the competition among the title character's suitors can easily be read as an international "struggle for control of the islands' material resources."[17] Finally, Valerie Forman reads the play as a rejection of the colonialist model embraced by both Portuguese and Dutch in favor of an English mercantile model in which economic exchange is not just uncoerced but actually liberating.[18]

While sympathetic to these interpretations, I approach Fletcher's tragicomedy first and foremost as a narrative of interracial desire—that is, as a plot that attempts to synchronize what Elizabeth Povinelli has called "the rhythms of politics and the market" to the rhythms of affective subjectivity.[19] I therefore read the play's erotic plot not as a mere metaphor for the political and economic dynamics of Europe's expansion overseas but rather as a point of imbrication between early modern ideologies of love and empire. More than a fantasy of imperial and sexual possession, I contend, *The Island Princess* is a fantasy of erotic conversion that is productive of both sexual and imperial outcomes. The processes through which the title character is conscripted into Christian marriage and the Molucca islands impressed into the service of European capitalism are coterminous to the process through which Quisara's and Armusia's erotic energies are recruited to the imperatives of domestic heterosexuality.

LOVE, LABOR, AND MERCANTILE IMPERIALISM

For all its eventual success as an interracial romance, *The Island Princess* began less as a love plot than as a prurient tale of murder and intrigue, presumably inserted in Argensola's *Conquista* as both an illustration of Moluccan disorder and a critique of Portugal's imperial ineptitude. The story is set on Tidore Island, whose king has just been captured by enemy Ternaten forces. In the power vacuum that follows, the king's sister, Quisara, proclaims that she will marry none but the man who shall bring her brother home, dead or alive. She hopes, in this manner, to have her brother killed while giving her secret lover, a Portuguese captain by the name of Ruy Dias, an opportunity to claim her hand in marriage.[20]

Much to Quisara's chagrin, Ruy Dias quickly proves unequal to the task. As he bides his time, unable or unwilling to act, a native suitor by the name of Salama reaches Ternate, frees the king, and returns home to claim the promised reward. The princess now goads Ruy Dias into murdering Salama, but is again disappointed by his inability to execute. Taking advantage of the situation, Ruy Dias's nephew, Pyniero, volunteers to kill both Salama and his uncle in exchange for the princess's affections. But no sooner has he dispatched Ruy Dias than he is in turn killed by Salama. Only "the slightest of violence" ("levissima violencia") is required at this point to convince the princess to fulfill her side of the bargain and marry her brother's rescuer.[21] And so the story ends with Quisara wedded to Salama, Ruy Dias and his nephew ignominiously dead, and the whole Portuguese nation shamed into disgrace. "And since the Portuguese make as much of honor lost or gained in love affairs . . . as the ancient Greeks made of winning the Olympic games," Argensola caustically concludes, "I will leave the vindication of these lovers to the care of those who are well skilled in these matters" ("Y pues del honor que se cobra, o pierde en los casos de amor . . . se haze entre la Nacion Portuguessa tanta estimacion, como la que otro tiempo se hizo en Grecia de la vitorias alcançadas en los juegos Olympicos, quedara reservada la defensa destos amantes, para la sutileza de los entendimientos que entienden la materia"; 153–54).

In picking up Argensola's story, Fletcher made significant changes. Among other things, he substituted for the devious Pyniero a cynical but dependable one, spared Ruy Dias from his untimely demise, and demoted the king of Ternate ("Ternata" in the play) to the rank of governor. He also added a religious twist by including a "Moore Priest" who brings the plot to the brink of tragedy, and replaced the native hero, Salama, with a Portuguese youth named Armusia.[22] And where the *Conquista*'s tale had closed with Quisara married to Salama, Ruy Dias murdered, and Pyniero bested, Fletcher closed with Quisara betrothed to Armusia, Pyniero in charge of Ternate, Ruy Dias alive and well, and the king of Tidore "halfe perswaded" to join the Christian fold (5.5.66). In this way, Fletcher radically altered the tenor of Argensola's plot: what was a story of European failure turned into a triumph of European prowess. What is more, Fletcher's obsessive categorization of Armusia as a Portuguese with a difference—a "stranger" as alien to his countrymen as he is to the Moluccan islanders (2.6.64, 2.6.80, 3.1.43, 3.2.76, 3.2.101, 4.2.75)—established a vantage point from which early-seventeenth-century Englishmen could envision their future in the region.

England's past record in insular Southeast Asia had been largely disappointing. Drake's landing at Ternate in 1579 had produced no commercial or political agreements, and Edward Fenton's 1582 venture to the Moluccas had not even made it to its intended destination.[23] An East India Company expedition had finally reached the islands in 1605, only to be overwhelmed by rival European forces. By the summer of 1619, however, things seemed poised for a change. First, the English had acquired factories—semisovereign toeholds usually obtained by concession from local authorities—in various parts of insular Southeast Asia, including Java, Sumatra, Sulawesi, and Borneo.[24] Second, East India Company merchants had claimed possession of several tiny islands in the Banda archipelago, planting St. George's flag on "Puloroon" (Pulau Run), "Puloway" (Pulau Ai), "the Countrey of *Wayre*," and the "Iland of *Rosinging*" (Pulau Hatta).[25] Third and most important, the ratification of the Anglo-Dutch "Treaty of Defence" had provided for the English and Dutch East India Companies to stop fighting, share in the spice trade, and create a joint fleet that could stand up to the Habsburg navy.[26] The hope, as one English diplomat put it, was "to beat the Spaniards out of the East Indies" and make the latter "as profitable unto us as the West Indies should be unto them."[27]

The cumulative effect of these advances was a wave of expansionist confidence and anti-Iberian buoyancy. Between 1620 and 1622, the English East India Company scored major victories at Jask and Mozambique, helped blockade Portuguese Goa and Spanish Manila, and assisted in the capture of Hormuz Island, which was regarded as a cornerstone of Portugal's Estado da Índia. In this light, Armusia's eventual conquest of Quisara can easily be read as a metaphor for England's mercantile and imperial success.[28] As I have noted elsewhere, there is much in the play that invites such an interpretation. Not only does Armusia's position as a "stranger" and a "gentleman scarce landed" (2.6.70) exactly mirror England's belated position as an imperial contender, but his name also carries topical implication that could hardly have been lost on seventeenth-century audiences:

during the early modern period, in fact, "Armusia" (or "Armuzia") was just another designation for Hormuz.[29] This important entrepôt at the mouth of the Persian Gulf had been a theater of mounting Anglo-Iberian hostilities since the late 1610s; by 26 December 1621, the date of *The Island Princess*'s first recorded performance, it was already the site of an offensive campaign that would soon oust the Portuguese from the island.[30] Thus overlaid with geopolitical allusions, Armusia's romantic exploits gloss England's imperial desires, and can even be understood as celebrating the country's encroachment into an area long considered an Iberian preserve.

At the root of the analogy between Armusia's courtship and England's interests in Asia lay the well-known homology between lands and female bodies.[31] If female anatomies were conceived as foreign lands to be discovered and explored, foreign lands were depicted as women to be seized and possessed. The relevance of this homology to the plot of *The Island Princess* is initially foregrounded by Pyniero, whose celebration of Portuguese imperialism is replete with bawdy allusions: "Where time is, and the sunne gives light, brave countrimen / Our names are known, new worlds disclose their riches, / Their beauties, and their prides to our embraces" (1.3.9–11). Activated by the pun on "pride" as estrus or sexual heat, Pyniero's innuendoes construe overseas expansion in explicitly sexual terms. Indeed, the fantasy conveyed by his lines—a striptease sequence where new worlds freely "disclose" themselves to male "embraces"—closely resembles the pattern of encounter traced by Camões in the Isle of Love episode. In both, radical asymmetries of power are naturalized, legitimized, and secured through the power of eros.

Armusia's rejoinder picks up Pyniero's homology but turns it in a new direction. His rapt description of the "blessed" Moluccas transforms every aspect of the surrounding landscape—trees, rivers, even the depths of the soil—into a gendered entity characterized by exceptional beauty and boundless fecundity.

> We are arriv'd among the blessed Islands,
> Where every wind that rises blowes perfumes,
> And every breath of aire is like an Incence:
> The treasure of the Sun dwels here, each tree
> As if it envied the old Paradice,
> Strives to bring forth immortall fruit; the spices
> Renewing nature, though not deifying,
> And when that fals by time, scorning the earth,
> The sullen earth, should taint or sucke their beauties,

But as we dreamt, for ever so preserve us:
Nothing we see, but breeds an admiration;
The very rivers as we floate along
Throw up their pearles, and curle their heads to court us;
The bowels of the earth swell with the births
Of thousand unknowne gems, and thousand riches;
Nothing that beares a life, but brings a treasure;
The people they shew brave too, civill manner'd,
Proportioned like the Mastres of great minds
(1.3.16–33)

It should perhaps come as no surprise that this rhetorical tour de force likely influenced Milton's vision of the Garden of Eden in *Paradise Lost*; in Armusia's description, the Moluccas are indeed a prelapsarian world closely mirroring "old Paradice" (1.3.20). The most important thing to note about this prelapsarian world is that it is, by and large, predicated on what Raymond Williams has called "the Penshurst fallacy"—the extraction of human labor from the landscape.[32] This Edenic understanding is already evident in sixteenth-century works that explicitly dissociate human labor from the riches of the Moluccas. "Everyone possesses some of these [clove] trees . . . but no one cultivates them," wrote Pigafetta in his *Relazione*. "[The natives do] no more than cleaning the ground where they collect the cloves," echoed the Portuguese naturalist Garcia da Orta.[33] Likewise, Armusia's description emphasizes the islands' complete independence from human labor: rivers regurgitate their riches, orchards produce by themselves, and precious gems come to the earth's surface like so many babies pushing their way out of the womb. The native men and women who dived for pearls, mined for minerals, planted, pruned, and harvested—these have all vanished without a trace. When they appear, as they do at the end of Armusia's description, they do so merely as a prop. "Brave," "civill manner'd," and "Proportioned like the Mastres of great minds," they add ornamental flourish to a self-sufficient system of production (1.3.32, 33).

Fletcher's presentation of the surrounding landscape may elide native labor, but this does not mean that all labor is absent from the play. As a matter of fact, there is plenty of labor even in Armusia's rapt description of the Moluccas as an earthly paradise. If we cannot locate it where we would expect it—that is, in the relationship between the islands and their native peoples—it is because islands and peoples slide seamlessly into one other. Fletcher's play merges both in a gendered anthropomorphization, a feminized Nature displayed in all her seductiveness and plenty. Transfigured, the labor of production reappears under the guise of reproductive labor, as the vocabulary of gestation and parturition that punctuates the islands' description—"bring[ing] forth," "breed[ing]," "swell[ing] with the births," "bear[ing] a life" (1.3.21, 27, 29)—makes abundantly clear. Conflating commodity production with sexual reproduction, Armusia's speech reduces both to natural forces, primal urges to be harnessed and directed. It will be the Europeans' task to inscribe both in a discourse of masculine wardship and exchange: the courtship that inscribes Quisara within a framework of (re)productive conjugality underwrites the process that inscribes the economy of distant lands within the framework of merchant capitalism. In this manner, *The Island Princess* gives Riche's conceit of the would-be husband as merchant venturer a literal equivalent: in his bid for the princess's hand, Armusia disguises himself as a "trading merchant" (2.2.30). The detail is borrowed from Argensola, but inserted in a larger lexical pattern tying the ventures of courtship to the hazards of mercantile imperialism. Quisara's suitors are asked to "travell" (1.3.126), Armusia's success is compared to that of a merchant who has "ended his Market" before everyone else (2.6.63), and the unenterprising Ruy Dias is scolded for not going "about his businesse sweating" (2.6.51).

CONVERTING DESIRE

If Armusia's description of the "blessed" Moluccas portrays Asian islands and female bodies as interchangeable objects easily yielding to European husbandry, the play's characterization of Quisara undoes this parallel: far from being a passive object of desire, the princess is presented from the outset as an actively desiring subject.[34] Hence the play's fundamental task is to "convert" Quisara's desire, to reshape it and make it conform to Armusia's. The narrative achieves this result by progressively foreclosing all the options available to the princess in the beginning of the play—becoming queen, choosing her own husband, remaining single, exercising cultural authority, being an equal partner—all the while insisting that the eventual outcome be taken as an elective choice.

This is the reason why Armusia emphatically rejects both rape and power play as viable models of interracial coupling. "Women are nice to wooe," he insists, and should not be approached with force, "For things compell'd and frighted of soft natures, / Turne into feares, and flye from their owne wishes" (2.6.162,164–65). Significantly, Armusia is the only character who sees it this way. Later in the play, his friend Soza suggests that a modicum of violence might very well expedite the marriage: "Doe what you should doe," he advises, "Take her and tosse her like a barre" (3.2.19, 24). Another friend, Emanuel, qualifies this suggestion by emphasizing the "slightness" of sexual violence vis-à-vis other kinds of violence: a good tossing "between a paire of sheets," he notes, will break Quisara's will but "bruise no bone" (3.2.26, 28). He then proceeds to propose that violence may even be welcome, since women "love a man that crushes 'em to verjuice" (3.2.40). But Armusia rebuffs both suggestions, explicitly distancing himself from any kind of violence: "I shall doe something," he promises, "But not your way, it shews too boisterous, / For my affections are as faire and gentle, / As her they serve" (3.2.42–45).

From Armusia's perspective, possession of the princess's body alone clearly will not do; for connubial consummation to take place, Quisara will have to conform her will to his out of her own volition. It is in this voluntarism that we can measure the ideological chasm dividing Fletcher's play from Camões's Isle of Love episode or even from Argensola's version of the Quisara story. In these narratives, a certain amount of violence—no matter how "slight" or staged—was necessarily embedded in the heteroerotics of marriage. In Fletcher's formulation, by contrast, external compulsion is wholly expunged from view. The play makes this point fully apparent later in the same act, when Armusia steals uninvited into the princess's bedchamber. It is late at night, and Quisara is alone—all favorable conditions for the kind of sexual consummation propounded by Soza and Emanuel. This the princess understands clearly, for she immediately vows strenuous resistance. But her fears are unfounded: in a scene rich with Petrarchan overtones, Armusia kneels humbly, complains of the princess's "fierce cruelty," and pledges his readiness to fulfill her every wish, obediently departing when she orders him to "quit this place presently" (3.3.86, 109).

Implicit in Armusia's rejection of sexual violence is nothing less than a plan of erotic refashioning—a process of psychological transformation that will eventually yield a Quisara as "faire and gentle" as Armusia sees her (3.2.44). For one thing is certain: while the princess may well be "faire" in terms of both beauty and skin color (although the exact nature of this fairness is a matter of debate early in the play), there is very little about her that could be defined as "gentle"—unless, of course, we take that "gentle" not as a synonym for "kind" or "tender" but merely as a reference to gentility. At the beginning of the play, Quisara is effectively poised to be Tidore's queen. As one of the characters points out, her brother's "ruine stiles her absolute" and "his imprisonment adds to her profit" (1.1.33, 34). In her first stage appearance, the princess admits that she could gain much from the king's death or perpetual captivity, yet protests that neither her "nature" nor her "faire affection" allows her to entertain such dreams of power:

> if I were ambitious,
> Gap'd for that glory was ne're borne with me,
> There he should lye his miseries upon him:
> If I were covetous, and my heart set
> On riches, and those base effects that follow
> On pleasures uncontroul'd, or safe revenges,
> There he should dye, his death would give me all these;
> For then stood I up absolute to do all;
> Yet all these flattering shews of dignity,
> These golden dreames of greatnesse cannot force me
> To forget nature and my faire affection.
> (1.3.137–47)

As it turns out, this is definitely a case in which the lady protests too much. For it soon becomes obvious that, despite her declarations of love and disinterestedness, Quisara harbors the hope to see her brother dead. Not only does she promise herself in marriage to the man who will bring the king home "Either alive or dead" (1.3.150)—a phrasing more suggestive of a bounty-hunting expedition than of a rescue mission—but she also makes clear that if her brother were to "be restor'd alive," then she and Ruy Dias would have to resign themselves to being mere "servants" (2.6.27, 28).

Fletcher's bleak characterization of his title character has generally gone unremarked, but it is crucial to a proper understanding of the play's erotic plot.[35] The point here is not just that Quisara's characterization as an actively desiring subject contradicts the fantasy of a feminine island passively yielding to European industry. The princess's behavior is also a perversion of feminine modesty and submissiveness. In naming herself as a reward for her brother's rescuer, the princess ostensibly constitutes herself in orthodox patriarchal terms: she is an object of exchange in a contract written for the benefit of men. Yet her actual plan is a negation of this patriarchal arrangement. The contract itself, one might argue, is a fraud: the goal of the agreement is not to redeem a king but to make Quisara a queen.

Argensola had portrayed Quisara as a latter-day Cleopatra: a (would-be) fratricide ruthlessly driven by political ambition, a woman in charge of her own sexuality, a skilled diplomat feeding all her suitors "with such hopes as lay no obligation on those who give them, but encourage those who value them" ("con aquellas esperanças que no obligan à quien las da, y animan à quien las estima"; 150). The early part of *The Island Princess* follows faithfully in Argensola's footsteps. Quisara eggs on Ruy Dias's courtship and even voices his desires when he proves unable to do so on his own. When Pyniero declares himself willing to kill for her—and not just Armusia but his own uncle as well—she neither accepts nor rebuffs the offer. Instead, she replies in terms that are at once elliptic and pellucid: she ends the conversation with a kiss, promising more the moment Pyniero will "deserve more" (3.1.264).

The play never distinguishes clearly between Quisara's political ambitions and her will to erotic self-determination, interpreting both as usurpations of male prerogative. But this entanglement is itself the relevant point: it reminds us that erotic representations are almost always about the ways that power can be bounded and distributed. Just as Linschoten's *Itinerario* makes the erotic desires of Indian women generally coterminous with murder, *The Island Princess* makes Quisara's desire for Ruy Dias virtually inextricable from her thirst for power. For this reason, Armusia's successful rescue of the king deals the princess a double blow: not only does she lose her bid for the throne, but she also finds herself obliged to marry a man she has not chosen. Of this she complains out loud: "Must I be given / Unto a man I never saw, ne're spoke with, / I know not of what Nation?" (2.6.85–87). Quisara's use of the passive voice is quite telling here: Armusia's success has placed her precisely in the position from which the pretended quest was meant to dislodge her.

Nevertheless, Quisara has not lost her power: as she claims in a later scene, the desire she inspires still puts at her command the "last services" (4.2.150) of the Portuguese and "even their lives" (4.2.151). The "utmost triall of . . . constancy" (4.5.29) she demands toward the end of the play is specifically construed as a show of strength; confident of her charm, the princess intends to prove "in what chaine" she can hold the people around her (4.2.170). It is in this spirit that, goaded by the "Moore Priest" (actually the governor of Ternate in disguise), she asks Armusia to renounce his religion in exchange for her agreement to marry him.

Demanding Armusia's apostasy as a conditio sine qua non for marriage, Quisara correctly identifies eros as a transformative force, a conduit through which people can become other to themselves. This identification is fully supported in the play by the frequent references to desire as an agent of psychological change. It might be worth remembering, in this context, that in an early conversation with Ruy Dias Quisara declares herself willing to convert for love, that murder is included among the "scurvy things this love *converts* us" (3.1.92, my emphasis), and that sexual intercourse is figured on occasion as a strategy of proselytization. "If thou wilt give me leave," Pyniero tells Quisara's waiting woman, "Ile get thee with Christian, / The best way to *convert* thee" (5.4.14–15, my emphasis). It is important to note that the terms remain strikingly consistent regardless of whether "love" and "conversion" pertain to murder or to procreation. That this should be the case suggests a remarkably value-neutral vision of eros: for most of the characters, desire seems to have no moral component, no other aim but its own satisfaction.

In Armusia's eyes, however, eros radically changes meaning depending on the kind of transformation it effects: identified as love when it bring about conversion to Christianity and European acculturation, it becomes unbridled lust when it brings about the opposite result. When Quisara invites him to "be of one beleefe" with her (4.5.35), Armusia recoils in indignation. He accuses the islanders of devil worship and human sacrifice, disparages their reverence for the sun and the moon, and reviles them for "mak[ing] offer" to "every bird that flies, and every worme" (4.5.41, 42). In the same breath, he also chides himself for lasciviousness, regrets having erred so far "the way of lust" (4.5.57), and marvels that he might have come so close to exchanging an "Eternitie of blessednesse for a woman" (4.5.61). Paradoxically, the more Armusia scorns her culture and insults her religion, the more Quisara "love[s] to hear him" (4.5.95)—with a hint of masochism suggesting, perhaps, that Soza might have been right all along.

As striking as it may appear today, Fletcher's construction of Moluccan religion as a hodgepodge of Satanism, animism, and paganism is almost entirely conventional. In part, this construction reflects Europe's preconceptions about Islam—the creed generally professed by Moluccan elites—as a "mungrull Religion compilde of shadowes and impostures."[36] In part, it points to the religious pluralism that seems to have characterized the region. Both Pigafetta's *Relazione* and Tomé Pires's *Suma Oriental*, for instance, mention that Islam was a relatively recent import in the Moluccas, and that it coexisted with other creeds. António Galvão, who was captain of the Portuguese forces on Ternate between 1536 and 1539, wrote that while the elites were Muslim, the lower classes clung to animist beliefs.[37] Even among Muslim converts, moreover, pre-Islamic manners and customs still survived. "So confusedly have these islanders received the rites of Mahometanism," summed up Argensola in his *Conquista*, "that they retain those of their ancient idolatry along with them, and mix up the ceremonies" ("tan indistintamente admiten estos Isleños los ritos del Mahometismo, que retienen con el, los de su antigua Idolatria, y confunden las ceremonias"; 80).

Also utterly conventional is Armusia's understanding of his own predicament. According to recent calculations, by the early seventeenth century there may have been as many as five thousand Christian "renegades" in South and Southeast Asia alone.[38] A portion of these might have abjured Christianity under duress (as Niccolò de' Conti claimed to have done), but many embraced Islam voluntarily. For some, this might have been a pragmatic choice to evade bondage or better their social standing; for others, it might have been the outcome of a moral choice rooted in spiritual experience.[39] Yet early modern representations of voluntary Islamization almost always identified eros as the primary motor of apostasy. The renegade met by Fernão Mendes Pinto in the Red Sea, for instance, had abandoned Christianity "for love of a Greek Moslem girl"; in Robert Daborne's *A Christian Turn'd Turke* (1612), Ward apostatizes in hopes of enjoying the Muslim Voada; and in Philip Massinger's *The Renegado* (1624), Vitelli considers doing the same for Donusa.[40] These representations of Christian apostasy went hand in hand with the belief that lubricity stood at the root of Islam's success as a religion. As Edward Aston put it in his 1611 translation of Johannes Boemus's *Omnium gentium mores, leges et ritus*, this was exactly how Islam had "crept into innumerable Nations"—by giving people "free liberty and power to pursue their lustes and all other pleasures."[41] The growing understanding of polygamy as both an outcome and an instrument of aberrancy turned Quranic allowances on plural marriage into yet another proof of Islam's unbridled carnality: in William Rowley's *All's Lost by Lust* (c. 1619), for example, a married man who finds himself attracted to another woman considers turning "Turk, or Moore Mahometan / For by the lustfull lawes of Mahomet / I may have three wives more."[42]

As a consequence, European notions of apostasy were intimately linked to the idea of sexual transgression. In reference to women, "to turn Turk" might mean not only to convert to Islam but also "to become a whore" or "to commit adultery."[43] It is precisely this connotation of "turning" that Pyniero invokes in two consecutive asides—"She turns for millions" (3.1.237); "For a tun of Crownes she turns" (3.1.239)—as he tests Quisara's inclination to pawn herself for political lucre. Although no exact male equivalent existed, "turning Turk" carried sexual implications for men as well, since converting to Islam was thought to open venues of behavior that ran the gamut from polygamy to sodomy.[44] More generally, "turning Turk" meant relinquishing the erotic self-control (*enkrateia*, the common antonym for *akrasia*) that formed the ideal backbone of European identity in general and of European masculinity in particular.[45] In one way or another, in fact, men who "turned Turk" were always men who loved excessively. This seems to be the sense in which the phrase is used in John Cooke's popular play *Greene's Tu Quoque* (1614)—"This is to turne Turke: from a most absolute compleat Gentleman to a most absurd ridiculouss and fond lover"—where Christian apostasy and conversion to Islam function as indictment of male prostration to the female beloved.[46] In both its gendered definitions, then, "turning Turk" suggests the ways in which sexuality was increasingly supplementing religion as a crucial category of identity. If acts of Christian apostasy were almost invariably infused with erotic frisson, sexual deviance was invariably imagined as an erasure of identity that was just as horrifying as apostasy.

These sexualized visions of apostasy both voiced and displaced the anxieties that dogged Europe's institutionalization of desire. Investing the business of marriage with the language of eros, domestic heterosexuality dangerously blurred the boundary between the adulterous and the conjugal. "Any love for another's wife is scandalous," had warned St. Jerome in the fourth century, purportedly quoting a lost text by the Roman philosopher Seneca. And "so is too much love for one's own wife. . . . A prudent man should love his wife with discretion, and so control his desire and not be led into copulation. *Nothing is more impure than to love one's wife as if she were a mistress.* . . . Men should appear before their wives not as lovers but as husbands."[47]

Since then, clergymen and laypeople alike had held it scandalous that spouses could treat one another as lovers would. "Those shamelesse endearings, which the first heate suggests unto us in that sportfull delight, are not onely undecently, but hurtfully employed towards our wives," wrote Michel de Montaigne in the late sixteenth century. "Marriage is a religious and devout bond: and that is the reason the pleasure a man hath of it, should be a moderate, staied, and serious pleasure."[48] In a similar vein, the German reformer Martin Luther enjoined moderation on both husbands and wives, while the English minister Richard Capel condemned the "immoderate desires" of married couples along with sodomy, adultery, and masturbation.[49] As late as 1727, Daniel Defoe referred to marital eroticism as "the first Branch of Matrimonial Whoredom." For while happiness in marriage effectively depended on the spouses' mutual affection, this affection was never supposed to venture beyond the "Bounds and Limitations of Decency, Modesty and Moderation."[50]

In Chapter 4, I suggested that the anxieties surrounding the emergence of domestic heterosexuality both inflected, and were inflected by, contemporary representations of the polygamous household. Interracial romances such as *The Island Princess*, I propose, performed related work, laying bare the contradictions of this new ideological formation while simultaneously displacing them onto the cross-racial couple. If interracial romances could freely dramatize the threat of male erotic dependence implicit in domestic heterosexuality, in other words, it was precisely because they could also contain this threat by assigning a racial meaning to it—thus marginalizing certain acts, affects, and behaviors as foreign or degenerate.

In *The Island Princess*, Armusia resists the lure of degeneracy and proves himself a "true" European. As he refuses to renounce Christianity, he also begins to see Quisara in a new light. Suddenly, her face "lookes ugly" (4.5.104), her eyes reflect "a thousand horrid ruines" (4.5.107), and her tongue betrays the "hideous murmurs of weake soules" (4.5.109). This startling metamorphosis echoes the well-established motif of the beautiful seductress exposed as an ugly witch—a motif that had roots in the mysterious figure of the Great Whore of Babylon (Revelation 17:3–7) and illustrious precedents in a variety of works such as Ludovico Ariosto's *Orlando Furioso* and Edmund Spenser's *The Faerie Queene*.[51] Given the long tradition associating apostasy with sorcery, Quisara's transformation is especially apposite to the circumstances.[52] By linking his Moluccan princess to characters such as Ariosto's Alcina and Spenser's Duessa, moreover, Fletcher also links Armusia's anagnorisis to those of Ruggiero and Redcrosse.

Just as the stripping of Alcina bares the dislocation of Ruggiero's masculinity, and the exposure of Duessa measures the depth of Redcrosse's enslavement to passion, the metamorphosis of Quisara holds the mirror to Armusia's abjection.

While depicting female sexuality as a form of radical alterity, the play also marginalizes the conventions of love as service. "Is this the venture? / The tryall that you talkt off?" (4.5.43–44), the hero asks incredulously, conveniently forgetting his earlier pledge of obeying Quisara's every command. In this manner, *The Island Princess* turns the threat of apostasy into an object lesson on the perils of heterosexual desire: at stake is not only religious orthodoxy but also the hero's sexual and racial identity. Read in this light, the "hideous murmurs" Armusia hears in Quisara's voice merely echo his own pleas for love; the "horrid ruines" he sees in her eyes are simply reflections of himself as a fond and ridiculous lover. In his sudden discovery of the princess's alterity, Armusia discovers, first and foremost, the untenability of an erotic script that the play decries as unfit for Europeans.

Armusia's anagnorisis opens the way to a more general recognition of Moluccan alterity. At the beginning of the play, the islanders are depicted in contradictory terms. On the one hand, they are "false and desperate people" characterized by "base breedings" and "base pleasures" (1.1.4, 18, 16); on the other hand, they are "brave," "civill manner'd," and "Proportioned like the Mastres of great minds" (1.3.32, 33). Once Armusia is faced with the threat of apostasy, however, this complex depiction is radically simplified. The islanders become "barbarians," "rascals" "rogues," "devils," "villaines," and "hounds," (5.1.24, 32, 33, 34, 35, 36)—in a crescendo of insults that eventually ascribes to the Moluccans the same canine lineage attributed to the Peguans and Siamese. As Pyniero puts it, "Hounds were their fathers, / Old blear-eyed bob-tail'd hounds" (5.1.36–37).

While "hound" was not uncommon as a generic term of opprobrium or contempt, the peculiar phrasing of Pyniero's insult points suggestively to the story according to which certain Southeast Asian peoples descended from the coupling of a woman and a dog. Detailed by Barros in the mid-sixteenth century to explain the wearing of penis bells (see chapter 1), this myth of origin had been popularized in England by the publication of Edward Grimston's *The estates, empires, & principallities of the world* (1615)—a massive geography derived from Pierre d'Avity's *Les Estats, empires, et principautez du monde* (1613)—and especially by the translation of Antonio de Torquemada's popular

Jardín de flores curiosas, which had appeared as *The Spanish Mandeville of Miracles* (1600; second ed. 1618):

> Writing certaine memorable thinges of the Kingdomes of Pegu and Sian [sic], which are on the other side of the River Ganges, [João de Barros] sayth, that the people of those Kingdoms, hold and affirme for a matter assured and indubitable, that of long time that Countrey was uninhabited. . . . It hapned on a time, that a ship comming from the Kingdome of Chinay, was through a violent tempest driven on that Coast among the Rocks, so that all those that were therein perrished, saving onely one woman, and a mighty great mastive, the which defended her from the furie of wilde beastes, using daily with her fleshlie copulation, in such sort, that she became great, and in proces of time was delivered of a sonne, she being at that present verie young, the boy in space of time had also acquaintance with her, and begat upon her other children, of whose multiplications those two kingdoms became to be inhabited.[53]

Echoing the outlines of this myth of origin, Pyniero's insult lends precise contours to the "base breedings" (1.1.18) imputed to the Moluccans early in the play. And because it foregrounds bestiality, it also infuses these "base breedings" with a distinct tinge of sexual deviance—thereby providing a specifically sexual connotation to the "base pleasures" (1.1.16) that the islanders putatively enjoy. Providing the Moluccans with a genealogy that makes them both sexually and racially other, the play opens an unbridgeable gap between Europeans and Asians, thereby naturalizing the plot's sudden switch from peace to war.

Meanwhile, Armusia's discovery of Quisara as a dangerous seductress turns the tables on the power dynamics between himself and to the princess. During the first three acts and much of the fourth, Armusia's language and behavior by and large conform to the standards of courtly and Petrarchan love poetry. In his interactions with Quisara, he consistently presents himself as a faithful and subservient lover, bound in service to a beautiful and unattainable mistress. No trace of this earlier characterization remains in the latter part of the play, as the character leaves the lover's posture behind to adopt the martyr's. Threatened with "tortures" (5.2.86), his reply is defiant: "Your worst and painful'st / I am joyfull to accept" (5.2.86–87). Fletcher possibly derived the idea of Armusia's martyrdom from Argensola's *Conquista*, which abounds with depictions of the persecutions suffered by Christians in the Moluccas. Yet the play's description of Armusia's resistance is also indebted to an autochthonous martyrological tradition that conceived of bodily disfigurement and dissolution as radical means of self-constitution.[54] Choosing to embrace martyrdom instead of Quisara, Armusia effectively reconfigures the play's erotic script: his "joyfull" acceptance of pain transforms abjection into agency, and suffering into an act of subversion undercutting the very political power capable of inflicting it.

It is only at this point that the princess decides to cross the cultural rift. Exhorting Armusia to stay the course of martyrdom, she pronounces herself "A virgin won" by his "faire constancy" (5.2.109). Eventually, she declares her willingness to die by his side:

I do embrace your faith sir, and your fortune;
Go one, I will assist ye, I feele a sparkle here,
A lively sparke that kindles my affection,
And tels me it will rise to flames of glory:
Let 'em put on their angers, suffer nobly,
Shew me the way, and when I faint instruct me
(5.2.121–26)

Quisara's conversion marks a major turning point in the play's structure—and a puzzling one to boot. Scholars have called it "an unmotivated capitulation," taken it as evidence of fickleness, or disparaged it as mere posturing.[55] And in truth, the Quisara who inhabits the latter part of the play hardly seems the same character: gone is the seductress who had men wrapped around her finger; gone is the culturally confident native upholding the value of her gods. Nevertheless, Quisara's transformation is much less of a turning point than it appears at first. The princess's fundamental characteristics—her will to power and erotic agency—are at play here just as they were before. First, by taking up the role of the martyred Christian virgin, Quisara successfully claims for herself an especially powerful subject position. This would have been almost obvious to Jacobean and even Restoration audiences accustomed to regard female martyrdom as an especially forceful demonstration of divine might.[56] Second, the role of the martyr affords, or better yet, *requires*, an actively desiring subjectivity. It is certainly significant that Quisara describes her conversion to Christianity as an "affection" rising to "flames of glory" (5.2.123, 124). Her careful wording conjures the bonfire of martyrdom while simultaneously evoking the image of sexual consummation; it is a language of mystical eroticism in which literal and metaphorical deaths merge and coalesce. Far from being a capitulation or even a radical turnabout, Quisara's acceptance of Christianity can be understood as a powerful act of erotic self-determination.

Thus religious conversion comes to seal a long process of inter-pellation or ideological self-constitution, the main goal of which has been to "turn" Quisara's desire in the right direction—to "convert" a perversely independent sexuality into proper connubiality. In the process, Quisara is made to learn a fundamental lesson: that wom-en's erotic fulfillment comes from following and not from leading, and that there is far greater pleasure in submitting than in dominat-ing. Hence the significance of her final words: "Which way you go, sir, I must *follow* necessary / One life, and one death" (5.5.41–42, my emphasis). As the Southeast Asian princess turns into a Christian wife, a specific vision of conjugality—passionate, reciprocal, hierar-chical, and unequal—is made a linchpin of European imperialism.

English Whiteness and the End of Romance

Just as Fletcher's *The Island Princess* consummated its happy ending on the stages of England, the spice race in Southeast Asia was taking a tragic turn. In theory, the Anglo-Dutch agreement of 2 June 1619 had ushered in an era of cooperation between the East India Company (EIC) and the Verenigde Oost-Indische Compagnie; thenceforth, the two would share in the spice trade, provide for their mutual defense, and hold jointly whatever taken by common "industry" and force.[1] In practice, the agreement did little or nothing to allay the tensions between the two corporations. Business went on as it had before the treaty, with the VOC decrying English activities as malicious hindrances, and the EIC accusing the Dutch of every possible crime. As paranoia mounted on both sides, a "horrible conspiracie" was uncovered in 1623 on Amboina, an island in the Banda Sea where both the EIC and the VOC had factories (Figure 10).[2] Informed that a Japanese soldier in VOC employ was asking questions about the strength of Castle Victoria (which the Dutch had taken from the Portuguese in 1605), Governor Harman van Speult had the soldier tortured, thereby obtaining a confession that implicated several Englishmen in a plot to seize control of the island.[3] In the end, twenty confessed conspirators—ten English factors, nine Japanese soldiers, and one Indo-Portuguese bailiff by the name of Augustine Perez—were publicly executed. Gabriel Towerson, the chief English merchant on Amboina, was decapitated and quartered, his severed head "set up upon the Gate" as a grim warning to prospective seditionists.[4]

Figure 10. A view of Castle Victoria on Amboina, as represented in a painting commissioned for the Amsterdam office of the VOC. Built by the Portuguese in 1580, the fortress fell to the Dutch in 1605 and would remain the principal overseas base of the VOC until the founding of Batavia in 1619. Courtesy of the Rijksmuseum, Amsterdam, The Netherlands.

British and Dutch historians still differ in their assessments as to how far, if at all, the defendants were guilty of the crimes of which they were accused. One thing is certain: the "massacre" of Amboina, as the incident would soon come to be known, marked England's retreat from the spice race.[5] "Upon the newes of this Tragedy," noted a 1632 pamphlet, "all the English as well at the Moluccoes and Banda, as the poore remnant at Amboyna . . . quitted their Factories in all those Islands: choosing rather to leave the places and their trade there, then their lives."[6] With the VOC tightening its grip on Southeast Asia, the EIC had no choice but to look for alternatives; by the middle of the seventeenth century, indigo, saltpeter, and especially calicoes had replaced pepper and fine spice as the mainstays of the company's business.[7] The reorientation turned out to be for the best: by the 1660s, England was witnessing a spectacular increase in the volume of its Asian commerce, with new factories springing up all the way from the Persian Gulf to the Bay of Bengal and beyond.[8] In 1661, these advances were supplemented by the acquisition of overseas settlements such as Galle (Sri Lanka) and Bombay (India), handed over to England (along with Tangier in Morocco) undert the terms of the marriage treaty between Charles II and the Portuguese infanta Catherine of Braganza. The same treaty also legalized English trade throughout Portuguese Asia, and licensed the establishment of new English posts at Goa, Diu, and Cochin.[9]

With these developments came more unions between Englishmen and Asian-born women. By 1642, "divers of the English souldiers" at Madras were finding wives from among the Indo-Portuguese population of nearby São Tomé—a practice that was not encouraged but had to be tolerated for fear that, as one EIC official put it, "the hotshots will take liberty otherwise to coole themselves."[10] Something of the sort must have happened at Bombay: noting that many of the English soldiers were involved with Indian women, EIC president Gerald Aungier begged the headquarters in London for a more suitable supply of female companions: "I could wish you would contrive some way to send out English women of the meaner sort, but of honest reputation," he wrote in a 1674 letter, "for the souldiers doe frequently converse with the Country women whoem wee force them to marry, for the preventing Sin & Gods Judgment thereon, but if they married with English women, surely it would be much better."[11]

Aungier was not alone in his uneasiness. As early as 1666, the EIC Council at Madras recommended to company headquarters that married employees be allowed to bring their wives and families to India. If this were done, they pointed out, "in a few Lusters of yeares, your Towne might be populous with a brood of our owne, and not a mixt Nation."[12] In response, small shipments of English women of "civil and sober behaviour" began making their way to India.[13] The company paid for the overseas passage and provided temporary employment; in return, sponsored immigrants were expected to marry no "other peoples but those of our owne nation, or such others as are Protestants."[14] But it soon became apparent that there were problems with this scheme. For one, English women in India did not marry as quickly as expected—and sometimes not at all. At least some of them, moreover, were proving neither civil nor sober. "Here is a scandallous woman or two that . . . daily dishonour the nation and their owne sect," lamented Deputy Governor Philip Giffard in a 1675 letter from Bombay. "No advise, no punishment will prevaile, therefor wee desire some of the Captains may have order to take them home with them, for we know noe other remidy."[15] To make matters worse, many of these female recruits had no stomach for the settler lifestyle—preferring instead to return for England with their husbands and children in tow. "Mrs. Williams is . . . Your Honours . . . humble petitioner for her owne & childs passage; Mr. Serle & his wife talk of going home, as also Corporall Browne with his wife & child," wrote a frustrated Philip Giffard in 1670.[16] By the following year, EIC agents in India were debating the wisdom of adopting a no-repatriation policy modeled after Dutch patterns. "Wee think it not consistent with the good of your Island that any women, especially those of ordinary Quallity, be suffred to leave it at their Pleasure," noted the EIC Council at Bombay in November 1671. "It is a wise Pollicy among the Dutch in these Indian Plantations, that whoever marrys with a Dutch woman is bound to live 15 years in India . . . and after the husbands decease, no woman is admitted to returne till she hath lived so many limmited yeares as she hath contracted for."[17]

Unsurprisingly, Englishmen in India continued to marry locally born women throughout the Restoration and beyond.[18] This seems to have been the case not only among sailors and common soldiers—that is, among those who could least afford the expenses that English wives were thought to comport—but also among company merchants and high-ranking officials. Gabriel Boughton, an EIC surgeon who served at Shah Shuja's court in the late 1640s, wedded "a Mogullana or Morish woman"; Thomas Chamber, who was chief agent at Madras between 1658 and 1661, married a "lady from the Indies."[19] Chamber's successor, Edward Winter, followed suit, as did Isfahan factor Thomas Codrington, Hughli factor William Pitt, and (presumably) Madras factors Henry Greenhill and Andrew Cogan.[20] The polyglot Henry Gary, who started out as a factor in 1645 and went on to hold a variety of important posts (including that of Bombay governor), also married in India.[21] At a time when EIC employees abroad rarely wrote about their private lives, Gary was remarkably open about the ties that bound him to the colonial periphery. In 1663, he declared himself unlikely to return for England, "in regaurd [that] his family" was "here in the country."[22] In 1667, in a plaintive letter that provides a rare emotional glimpse into the sexual interface of the Anglo-Indian encounter, he mourned the loss of his "deere consort" and detailed the arrangements made to fulfill her last wishes.[23] Preserved in lime, her corpse laid in state for eight days before being moved 163 miles to Surat, where it was buried near the grave of the couple's only son.[24] "Had it been possible to have done more for her, I had performed it," Gary wrote in closing. "Such was her merrits and such was the love I ever had for her."[25]

Interestingly, just as the number of officially sanctioned Anglo-Indian unions went up, English representations of the cross-racial

couple became increasingly problematic. A rhetoric of bodily difference began to accrete around the figure of the bride, eventually sev-
ering the connection between conubium and empire. In what follows, I chart the early moments of this transformation by way of two
generically discrepant but roughly coeval texts, Richard Head's *The
English Rogue: Described, In the Life of Meriton Latroon, a Witty
Extravagant* (1665) and John Dryden's *Amboyna; or, The Cruelties
of the Dutch to the English Merchants* (1673), both of which feature cross-racial couples. In *The English Rogue*, a tale of picaresque
adventure set in the Civil War era, the title character marries "an
Indian-Black."[26] In *Amboyna*, a tragedy purportedly dramatizing
the Amboina massacre of 1623, Gabriel Towerson weds the beautiful
Ysabinda, "a Native of this Iland of Amboyna" (1.1.118–19).[27] But
while these opening gambits may seem to reiterate the topoi of interracial romance, *Amboyna* and *The English Rogue* actually mark
a turning point in the tradition. Head's *English Rogue* retains the
connubial motif but renders it inoperative as a metaphor for imperial assimilation. Dryden's *Amboyna* goes even farther, sacrificing
interracial conubium on the altar of national and racial purity. In
the process, both texts disavow cross-racial desire and pathologize
interracial sexuality, expelling them from the domain of domestic
heterosexuality.

AMBOYNA

No less than half a century separated the Amboina massacre from
the first performance of Dryden's play *Amboyna; or, The Cruelties of
the Dutch to the English Merchants* in May 1673, in the midst of the
third Anglo-Dutch War. Yet the passage of time had hardly dimin-
ished the incident's currency; to the contrary, it had written this mercantile setback into national mythology. No sooner did news of the
massacre reach England than the EIC issued two pamphlets, *The Answer unto the Dutch Pamphlet, Made in Defence of the Uniust and
Barbarous Proceedings Against the English at Amboyna* (1624) and
*A True Relation of the Late Uniust, Cruell, and Barbarous Proceed-
ings against the English at Amboyna* (1624). The first ridiculed Dutch
claims of an English plot to take Castle Victoria as "A sweet conceit,
and such a service as perhaps hath bin somtimes represented upon a
stage, but never acted in surprise of a Castle in good earnest."[28] The

second built on the martyrological tradition of John Foxe's *Actes and Monuments*, turning the merchants' unglamorous ends into glorious *exempla* of martyrdom.[29] In 1632, the EIC published a new edition of *A True Relation* (reprinted in 1651 and 1665) and issued additional pamphlets; James Ramsey's *Bloudy Newes from the East-Indies* appeared in 1651; and the anonymous *Memento for Holland* followed two years later. Between 1652 and 1674, the massacre of Amboina was routinely rehashed in ballads, broadsides, and pamphlets; in 1672, on the eve of the third Anglo-Dutch War, the publication of *The Emblem of Ingratitude; or, A True Relation of the Unjust, Cruel, and Barbarous Proceedings against the English at Amboyna* made newly available the text of the 1624 *Relation*, expediently seasoned with additional crimes and misdemeanors. Thanks to this print history, the Amboina massacre came to connote much more than inter-European rivalries gone awry. As a byword of martyred English innocence in the colonial crucible, it proposed itself as a stark *theatrum* of Dutch cruelty and brutality.

That a play should eventually be cut out of such cloth is, in and of itself, not particularly striking. Emplotted from the beginning as a "sad Tragedie," the massacre of Amboina provided fitting material for dramatic performance, and more than one theatrical production on the subject had been either attempted or realized before 1673.[30] Far more striking are the choices Dryden made when he sat down to write his play. Given the premises provided by the EIC pamphlets—which Dryden almost certainly used as sources—one would expect Dutch machinations against the English to be central; instead, the alleged conspiracy is introduced only in the final act, and afforded a place merely as a pretext for the torture of the English merchants.[31]

With political and economic motives pushed to the plot's margins, the conflict of the play is essentially amatory, with the English hero, Captain Gabriel Towerson, and the Dutch antagonist, Harman Junior, vying for the beautiful Ysabinda. Their sentimental contest is mirrored by the rivalry between the English Beamont and the Dutch Fiscal (a "fiscaal" was the VOC official in charge of legal matters), both preening for Captain Perez's voluble wife, Julia. The insertion of Julia and Ysabinda into the cast of *Amboyna* represents a radical departure from the historical tradition handed down by the pamphlets. In these, Perez's wife is barely mentioned and Ysabinda makes an appearance only as the name of an executed Japanese soldier.[32] The innovation allowed Dryden to domesticate the massacre into a personal drama of erotic desire, and thereby mystify its actual motives of mercantile avarice and imperial cupidity. Even more important for my argument, the innovation anchored *Amboyna* to an interracial tradition that had been invigorated by the renewed success of *The Island Princess* in the 1660s.

Plots of interracial desire are relatively commonplace in Dryden's corpus; several of his plays romanticize the cross-cultural encounter, thus naturalizing contingent processes of acquisition, commodification, and exploitation. In *The Conquest of Granada* (1670–71), the Spaniard Almanzor weds the Moorish Almahide; in *Don Sebastian* (1689), the Portuguese Antonio courts the Arab Marayma; in *The Indian Emperour* (1665), the Spanish Cortez marries Montezuma's daughter. *Amboyna* is nevertheless unique in casting an Englishman, rather than a Spaniard or a Portuguese, as one half of the romantic pair. Dryden might have derived the idea from the increased incidence of Anglo-Asian unions, which had been on the uptick since the early 1640s. Or perhaps he had in mind Gabriel Towerson's real-life marriage to the daughter of Mubarak Khan, a former favorite of the Mughal emperor Akbar (1542–1605)—even though this union was not exactly the stuff of romance. An Armenian Christian, Mariam Khan had been the wife of William Hawkins, the commander of the first English ship to reach India. She and Towerson met shortly after Hawkins's death in 1613 and married within a few months. By report, Towerson had hoped to improve his fortunes with the help of his wife's relatives. When these hopes were disappointed, he returned to England and left Mariam behind at Agra. He evidently had no desire to rejoin her, for soon thereafter he sought employment from the East India Company as a principal factor in the Spice Islands.[33]

This drearily utilitarian attitude is neatly reversed in the main plot of *Amboyna*, where Towerson and Ysabinda's love is shown to override all other considerations. Ysabinda, for one, hardly seems aware of marrying beneath her station, or that her choice is "much against the will of all her friends" (1.1.122). As for Towerson, he is as oblivious to his betrothed's wealth as he is indifferent to the advantages he might derive from giving her up. When Harman Junior offers him "gain . . . beyond what you cou'd hope for" (2.1.78–79) in exchange for renouncing the wedding, Towerson's reaction is outright indignant: "Hold, you mistake me *Harman*, I never gave you just occasion to think I wou'd make Merchandise of Love; *Ysabinda* you know is mine, contracted to me e're I went for *England*, and must be so till death" (2.1.81–84). In this manner, the play construes the relationship between Towerson and Ysabinda as a purely romantic one, even as it makes clear that such a relationship could also stand for the rapport between England and the Spice Islands. There is, in fact, an obvious parallel between Ysabinda willingly giving herself away to Towerson and EIC claims that the East Indian islanders had freely yielded themselves and their islands "under the obeysance of the King of England."[34] The opening of *Amboyna* thus conforms to the patterns of interracial romance: on the one hand, the ideals of domestic heterosexuality are used to legitimize and naturalize England's lordship over the spice-producing polities of Southeast Asia; on the other hand, the political and economic asymmetries implicit in this relationship are used to stabilize the fluidities of eros, thus allaying at least some of the anxieties that attended the normalization of heterosexual desire.

Given these premises, it is no surprise to find that the initial characterization of Ysabinda meets and even exceeds the expectations of the genre. Not only does the play construe her as a somatic blank—all we know about her is that she is "beauteous . . . and young" (1.1.124)—it also sidesteps every possible index of her difference. She displays none of the exorbitant libido ascribed by Linschoten to all Asian women, and none of the waywardness that characterizes Fletcher's Quisara. Even her conversion to Christianity is placed in the past, thereby consigning her (unidentified) native religion to the play's prehistory; her speech, manners, and values are thoroughly assimilated to English standards. Indeed, she seems to consider herself more English than Ambonese: "Come, *Country woman*"—she tells a distraught English widow who appears in the third act—"I must call you so, since he who owns my Heart is English born" (3.3.152–53, my emphasis).

But while the play's opening may seem to embrace the conventions of interracial romance, the unfolding of the action exposes cross-racial sexuality as a site of defilement and degeneration. In doing so, *Amboyna* reveals a deep ambivalence about the very premises on which plots of interracial romance were based—which is to say, about the usefulness of eros as a means of negotiating identity. We might begin exploring this ambivalence by focusing on the tension between the main plot, which is centered on Ysabinda and organized around recognizable topoi of marriage-minded desire, and the subsidiary plot, which is structured around the illicit triangle composed by Beamont, the Fiscal, and Julia. The latter's name and role in the Amboina incident are Dryden's invention, but her figure is no less historically grounded than that of her husband, an Indo-Portuguese bailiff (a Spanish captain in the play), who was among the people actually executed in 1623. Trial records identify her as "a Slave of the honourable *Dutch East India* Company, who was given to . . . [the bailiff] Augustine [Perez] in hope of his good carriage." After Perez's conviction and execution, she was returned to bondage "untill such time that shee shall be otherwise disposed of by the Governour."[35] How she was "disposed of" is not known; one can only wonder whether she was simply assigned to a new board and a new bed.

Despite their scantiness, these documentary traces remind us not only that the VOC stood at the center of the most expansive slave trade in the history of Southeast Asia, but also that slaves performed much of the sexual/reproductive labor necessary for the survival of Dutch colonial settlements abroad.[36] As the VOC's governing board put it in 1643, "The Indian world is too big for us to possess for ourselves alone, and our country is too small to dispatch such a force as is needed for the stabilization of a colony."[37] In consequence, Dutch settlers in the East Indies frequently relied on female captives to serve as wives and mothers. Some of these captives were marriageable orphans from Portugal taken from defeated Habsburg vessels.[38] More often, they were slaves imported from various parts of Asia; Portuguese-speaking women from the Malabar and Coromandel coasts in southern India seem to have been especially prized.[39] Prospective grooms purchased their brides' freedoms and arranged for their christening. Their wives acquired Dutch status, but were prohibited from ever setting foot in the Netherlands.[40] The point of these arrangements was clear to all, including English East India Company observers. As Thomas Mills and John Milward wrote in 1622, it was on the foundation of these captive wombs that the Dutch planned to build a "perpetuall plantation in India." And this indeed might prove "the best designe" for them, they added tartly, for their tyrannies had made them "widowes of the world," unlikely to find partners any other way.[41]

Almost none of this historical context remains visible in Dryden's characterization of Julia. Far from being coerced, her sexual circulation among her Spanish husband, Perez, the Englishman Beamont, and the Dutch Fiscal is a function of her unrestrained libido. Her presence shatters the fantasy of reciprocity implicit in interracial romance by reproducing it ad libitum; her promiscuity dismantles the main plot's pretense of national distinctiveness by homologizing

Spanish, English, and Dutch. In many ways, Julia is the sheer antithesis of Ysabinda: she is as voracious as the latter is chaste, and as complicit in the Dutch plot as the latter is its innocent victim. At the same time, there are obvious parallels between the two characters: both are objects of competing Anglo-Dutch claims, and both are made to stand as personifications of the East Indies. If Harman Junior equates the sexual possession of Ysabinda to a "plenteous Harvest" (4.3.31), Beamont and the Fiscal compare Julia's body to a spice crop, to be shared according to the articles of the 1619 Agreement: [42]

Beam: Now Mr. *Fiscall*, you are the happy Man with the Ladies, and have
             got the precedence of Traffick here too; you've the *Indies* in your
             Arms, yet I hope a poor *English* Man may come in for a third part
             of the Merchandise.

Fisc: Oh Sir, in these Commodities, here's enough for both,
             here's Mace for you, and Nutmegg for me in the same Fruit;
             and yet the owner has to spare for other friends too.

Julia: My Husbands Plantation's like to thrive well betwixt you.

             (2.1.281–88)

In casting herself as her "Husbands Plantation," Julia extends the analogy between husbandry and sexual intercourse already proposed by Beamont and the Fiscal.[43] Before too long, however, her lovers develop the parallel in unexpected ways, turning the "drudgery" of the conjugal embrace into a medico-moral "venture" entailing personal and collective risks. In the process, national and individual bodies are constituted as vulnerable enclosures whose erotic apertures are, in Valerie Traub's well-chosen words, "sites and conduits for contamination":[44]

Beam: Betwixt you and me; 'tis a little kind of venture, that we make in
             doing this Dons drudgery for him; for the whole Nation of 'em is
             generally so Pocky, that 'tis no longer a Disease, but a second nature
             in 'em.

Fisc: I have heard indeed, that 'tis incorporated among 'em, as
             deeply as the *Moors* and *Jews* are; there's scarce a Family, but 'tis crept into their blood like the new Christians.

             (2.1.292–98)

The sudden shift from "drudgery" to "venture" turns Julia's account of cuckoldry-as-agricultural-cultivation into a cautionary tale about the pathological effects of interracial sex. Primary among these effects is the "incorporation" of supposedly alien elements (Moors, Jews) into the body politic, a phenomenon that is equated to the "incorporation" of venereal disease (the "pock" or syphilis) into the body natural. Simultaneously racializing and pathologizing the liaisons between Julia and her lovers, the subsidiary plot of *Amboyna* foregrounds precisely those aspects that the primary plot is so careful to occlude: where Towerson and Ysabinda's betrothal celebrates cross-racial desire as an instrument of colonial subordination, the ménage à trois among Julia, Beamont, and the Fiscal aligns it with aberrancy and disease. As a result, the very foundations of the primary plot are placed under stress, and Ysabinda's assimilability is called obliquely into question.

Nevertheless, it is only after her rape by Harman Junior that the play begins to insist on Ysabinda's alterity. When Towerson tries to console her by saying that her "breast" is still as white "as falling snow" (4.5.33, 34), she protests that Harman's rape has blackened and besmirched her: "My soul indeed is free from sin, but the *foul speckled stains are from my body ne'r to be wash'd out. . . .* Kill me, my Love, or I must kill my self; else you may think I was a *black Adulteress* in my mind, and some of me consented" (4.5.38–42, my emphasis). The black-white binarism that permeates the exchange aggressively colors the final act of the play. More to the point, it aggressively colors Ysabinda's body, implanting it with "foul speckled stains" never to be cleansed or erased. It is hardly a coincidence that the terms used by Ysabinda to describe her defilement carry evident racial overtones, as they recall both the classically derived proverb "to wash the Ethiop white is to labor in vain" and the closely related Jeremiah 13:23, which in the Geneva Bible reads, "Can the blacke More change his skin? or the leopard his spots?"[45] Both sayings locate truth in the surface of the body; both identify blackness not just as a marker of identity but as a deviance from whiteness—a "stain" that could be innate or acquired but was in any case intractable to change.[46] While putatively voicing her sexual shame, the terms in which Ysabinda represents herself toward the end of the play unmistakably constitute her as a racialized subject.

On the surface, the "blackening" of Ysabinda may be taken as an indication that eros and ethnos were as intertwined in the 1670s as they were in the earlier part of the century. But while this scene seems to uphold a straight equivalence between sexual propriety and racial privilege, other moments in the play destabilize the link between the two. Julia, for instance, is not openly racialized despite being depicted as a libidinous adulteress: Beamont and the Fiscal

may allegorize her as an East Indian plantation, but do not identify her as Asian—nor do they object when Julia implicitly catego-
rizes herself as a member of the "[Spanish] nation" (2.1.331). What
is more, *Amboyna* routinely undercuts the binary logic that would
sustain facile dichotomies between Asian and European, white and
black, chaste and unchaste.

We can see the strategy at play in the eerie symmetry between
the rape scene and the "wanton" epithalamium (3.3.28) anticipating
Towerson and Ysabinda's consummation of their marriage:

> The Bridegroom comes, He comes apace
> With Love and Fury in his Face;
> She shrinks away, He close pursues,
> And Prayers and Threats, at once do's use,
> She softly sighing begs delay,
> And with her hand puts his away,
> Now out aloud for help she cryes,
> And now despairing shuts her Eyes.
> (3.3.17–24)

From a structural point of view, the epithalamium belongs to an
anticipatory pattern that is part and parcel of *Amboyna*'s ham-fisted
irony. Just as Towerson's "pleasing dream" (3.2.24) of ascending into
the skies portends the massacre of the Englishmen at the hands of
their Dutch rivals, the epithalamium forecasts the rape of Ysabinda
at the hands of Harman Junior—or better yet, provides "a surrogate
'experience'" of it while simultaneously "withholding the visual spectacle" of the sexual violation.[47] Like the bridegroom of the epithalamium, Harman Junior pursues Ysabinda first with love and then with
fury. At first, he entreats her. Then his blandishments become threats:
"pray resolve to make me happy by your free consent," he warns her.
"I do not love these half Enjoyments, t' enervate my delights with
using force, and neither give my self nor you that full content, which
two can never have, but where both joyn with equal eagerness to bless
each other" (4.3.40–44). When Ysabinda still refuses, he pursues her
offstage; and the scene ends with Ysabinda crying in vain for help.

The precise symmetry between the epithalamium and the assault
scene brings conubium and rape into uncomfortable proximity. In
what is perhaps the most sustained reading of this contiguity to
date, Shankar Raman suggests that the play's movement from conjugal consummation to sexual violence "conceals the implicit English
rape of the colonized by explicitly assigning it elsewhere."[48] Hence

the epithalamium serves a paradoxical function: by bringing English East India Company and Dutch Verenigde Oost-Indische Compagnie into close contiguity, it distances and differentiates their respective East Indian projects. This is a suggestive hypothesis—not to mention a hypothesis that is easily supported by the contemporary record: after all, rape was an established metaphor for political tyranny since at least classical antiquity. There was, moreover, ample precedent for depicting Dutch behavior in the East Indies as sexual violence: describing English losses and Dutch advances in the Banda Islands, Samuel Purchas's 1625 *Pilgrimes* had compared the archipelago to "a beautiful and rich bride [who] was [once] envied to English Armes" and now lay "ravished from her new Husband."[49] Within this context, it is easy to read Ysabinda's rape at the hands of Harman Junior as an allegory of Dutch colonial policies; for where the English sought native "desire, consent, and good liking," the Dutch "laboured nothing more, than the conquests of Countries, and the acquiring of new dominion."[50] The rivalry between Towerson and Harman Junior thus makes manifest "the different end and designe of the English & Dutch Companies"—and obscures the fundamental identity of their respective mercantile-imperial pursuits.[51]

Perceptive and sophisticated in many respects, this reading nevertheless fails to take fully into account the disturbing symmetry between sexual violence and connubial consummation. For this is a symmetry that *connects* just as much as it separates, and *illuminates* just as much as it obscures: if it is true that the epithalamium provides a "surrogate 'experience'" of Ysabinda's rape at the hands of Harman Junior, it is also true that the rape provides a crucial interpretive key for the epithalamium. Scholars have long known that Dryden derived most of his epithalamium from the influential "Epithalamium" of Jan Everaerts, a Dutch neo-Latin poet more commonly known as Johannes Secundus.[52] In Secundus's original poem, the dynamics of the wedding night are not those of rape but rather those of power play; indeed, one could say that these dynamics are not too distant from those sketched by Camões in the Isle of Love episode. The struggle is part of an erotic script that deploys violence in the pursuit of pleasure—one in which, as the poem puts it, "pasci / Pugnando teneri volunt amores" (tender loves willingly feed on fighting).[53] If the bride resists at first, she later reciprocates the groom's caresses, and eventually grows bold enough to wrest the initiative away from him. Vestiges of this erotic mutuality are still traceable in Dryden's rendition of the epithalamium: the second stanza notes that the bride both "fears and wishes" the groom's arrival (3.3.16); and the third one describes her as "softly sighing" in her protestations (3.3.21), as if to suggest something of a halfhearted resistance. In the last two lines of the composition, however, Dryden turns erotic power play into sexual violence: soft sighs become cries for help, and wishful fears give way to desperation. Depriving the bride of the erotic agency with which Secundus's original poem had endowed her, Amboyna reframes connubial consummation as rape, and casts female marital sexuality as victimization.

This reframing of conubium may go a long way to illuminate the historical complexities of the European-Asian encounter, with its frequent circumstances of erotic coercion and sexual duress. Dryden's equation of rape and marital consummation recuperates in fact precisely those elements of sexual and colonial violence that the playwright had elided by casting Julia as a willful adulteress. At the same time, this equation questions the assumptions of a romance tradition in which asymmetries of power routinely coexisted with, and even underwrote, symmetries of pleasure and desire. In problematizing the tradition of interracial romance, *Amboyna* implicitly removes cross-racial desire from the domain of licit eroticism. Without conubium as a legitimizing outlet, this desire can only express itself as illicit sexuality—be it in the form of sexual violence, as in the primary plot, or in the form of adulterous promiscuity, as in the subsidiary plot. In the process, *Amboyna* also excludes the colonial contact zone from the domain of domestic heterosexuality, and construes interracial sexuality as the very antithesis of its ideals.

THE ENGLISH ROGUE

Although it is not widely known today, Richard Head's *The English Rogue: Described, In the Life of Meriton Latroon, a Witty Extravagant* was very popular during the Restoration. A first edition was issued in 1665, selling out within the year; second, third, and fourth editions were published in 1666; a fifth edition followed in 1667. By the first decade of the following century, the story had proven profitable enough to spawn five additional reprints, four sequels, one play, and two translations into Continental languages, plus a variety of imitations that included *The French Rogue* (1672), *The Dutch Rogue* (1683), *The Irish Rogue* (1690), and *The Scotch Rogue* (1706).[54] A mix of picaresque, criminal autobiography, moral resolve, captivity narrative, and Oriental travelogue, the book tells the story of Meriton Latroon, conceived by English parents in England but inevitably tainted by the climate of his native Ireland. "It is strange the Clymate should have more prevalency over the Nature of the Native, then the disposition of the Parent," muses the title character in the beginning of the story.[55] For although his father and mother could "neither flatter" nor "deceive, revenge, [and] equivocate," he had proven a crook, a hothead, and a liar since childhood, "according to the common custom of his [Irish] Countrymen" (sig. B2v).

Displaced by the Irish revolt of 1641, Latroon moves to England, where he joins a band of Gypsies, apprentices as a merchant, disguises himself as a lady's maid, fathers illegitimate children, marries an unfaithful wife, becomes a pimp, and turns into a highwayman. Caught and condemned to hang, he is granted a reprieve and sentenced to the American colonies. The character thus embarks for Virginia, but never makes it there. Captured by pirates and sold into slavery, he travels to Mauritius, Ceylon, India, Java, and Siam—rehearsing on the way many a topos obligé of Eastern travel. Within the space of ten chapters, he deflowers a Nair bride, witnesses a widow burning, describes a Jagannāth festival, explains the purpose of the penis bells, receives sexual advances from a Siamese talapoin (Buddhist monk), cons a banyan (Hindu merchant), and causes a "Running a Muck" (sig. Hhh2v).[56]

For the most part, Latroon's experiences in Asia are those of a lowly sailor: "None could distinguish me from one that received his first rocking in a Ship," he admits in his narrative (sig. Fff5r). "I could drink water that stunk . . . and eat beef and porke (that stirred as if it had received a second life, and was crawling out of the platter to seek out the rest of his Members). . . . And to make me the more compleat, I had forgot to wash either hands or face, or what the use of a comb or shirt was" (sig. Fff5r). Things suddenly change when Latroon reaches Bantam and marries an affluent "Indian-Black" (sig. Hhh4v). Using his wife's money, he begins buying and selling local commodities, quickly growing into a prosperous East India trader. It is at this point that Latroon experiences something of a spiritual awakening, pledging never again to neglect his duty to God, himself, and his neighbors. The book thus ends on a high moral note: metamorphosed into a respectable English businessman, the former rogue offers "wholesome advice" (largely ventriloquized from Owen Felltham's popular

Resolves) and voices the hope that others may benefit from the story of his past mistakes (sig. Hhh6v).

Latroon's striking metamorphosis underscores the importance of the East India trade in the social and economic imaginaries of seventeenth-century England: construed as an escape from the strictures and limitations of Europe, India was literally the place where even a convicted criminal could easily grow and prosper. By giving a central place to marriage, *The English Rogue* also underscores the role that Asian-born women could play in these dynamics of advancement. If private trade provided individuals with opportunities to grow rich, the key to a private trader's success were his business contacts—and this gave enterprising individuals every incentive to develop local kinship networks.[57] Of the several East India Company merchants known to have married in Asia around the middle of the seventeenth century, several made large fortunes through private trade, often in partnership with Asian merchants and sometimes to the detriment of company business. Thomas Chamber and his "lady from the Indies," for instance, grew rich enough to buy a manor in England and marry their son into a noble family. Their life stories, like those of many other seventeenth-century Europeans, suggest the emergence of a multinational merchant class that had Asian-born women as its linchpin.[58]

The English Rogue replicates this historical pattern by tying Latroon's economic success to his Asian marriage, yet goes beyond it by connecting both to his apparent reformation—that is, to his successful performance of sexual mastery, social propriety, and national belonging. "I was an absolute Monarch in my family," gloats the title character as he describes his household at Bantam, "yet though I thus enjoy'd the prerogative of an husband, yet I did not Lord it too much; which won so much upon my wifes affection . . . that assoon as I desired any thing, it was immediately performed, with much alacrity and expedition" (sig. Hhh5r). This self-description underscores Latroon's improved status by recalling the husband-as-king ideal so widely celebrated in European conduct books and marriage treatises. At the same time, it establishes a parallel between Latroon and Charles II. It is not only that Latroon's marriage to an "Indian-Black" echoes Charles II's marriage to Catherine of Braganza, whose swarthiness seems to have been both a subject of comment and an occasional source of ridicule.[59] More than that, Latroon's royal sway over his Asian household is described as an act of restoration mirroring the Stuart return to the English throne in 1660.

It is certainly not a coincidence that *The English Rogue* explicitly contrasts Latroon's marriage at Bantam with his earlier marriage in England—a period of "domestick civil wars" (sig. Cc4v), as the text defines it, that had left him socially and symbolically emasculated. Whereas Latroon's English wife had proven shrill, obstinate, and conniving, his Indian wife is altogether devoid of any "foolish self-will" (Hhh5r). Her submissiveness naturalizes Latroon's position as a benevolent patriarch, legitimizes his newfound status as a respectable trader, and secures his Englishness by reference to Stuart absolutism.[60]

In outline, the story of Latroon's marriage conforms to the tradition of interracial romance: it is an imperial narrative that describes and even celebrates the assimilation of Asian women to European manners and values. In the context of this tradition, Latroon's experience recalls the union of Armusia and Quisara in Fletcher's *The Island Princess*—which, incidentally, enjoyed a substantive revival right around the time of *The English Rogue*'s peak success.[61] Both narratives are set in the spice-producing islands of what is today Indonesia, both feature sexually aggressive East Indian women, both involve the bride's conversion to Christianity as a conditio sine qua non for marriage. Finally, they both construe marriage as a means of advancement for the groom: if the socially undistinguished Armusia rises so high as to get within reach of Tidore's throne, Latroon echoes the pattern in a bourgeois key.

Yet against the background of these superficial similarities, it is the differences that really stand out. Whereas *The Island Princess* focuses on Quisara's wayward eroticism as a key signifier of identity, *The English Rogue* concentrates on skin color instead. And whereas *The Island Princess* works to mystify the economic imperatives that propel the intermarriage plot, *The English Rogue* insists on these imperatives both frankly and unabashedly. Even as it deploys cherished topoi of interracial romance, then, *The English Rogue* problematizes the logic that sustained them. In this sense, Head's deployment of the intermarriage plot already anticipates Dryden's handling of *Amboyna*, where interracial romance is invoked only to be eventually dismissed.

In some respects, Latroon's insistence on the material dimensions of his East Indian marriage is merely genre appropriate—after all, the frank presentation of economic motives is a common feature of picaresque writing.[62] In other respects, however, this insistence is tied to an increasingly epidermal (and gender-neutral) understanding of racial difference. Here again, the differences between the title character's two marriages can be illuminating. In the case of the first marriage, contracted in England to an Englishwoman, the prospect of a rich dowry plays something of a role in Latroon's decision to propose, but only *after* he has already fallen for the woman's good looks and "Virgin whiteness" (sig. Cc4r). In the case of the second marriage, the prospect of a rich dowry plays a predominant role, and erotic desire has little or no part: as Latroon repeatedly informs us, his only reason for tying the knot in Asia is that his bride can offer financial security. Divested of its erotic component, intermarriage ceases to function as a means of and metaphor for European conquest, coming to mark instead Europe's surrender to the lure of gain: "By degrees, interest so over-power'd me, that I resolv'd to marry her," the title character confesses. "Thus many (nay most) for Money, stick not to give themselves to the Devil" (sig. Hhh3v).

Latroon's Faustian analogy implicitly portrays his marriage as a demonic bargain, yet spiritual and cultural differences play no part in *The English Rogue*. Whereas Fletcher's Quisara resists both marriage and conversion, Head's "Indian-Black" seems only too eager to embrace them. No sooner does Latroon decide to wed than she quickly renounces "her Paganism" and the couple is married "according to the Ceremonies of the [Anglican] Church" (Sig. Hhh5r); as a wife, she epitomizes European ideals of female behavior, striving to please her husband in every way. But where cultural differences recede from view, physical morphology quickly takes their place. As if reveling in what some critics have called "the monstrous union of white and black," the text misses no opportunity to underscore the swarthiness of Latroon's wife.[63] Indeed, as the narrative progresses, there is a significant slide in the way that her appearance is construed. Depicted as "tawny" or light brown at first, she grows progressively darker as she and Latroon become more intimate (sig. Hhh3r). For the title character, this darkness is an inescapable source of revulsion: for while acknowledging that his bride is both "well-featur'd and well-form'd," he also confesses that having sex with her "went against [his] stomach" (sigs. Hhh3r, Hhh3v). And although he later claims that "custom [had] made her become . . . as lovely in [his] eye, as if she had been the compleatest European beauty," he remains keenly aware of lying next to a woman "so contrary to [his] own complexion" (sig. Hhh5v).

Reduced to a synonym for pigmentation and construed as an ineradicable sign of difference, the complexion of Latroon's wife functions as a satirical gloss on the tradition of interracial romance. By and large, that tradition rested on two imbricated assumptions: first, that attraction was mutual, each lover equally desiring the other; second, that matters of difference could be effectively overcome if not altogether erased. In *The English Rogue*, both of these assumptions are undercut by a stark binarism of black and white. Because the text consistently associates whiteness with beauty and blackness with unsightliness, the darkness of Latroon's wife makes desire flow only in one direction. And because it inheres in the skin's surface, it can neither be erased nor forgotten. By implanting difference in the body, *The English Rogue* brings the assimilationist fantasy of interracial romance face to face with its own ultimate impossibility. Latroon's wife may convert to Christianity, marry in the Anglican Church, and even serve as a model of submissive femininity, but is not thereby admitted into the European fold. Quite to the contrary, the more she attempts to bridge the cultural gap, the more she becomes a figure of irreducible alterity.

WRITING ENGLISHNESS, WRITING WHITENESS

Until the second half of the seventeenth century, European understandings of human difference allowed eros to serve as a guarantor of racial identity: sexual arrangements and erotic proclivities functioned as carriers of ethnos, at once materially important and symbolically central to a people's sense of itself. It is precisely this articulation of eros and ethnos that underwrote the early modern vogue for interracial romance and helped enshrine domestic heterosexuality as culturally hegemonic. But as the end of the century approached, eros and ethnos began to grow apart. Sexual propriety became less and less convincing as an index of racial belonging. In turn, racial belonging ceased to function as a measure of sexual propriety, paving the way for the emergence of visible sexual minorities within Europe—the Portuguese "fanchono," the French "tribade," the English "molly," the Spanish "puto."[64] It is certainly suggestive that the earliest known account of London's molly subculture, Edward Ward's *Secret History of Clubs* (1709), depicts mollies as a separate race sprung from the unnatural coupling of some "Monster, Mad, or Drunk" with a "preposterous Punk."[65]

The emergence of a minoritizing discourse concerned with home-spun groups of sexual dissidents brought the process of "perverse implantation" from the contact zone back into the heart of Europe, but in no way lessened the salience of erotic deviance to the discourses of racial difference: stereotypes of non-European lechery and aberrance remained current well beyond the seventeenth century, as did the belief that same-sex practices were especially widespread among the "lower races."[66] But while "deviance" continued to form part and parcel of Europe's racial imagination, sexual orthodoxy progressively lost its ability to negotiate the boundaries of racial identity.

In the English context, this ineffectualness is already evident by the mid-Restoration period. Where late-sixteenth-century and early-seventeenth-century texts such as Linschoten's *Itinerario* and Fletcher's *The Island Princess* had conceptually tethered superior racial standing to the values of domestic heterosexuality, Dryden's *Amboyna* and Head's *The English Rogue* critiqued and complicated this link. Ysabinda may be a model of chastity and Latroon's unnamed wife a paragon of fidel-ity, yet their exemplary behavior cannot sanction their assimilation into the European fold. Dryden's and Head's reconfigurations of interracial romance thus testify to a fundamental rearticulation of eros and eth-nos: while recognizing the centrality of interracial sexuality to the pro-cess of Europe's expansion, they nevertheless exile it from the domain of domestic heterosexuality. *The English Rogue*, for instance, patterns Latroon's marriage at Bantam after the model of interracial romance, but evacuates this model of erotic mutuality. "Gold and Jewels she had great quantity, with an house richly furnished after the Indian fashion," the character confesses as he describes his Asian bride-to-be. "For this consideration, I perswaded my self to marry her; and with several argu-ments alleadged, *I gained so much conquest over my self, that I could kiss her without disgorging my self*; and by accustoming my self to her company, methought I began to take some delight in it" (sig. Hhh3v, my emphasis). Far from marking a victory of eros, conubial consum-mation signals Latroon's retreat from his own desires. In this avowed distaste for interracialism, Head's title character already anticipates the stance of Robert Knox (1641–1720), an Englishman who lived most of his adult life in Sri Lanka, yet declared to have always "abhor[red] all thoughts tending" toward a local companion.[67]

Something similar happens in *Amboyna*. Deprived of conubium as an outlet, interracial desire expresses itself only as illicit eroticism, be it adultery (as in the case of Beamont, Julia, and the Fiscal) or rape (as in the case of Towerson, Ysabinda, and Harman Junior). Such illicit eroticism, in turn, is construed as contagion—a sexual and racial pollution that threatens both the health of the natural body and the purity of the political one. This pathological valence is suggested as early as act 2, where Beamont and the Fiscal equate adultery with miscegenation (which deprives the political body of purity) and venereal disease (which deprives the natural body of health). It is only in the last act of the play, however, that this equation is brought to its logical conclusion. It is to this tragic climax that I now turn, to illuminate the ways that the torture of Beamont may be taken not only as a demonstration of Dutch cruelty but also as an illustration of the dangers inherent in interracialism.

As the only part of the play directly concerned with the 1623 massacre, the last act of *Amboyna* is the most obviously indebted to the EIC pamphlets on the subject. Towerson's forgiveness of his executioners (5.1.392) and Perez's confession of bigamy (5.1.442–45), for instance, come directly from *A True Relation*. Most of the torture details are lifted almost verbatim from the pamphlets; and the "smooth Apology" (5.1.467) promised by the Fiscal at the end of the play is a clear allusion to *A True Declaration* and *The Answer unto the Dutch Pamphlet* (both of which were bound together with *A True Relation*).[68] Nevertheless, there is at least one significant difference between the play and the pamphlets. The latter specify that Beamont was forced to drink water "till his inwards were ready to crack."[69] The former has the same character tortured with fire: he is brought on stage with "Matches" tied to his fingers (stage direction 5.1.326), exposed to candle flames "from the Wrists up to the Elbows" (5.1.342–3), and burned until he is "scorch'd and defac'd" (5.1.334). By replacing water with fire, the play builds on the equation among miscegenation, illicit sexuality, and venereal disease—and brings to fruition growing English anxieties about the potential effects of racial mixing. There is, in fact, an uncanny mimicry between Beamont's sufferings and the symptomatology of syphilis, with the painful lesions that felt as if one had "lyen in the fire" and the grotesque disfigurations that accompanied the disease's tertiary stage.[70] Read in this light, Beamont's torture by fire becomes an instantiation of the "burning disease" (as syphilis was then often called).

By denaturalizing racial mixing, Richard Head's *The English Rogue* and John Dryden's *Amboyna* signal the end of a long tradition built on the assimilative power of eros. Nor is this entirely surprising:

despite their overtly imperial character, these narratives are not—or at least not primarily—about England's power to woo, subordinate, and refashion foreign economies according to its desires. Their main concern lies, instead, with fashioning Englishness out of the multi-national, multifarious realities of the country's overseas expansion. Hence the conspicuous position assigned to the adjective "English" in both titles: by manipulating established topoi of interracial romance, Head and Dryden sought to define what it meant to be English. This is perhaps most evident in *The English Rogue*, since in the beginning of the narrative there is little or nothing that is specifically English about the title character. Not only is the young Latroon described as being just as much Irish as English, but his Irishness is also construed as a fundamental component of his identity as a rogue—as the prologue points out, it was the experience of being *"steept* for some years in an *Irish Bog"* that turned him into a seasoned crook (sig. A4r). Yet by the end of the story Latroon's rogue persona has been cast off, and his Irish characteristics are seemingly gone. The "Indian-Black" plays a crucial role in this ethnic metamorphosis. She provides Latroon with the financial resources to become a respectable trader, and she affords him the socio-symbolic tools to define himself as a successful head of household. Perhaps even more important, she secures Latroon's racial identity by means of her own inescapable blackness. Her function in the narrative can be compared to that of the black servant in seventeenth-century portraiture, whose presence made the master's (or mistress's) whiteness fully perceptible.[71] Juxtaposed against the body of a woman who looks *"all black,* as if she had had a *Mourning-Smock* on" (sig. Hhh3v), Latroon's Irish taint cannot but fade into insignificance: all that is left is his whiteness—a morphological meta-phor that was already becoming synonymous with Englishness (often at the expense of Scots and Irish).[72]

A related dynamic can be traced in *Amboyna*, where the figure of Ysabinda serves to catalyze the polarization between English and Dutch characters, driving a wedge between two nations that had, after all, strong political, religious, and intellectual ties. A spirit of invidious comparison is apparent from the play's inception: whereas the Fiscal is described as "a Petty-fogging Rogue" (1.1.153), Towerson is "daring," "apt to pitty the distress'd," and "liberal to relieve" those in need (1.1.129, 130); and whereas Dutch gentlemen "live like Bores" (2.1.393), English merchants "live like Noblemen" (2.1.392). Never-theless, for much of the play there is hardly a radical break between the Dutch and English: as the tense complicities between Beamont and the Fiscal suggest, there are just as many similarities between the two nations as there are differences. It is only after Harman Junior's rape of Ysabinda that the similarities vanish, leaving in their place a stark contraposition of values and behaviors. When the young Harman expresses some remorse, the Fiscal chides him for being *racially degenerate*: "Fits of Conscience in another might be excusable; but, in you, a *Dutchman*, who are of a Race that are born Rebels, and live every where on Rapine; Wou'd you degenerate, and have remorse?" (4.4.49–52). For the Fiscal, Harman Junior's violence is neither momentary nor conjunctural; rather, it is a manifestation of Dutch identity, the externalization of an inner essence that is imagined as both collective and transmissible. As the play draws toward its end, this inner essence acquires a mythical genealogy that is imbued with demonic otherness. "Are you Men or Devils?" (5.1.310) inveighs Towerson, as he is made to watch "*the* English *Tortur'd, and the* Dutch *tormenting them*" (stage direction 5.1.308):

> *D'Alva*, whom you condemn for cruelty did ne're the like; he knew original Villany was in your Blood: your Fathers are all damn'd for their Rebellion; when they Rebell'd they were well us'd to this: these Tortures ne're were hatch'd in Humane Breast, but as your Countrey lies confin'd on Hell, just on its Marches, your black Neighbors taught ye, and just such pains as you invent on Earth, Hell has reserv'd for you. (5.1.310–17)

Invoking the memory of the brutal reprisals carried out by Habsburg troops (under the command of Fernando Álvarez de Toledo, Duke of Alva) during the Dutch War of Independence, Towerson rehashes a common seventeenth-century parallel between Spanish behavior in the Low Countries and Dutch behavior in the East Indies.[73] In Towerson's formulation, however, even the memory of D'Alva's atrocities in the Netherlands is retorted against the Dutch. Spanish reprisals become instruments of a justice that is at once royal and divine—the appropriate punishment for a people whose ancestry is pointedly associated with Lucifer's revolt (the "original Villany" mentioned at 5.1.311–12). Moving from historical experience to Judeo-Christian myth, Towerson's outburst precipitates the Low Countries into Hell, and transforms their inhabitants into devils. Imbued with demonic darkness, the Dutch become epitomes of racial alterity. Their physiognomies may make them "pass" for white, but their actions show their true colors, a point the English printer John Crouch made quite bluntly in 1665, when he noted—in what is perhaps one of the earliest print instances of "white" as a racial noun—that the Dutch were "Whites" on the outside but "Blacks" on the inside.[74]

Against this background, Gabriel Towerson stands as an emblem of English whiteness. This is not merely an epidermal trait—the kind of whiteness that every Dutch character in the play could claim to possess. Nor is it merely an ethical quality—the kind of whiteness that characterizes Ysabinda throughout most if not all of the play. Rather, it is a mixture of both, and then some: the emblem of a purity that is not only physical and moral but also sociosexual. It is especially significant, in this regard, that the hero never gets to consummate his marriage to Ysabinda: in a world where interracial desire is but a vehicle of defilement, he remains unspoiled and unpolluted. It is for this reason that whereas the other Englishmen are scorched with fire or bloated with water, Towerson is spared from torture. His pristine body serves as a corporeal metaphor for English identity, defined both against the epidermal darkness of racial others and against the ethical blackness of England's imperial enemies.

INTRODUCTION

1. Consultation held at Surat, 20 Feb. 1625, British Library, India Office Records (hereafter IOR): G/36/1, 117.

2. Consultation held at Surat, 20 Feb. 1625, 117.

3. Richard C. Temple, ed., *The Travels of Peter Mundy in Europe and Asia, 1608–1667* (London: Hakluyt Society, 1914), 2: 354; see also William N. Sainsbury, ed., *Calendar of State Papers, Colonial Series*, vol. 2, *East Indies, China and Japan, 1617–21* (London, 1870), 263.

4. John Leachland's career in the East India Company is summarized by Temple in *The Travels of Peter Mundy*, 2: lxvi–lxx. Additional details can be gleaned from William Foster, ed., *The English Factories in India*, vol. 2, *1622–1623* (Oxford: Clarendon Press, 1908), 86, 205, 233, 345, as well as from vol. 3, *1624–1629* (1909), 1, 89, 119–120.

5. Consultation held at Surat, 20 Feb. 1625, 117.

6. Directions and instructions given to John Leachland and John Robinson, 23 Mar. 1632, British Library, IOR: G/36/1, 259–62. A summary of this document can be found in Foster, *The English Factories in India*, vol. 4, *1630–1633* (1910), 213–15.

7. Temple, *The Travels of Peter Mundy*, 2: 83.

8. Francis Breton et al. to the East India Company (hereafter EIC), 27 Jan. 1644, British Library, IOR: E/3/18 no. 1858, f. 336.

9. William Methwold et al. to the EIC, 29 Dec. 1634, British Library, IOR: E/3/15 no. 1543A, f. 84r. See also EIC Court of Committees, 25 Nov. 1635, British Library, IOR: B/18, 82; and Breton et al. to the EIC, 27 Jan. 1644, f. 336.

10. Consultation held at Surat on 22 Oct. 1634, British Library, IOR: G/36/1, 314. See also Consultation held at Surat on 30 June 1634, British Library, IOR: G/36/1, 300–303; Methwold et al. to the EIC, 29 Dec. 1634, f. 84r; EIC Court of Committees, 25 Nov. 1635, 82; Breton et al. to the EIC, 27 Jan. 1644, f. 336.

11. Breton et al. to the EIC, 27 Jan. 1644, f. 336. A partial transcription of this report can be found in Foster, *The English Factories in India*, vol. 7, *1642–1645* (1913), 135–53.

12. Breton et al. to the EIC, 27 Jan. 1644, f. 336.

13. Breton et al. to the EIC, 27 Jan. 1644, f. 336.

14. Breton et al. to the EIC, 27 Jan. 1644, f. 336.

15. Ann Laura Stoler, *Carnal Knowledge and Imperial Power: Race and the Intimate in Colonial Rule* (Berkeley: University of California Press, 2002), 43, and "Making Empire Respectable: The Politics of Race and Sexual Morality in 20th-Century Colonial Cultures," *American Ethnologist* 16, no. 4 (1989): 634–60.

16. William Biddulph to the EIC, 15 Feb. 1618, British Library, IOR: E/3/5, no. 614, f. 316v; William Foster, ed., *The Embassy of Sir Thomas Roe to the Court of the Great Mogul, 1615–1619.* . . . (London, 1899), 2: 552, n. 1.

17. Gary P. Leupp, *Interracial Intimacy in Japan: Western Men and Japanese Women, 1543–1900* (London: Continuum, 2003), 44–61; Derek Massarella, *A World Elsewhere: Europe's Encounter with Japan in the Sixteenth and Seventeenth Centuries* (New Haven, CT: Yale University Press, 1990).

18. One of Hawkins's servants officiated. "[This] I thought had beene lawfull," wrote the groom in a later account, "till I met with a Preacher that came with Sir Henry Middleton, and hee shewing me the error, I was new marryed againe: so ever after I lived content and without feare, she being willing to goe where I went, and live as I lived." William Hawkins, "Relations of the Occurents Which Happened in the Time of His Residence in India. . . ," in *Purchas his Pilgrimes*, comp. Samuel Purchas (London, 1625), 1: 206–26, quotation on 211.

19. John Keay, *The Honourable Company: A History of the English East India Company* (London: HarperCollins, 1991).

20. Temple, *The Travels of Peter Mundy*, 2: 356.

21. Consultation held at Surat on 30 June 1634, British Library, IOR: G/36 ff. 302–3; consultation held at Surat on 22 Oct. 1634, f. 313; a more circumspect report to company headquarters refers to Mānyā as the "woman called John Leachlands wife." See William Fremlin et al. to the EIC, 15 Jan. 1639, British Library, IOR: E/3/16, no. 1658, f. 224v.

22. On this point, made by Ruth Mazo Karras and reproposed in studies ranging from Gary Ferguson's *Queer (Re)readings in the French Renaissance: Homosexuality, Gender, Culture* (Burlington, VT: Ashgate, 2008) to Laura J. Rosenthal's *Infamous Commerce: Prostitution in Eighteenth-Century British Literature and Culture* (Ithaca, NY: Cornell University Press, 2006), see the debate among Karras ("Theoretical Issues: Prostitution and the Question of Sexual Identity in Medieval Europe" and "Response: Identity, Sexuality, and History"), Theo van der Meer ("Medieval Prostitution and the Case of a (Mistaken?) Sexual Identity"), and Carla Freccero ("Acts, Identities, and Sexuality in (Pre)Modern Regimes") in *Journal of Women's History* 11, no. 2 (1999): 159–98, as well as David M. Halperin's response to Karras in *How to Do the History of Homosexuality* (Chicago: University of Chicago Press, 2002), 66–68.

23. Consultation held at Surat, 20 Feb. 1625, f. 117.

24. Throughout the sixteenth century and into the seventeenth, the label "India" was so capacious as to accommodate not only most of the Asian

continent but also parts of east Africa. The first modern map of India, prepared by Martin Waldseemüller and published in the Strasbourg edition of Ptolemy's *Geographia* (1513), stretched as far west as modern-day Somalia. As late as 1626, the boundaries of India were still uncertain enough for Samuel Purchas to devote a full paragraph to the topic in *Purchas His Pilgrimage....* (London, 1626), 477.

25. Judith Butler, *Bodies That Matter: On the Discursive Limits of "Sex"* (New York: Routledge, 1993), 168. For examples of this scholarship, see notes 41 and 44 below, as well as Rudi C. Bleys, *The Geography of Perversion: Male-to-Male Sexual Behaviour Outside the West and the Ethnographic Imagination, 1750–1918* (New York: New York University Press, 1995); Abdul R. JanMohamed, "Sexuality on/of the Racial Border: Foucault, Wright, and the Articulation of Racialized Sexuality," in *Discourses of Sexuality: From Aristotle to AIDS*, ed. Domna C. Stanton (Ann Arbor: University of Michigan Press, 1992), 94–116; Ladelle McWhorter, "Sex, Race, and Biopower: A Foucauldian Genealogy," *Hypatia* 19, no. 3 (2004): 38–62; and Siobhan Somerville, *Queering the Color Line* (Durham, NC: Duke University Press, 2000).

26. Issues of intersectionality are broached in Ania Loomba, *Gender, Race, Renaissance Drama* (Manchester: Manchester University Press, 1989); Jonathan Goldberg, *Sodometries: Renaissance Texts, Modern Sexualities* (Stanford, CA: Stanford University Press, 1992); Kim F. Hall, *Things of Darkness: Economies of Race and Gender in Early Modern England* (Ithaca, NY: Cornell University Press, 1995); and several of the essays in Margo Hendricks and Patricia Parker, eds., *Women, "Race" and Writing in the Early Modern Period* (New York: Routledge, 1994). In recent years, intersectionality has moved center stage in the work of Valerie Traub, as suggested by "Mapping the Global Body," in *Early Modern Visual Culture: Representation, Race, and Empire in Renaissance England*, ed. Peter Erickson and Clark Hulse (Philadelphia: University of Pennsylvania Press, 2000), 44–97.

27. For a critique of the tendency to take "scientific" racism as paradigmatic of racial thinking *tout court*, see Geraldine Heng, "The Invention of Race in the European Middle Ages I: Race Studies, Modernity, and the Middle Ages," *Literature Compass* 8, no. 5 (2011): 315–31. Much of queer theory can be seen as a critique of identitarian epistemologies developed in the nineteenth century and still underpinning much contemporary thinking about sexuality.

28. The scholarship on the subject is too vast to be adequately summarized. What follows is a list of works that have informed my thinking. On the imbrications of race, geography, and religion, see Ania Loomba, *Shakespeare, Race, and Colonialism* (Oxford: Oxford University Press, 2002), and "'Delicious Traffick': Alterity and Exchange on Early Modern Stages," *Shakespeare Survey* 52 (1999): 201–14; Emily C. Bartels, *Speaking of the Moor: From* Alcazar *to* Othello (Philadelphia: University of Pennsylvania Press, 2008); Nabil Matar, *Turks, Moors, and Englishmen in the Age of Discovery* (New York: Columbia University Press, 1999); George Mariscal,

"The Role of Spain in Contemporary Race Theory," *Arizona Journal of Hispanic Cultural Studies* 2 (1998): 7–22; and James Shapiro, *Shakespeare and the Jews* (New York: Columbia University Press, 1996). On race and cultural habitus, see Etienne Balibar, "Is There a 'Neo-Racism'?" in Etienne Balibar and Immanuel Wallerstein, *Race, Nation, Class: Ambiguous Identities* (London: Verso, 1991), 17–28; as well as Stoler, *Carnal Knowledge and Imperial Power* 79–111. On climatology and race, see Mary Floyd-Wilson, *English Ethnicity and Race in Early Modern Drama* (Cambridge: Cambridge University Press, 2003); on race and class, see Jean E. Feerick, *Strangers in Blood: Relocating Race in the Renaissance* (Toronto: University of Toronto Press, 2010). For more general work on the unstable meanings of race during the early modern period, see Hendricks and Parker, *Women, "Race" and Writing*; Robert Bartlett, "Medieval and Modern Concepts of Race and Ethnicity," *Journal of Medieval and Early Modern Studies* 31, no. 1 (2001): 39–56; Margo Hendricks, "Race: A Renaissance Category?" in *A Companion to English Renaissance Literature and Culture*, ed. Michael Hattaway (Malden, MA: Blackwell, 2001), 690–98; Ania Loomba and Jonathan Burton, *Race in Early Modern England: A Documentary Companion* (New York: Palgrave, 2007), 1–36; Michael Giffert, ed., "Constructing Race: Differentiating Peoples in the Early Modern World," special issue of *William and Mary Quarterly* 54, no. 1 (1997); and the forum on "Race and the Study of Shakespeare" edited by Leeds Barroll and contained in *Shakespeare Studies* 26 (1998): 19–82. In a parallel but distinct vein, Laura Bovilsky's *Barbarous Play: Race on the English Stage* (Minneapolis: University of Minnesota Press, 2008); Ian Smith's *Race and Rhetoric in the Renaissance: Barbarian Errors* (New York: Palgrave Macmillan, 2009); and Ayanna Thompson's *Performing Race and Torture on the Early Modern Stage* (New York: Routledge, 2007) insist on the performative nature of race, both in the early modern period and in our day.

29. Katherine Crawford, *European Sexualities, 1400–1800* (Cambridge: Cambridge University Press, 2007); Merry E. Wiesner-Hanks, *Sexuality and Christianity in the Early Modern World* (New York: Routledge, 2000); and James Knowles, "Sexuality: A Renaissance Category?" in Hattaway, *Companion*, 674–89.

30. Michel Foucault, *The History of Sexuality*, vol. 1, *An Introduction* (New York: Random House, 1990), 101. On the capaciousness of the term "sodomy," see Alan Bray, *Homosexuality in Renaissance England: With a New Afterword* (New York: Columbia University Press, 1995), 14–17; and David F. Greenberg, *The Construction of Homosexuality* (Chicago: University of Chicago Press, 1988), 274–75; on marital intercourse without possibility of conception, see Michel de Montaigne's opinion in *Les Essais de Michel, Seigneur de Montaigne* (1595), trans. John Florio as *Essayes Written in French by Michael Lord of Montaigne*. . . . (London, 1613), 98.

31. Loomba, *Shakespeare, Race, and Colonialism*, 2–4; Peter Erickson makes a similar point in "The Moment of Race in Renaissance Studies," *Shakespeare Studies* 26 (1998): 27–36.

32. Halperin, *How to Do the History of Homosexuality*, 109. Several scholars have also emphasized how older constructions of sexuality often coexist along newer ones; for an example, see Eve K. Sedgwick, *Epistemology of the Closet* (Berkeley: University of California Press, 1990), 44–48.

33. Jean Bodin, *Methodus ad facilem historiarum cognitionem* (1566), trans. Beatrice Reynolds as *Method for the Easy Comprehension of History* (New York: W. W. Norton, 1969), 85–106.

34. Bernhard Varen, *Geographia generalis. . . .* (Amsterdam, 1650), 4; William Petty, "The Scale of Animals," in *The Petty Papers: Some Unpublished Writings of Sir William Petty*, ed. Marquis of Lansdowne (Boston: Houghton Mifflin, 1927), 2: 25–34.

35. John Bulwer, *Anthropometamorphosis. . . .* (London, 1653).

36. Wiesner-Hanks, *Sexuality and Christianity*, 107. See also Crawford, *European Sexualities*, 13–19; Kathleen M. Davies, "Continuity and Change in Literary Advice on Marriage," in *Marriage and Society: Studies in the Social History of Marriage*, ed. R. B. Outhwaite (New York: St. Martin's Press, 1981), 58–80; and Shaji George Kochuthara, *The Concept of Sexual Pleasure in the Catholic Moral Tradition* (Rome: Editrice Pontificia Università Gregoriana, 2007).

37. Valerie Traub, *The Renaissance of Lesbianism in Early Modern England* (Cambridge: Cambridge University Press, 2002), 265. Although Traub focuses exclusively on seventeenth-century England, the scholarship cited above suggests that similar developments occurred in others countries as well.

38. Prosecutions for bigamy and sodomy (the latter involving for the most part same-sex relations between males, although cases of bestiality and non-reproductive sexual practices between males and females were occasionally brought to trial) increased trough much of Europe, and harsher penalties for convicted offenders were adopted or advocated. In fifteenth-century Florence, new laws stripped convicted sodomites of their civic rights; in Venice, sodomy trials multiplied over two thousand–fold. In Portugal and Spain, the rate of prosecution stepped up significantly after the mid-sixteenth century; in the Netherlands, it began rising steadily during the final quarter of the seventeenth century. In England, where sodomy trials remained relatively rare until the early decades of the eighteenth century, legislation passed during the reign of Henry VIII and reenacted under Elizabeth I introduced the death penalty for convicted offenders. For Venice and Florence, see Guido Ruggiero, *The Boundaries of Eros: Sex Crime and Sexuality in Renaissance Venice* (Oxford: Oxford University Press, 1985), 109–45; and Michael Rocke, *Forbidden Friendships: Homosexuality and Male Culture in Renaissance Florence* (Oxford: Oxford University Press, 1996). For Portugal and Spain, see Luiz R. B. Mott, "Justitia et misericordia: A Inquisição portuguesa e a repressão ao nefando pecado de sodomia," in *Inquisição: Ensaios sobre mentalidade, heresias e arte*, ed. Anita Novinsky and Maria Luiza Tucci Carneiro (São Paulo: EDUSP, 1992), 703–38; Bartolomé Bennassar, "Le modèle sexuel: l'Inquisition d'Aragon et la répression des péchés 'abominables,'" in *L'Inquisition espagnole XVe–XIXe siècles*, ed. Bartolomé Bennassar (Paris: Hachette, 1979), 339–69; and Mary

E. Perry, "The 'Nefarious Sin' in Early Modern Seville," in *The Pursuit of Sodomy: Male Homosexuality in Renaissance and Enlightenment Europe*, ed. Kent Gerard and Gert Hekma (New York: Harrington Park Press, 1989), 67–89. For the Netherlands, see Theo van der Meer, "Sodom's Seed in the Netherlands: The Emergence of Homosexuality in the Early Modern Period," *Journal of Homosexuality* 34, no. 1 (1997): 1–16; and Dirk Jaap Noordam, "Sodomy in the Dutch Republic, 1600–1725," in Gerard and Hekma, *Pursuit of Sodomy*, 207–28. For England, see Bray, *Homosexuality in Renaissance England*; and Caroline Bingham, "Seventeenth-Century Attitudes to Deviant Sex," *Journal of Interdisciplinary History* 1 (1971): 447–67. Kenneth Borris offers a helpful overview of the English legal system and how this might have affected the rate of sodomy prosecutions in *Same-Sex Desire in the English Renaissance: A Sourcebook of Texts, 1470–1650* (New York: Routledge, 2004), 1–17. Readers interested in Switzerland, Germany, and France may wish to consult E. William Monter, "Sodomy and Heresy in Early Modern Switzerland," *Journal of Homosexuality* 6, nos. 1–2 (1980): 41–55; Helmut Puff, *Sodomy in Reformation Germany and Switzerland, 1400–1600* (Chicago: University of Chicago Press, 2003); Michael Sibalis, "Homosexuality in Early Modern France," in *Queer Masculinities, 1550–1800: Siting Same-Sex Desire in the Early Modern World*, ed. Michael O' Rourke and Katherine O'Donnell (London: Palgrave, 2006), 211–31; and Alfred Soman, "The Parliament of Paris and the Great Witch-Hunt," *Sixteenth Century Journal* 9, no. 2 (1978): 31–44, esp. 36.

A fairly similar pattern is observable for bigamy: between the second half of the sixteenth century and the end of the seventeenth, plural marriage cases made over 11 percent of all Inquisition prosecutions in Galicia and about 6 percent of all Inquisition prosecutions in Spain. Penalties also became more severe: in Portugal, plural marriage was made a capital offense in 1603 (albeit with allowances for extenuating circumstances); in England, it became a felony for the first time in 1604. In the Holy Roman Empire, the Constitutio Criminalis Carolina, promulgated by Charles V and ratified in 1532, prescribed the death penalty for both sodomy and bigamy. See Wiesner-Hanks, *Sexuality and Christianity*, 110; Allyson M. Poska, "When Bigamy Is the Charge: Gallegan Women in the Holy Office," in *Women in the Inquisition: Spain and the New World*, ed. Mary E. Giles (Baltimore, MD: Johns Hopkins University Press, 1999), 189–205, 192; Silvia Hunold Lara, ed., *Ordenações Filipinas: Livro V* (São Paulo: Companhia das Letras, 1999), 106–9; 1 James I, ch. 11, in John Raithby, ed., *Statutes at Large of England and Great Britain: From Magna Carta to the Union of the Kingdoms of Great Britain and Ireland* (London, 1811), 4: 598; and Isabel V. Hull, *Sexuality, State and Civil Society in Germany, 1700–1815* (Ithaca, NY: Cornell University Press, 1996), 61–66.

39. I borrow this phrase from Paul Rabinow, *French Modern: Norms and Forms of the Social Environment* (Cambridge, MA: Massachusetts Institute of Technology Press, 1989), 277.

40. Kobena Mercer and Isaac Julien, "Race, Sexual Politics and Black Masculinity: A Dossier," in *Male Order: Unwrapping Masculinity*, ed.

Rowena Chapman and Jonathan Rutherford (London: Lawrence & Wishart, 1988), 97–164, quotation on 106.

41. On the Dutch East Indies and French Indochina, see Stoler, *Carnal Knowledge and Imperial Power*. On British India, see Durba Ghosh, *Sex and the Family in Colonial India* (Cambridge: Cambridge University Press, 2006); and Kenneth Ballhatchet, *Race, Sex, and Class Under the Raj: Imperial Attitudes and Policies and Their Critics, 1793–1905* (New York: St. Martin's Press, 1980). On Spanish Mexico, see Patricia Seed, *To Love, Honor, and Obey in Colonial Mexico: Conflicts over Marriage Choice, 1574–1821* (Stanford, CA: Stanford University Press, 1988). For other colonial locales, see Philippa Levine, *Prostitution, Race, and Politics: Policing Venereal Disease in the British Empire* (New York: Routledge, 2003); Lenore Manderson, "Colonial Desires: Sexuality, Race, and Gender in British Malaya," *Journal of the History of Sexuality* 7, no. 2 (1997): 372–88; and Richard Phillips, *Sex, Politics and Empire: A Postcolonial Geography* (Manchester: University of Manchester Press, 2006).

42. Stoler, *Carnal Knowledge and Imperial Power*, 47.

43. Ann Laura Stoler, *Race and the Education of Desire: Foucault's History of Sexuality and the Colonial Order of Things* (Durham, NC: Duke University Press, 1995), 11.

44. Stoler, *Race and the Education of Desire*; Anne McClintock, *Imperial Leather: Race, Gender and Sexuality in the Colonial Context* (New York: Routledge, 1995); and Philip Howell, *Geographies of Regulation: Policing Prostitution in Nineteenth-Century Britain and the Empire* (Cambridge: Cambridge University Press, 2009).

45. Norman Daniel, *Islam and the West: The Making of an Image* (Edinburgh: Edinburgh University Press, 1960), 150–85.

46. Jeffrey J. Cohen, *Medieval Identity Machines* (Minneapolis: University of Minnesota Press, 2003), 208. On the influence of these stereotypes in medieval Spain, see Gregory S. Hutcheson, "The Sodomitic Moor: Queerness in the Narrative of Reconquista," in *Queering the Middle Ages*, ed. Glenn Burger and Steven F. Kruger (Minneapolis: University of Minnesota Press, 2001), 99–122.

47. Carolyn Brewer, *Shamanism, Catholicism and Gender Relations in Colonial Philippines, 1521–1685* (Burlington, VT: Ashgate, 2004); Ramón Gutierrez, *When Jesus Came, the Corn Mothers Went Away: Marriage, Sexuality, and Power in New Mexico, 1500–1846* (Stanford, CA: Stanford University Press, 1991); Ann Marie Plane, *Colonial Intimacies: Indian Marriage in Early New England* (Ithaca, NY: Cornell University Press, 2000); Irene Silverblatt, "Honor, Sex, and Civilizing Missions in the Making of Seventeenth Century Peru," *Journal of the Steward Anthropological Society* 25, nos. 1–2 (1997): 181–98; and Neil L. Whitehead, Peter Sigal, and John F. Chuchiak, eds., "Sexual Encounters/Sexual Collisions: Alternative Sexualities in Colonial Mesoamerica," special issue of *Ethnohistory* 54, no. 1 (2007).

48. John W. McCrindle, ed., *Ancient India as Described in Classical Literature*, vol. 6 (Westminster, UK: Archibald Constable, 1901).

49. Joan-Pau Rubiés, "New Worlds and Renaissance Ethnology," *History and Anthropology* 6, nos. 2–3 (1993): 157–97.

50. Diodorus Siculus, *The Library of History*, vol. 9, *Books 18–19.65*, trans. Russell M. Geer and ed. George P. Goold (Cambridge, MA: Harvard University Press, 1947), 321. For the full passage, see note 36 in Chapter 3.

51. In 1614, for example, the East India Company denied passage to the English wives of "three Indians" in its employ on the grounds that it would be inappropriate for them "to go among so many unruly sailors in a ship." Sainsbury, *Calendar of State Papers*, 2: 275.

52. The policy and its effects are discussed in António da Silva Rêgo, *História das missões do padroado português do Oriente: Índia, 1500–1542* (Lisbon: Divisão de Publicações e Biblioteca, Agência Geral das Colónias, 1949), 174–85; Charles R. Boxer, *Race Relations in the Portuguese Colonial Empire, 1415–1825* (Oxford: Clarendon Press, 1963); Ian A. MacGregor, "Notes on the Portuguese in Malaya," *Journal of the Malayan Branch of the Royal Asiatic Society* 28, no. 2 (1955): 5–47; and Fátima da Silva Gracias, *Kaleidoscope of Women in Goa: 1510–1961* (New Delhi: Concept, 1996).

53. "Memorial to the Council by Citizens of the Filipinas Islands, 26 July 1586," in *The Philippine Islands, 1493–1803*, ed. Emma H. Blair and James A. Robertson (Cleveland: Arthur H. Clark, 1903), 6: 157–233, on 172; Alonso Sánchez, "De la entrada de la China en particular," in *Labor Evangelica de los Obreros de la Compañía de Jesús en las Islas Filipinas*, ed. Francisco Colín and Pablo Pastells (Barcelona: Henrich, 1904), 1: 443.

54. Jean G. Taylor, *The Social World of Batavia: European and Eurasian in Dutch Asia* (Madison: University of Wisconsin Press, 1983), 16–17.

55. Qtd. in Stephen Neill, *A History of Christianity in India: The Beginnings to ad 1707* (Cambridge: Cambridge University Press, 1984), 372. Adrian Carton provides an insightful contextualization of this decree in "Historicizing Hybridity and the Politics of Location: Three Early Colonial Indian Narratives," *Journal of Intercultural Studies* 28, no. 1 (2007): 143–55.

56. Consultation held at Fort St. George, 22 Mar. 1680, British Library, IOR: G/19/2, f. 33. See also Frank Penny, *The Church in Madras: Being the History of the Ecclesiastical and Missionary Action of the East India Company in the Presidency of Madras in the Seventeenth and Eighteenth Centuries* (London: Smith and Elder, 1904), 1: 78–79.

57. Marcus Zuerius van Boxhorn, *Commentariolus de Statu Confoederatarum Provinciarum Belgii* (The Hague, 1649), 81. See also Leonard Blussé, *Strange Company: Chinese Settlers, Mestizo Women and the Dutch in VOC Batavia* (Dordrecht: Foris, 1986), 161; and Taylor, *Social World of Batavia*, 16–17.

58. On the mimetic rivalries that characterized Europe's early modern expansion, see Barbara Fuchs, *Mimesis and Empire: The New World, Islam, and European Identity* (Cambridge: Cambridge University Press, 2001); and Carmen Nocentelli, "Spice Race: *The Island Princess* and the Politics of Transnational Appropriation," *PMLA* 125, no. 3 (2010): 572–88.

59. Richard C. Temple, ed., *The Diaries of Streynsham Master, 1675–1680* (London: John Murray, 1911), 1: 201–2.

60. Philip Holden, "Rethinking Colonial Discourse Analysis and Queer Studies," in *Imperial Desire: Dissident Sexualities and Colonial Literature*, ed. Philip Holden and Richard J. Ruppel (Minneapolis: University of Minnesota Press, 2003), 291–321, on 316. The phrase "portable machine" comes from Simon During, "Postcolonialism and Globalisation: A Dialectical Relation After All?" *Postcolonial Studies* 1 (1998): 31–47, quotation on 44.

61. In Roman law, conubium identified each partner's legal capacity to marry the other one; I use the term in its extended sense of legal marriage.

62. On the "enamored Moslem princess" topos, see F. M. Warren, "The Enamored Moslem Princess in Orderic Vital and the French Epic," *PMLA* 29, no. 3 (1914): 341–58; Dorothee Metlitzki, *The Matter of Araby in Medieval England* (New Haven, CT: Yale University Press, 1977); Sharon Kinoshita, *Medieval Boundaries: Rethinking Difference in Old French Literature* (Philadelphia: University of Pennsylvania Press, 2006); Jacqueline de Weever, *Sheba's Daughters: Whitening and Demonizing the Saracen Woman in Medieval French Epic* (New York: Garland, 1998); and Jennifer R. Goodman, "Marriage and Conversion in Late Medieval Romance," in *Varieties of Religious Conversion in the Middle Ages*, ed. James Mouldon (Gainesville: University Press of Florida, 1997), 115–28.

63. Richard Head, *The English Rogue. . . .* (London, 1665), sig. Hhh4v. On color consciousness, see Kim F. Hall, *Things of Darkness*, and "Object into Object? Some Thoughts on the Presence of Black Women in Early Modern Culture," in *Early Modern Visual Culture: Representation, Race, and Empire in Renaissance England*, ed. Peter Erickson and Clarke Hulse (Philadelphia: University of Pennsylvania Press, 2000), 346–79; Michael Neill, "'Mulattos,' 'Blacks,' and 'Indian Moors': *Othello* and Early Modern Constructions of Human Difference," *Shakespeare Quarterly* 49, no. 4 (1998): 361–74; and Sujata Iyengar, *Shades of Difference: Mythologies of Skin Color in Early Modern England* (Philadelphia: University of Pennsylvania Press, 2004).

CHAPTER 1

1. The indigenous nomenclature is far from uniform; for an overview of terms used in Sulawesi, Borneo, and the Philippines, see Donald E. Brown, James W. Edwards, and Ruth P. Moore, *The Penis Inserts of Southeast Asia: An Annotated Bibliography with an Overview and Comparative Perspectives* (Berkeley: Center for South and Southeast Asia Studies, University of California, 1988); Alonso de Méntrida's seventeenth-century *Diccionario de la lengua bisaya, hiligueina y haraya de la Isla de Panay* ([Manila], 1841) lists "tugbuc" for the Philippines (311).

2. Vātsyāyana, *The Complete Kāma Sūtra: The First Unabridged Modern Translation of the Classic Indian Text by Vātsyāyana*, trans. Alain Daniélou (Rochester, VT: Park Street Press, 1994), 514. The practice has been variously explained: Charles Miller interprets it as a chastity device; G. N. Appel suggests its potential as a form of population control; Friedrich Seltmann links it to ancient fertility cults; Tom Harrisson and Carolyn Brewer take

it as a maturity rite; Raven Rowanchilde and Herwig Zahorka emphasize its sacrificial aspects. For most of these writers, the device also enhances female pleasure by "stimulating and extending the inner walls of the vagina." Tom Harrisson, "Rhinoceros in Borneo: And Traded to China," *The Sarawak Museum Journal* 7 (1956): 263–74, quotation on 270. See also G. N. Appel, "The Penis Pin at Peabody Museum, Harvard University," *Journal of the Malaysian Branch, Royal Asiatic Society* 41 (1968): 202–5; Carolyn Brewer, *Shamanism, Catholicism and Gender Relations in Colonial Philippines, 1521–1685* (Burlington, VT: Ashgate, 2004); Donald E. Brown, "The Penis Pin: An Unresolved Problem in the Relation Between the Sexes in Borneo," in *Borneo: Contributions to Gender Studies*, ed. Vinson H. Sutlive (Williamsburg, VA: Borneo Research Council, 1991), 435–54; Tom Harrisson, "The 'Palang,' Its History and Proto-History in West Borneo and the Philippines," *Journal of the Malaysian Branch, Royal Asiatic Society* 37, no. 2 (1964): 162–74; Charles Miller, *Black Borneo* (New York: Modern Age Books, 1942), 150; Raven Rowenchilde, "Male Genital Modification," *Human Nature* 7, no. 2 (1996): 189–215; Friedrich Seltmann, "Palang and Pûjâ: An Analysis of Studies of the Use of Penis-Pins and Related Paraphernalia in Certain Southeast Asian Countries and an Initial Treatment of Their Former Ritualistic Use in Java," *Tribus: Jahrbuch des Linden-Museums* 24 (1975): 67–78; and Herwig Zahorca, "The Palang Phenomenon and Its Historic and Socio-Cultural Background in Southeast Asia," *Tribus: Jahrbuch des Linden-Museums* 53 (2004): 185–202.

3. Francisco Ignacio Alcina, *La Historia de las islas e indios Visayas del Padre Alcina, 1668*, ed. María Luisa Martin-Merás and María Dolores Higueras (Madrid: Instituto Historico de Marina, 1974), f. 13r. All quotations are from this facsimile edition of the MS conserved in the Museo Naval, Madrid.

4. Ralph Fitch, "The Voyage of Master Ralph Fitch Merchant of London to Ormus, and so to Goa in the East India . . . begun in the yeere of our Lord 1583 and ended 1591," in *Purchas his Pilgrimes*, comp. Samuel Purchas (London, 1625), 2: 1741.

5. Jacques de Coutre, "Vida de Iaques de Couttre natural de la ciudad de la Brugas" (1640), published as *Andanzas asiáticas*, ed. Eddy Stols, Benjamin Teensma, and Johan Verberckmoes (Madrid: Historia 16, 1991), 135; Thomas Herbert, *A Relation of Some Yeares Travaile* (London, 1634), 41, 195; John Bulwer, *Anthropometamorphosis* (London, 1653), 348. Chinese sources refer to the same inserts as "Mianling" (meaning "Burmese bell"). See Sun Laichen, "Burmese Bells and Chinese Eroticism: Southeast Asia's Cultural Influence on China," *Journal of Southeast Asian Studies* 38, no. 2 (2007): 247–73.

6. Antonio Pigafetta, *Relazione del primo viaggio attorno al mondo*, ed. Andrea Canova (Padua: Antenore, 1999), 240–41. All quotations are from this edition.

7. Andrea Canova includes the palang among the "wonders" scattered throughout Pigafetta's narrative in "Faraway Countries and Useful Books: Some Remarks on Antonio Pigafetta and Other Travellers in the Pacific at

the Beginning of the Sixteenth Century," *Studies in Travel Writing* 5 (2001): 1–34. The epistemological tensions of Pigafetta's account are briefly but insightfully treated in Joan-Pau Rubiés, "The Spanish Contribution to the Ethnology of Asia in the Sixteenth and Seventeenth Centuries," *Renaissance Studies* 17, no. 3 (2003): 418–48, on 418–19.

8. On the classical distinction between penetrator and penetrated, see David Halperin, *How to Do the History of Homosexuality* (Chicago: University of Chicago Press, 2002), 113–17, and *One Hundred Years of Homosexuality and Other Essays on Greek Love* (New York: Routledge, 1990), 18–36; as well as several of the essays in Judith Hallett and Marilyn Skinner, eds., *Roman Sexualities* (Princeton, NJ: Princeton University Press, 1997). For the persistence of this distinction during the Middle Ages and into the early modern period see Ruth Mazo Karras, *Sexuality in Medieval Europe: Doing onto Others* (New York: Routledge, 2005), 3–5; Mary E. Perry, *Gender and Disorder in Early Modern Seville* (Princeton, NJ: Princeton University Press, 1990), 125; Michael Rocke, "Gender and Sexual Culture in Renaissance Italy," in *Gender and Society in Renaissance Italy*, ed. Judith C. Brown and Robert C. Davis (New York: Longman, 1998), 150–70; and Jonathan Goldberg, *Sodometries: Renaissance Texts, Modern Sexualities* (Stanford, CA: Stanford University Press, 1992), 121.

9. Rhetorics of self-mastery have long been shown to be a crucial component of colonial discourse. See Louis Montrose, "The Work of Gender in the Discourse of Discovery," *Representations* 33 (1991): 1–41.

10. Lorraine Daston and Katharine Park, "The Hermaphrodite and the Orders of Nature," in *Premodern Sexualities*, ed. Louise Fradenburg and Carla Freccero (New York: Routledge, 1996), 126.

11. According to Antonio de Morga, a high-ranking Spanish official who resided in the Philippines between 1595 and 1603, native Visayans were so fond of their piercings "that although they shed much blood, and receive other injuries, they use them commonly." Antonio de Morga, *Sucesos de las Islas Filipinas* (Mexico City, 1609), fol. 145r. All references are to this edition.

12. "An tenido muy especial cuidado los españoles despues que estan entre estas gentes de quitar esta abominable y bestial costumbre y an quitado munchas de ellas a los naturales y castigadoles con açotes porque las traen y con todo esto no aprovecha nada porque las traen y husan muy de hordinario traer el pernete o clavo que entra . . . por el miembro del hombre continuamente puesto en el mismo membro." Boxer Codex, f. 41r–41v; all quotations are from this manuscript. A portion of the text has been transcribed, translated, and annotated by Carlos Quirino and Mauro Garcia in "The Manners, Customs and Beliefs of the Philippine Inhabitants of Long Ago," *Philippines Journal of Science* 87, no. 4 (1958): 324–449.

13. Like the abridged French edition from which they directly or indirectly derive, these publications omit Pigafetta's account of Visayan intercourse but reproduce his description of the palang. The full account is conserved in two of the five manuscript sources that have come down to us. On the circulation of the *Relazione*—the influence of which can be traced in works as diverse

as Antonio de Torquemada's *Jardín de flores curiosas* (1570), Torquato Tasso's *Gerusalemme liberata* (1581), and William Shakespeare's *The Tempest* (1611)—see Antonio Canova, "Esperienza e letteratura nella *Relazione*," in Pigafetta, *Relazione, 62–102.*

14. Pretty's account was included in the second edition of Richard Hakluyt's *Principal Navigations* (1598–1600) and reprinted, in abbreviated form, in Purchas's *Pilgrimes* (1625). See Francis Pretty, "The Admirable and Prosperous Voyage. . . . ," in *The Principal Navigations, Voyages, Traffiques, and Discoveries of the English Nation. . . .*, comp. Richard Hakluyt (London, 1600), 3: 803–25, quotation on 819; and *Purchas his Pilgrimes*, comp. Samuel Purchas 1(bk.2): 57–70, quotation on 67.

15. Gabriel Rebelo, "Informação das cousas do Maluco," in *Documentação para a história das missões do padroado português do Oriente: Insulíndia*, vol. 3, *(1563–1567)*, ed. Artur Basilio de Sá (Lisbon: Divisão de Publicações e Biblioteca, Agência Geral do Ultramar, 1955), 345–508; Gonzalo Fernández de Oviedo y Valdés, *Historia general y natural de las Indias, islas y tierra-firme del Mar Océano*, ed. José Amador de los Rios (Madrid, 1852), 2: 105; and Alcina, *Historia de las islas*, f. 13r.

16. Oviedo y Valdés, *Historia general*, 105; Juan de Medina, *Historia de los sucesos de la Orden de N. Gran P. S. Agustin de estas Islas Filipinas* (Manila, 1893), 59.

17. Morga, *Sucesos de las islas Filipinas*, f. 145r; Alcina, *Historia de las islas*, f. 13r.

18. For this attribution, see Charles R. Boxer, "A Late Sixteenth Century Manila Manuscript," *Journal of the Royal Asiatic Society of Great Britain and Ireland* 87 (1950): 37–49. For an alternative hypothesis, see Quirino and Garcia, "Manners," 337–40.

19. Quirino and Garcia, "Manners," 341.

20. Boxer Codex, f. 41r (my emphasis).

21. Medina, *Historia de los sucesos*, 58–59.

22. John Sadler, *The Sicke Womans Private Looking-Glasse* (London, 1636), 108–9. Sadler's phrasing clearly echoes Ambroise Paré's *Des monstres et prodiges* (Paris, 1573), trans. Janis L. Pallister as *On Monsters and Marvels* (Chicago: University of Chicago Press, 1982), 849. See also Realdo Colombo, *De Re Anatomica Libri XV* (Venice, 1559), 243.

23. The role of female pleasure in reproduction has been extensively studied, most notably by Thomas Laqueur, "Orgasm, Generation, and the Politics of Reproductive Biology," *Representations* 14 (1986): 1–41, and *Making Sex: Body and Gender from the Greeks to Freud* (Cambridge, MA: Harvard University Press, 1990). See also Joan Cadden, *Meanings of Sex Difference in the Middle Ages: Medicine, Science, and Culture* (Cambridge: Cambridge University Press, 1993); and Audrey Eccles, *Obstetrics and Gynaecology in Tudor and Stuart England* (Kent, OH: Kent State University Press, 1982).

24. Cristina Blanc-Szanton, "Collision of Cultures: Historical Reformulations of Gender in the Lowland Visayas, Philippines," in *Power and Difference: Gender in Island Southeast Asia*, ed. Jane Monnig Atkinson and Shelly Errington (Stanford, CA: Stanford University Press, 1990), 345–84.

25. Pigafetta, *Relazione*, 240. James A. Boon makes a related point with regard to Francis Pretty's account, pointing out that the sagra device can be read as an emblem of false kingship. Boon, *Other Tribes, Other Scribes: Symbolic Anthropology in the Comparative Study of Cultures, Histories, Religions, and Texts* (Cambridge: Cambridge University Press, 1982), 167.

26. Peter Brown, *The Body and Society: Men, Women, and Sexual Renunciation in Early Christianity* (New York: Columbia University Press, 2008), 432; and Keith Thomas, *Man and the Natural World: A History of Modern Sensibility* (New York: Pantheon, 1983), 39.

27. Thomas Aquinas, *Summa Theologica*, trans. Fathers of the English Dominican Province (New York: Benzinger, 1947), 2: 1826.

28. Medina, *Historia de los sucesos*, 59. A similar point is made by Juan Martínez, "Relación detallada de los sucesos ocurridos durante el viaje de la nao San Jerónimo," in *Colección de documentos inéditos relativos al descubrimiento, conquista y organización de las antiguas posesiones españolas de Ultramar* (Madrid, 1887), 3: 371–475, on 461.

29. Maximilianus Transylvanus, *De Moluccis insulis....* (Cologne, 1523), sigs. B2v–B3r.

30. According to Pietro Martire d'Anghiera, who interviewed the expedition's survivors, the rape of native women was likely a factor in Humabon's about-face. See *Decadas de Orbe Novo* (Alcalá, 1530), trans. Francis Augustus MacNutt as *De Orbe Novo: The Eight Decades of Peter Martyr D'Anghera* (New York: G. P. Putnam's Sons, 1912), 2: 159.

31. Richard Eden, comp., *The decades of the newe worlde....* (London, 1555), f. 227r; Pretty, "Admirable and Prosperous Voyage," 819.

32. Geraldine Heng, "The Invention of Race in the European Middle Ages II: Locations of Medieval Race," *Literature Compass* 8, no. 5 (2011): 332–50, on 332. See also Denise Kimber Buell, *Why This New Race: Ethnic Reasoning in Early Christianity* (New York: Columbia University Press, 2005).

33. David Nirenberg, "Mass Conversion and Genealogical Mentalities: Jews and Christians in Fifteenth-Century Spain," *Past and Present* 174 (2002): 3–41; Jerome Friedman, "Jewish Conversion, the Spanish Pure Blood Laws and Reformation: A Revisionist View of Racial and Religious Antisemitism," *Sixteenth Century Journal* 18, no. 1 (1987): 3–30; and Kathryn Burns, "Unfixing Race," in *Rereading the Black Legend: The Discourses of Religious and Racial Difference in the Renaissance Empires*, ed. Margaret Greer, Walter D. Mignolo, and Maureen Quilligan (Chicago: University of Chicago Press, 2007), 188–202.

34. The scholarship on the subject is too vast to be adequately summarized. Works that have shaped my thinking include Etienne Balibar, "Is There a 'Neo-Racism'?," in Etienne Balibar and Immanuel Wallerstein, *Race, Nation, Class: Ambiguous Identities* (London: Verso, 1991), 17–28; George Mariscal, "The Role of Spain in Contemporary Race Theory," *Arizona Journal of Hispanic Cultural Studies* 2 (1988): 7–22; Mary Floyd-Wilson, *English Ethnicity and Race in Early Modern Drama* (Cambridge: Cambridge University Press, 2003); Paul Hazard, *The European Mind,*

1680–1715 (Cleveland: Meridian, 1963), esp. 364–65; and Jean Feerick, "'A Nation Now Degenerate': Shakespeare's *Cymbeline*, Nova Britannia, and the Role of Diet and Climate in Reproducing Races," *Early American Studies* 1, no. 2 (2003): 30–70.

35. The passage is discussed in James A. Boon, "'Extravagant Art' and Balinese Ritual," in *Recovering the Orient: Artists, Scholars, Appropriations*, ed. C. Andrew Gerstle and Anthony Crothers Milner (New York: Routledge, 1994), 339–56.

36. Tomé Pires, *The Suma Oriental of Tomé Pires*, trans. and ed. Armando Cortesão (London: Hakluyt Society, 1944), 1: 102–3, 2: 384. All quotations are from this edition.

37. In his preface to the first Italian translation of Conti's travelogue, for instance, Giovan Battista Ramusio wrote: "Having been forced to abjure the Christian faith in order to save his life, after his return [Niccolò de' Conti] went to the Pope to be absolved . . . [and] the latter, after blessing him, gave him as a penance the task of narrating all his travels truthfully." Giovan Battista Ramusio, *Delle navigationi et viaggi* (Venice, 1550), 1: f. 364v. Contemporary scholars reject the story as spurious, noting that there is no reference to Conti's "penance" before the Portuguese edition of 1502. See Anca Crivat-Vasile, "El viaje de Nicolò dei Conti en los relatos de Pero Tafur y Poggio Bracciolini," *Revista de Filología Románica* 13 (1996): 231–52.

38. Until 1492, Conti's relation seems to have circulated primarily as part of Poggio Bracciolini's *De Varietate Fortunae*. See Mario Longhena, "I manoscritti del IV libro del *De Varietate Fortunae* di Poggio Bracciolini," *Bollettino della Società Geografica Italiana* 6, no. 1 (1925): 191–215; and Renata Cusmai Belardinelli, "Discorso sopra il viaggio di Nicolò di Conti veneziano," *Accademie e biblioteche d'Italia* 53 (1985): 155–70.

39. Kennon Breazeale, "Editorial Introduction to Nicolò de' Conti's Account," *SOAS Bulletin of Burma Research* 2, no. 2 (2004): 100–109.

40. Dorothy Figueira, "Civilization and the Problem of Race: Portuguese and Italian Travel Narratives to India," in *Imperialisms: Historical and Literary Investigations, 1500–1900*, ed. Anthony Pagden, Balachandra Rajan, and Elizabeth Sauer (New York: Macmillan, 2004), 75–92; and Richard Trexler, *Sex and Conquest: Gendered Violence, Political Order, and the European Conquest of the Americas* (Ithaca, NY: Cornell University Press, 1995), 61.

41. Niccolò de' Conti and Poggio Bracciolini, *India Recognita* (Milan, 1492), sigs. A5r–A5v. All quotations are from this first print edition.

42. Although circumcision was sometimes linked to sexual desire, I am not aware of works stipulating a libidinous etiology for the practice. On the contrary, circumcision seems to have been envisioned quite consistently as a remedy against lust. See Shaye J. D. Cohen, *Why Aren't Jewish Women Circumcised? Gender and Covenant in Judaism* (Berkeley: University of California Press, 2005), 143–53; and Rogaia Mustafa Abusharaf, *Female Circumcision: Multicultural Perspectives* (Philadelphia: University of Pennsylvania Press, 2006), 62–64.

43. The classical study on the subject is Sander L. Gilman's "Black Bodies, White Bodies: Toward an Iconography of Female Sexuality in Late Nineteenth-Century Art, Medicine, and Literature," *Critical Inquiry* 12, no. 1 (1985): 204–42. See also Gilman's *Difference and Pathology: Stereotypes of Sexuality, Race, and Madness* (Ithaca, NY: Cornell University Press, 1985), 76–108; and Anne Fausto-Sterling, "Gender, Race, and Nation: The Comparative Anatomy of 'Hottentot' Women in Europe, 1815–1817," in *Deviant Bodies: Critical Perspectives on Difference in Science and Popular Culture*, ed. Jennifer Terry and Jacqueline Urla (Bloomington: Indiana University Press, 1995), 19–48.

44. Laichen, "Burmese Bells," 257.

45. Fitch, "Voyage," 1741.

46. Herbert, *Relation of Some Yeares Travaile*, 41.

47. Fitch, "Voyage,"1741.

48. João de Barros, *Ásia de João de Barros: Dos feitos que os portugueses fizeram no descobrimento e conquista dos mares e terras do Oriente*, vol. 3, *Terceira Década*, ed. Hernâni Cidade and Manuel Múrias (Lisbon: Divisão de Publicações e Biblioteca, Agência Geral das Colónias, 1946), 130; all quotations are from this edition. The same story appears, with minor variants, in Camões's *Os Lusíadas* (1572); Torquemada's *Jardín de flores curiosas* (1570); Lope de Vega's *La hermosura de Angélica* (1602) ; Pierre d'Avity's *Les Estats, empires, et principautez du monde* (1613); and Manuel de Faria e Sousa's *Asia portuguesa* (1666–75).

49. The point is made quite explicitly by Luís de Camões who, in *Os Lusíadas* 10.122, defines Peguans and Siamese as "Monstros filhos do feio ajuntamento / De ũa mulher e um cão" (monstrous offspring of the foul union / Of a woman and a dog). Camões, *Os Lusíadas*, ed. Frank Pierce (Oxford: Clarendon Press, 1973), trans. Landeg White as *The Lusíads* (Oxford: Oxford University Press, 1997). There is a large body of recent scholarship on monsters; for representative examples, see Michel Foucault, *Abnormal: Lectures at the Collège de France, 1974–1975* (New York: Picador, 2003); Arnold I. Davidson, "The Horror of Monsters," in *The Emergence of Sexuality: Historical Epistemology and the Formation of Concepts* (Cambridge, MA: Harvard University Press, 2002), 93–124; Lorraine Daston and Katharine Park, *Wonders and the Order of Nature: 1150–1750* (New York: Zone Books, 1998); and Jeffrey J. Cohen, "Monster Culture (Seven Theses)," in *Monster Theory: Reading Culture*, ed. Jeffrey J. Cohen (Minneapolis: University of Minnesota Press, 1996), 3–25.

50. Paré, *Des monstres et prodiges*, 67.

51. Camões, *Os Lusíadas*, 2.7. See also Afonso de Albuquerque, *Cartas de Affonso de Albuquerque, seguidas de documentos que as elucidam*, ed. Raymundo A. de Bulhão Pato and Henrique Lopes de Mendonça, 7 vols. (Lisbon: Academia das Ciências de Lisboa/Imprensa Nacional, 1884–1935); and Charles R. Boxer, *The Portuguese Seaborne Empire, 1415–1825* (London: Hutchinson, 1969), 90. As Timothy Coates observes in *Convicts and Orphans: Forced and State-Sponsored Colonizers in the Portuguese Empire, 1550–1755* (Stanford, CA: Stanford University Press, 2001), Portugal's

experiments with forced colonization were harbingers of a larger European trend: in England, exile overseas was already a punitive alternative by 1615, and grew more common during the course of the seventeenth century (xv–xvii).

52. For details on the legislation concerning the punishment of heretics, counterfeiters, traitors, and sodomites, see Liv. 5 tit. 2, 3, 6, and 12, *Ordenações manuelinas On-line*, http://www1.ci.uc.pt/ihti/proj/manuelinas/.

53. Coates, *Convicts and Orphans*, 24–27. The same seems to have occurred in other parts of Europe; after 1539, for instance, men convicted of sodomy in Venice were punished by galley service or a prison sentence rather than by death as the law would require. Nicholas Davidson, "Theology, Nature and the Law: Sexual Sin and Sexual Crime in Italy from the Fourteenth to the Seventeenth Century," in *Crime, Society and the Law in Renaissance Italy*, ed. Trevor Dean and K. J. P. Lowe (Cambridge: Cambridge University Press, 1994), 74–98.

54. Jan Huygen van Linschoten, *Itinerario.* . . . (Amsterdam, 1596), trans. William Phillip as *The Voyage of John Huyghen Van Linschoten to the East Indies.* . . . , ed. Arthur Coke Burnell and Pieter Anton Tiele (London, 1885), 1: 100. All references are to this edition.

55. Fitch, "Voyage," 1741.

56. Herbert, *Relation of Some Yeares Travaile*, 195. This myth of origin is ubiquitous in early modern writing, being featured in the "Tratado de las yslas de los Malucos" as well as in Barros's *Décadas da Ásia*, Camões's *Os Lusíadas*, Gasparo Balbi's *Viaggio dell'Indie orientali*, Francesco Carletti's *Ragionamenti del mio viaggio attorno al mondo*; and Faria e Sousa's *Asia portuguesa*.

57. Michel Foucault, *Society Must Be Defended* (New York: Picador, 2003), esp. 241; see also Michel Foucault, *The History of Sexuality*, vol. 1, *An Introduction* (New York: Vintage, 1990), 36–49.

58. John Bulwer, *Anthropometamorphosis.* . . . (London, 1650), 198.

59. Pretty, "Admirable and Prosperous Voyage," 819.

60. Alcina, *Historia de las islas*, f. 13r.

61. Herbert, *Relation of Some Yeares Travaile*, 195.

62. Gasparo Balbi, *Viaggio dell'Indie Orientali* (Venice, 1590), f. 126v; see also Herbert, *Relation of Some Yeares Travaile*, 195.

63. Conti and Bracciolini, *India Recognita*, sig. B1r.

64. "Tratado de las yslas Malucas," trans. and ed. Hubert M. Jacobs as *A Treatise on the Moluccas (c. 1544): Probably the Preliminary Version of António Galvão's Lost* História das Molucas (Rome: IHSI, 1970), 118–19.

65. The dubious claim is discussed in John L. Phelan, *The Hispanization of the Philippines: Spanish Aims and Filipino Responses, 1565–1700* (Madison: University of Wisconsin Press, 1959), 186–87.

66. Linschoten, *Itinerario*, 1: 100.

67. Ernst van den Boogaart, *Civil and Corrupt Asia: Image and Text in the* Itinerario *and the* Icones *of Jan Huygen van Linschoten* (Chicago: University of Chicago Press, 2003), 12.

68. Foucault, *History of Sexuality*, 1: 43.

69. Charles R. Boxer, ed., *A True Description of the Mighty Kingdoms of Japan and Siam by François Caron and Joost Schouten* (London: Argonaut Press, 1935), 139–43. In consideration of the services he had rendered during the course of his career, Schouten was strangled before being burned. Schoten's partners were "smothered under water since they were unworthy to continue living among humans—which is a fitting recompense and retribution for their gruesome life on earth." Qtd. in Barend Jan Terwiel, "The Body and Sexuality in Siam: A First Exploration in Early Sources," *Manusya: Journal of Humanities* 14 (2007): 42–52.

70. Richard Head, *The English Rogue: Described, In the Life of Meriton Latroon, a Witty Extravagant. . . .* (London, 1665), sig. Ggg3r. Unless otherwise noted, all quotations are from this erratically paginated edition. Signature references have been provided in lieu of page numbers.

71. Herbert, *Relation of Some Yeares Travaile*, 197.

72. Richard Head, *The English Rogue. Described, In the Life of Meriton Latroon, a Witty Extravagant. . . .* (London, 1668), 131.

73. Pigafetta, *Relazione*, 241.

74. Morga, *Sucesos*, f. 145r.

75. Brewer, *Shamanism*, 29.

76. Balbi, *Viaggio dell'Indie Orientali*, f. 126v; and Herbert, *Relation of Some Yeares Travaile*, 195–96. The claim is repeated in Bulwer's *Anthropometamorphosis* (1653), 393–94.

77. Francesco Carletti, *Ragionamenti del mio viaggio attorno al mondo*, ed. Paolo Collo (Torino: Giulio Einaudi Editore, 1989), 137. Carletti's claim is contradicted by a fifteenth-century Chinese source, according to which it was men rather than women who specialized in the soldering of these inserts. Ma Huan, *Ying-Yai Sheng-Lan: The Overall Survey of the Ocean's Shores*, trans. J. V. G. Mills (Cambridge: Hakluyt Society, 1970), 104.

78. James Shapiro advances a similar hypothesis to account for the popularity of early modern narratives featuring the conversion and assimilation of Jewish women to Christian values and mores. "It was also clear to Christian theologians that for the Jews who literally circumcised the flesh, the Covenant could only be transmitted through men," Shapiro writes in *Shakespeare and the Jews* (New York: Columbia University Press, 1996). "This helps explain why Jewish daughters like Jessica in *The Merchant of Venice* and Abigail in *The Jew of Malta* can so easily cross the religious boundaries that divide their stigmatized fathers from the dominant Christian community" (120).

79. Elizabeth Kuznesof, "Ethnic and Gender Influences on 'Spanish' Creole Society," *Colonial Latin American Review* 4, no. 1 (1995): 153–76.

CHAPTER 2

1. António Baião, Artur de Magalhães Basto, and Damião Peres, eds., *Diário da viagem de Vasco da Gama* (Porto: Livraria Civilização, 1945), 1: 110; and Felipe Fernández-Armesto, "Times and Tides," *History Today* 47, no. 12 (1997): 9–11, on 8.

2. "Senhor da conquista, navegação e comércio da Ethiopia, Arabia, Persia, e India." João de Barros, *Ásia de João de Barros: Dos feitos que os portugueses fizeram no descobrimento e conquista dos mares e terras do Oriente*, vol. 1, *Primeira Década*, ed. Hernâni Cidade and Manuel Múrias (Lisbon: Divisão de Publicações e Biblioteca, Agência Geral das Colónias, 1945), 164; Michael N. Pearson, *The Portuguese in India* (Cambridge: Cambridge University Press, 1987), 30–32.

3. "A melhor parte . . . de tantas regiões e províncias ficou pera nós, e nós lhe levámos a virgindade." Duarte Pacheco Pereira, *Esmeraldo de Situ Orbis*, ed. Damião Peres (Lisbon: Academia portuguesa da história, 1954), 167. Although presumably complete by 1508, the *Esmeraldo de Situ Orbis* was ignored for centuries, being first published only in 1892. See Joaquim Barradas de Carvalho, *A la recherche de la spécificité de la Renaissance portugaise: L' "Esmeraldo de Situ Orbis" de Duarte Pacheco Pereira et la littérature portugaise de voyages à l'époque des grandes découvertes*, 2 vols. (Paris: Fundação Calouste Gulbenkian, 1983); as well as George H. T. Kimble, introduction to *Esmeraldo de Situ Orbis*, by Duarte Pacheco Pereira, trans. and ed. George H. T. Kimble (London: Hakluyt Society, 1937), xi–xxxii.

4. The "Piscos" edition, which was published only a few years after Camões's death, excised many of the passages considered in this chapter, including most of the hunting scene (9.71–73), much of Lionardo's plea to Ephyre (9.78), and the entire episode's climax (9.83). A useful list of variants is provided in A. J. Gonçálvez Guimarãis, "Variantes da segunda edição d'*Os Lusíadas* (1584)," in *Os Lusíadas de Luis de Camões*, ed. A. J. Gonçálvez Guimarãis (Coimbra: Universidade, 1919), 375–85. After the sixteenth century, outright censorship was replaced by critical commentary. In response to Voltaire's criticism, for instance, William Mickle buried the Isle of Love under a thick layer of whitewash. "Though the nymphs in Camões are detected naked," he wrote in a gloss to his translation, "still their behavior is that of the virgin who hopes to be the spouse. They act the part of offended modesty; even when they yield they are silent, and behave in every respect like Milton's Eve in the state of innocence." William J. Mickle, trans., *The Lusiad; or, The Discovery of India: An Epic Poem Translated from the Portuguese of Luis de Camoëns* (London, 1877), 280–81.

5. Portuguese quotations are from Luís Vaz de Camões, *Os Lusíadas*, ed. Frank Pierce (Oxford: Clarendon Press, 1973), and identified in the text by canto and stanza. English quotations are from Landeg White's award-winning translation, *The Lusíads*, by Luís Vaz de Camões (Oxford: Oxford University Press, 1997), although I have occasionally made minor changes to drive a point home. White's critical notations are from the same volume.

6. On *Os Lusíadas* and High Renaissance painting, see Américo da Costa Ramalho, *Estudos Camonianos* (Lisbon: Instituto Nacional de Investigação Científica, 1980), 58.

7. On Actæon as a victim of sexual violence, see Ann Olga Koloski-Ostrow, "Violent Stages in Two Pompeian Houses: Imperial Taste, Aristocratic Response, and Messages of Male Control," in *Naked Truths: Women,*

Sexuality, and Gender in Classical Art and Archaeology, ed. Olga Koloski-Ostrow and Claire L. Lyons (New York: Routledge, 1997), 256–57.

8. Anna Klobucka, "Lusotropical Romance: Camões, Gilberto Freyre, and the Isle of Love," *Portuguese Literary and Cultural Studies* 9 (2002): 121–38, on 128–29.

9. A useful discussion of Camões's historical sources can be found in Rebecca Catz, "Camões and the Writers of the Discoveries," in *Camoniana Californiana,* ed. Maria de Lourdes Belchior and Enrique Martínez-López (Santa Barbara, CA: Jorge de Sena Center for Portuguese Studies, 1985), 147–53.

10. Robert M. Torrance, "Se fantasticas são, se verdadeiras: The Gods of the *Lusiads* in the Isle of Love," *Modern Language Notes* 80, no. 2 (1965): 210–34, on 210–11. To be sure, stanza 9.89 instructs us to read the painted island as an allegory of the fame won by the Portuguese. Yet the censors of the Piscos edition found the explanation unconvincing, and many critics have echoed their sentiments. See A. Bartlett Giamatti, *The Earthly Paradise and the Renaissance Epic* (Princeton, NJ: Princeton University Press, 1996), 224; Joaquim Nabuco, *Camões: Discurso pronunciado a 10 de Junho de 1880* (Rio de Janeiro: Biblioteca Nacional, 1980), 19; and Frank Pierce, "The Place of Mythology in the *Lusiads,*" *Comparative Literature* 6 (1954): 97–122.

11. Voltaire, "Essai sur la poésie épique," *Oeuvres complètes de Voltaire* (Paris, 1828), 13: 429–533, on 484; and Cecil Maurice Bowra, *From Virgil to Milton* (London: Macmillan, 1948), 130.

12. Vítor Manuel de Aguiar e Silva, *Camões: Labirintos e Fascínios* (Lisbon: Cotovia, 1994), 133.

13. Landeg White, explanatory notes to Camões, *The Lusíads,* 251–52.

14. Helder Macedo, *Camões e a viagem iniciática* (Lisbon: Moraes, 1980), 3.

15. David Quint, *Epic and Empire: Politics and Generic Form from Virgil to Milton* (Princeton, NJ: Princeton University Press, 1993), 119. Jonathan Crewe makes a similar point in "Recalling Adamastor: Literature as Cultural Memory in 'White' South Africa," in *Acts of Memory: Cultural Recall in the Present,* ed. Mieke Bal, Jonathan V. Crewe, and Leo Spitzer (Hanover, NH: University Press of New England, 1999), 75–86, on 81.

16. Quint, *Epic and Empire,* 119.

17. René P. Garay, "Camões, Luíz Vaz de. . . . ," in *Literature of Travel and Exploration: An Encyclopedia,* ed Jennifer Sparke (New York: Routledge, 2003), 1: 177. For a critique of readings that reduce sexual relations to a a mere trope, see Ann Laura Stoler, *Carnal Knowledge and Imperial Power: Race and the Intimate in Colonial Rule* (Berkeley: University of California Press, 2002), esp. 43–46.

18. Stoler, *Carnal Knowledge and Imperial Power,* 47. Among the many empirical studies that support Stoler's claims are Kenneth Ballhatchet, *Race, Sex, and Class Under the Raj: Imperial Attitudes and Policies and Their Critics, 1793–1905* (New York: St. Martin's Press, 1980); Kirsten Fischer, *Suspect Relations: Sex, Race, and Resistance in Colonial North Carolina*

(Ithaca, NY: Cornell University Press, 2002); and Durba Ghosh, *Sex and the Family in Colonial India* (Cambridge: Cambridge University Press, 2006).

19. Ann Laura Stoler, "Rethinking Colonial Categories: European Communities and the Boundaries of Rule," *Comparative Studies in Society and History* 31, no. 1 (1989): 134–61, quotation on 138.

20. For an example, see the case of Ortiga and King Ramiro in José Mattoso, ed., *Narrativas dos livros de linhagens* (Lisbon: Imprensa Nacional, 1983), 49–61.

21. The legend is retold in Bernardo de Brito's *Primeyra parte da Chronica de Cister. . . .* (Lisbon, 1602), ff. 369v–371v.

22. Robert Harder, "The Element of Love in the Chansons de Geste," *Annuale Mediaevale* 5 (1963): 65–80; see also Dorothee Metlitzki, *The Matter of Araby in Medieval England* (New Haven, CT: Yale University Press, 1977); Louise O. Vasvári, *The Heterotextual Body of the Mora Morilla* (London: Queen Mary and Westfield College, 1999); and F. M. Warren, "The Enamoured Moslem Princess in Orderic Vital and the French Epic," *PMLA* 29, no. 3 (1914): 341–58.

23. "Aqy se tomárão allgũas mouras, molheres alvas e de bom parecer, e alguuns homens limpos e de bem quiseram casar com ellas e fiqar aquy nesta terraa, e me pediram fazemda, e eu os casei com elas e lhe dei o casamento ordenado de vosa alteza, e a cada hum seu cavalo e casas e terras e gado." Afonso de Albuquerque to King Manuel, 22 Dec. 1510, in Afonso de Albuquerque, *Cartas de Affonso de Albuquerque, seguidas de documentos que as elucidam*, vol. 1, ed. Raymundo A. de Bulhão Pato (Lisbon: Academia das Ciências de Lisboa, 1884), 27.

24. Albuquerque, *Cartas. . . .* , vol. 5, ed. Raymundo A. de Bulhão Pato and Henrique Lopes de Mendonça (Lisbon: Imprensa Nacional, 1915), 9–172.

25. "Ho feito dos casados vay muyto avamte . . . averá em cananor e cochim cem casados, e em goa perto de duzentos. . . . Se pela vemtura a jemte casar desta maneira, parece me que será necessareo mandar voss alteza botar fora os naturaees da ilha e dar as terras e lavoyras aos casados." Albuquerque to King Manuel, 1 Apr. 1512, in Albuquerque, *Cartas*, 1: 63.

26. "A imcrinaçam da jemte e desejos de casar em goa, se ho voss alteza vise bem, espamtar s ya; e parece cousa de deus desejarem os portugueses tamto de casar e viver em Goa. . . . [A] mim me parece que noso senhor ordena isto e imcrina os coraçõees dos homeens por algũa cousa de muyto seu serviço escomdida a nós." Albuquerque to King Manuel, 1 Apr. 1512, 56–57.

27. António da Silva Rêgo, *Portuguese Colonization in the Sixteenth Century: A Study of the Royal Ordinances* (Johannesburg: Witwaresrand University Press, 1965), 55.

28. Around the mid-sixteenth century, shipments of marriageable orphan girls began injecting Portugal's outposts in Asia with small doses of "white" blood. Even so, sex ratios remained grossly uneven—as Charles Boxer has noted, there would rarely be more than a few immigrant women aboard a vessel that could carry over a thousand men—and racial mixing more the rule than the exception. Charles R. Boxer, *Women in Iberian Expansion*

Overseas, 1415–1815 (Cambridge: Cambridge University Press, 1975), 66–67; see also Timothy J. Coates, *Convicts and Orphans: Forced and State-Sponsored Colonizers in the Portuguese Empire, 1550–1755* (Stanford, CA: Stanford University Press, 2001); and Dejanirah Couto, "Alguns dados para um estudo ulterior sobre a 'sociedade espontânea' no *Estado da Índia* na primeira metade do séc. XVI," in *Metahistory: History Questioning History*, ed. Teotónio R. de Souza, Charles J. Borges, and Michael N. Pearson (Lisbon: Nova Vega, 2007), 283–301.

29. For a discussion of early modern reproductive theories, see Valeria Finucci, "Maternal Imagination and Monstrous Birth: Tasso's *Gerusalemme Liberata*," in *Generation and Degeneration: Tropes of Reproduction in Literature and History from Antiquity Through Early Modern Europe*, ed. Valeria Finucci and Kevin Brownlee (Durham, NC: Duke University Press, 2001), 41–77; and Ian Maclean, *The Renaissance Notion of Woman* (Cambridge: Cambridge University Press, 1980).

30. "Los nacidos en la India son de quatro suertes o naturales de la tierra, o mestiços que son hijos de portugueses y de natural, o castiços que son hijos de Portugueses y mestiça, o portugueses porque nacieron de padre y madre portugueses." Alessandro Valignano, "Sumario de las cosas que perteneçen a la provincia de la Yndia Oriental. . . . ," in *Documentação para a história das missões do padroado português do Oriente: Índia*, vol 12, *1572–1582*, ed. António da Silva Rêgo (Lisbon: Divisão de Publicações e Biblioteca, Agência Geral do Ultramar, 1958), 577.

31. The idea that it took three generations for European-Indian families to return to "pure" European status was also common in Spanish America, despite the formation of a much more elaborate caste system. Ilona Katzew, *Casta Painting: Images of Race in Eighteenth-Century Mexico* (New Haven, CT: Yale University Press, 2005), 49.

32. On this subject, although in a different geographical and historical context, see John Comaroff and Jean L. Comaroff, "Home-Made Hegemony: Modernity, Domesticity, and Colonialism in South Africa," in *African Encounters with Domesticity*, ed. Karen T. Hansen (New Brunswick, NJ: Rutgers University Press, 1992), 37–74.

33. "Todo foi povoado de mais baixos princípios, e de gente a que podemos chamar enxurro de homens. Ca se êles olharam aos princípios de Roma . . . monarca do Império Romano . . . acharam que foi um consórcio de gente pastoril, ou (per melhor dizer) ũa acolheita de malfeitores; e que as moças sabinas, que êles teveram pera ter por mulheres, se eram mais alvas por razão do clima, não seriam de mais nobre sangue, que as canaris, nem tinham mais conhecimento de Deus . . . nem em os seus esposórios concorreram duas tenções em um vínculo de consentimento, como quere o auto matrimonial: sòmente um ímpeto de fôrça, cujo fim foi um comum estrupo." Barros, *Ásia de João de Barros. . . .* , vol. 2, *Segunda Década*, ed. Hernâni Cidade and Manuel Múrias (Lisbon: Divisão de Publicações e Biblioteca, Agência Geral das Colónias, 1946), 243–44. The term "Canarins" was used by the Portuguese to designate the people of Goa and more generally native Indians. See Rafael Bluteau, *Vocabulario Portuguez e Latino* (Coimbra,

1712), 2: 93; and Charles R. Boxer, *Race Relations in the Portuguese Colonial Empire, 1415–1825* (Oxford: Clarendon Press, 1963), 79.

34. José Filgueira Valverde, *Camões: Comemoração do Centenário de Os Lusíadas* (Coimbra: Almedina, 1981), 290; da Costa Ramalho, *Estudos Camonianos*, 58. Scholars have identified a whole spectrum of literary sources for the Isle of Love episode. Chief among them are the *Odyssey* (the Gardens of Alcinoo) and the *Aeneid* (boob 6); Cicero's *Somnium Scipionis*; Apollonis of Rodhe's *Argonautica*; Petrarch's *Triumphs* (the garden of Venus); Poliziano's *Stanze* (the kingdom of Venus); and Ariosto's *Orlando Furioso*. See Aguiar e Silva, *Camões*, 84–85.

35. On heroic rape, see Susan Brownmiller, *Against Our Will: Men, Women and Rape* (New York: Simon and Schuster, 1975), 313–42; Diane Wolfthal, *Images of Rape: The "Heroic Tradition" and Its Alternatives* (Cambridge: Cambridge University Press, 1999); and Margaret D. Carroll, "The Erotics of Absolutism: Rubens and the Mystification of Sexual Violence," in *The Expanding Discourse: Feminism and Art History*, ed. Norma Broude and Mary D. Garrard (New York: HarperCollins, 1992), 139–59.

36. Camões's conjoined reference to Byblis and Myrrha (9.34), for instance, distinctly echoes *The Art of Love* 1: 283–85; 9.34, 9.61, and 9.83 have been traced to *The Art of Love* 2: 561, 1: 729, and 2: 724, respectively. See Leonard Bacon, trans. and ed., *The Lusiads of Camões* (New York: Hispanic Society of America, 1950), 342, 344, 345.

37. Mary Beard, "The Erotics of Rape: Livy, Ovid and the Sabine Women," in *Female Network and the Public Sphere in Roman Society*, ed. Päivi Setälä and Liisa Savunen (Rome: Institutum Romanum Finlandiae, 1999), 1–10. As historians have pointed out, the classical concept of *raptus* involved abduction rather than sexual violence—and should therefore be kept apart from rape. The distinction is moot in the Sabines' case, since sexual violence accompanied the abduction.

38. Livy, *Ab Urbe Condita* 1.9. Building on Livy, Plutarch read the rape as a diplomatic event born not out of "wantonness," but rather of the desire to unite Romans and Sabines "in the strongest bonds." See Mestrius Plutarchus, *Plutarch: Lives*, vol. 1, *Theseus and Romulus, Lycurgus and Numa, Solon and Publicola*, trans. Bernadotte Perrin (Cambridge, MA: Harvard University Press, 1914), 131.

39. "Romule, militibus scisti dare commoda solus / Haec mihi si dederis commoda, miles ero." Publius Ovidius Naso, *Ovid in Six Volumes*, vol. 2, *The Art of Love, and Other Poems*, trans. John H. Mozley, ed. George P. Goold (Cambridge, MA: Harvard University Press, 1979), 20, 21.

40. I borrow the term *libido dominandi* from Leslie Cahoon, "The Bed as Battlefield: Erotic Conquest and Military Metaphor in Ovid's *Amores*," *Transactions of the American Philological Association* 118 (1988): 293–307.

41. In BDSM, "power exchange" refers to a relationship or activity in which the submissive partner exchanges his or her authority to make decisions for the dominant partner's agreement to take responsibility for the submissive partner's well-being.

42. Richard Helgerson, *Forms of Nationhood: The Elizabethan Writing of England* (Chicago: University of Chicago Press, 1992), 155–56.

43. Helder Macedo, "*The Lusiads*: Epic Celebration and Pastoral Regret," *Portuguese Studies* 6 (1990): 32–37.

44. Valerie Traub, *The Renaissance of Lesbianism in Early Modern England* (Cambridge: Cambridge University Press, 2002), 265.

45. "Esta voz, *nefando* en tal ocasion suena sin duda más de lo que yo pienso quiere el Poeta dezir en ella: i tambien se puede pensar que lo dize." Manuel de Faria y Sousa, *Lusiadas de Luis de Camoens, principe de los poetas de España. . . . Comentadas por Manuel de Faria i Sousa, Cavallero de la Orden de Christo, i de la Casa Real* (Madrid, 1639), 4: 81. In legal parlance, *nefando* stood for sodomy. Inquisitorial registers of sodomy cases, for instance, were known as "Repertórios do nefando." For the pervasiveness of the nefando in the Inquisitorial record of Portugal, see Luiz Mott, *O sexo proibido: Virgens, gays e escravos nas garras da Inquisição* (Campina: Papirus, 1988), and "Justitia et misericordia: A Inquisição portuguesa e a repressão ao nefando pecado de sodomia," in *Inquisição: Ensaios sobre mentalidade, heresias e arte,* ed. Anita Novinsky and Maria Luiza Tucci Carneiro (São Paulo: EDUSP, 1992), 703–38; as well as some of the essays in Pete Sigal, ed., *Infamous Desire: Male Homosexuality in Colonial Latin America* (Chicago: University of Chicago Press, 2003).

46. Klobucka, "Lusotropical Romance," 133.

47. Thomas Biolsi, "Race Technologies," in *A Companion to the Anthropology of Politics*, ed. David Nugent and Joan Vincent (Oxford: Blackwell, 2004); and Stoler, *Carnal Knowledge and Imperial Power*, 79–111.

48. "[Afonso de Albuquerque] esperava em Deus de arrincar as cepas da má casta que havia naquela cidade, que eram os mouros, e plantar cepas católicas, que frutificassem em louvor de Deus, dando povo que por seu nome com prègação e armas conquistassem todo aquêle Oriente.

Ao que deziam êstes mofadores entre si que aquêle seu bacelo era de vidonho labrusco em ser mistiço, principalmente por ser da mais baixa planta do reino, que seria para êle parreiras de ante a porta, que o primeiro asno de trabalho que viesse àquela cidade lhas havia de roer: porque de gente tam vil como era aquela, que aceitava casar per aquêle modo, não se podia esperar fruito que tivesse honra, nem as calidades pera aquelas grandes esperanças de Afonso de Albuquerque." Barros, *Ásia de João de Barros*, vol. 2, *Segunda Década*, 243.

49. Qtd. in Boxer, *Race Relations*, 67.

50. Barros, *Ásia de João de Barros*, vol. 2, *Segunda Década*, 243. For the original Portuguese, see note 48 above.

51. "Eu nunqua tive devaçam de casar homens com estas molheres malavares, porque sam negras e mulheres currutas em seu viver per seus custumes; e as molheres que foram mouras, sam alvas e castas e Retraydas em suas casas e no modo de seu viver . . . e as molheres de bramenes e filhas delles tambem sam castas molheres e de bom viver, e sam alvas e de boma presemça; asy, senhor, em quallquer parte homde se tomava molher bramqua, nom se vendia, nem se Resgatava, todas se davam a homens de beem que

quyryam casar com elas." Albuquerque to King Manuel, 4 Nov. 1514, in Albuquerque, *Cartas*, 1: 338. See also Boxer, *Race Relations*, 64–65.

52. Sanjay Subrahmanyam, *The Portuguese Empire in Asia, 1500–1700: A Political and Economic History* (New York: Longman, 1993), 220; see also Fátima da Silva Gracias, *Kaleidoscope of Women in Goa, 1510–1961* (New Delhi: Concept, 1996), 33.

53. "Os casados que se ca casam, nam crea Vossa Alteza que sam os que vos desejaes . . . tegora, nam casou ca nemgem, senam homens vys e velhacos, que casam com suas escravas cativas, por averem casamentos e gozarem dos pryvilegios e omrra que lhes faz; e outros, desesperados de os nam quererem leyxar hyr pera portugall ou de se verem mall tratados, por isso casam, e dahy a dous dias, fogem pera os mouros, deles com as molheres e deles sem ellas, ou elas sem eles, com quamto tem." António Real to King Manuel, 12 Dec. 1512, in Albuquerque, *Cartas. . .* , vol. 3, ed. Raymundo A. de Bulhão Pato (Lisbon: Academia das Ciências de Lisboa, 1903), 351.

54. Silva Rêgo, *Portuguese Colonization*, 39.

55. Real to King Manuel, 12 Dec. 1512, 3: 351. On the complexities of apostasy during the first half of the sixteenth century, see Dejanirah Couto, "Some Observations on Portuguese Renegades in Asia in the Sixteenth Century," in *Vasco da Gama and the Linking of Europe and Asia*, ed. Anthony Disney and Emily Booth (New Delhi: Oxford University Press, 2001), 178–201.

56. "Sómente algūuas vehuvas que tinham arrezoada fazemda e casamento, dey lugar que casasem, sem lhe ser dado da vosa fazemda cousa algūua, por nam amdarem ao huso dos homeens, e por darmos aos imigos boom emxempro de nós e de nosas vidas e costumis." Albuquerque to King Manuel, 25 Oct. 1514, in Albuquerque, *Cartas*, 1: 298. On the popularity of intermarriage among seventeenth-century immigrants, see Fernão de Albuquerque's letter of 1621 in António da Silva Rêgo, ed., *Documentos remettidos da Índia; ou, Livros das Monções* (Lisbon: Imprensa Nacional, 1975), 7: 150–51.

57. Ann Laura Stoler, *Race and the Education of Desire: Foucault's History of Sexuality and the Colonial Order of Things* (Durham, NC: Duke University Press, 1995), 114.

58. Barros, *Ásia de João de Barros*, vol. 2, *Segunda Década*, 221. According to Fernão Lopes de Castanheda, Albuquerque intended to send these captives to Portugal, as a gift to the queen. Castanheda, *História do descobrimento e conquista da Índia pelos Portugueses* (Lisbon, 1833), 3: 94. Following Henry Morse Stephens, William Freitas postulates that suspicions of treason might have been at the root of the execution. See Freitas, *Camoes and His Epic: A Historic, Geographic and Cultural Survey* (Stanford, CA: Institute of Hispanic and Luso-Brazilian Studies, 1963), 72; as well as Stephens, *Albuquerque* (London, 1897), 81.

59. Brás de Albuquerque, *The Commentaries of the Great Afonso Dalbuquerque. . . .* , trans. and ed. Walter De Gray Birch (London, 1878), 2: 188.

CHAPTER 3

1. Jan Huygen van Linschoten, *Itinerario*. . . . (Amsterdam, 1596), trans. William Phillip as *The Voyage of John Huyghen van Linschoten to the East Indies*. . . . , ed. Arthur Coke Burnell and Pieter Anton Tiele (London, 1885), 1: 1. All quotations are from this edition, which reproduces the 1598 English translation of the Dutch original. Square brackets indicate English additions that have no equivalent in Dutch.

2. Pieter Anton Tiele, introduction to *Voyage of Linschoten*, 1: xl. Although not always included in the reprints and translations issued after 1596, the *Itinerario*'s engravings circulated just as widely as the text. Their popularity and influence can be inferred not only from Johann Theodor and Johann Israel de Bry's India *Oriental Series*—which is heavily indebted to the *Itinerario* copper plates—but also from the many borrowings and recyclings that took place in the following centuries. See Ernst van den Boogaart, ed., *Jan Huygen van Linschoten and the Moral Map of Asia: The Plates and Text of the* Itinerario *and* Icones, *habitus gestusque indorum ac lusitanorum per Indiam viventium* (London: Roxburghe Club, 1999), 11; and Donald Lach, *Asia in the Making of Europe*, vol. 2, *A Century of Wonder* (Chicago: University of Chicago Press, 1970), bk. 1: 94.

3. Qtd. in Charles McKew Parr, *Jan van Linschoten: The Dutch Marco Polo* (New York: Thomas Y. Crowell, 1964), xxvi.

4. Karel Steenbrink, *Dutch Colonialism and Indonesian Islam: Contacts and Conflicts, 1596–1950* (Amsterdam: Rodopi, 1993), 25.

5. The notion of an actual "decadência" has been largely dismantled in recent times. According to James Boyajian and Sanjay Subrahmanyam, for instance, the only thing that declined during the alleged decadência was the Crown's role as a trader, in part because of a policy shift toward territorial adventurism in the second half of the sixteenth century. The shift accelerated after 1580, as the Habsburg Crown hatched ambitious plans for the subjugation of Malaya, Siam, Cambodia, Vietnam, and China. See James C. Boyajian, *Portuguese Trade in Asia Under the Habsburgs, 1580–1640* (Baltimore: Johns Hopkins University Press, 1993); Sanjay Subrahmanyam, *The Portuguese Empire in Asia, 1500–1700: A Political and Economic History* (New York: Longman, 1993), 107–43; and Charles R. Boxer, "Portuguese and Spanish Projects for the Conquest of Southeast Asia, 1580–1600," in *Portuguese Conquest and Commerce in Southern Asia 1500–1750* (London: Variorum, 1985), 118–36.

6. Filippo Sassetti, *Lettere dall'India, 1583–1588*, ed. Adele Dei (Rome: Salerno Editrice, 1995), 78.

7. Diogo do Couto, *O Soldado Prático*, ed. Manuel Rodrigues Lapa (Lisbon: Livraria Sá da Costa, 1937), 115, 150.

8. George D. Winius, "The Portuguese Asian 'Decadência' Revisited," in *Empire in Transition: The Portuguese World in the Time of Camões*, ed. Alfred Hower and Richard A. Preto-Rodas (Gainesville: University of Florida

Press, 1985), 112–13, and *The Black Legend of Portuguese India: Diogo do Couto, His Contemporaries and the 'Soldado Prático'* (New Delhi: Concept, 1985).

9. Couto's *Soldado Prático* did not appear in print until 1790, and Silveira's *Reformação* was published for the first time in 1996. As for Sassetti, the earliest (and partial) edition of its letters dates to 1743; the complete corpus was published only in 1970.

10. Tiele, introduction to *Voyage of Linschoten*, 1: xl.

11. Ivo Kamps, "Colonizing the Colonizer: A Dutchman in Asia Portuguesa," in *Travel Knowledge: European "Discoveries" in the Early Modern Period*, ed. Ivo Kamps and Jyotsna C. Singh (New York: Palgrave, 2001), 163. Although my overall argument differs from Kamps's, I am greatly indebted to his work throughout this chapter.

12. Philip S. Gorski, "The Protestant Ethic Revisited: Disciplinary Revolution and State Formation in Holland and Prussia," *American Journal of Sociology* 99.2 (1993): 265–316, on 276–77.

13. Parr, *Jan van Linschoten*, 188, 34.

14. By portraying Antony like an Oriental despot dominated by his Egyptian queen, Octavian turned the civil war into a confrontation between East and West. See Mary Hamer, *Signs of Cleopatra: History, Politics, Representation* (New York: Routledge, 1993), 36.

15. Grant Parker, "*Ex Oriente Luxuria*: Indian Commodities and Roman Experience," *Journal of Economic and Social History of the Orient* 45, no.1 (2002): 40–95.

16. Giovanni Pietro Maffei, *Historiarum Indicarum libri XVI* (Florence, 1588), trans. Francesco Serdonati as *Le istorie delle Indie orientali* (Bergamo: Pietro Lancellotti, 1749), 1: 361.

17. Francesco Carletti, *Ragionamenti del mio viaggio intorno al mondo*, ed. Paolo Collo (Torino: Giulio Einaudi Editore, 1989), 181–82. All quotations are from this edition.

18. Henry Yule, *Hobson-Jobson: A Glossary of Colloquial Anglo-Indian Words and Phrases, and of Kindred Terms, Etymological, Historical, Geographical and Discursive*, ed. William Crooke (Delhi: Munshiram Manoharlal, 1968), 659.

19. Joaquim Heliodoro da Cunha Rivara, ed., *Archivo Portuguez-Oriental* (Nova-Goa, 1861), fasc. 3: 324–25.

20. Rivara, *Archivo Portuguez-Oriental* (1862), fasc. 4: 273. This edict likely remained unimplemented: the citizenry of Goa found the idea that "palanquins should travel in such a fashion that it could be seen who was in them" utterly odious, and begged the king "to make no new rule." See Rivara, *Archivo Portuguez-Oriental* (1876), fasc. 1, pt. 2: 186. On the perceived dangers of covered palanquins, see Raymundo A. Bulhão Pato, ed., *Documentos remettidos da Índia; ou, Livros das Monções* (Lisbon, 1880), 1: 156.

21. Pietro della Valle, *Viaggi di Pietro della Valle il pellegrino* (Rome, 1650), trans. George Havers as *The Travels of Pietro della Valle in India:*

From the Old English Translation of 1664, ed. Edward Grey (London, 1892), 1: 31, my emphasis.

22. In the attempt to make distinctions between groups immediately visible, the 1567 Council of Goa promulgated sumptuary laws prohibiting "Moors" from dressing as Christians. See Rivara, *Archivo Portuguez-Oriental*, fasc. 4: 29–30.

23. I have deliberately adopted the obsolete "mean" as a way of rendering the clandestine implications of the Italian "mezzano" as a term that could mean both "means" and "pimp."

24. Ines G. Županov, "Lust, Marriage and Free Will: Jesuit Critique of Paganism in South India (Seventeenth Century)," *Studies in History* 16, no. 2 (2000): 199–220, quotation on 210.

25. Josef Wicki, ed., *Documenta Indica* (Rome: IHSI, 1975), 13: 271–72.

26. On the effects of datura, see also Garcia da Orta, *Colóquios dos simples e drogas e cousas medicinais da India*. . . . (1563; Lisbon: Academia das Ciências de Lisboa, 1963), trans. Clements Markham as *Colloquies on the Simples and Drugs of India*, ed. Conde de Ficalho (London: Henry Sotheran, 1913), 81–83.

27. Kamps, "Colonizing the Colonizer," 168.

28. For much of the sixteenth century, the term *castiços* had denoted children "born of Portuguese father and mestiço mother"—a formulation deployed as late as Alessandro Valignano's 1579 "Sumario de las cosas. . . . ," in *Documentação*. . . . , vol. 12, *1572–1582*, ed. António da Silva Rêgo (Lisbon: Divisão de Publicações e Biblioteca, Agência Geral do Ultramar, 1958), 577. With the approach of the seventeenth century, however, the label came to be increasingly applied to those born in India of allegedly pure European parentage. Linschoten's gloss for *castiços*— "children of the Portingales . . . borne in India"—testifies to this semantic shift, anticipating by several years François Pyrard de Laval's definition of *castiços* as "born in India of Portuguese father and mother" (nez en Inde de pere & mere Portugais). François Pyrard, *Voyage de François Pyrard*. . . . (Paris 1619), 1 :39. See also Charles R. Boxer, *Race Relations in the Portuguese Colonial Empire, 1415–1825* (Oxford: Clarendon Press, 1963), 63, n. 18; and Sebastião R. Dalgado, *Glossário Luso-Asiático*, (Coimbra: Imprensa da Universidade, 1919), 1: 229.

29. Ann Laura Stoler, *Carnal Knowledge and Imperial Power: Race and the Intimate in Colonial Rule* (Berkeley: University of California Press, 2002), 62.

30. Panduronga Pissurlencar, ed., *Roteiro dos Arquivos da Índia Portuguesa* (Bastorá: Rangel, 1955), 82, 83; Boxer, *Race Relations*, 69–71; John Villiers, "The Estado da India in Southeast Asia," in *The First Portuguese Colonial Empire*, ed. Malyn Newitt (Exeter: University of Exeter Press, 1986), 37–67, on 48.

31. Michael N. Pearson, *The Portuguese in India* (Cambridge: Cambridge University Press, 1987), 95; Josef Wicki, "Duas cartas oficiais de Vice-Reis da Índia, escritas em 1561 e 1564," *Studia* 3 (1959): 36–89, on 59.

32. Valignano, "Sumario de las cosas," 577–78. Similar opinions are expressed in a series of manuscript notes conserved in the Biblioteca Nazionale in Rome (Manoscritti Gesuitici 1255, n. 47).

33. Kamps, "Colonizing the Colonizer," 173.

34. Domingo Fernández Navarrete, *Tratados historicos*. . . . (Madrid, 1676), partially trans. James S. Cummins in *The Travels and Controversies of Friar Domingo Navarrete* (London: Hakluyt Society, 1960), 1: 162.

35. "Tratado de las yslas de los Malucos," trans. and ed. Hubert M. Jacobs as *A Treatise on the Moluccas (c. 1544): Probably the Preliminary Version of António Galvão's Lost* História das Molucas (Rome: IHSI, 1970) 89.

36. The earliest classical source on the origins of sati is Diodorus Siculus's *Bibliotheca Historica*, which was composed in the second half of the first century B.C.: "It is an ancient custom among the Indians that the men who marry and the maidens who are married do not do so as a result of the decision of their parents but by mutual persuasion. Formerly, since the wooing was done by persons who were too young, it often happened that, the choice turning out badly, both would quickly regret their act, and that many wives were first seduced, then through wantonness gave their love to other men, and finally, not being able without disgrace to leave the mates whom they had first selected, would kill their husbands by poison. . . . But when this evil became fashionable, and many were murdered in this way, the Indians, although they punished those guilty of the crime, since they were not able to deter the others from wrongdoing, established a law that wives, except such as were pregnant or had children, should be cremated along with their deceased husbands, and that one who was not willing to obey this law should not only be a widow for life but also be entirely debarred from sacrifices and other religious observances as unclean." Diodorus Siculus, *The Library of History*, vol. 9, *Books 18–19.65*, trans. Russell M. Geer, ed. George P. Goold, (Cambridge, MA: Harvard University Press, 1947), 321. Strabo provides a similar (albeit more skeptical) account in *Geographika* 15.1.30.30.

37. On the conversion of this personage, see Diogo do Couto, *Da Ásia de Diogo de Couto . . . Década decima, parte segunda*, vol. 21 of *Da Asia de João de Barros e de Diogo de Couto* (Lisbon, 1788), 325; "Missões dos religiosos agostinhos na Índia," in Silva Rêgo, *Documentação*, 12: 99–233, on 171; and Sebastião de San Pedro, "Retrato da perdição que teve o Padre Frey Sebastião de S. Pedro, da Ordem de Sto. Agostinho, indo pera Ormus o anno de 1592. . . . ," in *Analecta Augustiniana* 47 (1984): 48–73, on 71–72.

38. For a concise but vivid description of the conquest of Hormuz, in which "an infinite number of Moors were killed," see Martín Fernández de Figueroa, *Conquista de las Indias*. . . . , trans. and ed. James McKenna as *A Spaniard in the Portuguese Indies: The Narrative of Martín Fernández de Figueroa* (Cambridge, MA: Harvard University University Press, 1967), 89.

39. Nicola Lancillotto, "Carta ao Padre Inácio de Loiola," 5 Dec. 1550, in *Documentacão*. . . . , vol. 7, *1559*, ed. António da Silva Rêgo (Lisbon: Divisão de Publicações e Biblioteca, Agência Geral do Ultramar, 1952), 33.

40. Gaspar Barzeu, "Carta ao Padre Inácio de Loiola," 16 Dec. 1551, in Silva Rêgo, *Documentacão*, 7: 74.

41. Diogo Gonçalves, *História do Malavar*, ed. Josef Wicki (Rome: IHSI, 1953), 96, my emphasis.

CHAPTER 4

1. Antonio de Morga, *Sucesos de las islas Filipinas* (Mexico City, 1609), f. 119r; see also Leonard Y. Andaya, *The World of Maluku: Eastern Indonesia in the Early Modern Period* (Honolulu: University of Hawaii Press, 1993), 152. Today, the Moluccas comprise about one thousand islands stretching between Sulawesi and New Guinea; during the early modern period, however, the term denoted only the five islands of Ternate, Tidore, Makian, Moti, and Bacan (with their dependent islets).

2. The traditional rivalry between Ternate and Tidore is insightfully detailed by Andaya, *The World of Maluku*, 47–112.

3. Jacob Corneliszoon van Neck, *Journael ofte Dagh-register. . . .* ([Amsterdam], 1600), trans. William Walker as *The Iournall, or Dayly Register. . . .* (London, 1601), fol. 46r. See also Donald F. Lach and Edwin J. Van Kley, *Asia in the Making of Europe*, vol. 3, *A Century of Advance* (Chicago: University of Chicago Press, 1993), bk. 3: 1398.

4. Gary W. Bohigian, "Life on the Rim of Spain's Pacific-American Empire" (PhD diss., University of California, Los Angeles, 1994), 141–42.

5. I quote throughout from the third and most complete edition of Pyrard's text, which appeared in two volumes under the title *Voyage de François Pyrard, de Laval, contenant sa navigation aux Indes Orientales, Maldives, Moluques, Bresil. . . .* (Paris, 1619), 2: 175. The English translations are mine, wherever possible in consultation with those by Albert Gray and H. C. P. Bell in *The Voyage of François Pyrard of Laval to the East Indies, the Maldives, the Moluccas and Brazil* (London, 1887–90). For useful overviews of Pyrard's account, see Lach and Van Kley, *Asia in the Making of Europe*, vol. 3, *A Century of Advance*, bk. 2: 935–45; and Diane C. Margolf, "Wonders of Nature, Diversity of Events: The *Voyage de François Pyrard de Laval*," in *Distant Lands and Diverse Cultures: The French Experience in Asia, 1600–1700*, ed. Glenn J. Ames and Ronald S. Love (Westport, CT: Praeger, 2003), 111–33.

6. Qtd. in Miguel Mir, "Estudio literario sobre el doctor Bartolomé Leonardo de Argensola," in *Conquista de las Islas Malucas. . . .*, by Bartolomé Leonardo de Argensola (Zaragoza, 1891), lxxxiv. For recent assessments of the *Conquista*, see John Villiers, "'A Truthful Pen and an Impartial Spirit': Bartolomé Leonardo de Argensola and the *Conquista de las Islas Malucas*," *Renaissance Studies* 17, no. 3 (2003): 449–73; and Joan-Pau Rubiés, "The Spanish Contribution to the Ethnology of Asia in the Sixteenth and Seventeenth Centuries," *Renaissance Studies* 17, no. 3 (2003): 418–48.

7. The formula "plures simul habere uxores" can be found in numerous early modern texts, including Tomás Sanchez's *De Sancto Matrimonii Sacramento* (Antwerp, 1607), 2: 286, 288; and the canons and decrees of the Council of Trent.

8. Monja Kahf, *Western Representations of the Muslim Woman: From Termagant to Odalisque* (Austin: University of Texas Press, 1999), 15–18.

9. Ruby Lal, *Domesticity and Power in the Early Mughal World* (Cambridge: Cambridge University Press, 2005), 24–49.

10. Anthony Reid, *Southeast Asia in the Age of Commerce, 1450–1680* (New Haven, CT: Yale University Press, 1992), 151.

11. Catherine Belsey, "The Serpent in the Garden: Shakespeare, Marriage, and Material Culture," *Seventeenth Century* 11, no. 1 (1996): 1–20.

12. Catherine Belsey, "Love as Trompe-l'oeil: Taxonomies of Desire in *Venus and Adonis*," *Shakespeare Quarterly* 46, no. 3 (1995): 257–76. Although Belsey works exclusively with English sources, her argument can be extended to other linguistic and national contexts; in his novella "La fuerza de la sangre," for instance, Cervantes makes a radical distinction between lust (lascivia) and love (amor).

13. Perhaps the bluntest statement in this regard is Reynolds vs. U.S., 98 U.S. 145 (1878): "Polygamy has always been odious among the northern and western nations of Europe, and, until the establishment of the Mormon Church, was almost exclusively a feature of the life of Asiatic and of African people."

14. Laura Betzig, "Roman Polygyny," *Ethnology and Sociobiology* 13 (1992): 309–49; Sara E. Phang, *The Marriage of Roman Soldiers, 13 B.C.–A.D. 235: Law and Family in the Imperial Army* (Leiden: Brill, 2001), 412–13; and Raimund Friedl, *Der Konkubinat im kaiserzeitlichen Rom: Von Augustus bis Septimius Severus* (Stuttgart: Steiner, 1996), 214–15, 256–57. See also Walter Schedeil, "A Peculiar Institution? Greco–Roman Monogamy in Global Context," *History of the Family* 14, no. 3 (2009): 280–91.

15. *Justinian's Institutes*, trans. Peter Birks and Grant McLeod (Ithaca, NY: Cornell University Press, 1987), 43.

16. John Cairncross, *After Polygamy Was Made a Sin: The Social History of Christian Polygamy* (London: Routledge & Kegan Paul, 1974), 59; and Anne McLaren, "Monogamy, Polygamy and the True State: James I's Rhetoric of Empire," *History of Political Thought* 25, no. 3 (2004): 446–80, on 469–70.

17. Augustine, *Contra Faustum Manichaeum*, in *A Select Library of Nicene and Post-Nicene Fathers of the Christian Church*, ed. Philip Schaff (Buffalo, 1887), 4: 151–345, quotation on 289.

18. James A. Brundage, *Law, Sex and Christian Society in Medieval Europe* (Chicago: University of Chicago Press, 1987).

19. Cairncross, *After Polygamy*, 59; McLaren, "Monogamy, Polygamy," 470.

20. Eugene Hillman, "Polygamy and the Council of Trent," *The Jurist* 33 (1973): 358–76, on 365–66.

21. Cairncross, *After Polygamy*, 70. See also John L. Thompson, "Patriarchs, Polygamy, and Private Resistance: John Calvin and Others on Breaking God's Rules," *Sixteenth Century Journal* 25, no. 1 (1994): 3–27.

22. For women the matter was different, as no one seemed to doubt that they should be monogamous at all times. This explains why Asian polyandry

and group marriage, although mentioned by several European travelers, failed to elicit the copious attention devoted to Asian polygyny.

23. Ursula Vogel, "Political Philosophers and the Trouble with Polygamy: Patriarchal Reasoning in Modern Natural Law," *History of Political Thought* 12, no. 2 (1991): 229–51, quotation on 230.

24. Geoffrey Bullough, "Polygamy among the Reformers," in *Renaissance and Modern Essays*, ed. G. R. Hibbard (London: Routledge & Kegan Paul, 1966), 5–24, on 6. It was probably these biblical precedents that the German reformer Bernhard Rothmann had in mind in 1534 when he claimed that polygamy was closer to "the true practice of holy matrimony" than monogamy. See Lowell H. Zuck, ed., *Christianity and Revolution: Radical Christian Testimonies, 1520–1650* (Philadelphia: Temple University Press, 1975), 98–104, quotation on 101.

25. John Milton, *The Complete Prose Works of John Milton*, vol. 6, (*ca. 1658–ca. 1660*) trans. John Carey, ed. Maurice Kelly, (New Haven, CT: Yale University Press, 1973), 360. Although for different reasons, John Dryden reached a similar conclusion in *Absalom and Achitophel*.

26. Leo Miller, *Milton among the Poligamophiles* (New York: Loewenthal Press, 1974), 15, 17, 18–19.

27. Bernardino Ochino, *A Dialogue of Polygamy....* (London, 1657), 66. Ochino's discussion of polygamy had originally appeared as part of the *Dialogi XXX*, published in Basel in 1563.

28. Lyndal Roper, "Sexual Utopianism in the German Reformation," *Journal of Ecclesiastical History* 42, no. 3 (1991): 394–418; and L. G. Jasma, "Crime in the Netherlands in the Sixteenth Century: The Batenburg Bands After 1540," *Mennonite Quarterly Review* 62 (1988): 221–35.

29. Paracelsus, *Selected Writings*, trans. Norbert Guterman, ed. Jolande Székács Jacobi (New York: Pantheon, 1951), 110.

30. Giordano Bruno, *Lo spaccio della bestia trionfante* (London, 1584), trans. Arthur D. Imerti as *The Expulsion of the Triumphant Beast* (Lincoln: University of Nebraska Press, 2004), 96.

31. Tommaso Campanella, "De Matrimonio," in *I sacri segni*, ed. Romano Amerio (Rome: Centro Internazionale di Studi Umanistici, 1968), 6: 160. All quotations are from this edition.

32. Giovanni Botero, *Della ragion di stato* (Venice, 1589), trans. P. J. Waley and D. P. Waley as *The Reason of State* (New Haven, CT: Yale University Press, 1956), 155; and Philippe de Béthune, *Le conseiller d'État....* (Paris, 1632), trans. Edward Grimston as *The Counsellor of Estate* (London, 1634), 326.

33. Cairncross, *After Polygamy*, 46.

34. Campanella, "De Matrimonio," 162.

35. "Altitudo Divini Consilii" (1 June 1537), in *Enchiridion Symbolorum: Definitionum et Declarationum de Rebus Fidei et Morum*, ed. Henry Denziger (Freiburg: Herder, 1965), 363. By and large, the bull confirmed the decretal "Gaudemus in Domino" issued by Pope Innocent III in 1201.

36. In a concession to practicality, the bull stipulated that polygamous converts might be allowed to choose whatever wife they preferred, provided

they could "not remember which wife they had married first." Francisco J. Hernáez, ed., *Colección de bulas, breves y otros documentos relativos a la Iglesia de America y Filipinas* (Vaduz: Kraus Reprint, 1964), 1: 66. In 1571, Pope Pius V granted a new exception to polygamists whose first wife (although known) refused baptism. In this case, a neophyte could legitimately marry whatever spouse converted with him. A later directive, issued in 1585, allowed neophytes who had been forcibly removed from their countries of origin to marry again.

37. Helen Rawlings, *The Spanish Inquisition* (Malden, MA: Blackwell, 2006), 122; and Sara McDougall, "The Punishment of Bigamy in Late-Medieval Troyes," *Imago Temporis: Medium Aevum* 3 (2009): 189–204.

38. James Waterworth, trans., *The Canons and Decrees of the Sacred and Oecumenical Council of Trent* (London, 1848), 201–2.

39. Nicola Lancillotto, "Carta ao Padre Inácio de Loiola," in *Documentacão para a história das missões do padroado português do Oriente: Índia*, vol. 7, *1559*, ed. António da Silva Rêgo (Lisbon: Divisão de Publicações e Biblioteca, Agência Geral do Ultramar, 1952), 32–38. My translation follows that provided by Charles R. Boxer in *Race Relations in the Portuguese Colonial Empire, 1415–1825* (Oxford: Clarendon Press, 1963), 62.

40. Joaquim Heliodoro da Cunha Rivara, ed., *Archivo Portuguez-Oriental* (Nova-Goa, 1862), fasc. 4: 12–13, 70. As Fátima da Silva Gracias notes in *Kaleidoscope of Women in Goa, 1510–1961* (New Delhi: Concept, 1996), 97–98, the decree was often ignored. Unable to stamp out polygamy, colonial authorities sought nevertheless to control it: starting in 1614, non-Christians who desired to have another wife had to seek permission from the state. See also Merry E. Wiesner-Hanks, *Christianity and Sexuality in the Early Modern World: Regulating Desire, Reforming Practice* (London: Routledge, 2000), 190–91.

41. Rivara, *Archivo Portuguez-Oriental* (Nova-Goa, 1865), fasc. 5, pt. 2: 777.

42. Rivara, *Archivo Portuguez-Oriental*, fasc. 4: 263.

43. Francisco de Sande, "Relacion," trans. José M. Ascencio as "Relation and Description of the Phelipinas Islands," in *The Philippine Islands, 1493–1803*, ed. Emma H. Blair and James A. Robertson (Cleveland: Arthur H. Clark, 1903), 4: 98–118, on 107. See also Juan de la Concepción, *Historia general de Philipinas. . . .* (Manila, 1788), 3: 409–12.

44. Johan Karel Jakob de Jonge et al., eds., *De Opkomst van het Nederlandsch gezag in Oost-Indië. . . .* (The Hague, 1869), 4: 242. See also Ulbe Bosma and Remco Raben, *Being "Dutch" in the Indies: A History of Creolisation and Empire, 1500–1920*, trans. Wendie Shaffer (Athens: Ohio University Press, 2008), 27–28; and Eric Jones, *Wives, Slaves and Concubines: A History of the Female Underclass in Dutch Asia* (DeKalb: Northern Illinois University Press, 2010).

45. Jacobus A. van der Chijs, *Nederlandsch-Indisch Plakaatboek, 1602–1811* (Batavia, 1885), 1: 99. All quotations are from this edition.

46. Chijs, *Nederlandsch-Indisch Plakaatboek*, 1: 102.

47. Chijs, *Nederlandsch-Indisch Plakaatboek*, 1: 101.

48. Thomas Mills and John Milward to the president at Surat, 14 Nov. 1622, British Library, IOR: G/36/102, 275. A summary of the letter is given in William Foster, ed., *The English Factories in India*, vol. 2, *1622–1623* (Oxford: Clarendon Press, 1908), 145–47.

49. Mills and Milward to the president, 276.

50. As Andaya has observed, European models of kingship do not adequately capture the position of Moluccan leaders during the early modern period. Andaya, *World of Maluku*, 60. Since my sources routinely call these leaders kings, however, I have chosen to follow their usage.

51. Antonio Pigafetta, *Relazione del primo viaggio attorno al mondo*, ed. Andrea Canova (Padua: Antenore, 1999), 280. All quotations are from this edition.

52. Numerous scholars have examined Orientalist discourses on the harem. For examples, see Malek Alloula, *The Colonial Harem* (Minneapolis: University of Minnesota Press, 1986); Caren Kaplan, "'Getting to Know You': Travel, Gender, and the Politics of Representation in *Anna and the King of Siam* and *The King and I*," in *Late Imperial Culture*, ed. Román de la Campa, E. Ann Kaplan, and Michael Sprink (New York: Verso, 1995), 33–52; Inderpal Grewal, *Home and Harem: Nation, Gender, Empire and the Cultures of Travel* (Durham, NC: Duke University Press, 1996); Alain Grosrichard, *The Sultan's Court: European Fantasies of the East* (London: Verso, 1999); Reina Lewis, *Rethinking Orientalism: Women, Travel and the Ottoman Harem* (New Brunswick, NJ: Rutgers University Press, 2004); Billie Melman, *Women's Orients: English Women and the Middle East, 1718–1918* (Ann Arbor: University of Michigan Press, 1992); Gayatri Spivak, "Three Women's Texts and a Critique of Imperialism," *Critical Inquiry* 12 (1985): 243–261; and Ruth B. Yeazell, *Harems of the Mind: Passages of Western Art and Literature* (New Haven, CT: Yale University Press, 2000).

53. Grewal, *Home and Harem*, 26. For a discussion of panopticism, see Michel Foucault, *Discipline and Punish: The Birth of the Prison* (New York: Vintage, 1995), 195–228, and "The Eye of Power," in *Power/Knowledge: Selected Interviews and Other Writings, 1972–1977*, ed. Colin Gordon (New York: Pantheon, 1980), 146–65.

54. Included in Jacob Corneliszoon van Neck, *Het Tweede Boeck. . . . ,* published by Cornelis Claeszoon in 1601, the plate was reprinted (with minor modifications) in the fifth volume of Johann Theodor and Johann Israel de Bry's *Quinta pars Indiae Orientalis. . . .* (Frankfurt, 1601), as well as in Jacob Corneliszoon van Neck, *Historiale beschrijvinghe, inhoudende een waerachtich verhael vande reyse ghedaen met acht schepen van Amsterdam. . . .* (Amsterdam, 1619), and *Waerachtigh verhael van de schipvaert op Oost-Indien. . . .* (Amsterdam, 1646).

55. Francisco Pelsaert, "Remonstrantie" (ca. 1626), trans. and ed. W. H. Moreland and Pieter Geyl as *Jahangir's India: The Remonstrantie of Francisco Pelsaert* (Cambridge: W. Heffer, 1925), 64.

56. "A letter of Father Diego de Pantoia . . . written in Paquin, which is the Court of the King of China, the ninth of March, the yeere 1602," in

Purchas his Pilgrimes. . . . , comp. Samuel Purchas (London, 1625), 3: 350–411, quotation on 399. On the letter's publication history, see Donald F. Lach, *Asia in the Making of Europe* (Chicago: University of Chicago Press, 1977), vol. 2, *A Century of Wonder*, bk. 3: 320, n. 71.

57. "Letter of Father Diego de Pantoia," 400.

58. Pedro Chirino, *Relacion de las islas Filipinas i de lo que en ellas an trabaiado los Padres de la Compañia de Iesus* (Rome, 1604), trans. Frederic W. Morrison and Emma H. Blair as "Relation of the Filipinas Islands. . . . ," in *The Philippine Islands, 1493–1803*, ed. Emma H. Blair and James A. Robertson (Cleveland: Arthur H. Clark, 1904), 13: 74; and Alexandre de Rhodes, *Relazione de' felici successi della santa fede predicata da' padri della Compagnia di Giesu nel regno di Tunchino* (Rome, 1650), 187–88.

59. Manuel Gomes to the Jesuits in Goa, in Hubert M. Jacobs, ed., *Documenta Malucensia* (Rome: IHSI, 1974), 1: 464–72, on 467.

60. Francis Xavier to the Jesuits in Rome, in Jacobs, *Documenta Malucensia*, 1: 40.

61. Pierre du Jarric, *Histoire des choses plus memorable.* . . . (Bourdeaux, 1608–14), partially trans. Charles H. Payne as *Akbar and the Jesuits: An Account of the Jesuit Missions to the Court of Akbar by Father Pierre du Jarric, S. J.*, ed. E. Denison Ross and Eileen Power (New Delhi: Tulsi, 1979), 30; Rodolfo Acquaviva et al. to Rodrigo Vicente, in Josef Wicki, ed., *Documenta Indica* (Rome: IHSI, 1972), 12: 41, 50; and Liam M. Brockey, *Journey to the East: The Jesuit Mission to China, 1579–1724* (Cambridge, MA: Harvard University Press, 2007), 301.

62. "Niun'altro abuso è così largamente sparso per quelle parti dell'Oriente . . . quanto questo. . . . Non v'è casa di persone bene stanti . . . e non v'è Reggia di quei Principi regnanti, che non sia . . . contaminata da mandre di femmine impudiche. Nè vi è vitio, che più malagevolmente si possa diradicare dagli animi di questi homini effeminati, e molli, quanto la Poligamia." Clemente Tosi, *Dell'india Orientale* (Rome, 1669), 2: 352.

63. William Foster, ed., *The Voyage of Thomas Best to the East Indies, 1612–1614* (London: Hakluyt Society, 1934), 213–14. Although an English "gentleman of honorable parentage" volunteered his daughters, nothing seems to have come out of this proposal.

64. "Tratado de las yslas de los Malucos," trans. and ed. Hubert M. Jacobs as *A Treatise on the Moluccas: (c. 1544): Probably the Preliminary Version of António Galvão's Lost* História das Molucas (Rome: IHSI, 1970), 89. All citations are from this edition.

65. António Monserrate, "Mongolicae Legationis Commentarius" (ca. 1582), trans. John S. Hoyland as *The Commentary of Father Monserrate, S. J., on His Journey to the Court of Akbar*, ann. S. N. Banerjee (London: Oxford University Press, 1922), 202. This Jesuit mission took place in 1580–83.

66. There are exceptions, of course. According to Alexandre de Rhodes, for example, polygamy served a demographic (and therefore political) purpose. "You want my subjects to have only one wife," the king of Tonquin had told him, "and I want them to have more, so that they might have more

children to be my faithful subjects" ("volete che i miei sudditi habbiano una sola moglie ed io voglio che ne habbiano più, perche possano fare più figliuoli, che mi siano sudditi fedeli"). De Rhodes, *Relazione de' felici successi*, 187.

67. Edmund Scott, *An Exact Discourse of the Subtilties . . . and ceremonies of the East Indians* (London, 1606), sig. N1v my emphasis; reprinted, with additions, in Purchas's *Pilgrimes*, 1 (bk. 3): 164–84, quotation on 166. Echoing attitudes and concerns typical of missionary writing, *An Exact Discourse* evinces the extent to which religious writers in general, and the Jesuits in particular, had shaped European discourses on polygamy.

68. Jean Bodin, *Les Six livres de la République* (Paris, 1576), trans. Richard Knolles as *The Six Books of a Commonweale*, (London, 1606), 557.

69. Bartolomé Leonardo de Argensola, *Conquista de las Islas Malucas. . . .* (Madrid, 1609), 1. All quotations are from this edition; all translations are mine, if possible in consultation with those of John Stevens in *The Discovery and Conquest of the Molucco and Philippine Islands. . . .* (London, 1708).

70. Anthony Pagden, *Lords of All the World: Ideologies of Empire in Spain, Britain and France c. 1500–c. 1800* (New Haven, CT: Yale University Press, 1995), 41.

71. Since the early 1570s, the term could also be used to identify programs of resettlement and acculturation entrusted to religious orders. See Cynthia Radding, "The Común, Local Governance, and Defiance in Colonial Sonora," in *Choice, Persuasion, and Coercion: Social Control on Spain's North American Frontiers*, ed. Jesús F. de la Teja and Ross Frank (Albuquerque: University of New Mexico Press, 2005), 179–200, on 180.

72. "Tratado de las yslas de los Malucos," 169. See also Gabriel Rebelo's "Historia das Ilhas de Maluco escripta no anno de 1561" and "Informação das cousas de Maluco," in *Documentação para a história das missões do padroado português do Oriente: Insulíndia*, vol. 3, 1563–1567, ed. Artur Basilio de Sá (Lisbon: Divisão de Publicações e Biblioteca, Agência Geral do Ultramar, 1955), 192–343, 345–508.

73. Giovanni Botero, *Le Relationi Universali* (Venice, 1596), 145.

74. Margo Todd, *Christian Humanism and the Puritan Social Order* (Cambridge: Cambridge University Press, 1987).

75. For Peru and New Spain, see Mariano Galván Rivera, ed., *Concilio III Provincial Mexicano, celebrado en México el año de 1585. . . .* (Mexico City, 1859), 348–51. For India and its subordinate jurisdictions, see Rivara, *Archivo Portuguez-Oriental*, fasc. 4: 16, 70, 217, 263, 452.

76. Botero, *Della ragion di stato*, 155. On Botero's use of sixteenth-century travel writing, see Joan-Pau Rubiés, "Oriental Despotism and European Orientalism: Botero to Montesquieu," *Journal of Early Modern History* 9, nos. 1–2 (2005): 109–80.

77. For popular pronouncements on the rewards of marriage, see Luis Vives, *De institutione foeminae Christianae* (Antwerp, 1524), trans. Charles Fantazzi as *The Education of a Christian Woman: A Sixteenth-Century Manual* (Chicago: University of Chicago Press, 2000), 172; and Antonio de

Guevara, *Relox de Príncipes* (Valladolid, 1529), in *Obras Completas de Fray Antonio de Guevara*, ed. Emilio Blanco (Madrid: Fundación José Antonio de Castro, 1994), 2: 355.

78. Adam Olearius and Johann Albrecht von Mandelslo, *Morgenländische Reyse-Beschreibung* (Schleßwig, 1658), trans. John Davies as *The voyages & travels of the ambassadors sent by Frederick, Duke of Holstein. . . .* (London 1662), 81.

79. Valerie Traub, *The Renaissance of Lesbianism in Early Modern England* (Cambridge: Cambridge University Press, 2002), 98.

CHAPTER 5

1. William Ravenhill, *A Short Account of the Company of Grocers* (London, 1689), 1. The very career of George Bowles testifies to the relationship between the Society of Grocers and the East India Company. A prominent grocer, he was among the incorporators of the East India Company in 1600 and 1609.

2. Thomas Middleton, *The Tryumphs of Honor and Industry* (London, 1617), sigs. A4v, B1r.

3. Linschoten's English printer, for instance, compared merchant venturers to Hercules "when hee fetched away the *Golden Apples* out of the *Garden* of the *Hesperides*." John Wolfe, "To the Reader," in *The Voyage of John Huyghen Van Linschoten to the East Indies. . . .* , ed. Arthur Coke Burnell and Pieter Anton Tiele (London, 1885), 1: lii.

4. Jane Kingsley-Smith, *Cupid in Early Modern Literature and Culture* (Cambridge: Cambridge University Press, 2010), 4.

5. Roland Greene, *Unrequited Conquests: Love and Empire in the Colonial Americas* (Chicago: University of Chicago Press, 1999), 9.

6. Qtd. in John Lynch, *Spain Under the Habsburgs*, vol. 2, *Spain and America 1598–1700* (Oxford: Blackwell, 1981), 65.

7. Barnabe Riche, *The Excellency of Good Women* (London, 1613), 9.

8. Peter Hulme, *Colonial Encounters: Europe and the Native Caribbean, 1492–1797* (London: Routledge, 1992), 141.

9. Carmen Nocentelli, "The Erotics of Mercantile Imperialism: Cross-cultural Requitedness in the Early Modern Period," *Journal for Early Modern Cultural Studies* 8, no. 1 (2008): 134–52.

10. Examples of "industrious love" can be found in the first English translation of Giambattista Guarini's *Pastor Fido; or, The Faithfull Shepheard* (London, 1602), sig. E1v, as well as in Thomas Shadwell's *Psyche* (London, 1675), 7.

11. Valerie Traub, *The Renaissance of Lesbianism in Early Modern England* (Cambridge: Cambridge University Press, 2002), 268.

12. My hypothesis finds support in the findings of numerous scholars—including Martha Howell, Alan Macfarlane, and Lawrence Stone—all of whom posit a connection between the socioeconomic dislocations of incipient capitalism and the emergence of a new ideology of marriage. See Martha Howell, *Commerce Before Capitalism in Europe, 1300–1600* (Cambridge:

Cambridge University Press, 2010); Alan J. Macfarlane, "Love and Capitalism," *Cambridge Anthropology* 11 (1987): 22–39; and Lawrence Stone, *Family, Sex, and Marriage in England, 1500–1800* (New York: Harper and Row, 1977). See also Friedrich Engels, *The Origin of the Family, Private Property, and the State*, ed. Eleanor B. Leacock (New York: International, 1972).

13. Louis Althusser defines "interpellation" as the process through which ideology constitutes concrete individuals as subjects. See Althusser, "Ideology and Ideological State Apparatuses," in *Lenin and Philosophy and Other Essays* (New York: Monthly Review Press, 1971), 160.

14. The threat of effeminacy implicit in heterosexual relations is perceptively discussed in Ian F. Moulton, *Before Pornography: Erotic Writing in Early Modern England* (Oxford: Oxford University Press, 2000), esp. 74–79.

15. Arthur C. Sprague, *Beaumont and Fletcher on the Restoration Stage* (Cambridge, MA: Harvard University Press, 1926); Curtis Price and Robert D. Hume, eds., *The Island Princess: A Semi-Opera* (Tunbridge Wells: Richard Macnutt, 1985). In addition to Argensola's *Conquista*, Fletcher also used a French retelling of the story penned by Louis Gédoyn de Bellan, "Histoire memorable de Dias Espagnol, et de Quixaire Princesse des Moluques" (Paris, 1615). For a full account of the narrative's movement from Portugal's imperial periphery to Spain, from Spain to France, and from France to England, see Carmen Nocentelli, "Spice Race: *The Island Princess* and the Politics of Transnational Appropriation," *PMLA* 125, no. 3 (2010): 572–88. Fletcher's sources are also discussed by A. L. Stiefel, "Uber die Quelle von J. Fletcher's *Island Princess*," *Archiv fur das Studium der neueren Sprachen* 103 (1899): 277–308; Felix E. Schelling, *Elizabethan Drama* (Boston: Houghton Mifflin, 1908), 2: 211; and Edward M. Wilson, "Did Fletcher Read Spanish?," *Philological Quarterly* 27, no. 2 (1948): 187–90. Andrew Hadfield identifies John Saris's account of the first English voyage to Japan as another possible source in *Literature, Travel and Colonial Writing in the English Renaissance* (Oxford: Clarendon Press, 1998), 262.

16. Ania Loomba, "'Break Her Will, and Bruise No Bone Sir': Colonial and Sexual Mastery in Fletcher's *The Island Princess*," *Journal for Early Modern Cultural Studies* 2, no. 1 (2002): 68–108; Shankar Raman, *Framing "India": The Colonial Imaginary in Early Modern Culture* (Stanford, CA: Stanford University Press, 2001), 155–88.

17. Michael Neill, *Putting History to the Question: Power, Politics, and Society in English Renaissance Drama* (New York: Columbia University Press, 2002), 325.

18. Valerie Forman, *Tragicomic Redemptions: Global Economics and the Early Modern English Stage* (Philadelphia: University of Pennsylvania Press, 2008), 113–45.

19. Elizabeth A. Povinelli, *The Empire of Love: Toward a Theory of Intimacy, Genealogy, and Carnality* (Durham, NC: Duke University Press, 2006), 190.

20. Argensola gives the name of the Portuguese captain as Ruy Diaz de Acuña and that of his nephew as Roque Piñeyro; he also gives the princess's

name as Quisayra. For consistency, I have adopted Fletcher's spellings through-out.

21. Argensola, *Conquista de las Islas Malucas* (Madrid, 1609), 153. All quotations are from this edition.

22. John Fletcher, *The Island Princess*, ed. George W. Williams, vol. 5 of *The Dramatic Works in the Beaumont and Fletcher Canon*, ed. Fredson Bowers (Cambridge: Cambridge University Press, 1982), 552–651, on 552, 609. All references to the play are from this edition.

23. During the course of his stay at Ternate, Francis Drake presumably obtained from King Baab Ullah the promise "that hee would yeeld himselfe, and the right of his Island to bee at the pleasure and commandement" of the English Crown. "The famous voyage of Sir Francis Drake into the South Sea. . . . ," in the *The Principal Navigations, Voyages, Traffiques, and Discoveries of the English Nation. . . .*, comp. Richard Hakluy (London, 1600) 3: 730–42, quotation on 739. Despite these promising overtures, no one followed in Drake's footsteps for over twenty years. See Kenneth Andrews, *Trade, Plunder, and Settlement: Maritime Enterprise and the Genesis of the British Empire, 1480–1630* (Cambridge: Cambridge University Press, 1984); William Foster, ed., *The Voyages of Sir James Lancaster to Brazil and the East Indies, 1591–1603* (London: Hakluyt Society, 1940); and R. T. Fell, *Early Maps of South-East Asia* (Oxford: Oxford University Press, 1991), 41–56.

24. By 1616, the company also had establishments in India, Thailand, and Japan. John Bruce, *Annals of the Honourable East India Company* (London, 1810), 1:188–90.

25. Samuel Purchas, comp., *Purchas his Pilgrimes* (London, 1625), 1: 702. See also "Nathaniel Courthope and Thomas Spurway to the Chief at Bantam, Poloronne 15 April 1617," in *Letters Received by the East India Company by Its Servants in the East*, vol. 5, *January to June 1617*, ed. William Foster (London: Sampson, Low, Marston, 1901), 345–52, on 351. Outmanned and outgunned, the English were soon forced to relinquish their acquisitions. Only Pulau Run was to remain, at least nominally, under English suzerainty; it was eventually surrendered to the Dutch in 1667, in exchange for Manhattan Island in North America.

26. K. N. Chaudhuri, *The English East India Company: The Study of an Early Joint-Stock Company, 1600–1640* (New York: AMK, 1965), 49.

27. Qtd. in Giles Milton, *Nathaniel's Nutmeg or, The True and Incredible Adventures of the Spice Trader Who Changed the Course of History* (New York: Farrar, Straus and Giroux, 1999), 265.

28. Neill, *Putting History to the Question*, 112.

29. Nocentelli, "Spice Race," 583-84. For examples of Armusia as a geographic name, see James Ussher, *The annals of the world. . . .* (London, 1658), 272; and Edmund Bohun, *A geographical dictionary. . . .* (London, 1693), 165.

30. Niels Steensgaard, *The Asian Trade Revolution of the Seventeenth Century: The East India Companies and the Decline of the Caravan Trade* (Chicago: University of Chicago Press, 1973), 331–43; and Charles R. Boxer,

"Anglo-Portuguese Rivalry in the Persian Gulf, 1615–1635," in *Chapters in Anglo-Portuguese Relations*, ed. Edgar Prestage (London: Watford, 1935), 46–129.

31. This homology is perceptively explored by Anne McClintock in *Imperial Leather: Race, Gender, and Sexuality in the Colonial Context* (New York: Routledge, 1995), 21–31.

32. Raymond Williams, *The Country and the City* (New York: Oxford University Press, 1973), 26–34.

33. Antonio Pigafetta, *Relazione del primo viaggio attorno al mondo*, ed. Andrea Canova (Padua: Antenore, 1999), 168; Garcia da Orta, *Colóquios dos simples e drogas e cousas medicinais da India. . . .* (1563; Lisbon: Academia das Ciências de Lisboa, 1963), trans. Clements Markham as *Colloquies on the Simples and Drugs of India*, ed. Conde de Ficalho (London: Henry Sotheran, 1913), 218.

34. Mario Di Gangi, *The Homoerotics of Early Modern Drama* (Cambridge: Cambridge University Press, 1997), 156.

35. Studies by Jean Feerick and Claire Jowitt seem to point in this direction, but without underscoring the relevance of Quisara's characterization to the play's construction of racial difference. Jean Feerick, "Tragicomic Transformations: Passion, Politics, and the 'Art to Turn' in Fletcher's *Island Princess*," *Early Modern Literary Studies* 19, no. 3 (2009): 1–24; and Claire Jowitt, "*The Island Princess* and Race," in *Early Modern English Drama: A Critical Companion*, ed. Patrick Cheney, Andrew Hadfield, and Garrett A. Sullivan (Oxford: Oxford University Press, 2006), 287–97.

36. Joseph Wybarne, *The New Age of Old Names* (London, 1609), qtd. in Samuel C. Chew, *The Crescent and the Rose: Islam and England During the Renaissance* (New York: Oxford University Press, 1937), 446; see also Daniel J. Vitkus, "Early Modern Orientalism: Representations of Islam in Sixteenth- and Seventeenth-Century Europe," in *Western Views of Islam in Medieval and Early Modern Europe*, ed. David R. Blanks and Michael Frassetto (New York: St. Martin's Press, 1999), 207–30, esp. 216–17.

37. Anthony Reid offers a useful overview of Islamization in Southeast Asia in *Charting the Shape of Early Modern Southeast Asia* (Bangkok: Silkworm, 1999), 15–38, and "Islamization and Christianization in Southeast Asia: The Critical Phase, 1550–1650," in *Southeast Asia in the Early Modern Era: Trade, Power, and Belief*, ed. Anthony Reid (Ithaca, NY: Cornell University Press, 1993), 151–79.

38. Geoffrey Parker, "Europe and the Wider World, 1500–1750: The Military Balance," in *The Political Economy of Merchant Empires: State Power and World Trade, 1350–1750*, ed. James D. Tracy (Cambridge: Cambridge University Press, 1991), 177; and Mario Longhena, *Viaggi in Persia, India e Giava di Nicolò de' Conti, Girolamo Adorno e Girolamo di Santo Stefano* (Milan: Istituto Editoriale Italiano, 1960).

39. Jonathan Burton, "English Anxiety and the Muslim Power of Conversion: Five Perspectives on 'Turning Turk' in Early Modern Texts," *Journal for Early Modern Cultural Studies* 2, no. 1 (2002): 35–67, on 60.

40. Fernão Mendes Pinto, *Peregrinaçam de Fernam Mendez Pinto* (Lisbon, 1614), ed. and trans. Rebecca D. Catz as *The Travels of Mendes Pinto* (Chicago: University of Chicago Press, 1989), 5. As Nabil Matar has observed, the link between apostasy and sexual desire is pervasive in early modern travel writing. Matar, *Islam in Britain, 1558–1685* (Cambridge: Cambridge University Press, 1998), 60, n. 25.

41. Johannes Boemus, *Omnium gentium mores, leges et ritus. . . .* (Augsburg, 1520), trans. Edward Aston as *The Manners, Lawes and Customes of all Nations* (London, 1611), 137. An extensive account of European stereotypes on the alleged carnality of Islam is provided in Norman Daniel, *Islam and the West: The Making of an Image* (Edinburgh: Edinburgh University Press, 1960), esp. 118–25.

42. William Rowley, *A Tragedy Called Alls Lost by Lust* (London, 1633), sig. D3v.

43. Daniel J. Vitkus, *Turning Turk: English Theater and the Multicultural Mediterranean, 1570–1630* (New York: Palgrave, 2003), 88; and Warner G. Rice, "To Turn Turk," *Modern Language Notes* 46, no. 3 (1931): 153–54. See also Bernadette D. Andrea, *Women and Islam in Early Modern English Literature* (Cambridge: Cambridge University Press, 2008); Jonathan Burton, *Traffic and Turning: Islam and English Drama, 1579–1624* (Cranbury: University of Delaware Press, 2005), and "English Anxiety and the Muslim Power of Conversion," 60; Barbara Fuchs, "Faithless Empires: Pirates, Renegadoes and the English Nation," *ELH* 67, no. 1 (2000): 45–69; Gerald MacLean, "On Turning Turk, or Trying To: National Identity in Robert Daborne's *A Christian Turn'd Turk*," *Explorations in Renaissance Culture* 29 (2003): 225–52; Matar, *Islam in Britain,* esp. 21–49; and Lois Potter, "Pirates and Turning Turk in Renaissance Drama," in *Travel and Drama in Shakespeare's Time,* ed. Jean-Pierre Maquerlot and Michèle Williams (Cambridge: Cambridge University Press, 1996), 124–40.

44. Patricia Parker, "Preposterous Conversions: Turning Turk and Its Pauline Righting," *Journal for Early Modern Cultural Studies* 2, no. 1 (2002): 1–34. Male sodomy held a paramount place in the list of behaviors associated with Islam, even though several European writers also understood the Quran to proscribe it. The "Tratado del las yslas de los Malucos," for instance, mentions that "although some think that Muslims have [sodomy] as a rule of conduct, they are mistaken, because the sixth commandment forbids it." "Tratado de las yslas de los Malucos," trans. and ed. Hubert M. Jacobs as *A Treatise on the Moluccas (c. 1544): Probably the Preliminary Version of António Galvão's Lost* História das Molucas (Rome: IHSI, 1970), 120–21.

45. The pervasive link between erotic self-control and early modern understandings of masculinity is discussed in a number of recent studies, including Todd Reeser's *Moderating Masculinity in Early Modern Culture* (Chapel Hill: University of North Carolina Press, 2006); and Bruce R. Smith's *Homosexual Desire in Shakespeare's England: A Cultural Poetics* (Chicago: University of Chicago Press, 1991), esp. 196–97. Michel Foucault's

well-known exploration of classical enkrateia can be found in *The History of Sexuality*, vol. 2, *The Use of Pleasure*, (New York: Vintage, 1990).

46. John Cooke, *Greenes Tu Quoque; or, The Cittie Gallant* (London, 1614) sig. F1r.

47. Qtd. in Philippe Ariès, "Love in Married Life," in *Western Sexuality: Practice and Precept in Past and Present Times*, ed. Philippe Ariès and André Béjin (Oxford: Blackwell, 1985), 130–39, quotation on 134.

48. Michel de Montaigne, *Les Essais de Michel, Seigneur de Montaigne* (Paris, 1595), trans. John Florio as *Essayes Written in French by Michael Lord of Montaigne. . . .* (London, 1613), 98.

49. Martin Luther, "A Sermon on the Estate of Marriage," in *Luther on Women: A Sourcebook*, Susan C. Karant-Nunn and Merry E. Wiesner-Hanks, eds., (Cambridge: Cambridge University Press, 2003), 91; and Richard Capel, *Tentations: Their Nature, Danger, Cure* (London, 1633), 395.

50. Daniel Defoe, *Conjugal Lewdness; or, Matrimonial Whoredom. A Treatise Concerning the Use and Abuse of the Marriage Bed* (London 1727), 57, 61. On the dangers of lust in marriage, see Jean-Louis Flandrin, "Sex in Married Life in the Early Middle Ages: The Church's Teaching and Behavioural Reality," in Ariès and Béjin, *Western Sexuality,* 114–29; and Lawrence Stone, *The Past and Present Revisited* (London: Routledge and Kegan Paul, 1987), 347–48.

51. Melinda J. Gough, "'Her Filthy Feature Open Showne' in Ariosto, Spenser, and *Much Ado About Nothing*," *Studies in English Literature* 39, no. 1 (1999): 41–67, on 41.

52. P. Parker, "Preposterous Conversions," esp. 8–9.

53. Antonio de Torquemada, *Jardín de flores curiosas* (Salamanca, 1570), trans. Lewes Lewkenor as *The Spanish Mandevile of Miracles* (London, 1600), ff. 33r–33v.

54. James C. W. Truman, "John Foxe and the Desires of Reformation Martyrology," *ELH* 70, no. 1 (2003): 35–66. It is useful to remember, in this context, that Fletcher's family was staunchly Protestant: John Fletcher's grandfather was one of the first English Reformation ministers; his father was chaplain-in-ordinary of Queen Elizabeth. See Gordon McMullan, *The Politics of Unease in the Plays of John Fletcher* (Amherst: University of Massachusetts Press, 1994), 1–7.

55. Andrea R. Salomon, "'A Wild Shambles of Strange Gods': The Conversion of Quisara in Fletcher's *The Island Princess*," in *Christian Encounters with the Other*, ed. John C. Hawley (New York: New York University Press, 1998), 17–32, quotation on 27; William Appleton, *Beaumont and Fletcher: A Critical Study* (London: Allen and Unwin, 1956), 66–67; and Philip J. Finkelpearl, "Fletcher as a Spenserian Playwright: *The Faithful Shepherdess* and *The Island Princess*," *Studies in English Literature* 27 (1987): 285–302.

56. Susannah B. Monta, *Martyrdom and Literature in Early Modern England* (Cambridge: Cambridge University Press, 2005), 197–98.

CHAPTER 6

1. "Traité fait entre les Compagnies des Indes Orientales, Angloise & Hollandoise, au sujet des differens survenus entre elles. A Londres, le 2 Juin, 1619," in *Corps universel diplomatique du droit des gens* comp. Jean Dumont (Amsterdam, 1723), 5: 333–35, on 335.

2. The island is known today as Ambon (Indonesia). Throughout this chapter, I refer to this island as Amboina, as it was called in the seventeenth century.

3. "A True Declaration of the News that Came out of the East-Indies. . . . " (London, 1624), 4.

4. "An Authentick Copy of the Confessions and Sentences against M. Towerson, and Complices, Concerning the Bloudy Conspiracy enterprised against the Castle of Amboyna," in *A Remonstrance of the Directors of the Netherlands East India Company presented to the Lords States Generall of the United Provinces. . . .* (London, 1632), 31.

5. Philip D. Curtin, *Cross-Cultural Trade in World History* (Cambridge: Cambridge University Press, 1984), 155; and Om Prakash, *The Dutch East India Company and the Economy of Bengal, 1630–1720* (Princeton, NJ: Princeton University Press, 1984), 16. The Amboina massacre probably hastened England's retreat from the Spice Islands, but did not cause it. The EIC had been considering this option since at least 1622, when it was suggested that it might "be more wise to withdraw their factories from Amboyna, Banda, and the Moluccas . . . than to expose the Company to ruin, by incurring charges, and yet being excluded from the trade." John Bruce, *Annals of the Honorable East India Company* (London, 1810), 1:238.

6. "A Reply to the Remonstrance of the Bewinthebbers or Directors of the Netherlands East-India Companie," in *Remonstrance of the Directors*, 27.

7. C. G. A. Clay, *Economic Expansion and Social Change: Industry, Trade, and Government* (Cambridge: Cambridge University Press, 1984), 130; P. J. Marshall, "The English in Asia to 1700," in *The Origins of Empire: British Overseas Enterprise to the Close of the Seventeenth Century*, ed. Nicholas Canny (Oxford: Oxford University Press, 1998), 264–85, on 274.

8. K. N. Chaudhuri, *The Trading World of Asia and the English East India Company: 1660–1760* (Cambridge: Cambridge University Press, 2006), 7.

9. George Chalmers, ed., *A Collection of Treaties Between Great Britain and Other Powers* (London, 1790), 2: 291–92. Bombay was ruled directly by the English Crown from 1662 to 1667, but formally occupied only in 1665; it was leased to the East India Company in 1668. The Mediterranean port of Tangier was occupied in 1661 and abandoned in 1684. Galle was not actually acquired until the nineteenth century.

10. William Foster, ed., *The English Factories in India*, vol. 7, *1642–1645* (Oxford: Clarendon Press, 1913), 12.

11. Gerald Aungier to the EIC, 15 Jan. 1674, British Library, IOR: E/3/34, f. 342r; see also Charles Fawcett, ed., *The English Factories in India*, new

series, vol. 1, *The Western Presidency, 1670–1677* (Oxford: Clarendon Press, 1936), 73.

12. Foster, *The English Factories in India*, vol. 12, *1665–1667* (1925), 130. Similar requests were made on behalf of the Bombay colony in 1671. See George W. Forrest, ed., *Selections from the Letters, Despatches, and Other State Papers Preserved in the Bombay Secretariat*. Home Series (Bombay, 1887), 1: 55.

13. Ethel B. Sainsbury, ed., *A Calendar of the Court Minutes Etc. of the East India Company*, vol. 8, *1668–1670* (Oxford: Clarendon Press, 1929), 250.

14. Foster, *The English Factories in India*, vol. 13, *1668–1669* (1927), 237–38.

15. Philip Giffard to the EIC, 19 Nov. 1675, British Library, IOR: G/3/7, 169; Philip Giffard to the EIC, 4 Dec. 1675, British Library, IOR: G/3/7, 171.

16. Philip Giffard et al. to the EIC, 3 Nov. 1670, British Library, IOR: E/3/31 no. 3509, ff. 140r–140v.

17. Gerald Aungier et al. to the EIC, 7 Nov. 1671, British Library, IOR: E/3/32 no. 3594, ff. 95v–96r.

18. This was especially the case where EIC authorities forced concubinaries into marriage. See J. Talboys Wheeler, *Madras in the Olden Time: Being a History of the Presidency from the First Foundation of Fort St. George to the French Occupation of Madras* (Madras, 1862), 454.

19. Foster, *The English Factories in India*, vol. 10, *1655–60* (1921), 108; Ethel B. Sainsbury, ed., *A Calendar of the Court Minutes etc. of the East India Company*, vol. 7, *1664–1667* (1925), 158. An overview of Gabriel Boughton's career can be found in Foster, *The English Factories in India*, vol. 7, *1642–1645*, xxv–xxvi.

20. Henry D. Love, *Vestiges of Old Madras, 1640–1800* (London: John Murray, 1913), 1: 185, 262; Sainsbury, *A Calendar of the Court Minutes Etc. of the East India Company*, vol. 3, *1644–1649* (1912), 255; Foster, *The English Factories in India*, vol. 7, *1642–1645*, 76, and vol. 10, *1655–1660*, 402.

21. Ray Strachey and Oliver Strachey, *Keigwin's Rebellion, (1683–4): An Episode in the History of Bombay* (Oxford: Clarendon Press, 1916), 10–11. Henry Gary's wife, Maria, was presumably an Indo-Portuguese from Surat. Although the marriage cannot be dated with certainty, it probably occurred at some point before 1658, for in this year the couple buried their only son. See Foster, *The English Factories in India*, vol. 11, *1661–1664* (1923), 209; and Forrest, *Selections*, 1: 17.

22. Forrest, *Selections*, 1: 14.

23. Foster, *The English Factories in India*, vol. 12, *1665–1667*, 299.

24. Curiously, a 1865 list of English tombstones at Surat mentions Henry Gary's son but has nothing to say about his wife. Augustus Fortunatus Bellasis, "Monumental Inscriptions in the English and Dutch Cemeteries at Surat," British Library, MS Add. 44948, f. 1r.

25. Foster, *The English Factories in India*, vol. 12, *1665–1667*, 299.

26. Richard Head, *The English Rogue: Described, in the Life of Meriton Latroon, a Witty Extravagant* (London, 1665), sig. Hhh4v. All quotations

are from this erratically paginated edition. Signature references have been provided in lieu of page numbers.

27. John Dryden, *Amboyna; or, The Cruelties of the Dutch to the English Merchants*, in *The Works of John Dryden*, vol. 12 ed. Vinton A. Dearing (Berkeley: University of California Press, 1994), 3–77. All citations are from this edition.

28. *The Answer unto the Dutch Pamphlet.* . . . (London, 1624), 13. The EIC also ordered "a detailed picture of all the tortures inflicted on the English at Amboyna," commissioned a play on the subject, and supported the publication of *The Stripping of Joseph*, a sermon comparing the treatment Joseph had received from his brothers to the fate the Dutch had meted out to the English. Mary Ann E. Green, ed., *Calendar of State Papers, Domestic: 1623–25* (London, 1859), 481.

29. On the role of merchants in the English martyrological tradition, see Laura C. Stevenson, *Praise and Paradox: Merchants and Craftsmen in Elizabethan Popular Literature* (Cambridge: Cambridge University Press, 1984), 78; John R. Knott, *Discourses of Martyrdom in English Literature, 1563–1694* (Cambridge: Cambridge University Press, 1993); and Helen C. White, *Tudor Books of Martyrs* (Madison: University of Wisconsin Press, 1963).

30. *A True Relation*, 2. A play on Amboina was commissioned in 1624–25, but immediately suppressed; another play on the subject was produced in November 1672 by one Anthony Di Voto. See James A. Winn, *John Dryden and His World* (New Haven, CT: Yale University Press, 1987), 239.

31. Scholars have long identified Dryden's principal sources as *A True Relation*—often attributed to Dudley Digges—and John Darrell's *A True and Compendious Narration.* . . . (London, 1665). See Robert Markley, "Violence and Profits on the Restoration Stage: Trade, Nationalism, and Insecurity in Dryden's *Amboyna*," *Eighteenth-Century Life* 22, no. 1 (1998): 2–17; Yoichi Onishi, "In Quest of National Solidarity: Gender and Empire in John Dryden's *Amboyna*," *Shiron* 35 (1996): 1–18; and Anne B. Gardiner, "Dating Dryden's *Amboyna*: Allusions in the Text to 1672–1673 Politics," *Restoration and Eighteenth Century Theatre Research* 1, no. 1 (1990): 18–27.

32. The pamphlets actually give this name as "Tsabinda." As Colin Visser has suggested, Dryden's spelling of the name probably derives from the 1672 *Emblem of Ingratitude*, where the "T" of Tsabinda is printed in italics and can be easily misread as a "Y." Visser, "John Dryden's *Amboyna* at Lincoln's Inn Fields, 1673," *Restoration and Eighteenth Century Theatre Research* 15, no. 1 (1976): 1–11.

33. Michael H. Fisher, *Counterflows to Colonialism: Indian Travellers and Settlers in Britain, 1600–1685* (Delhi: Permanent Black, 2004), 23–29; William Foster, ed., *The Embassy of Sir Thomas Roe to the Court of the Great Mogul, 1615–1619.* . . . (London, 1899), 2: 477–78; and William Foster, *Early Travels in India, 1583–1619* (1921; New York: AMS Press, 1975), 69–70.

34. *An answere to the Hollanders Declaration, Concerning the Occurrents of the East-India* (London, 1622), 5.

35. "An Authentick Copy," 35.

36. James Fox, "'For Good and Sufficient Reasons': An Examination of Early Dutch East India Company Ordinances on Slaves and Slavery," in *Slavery, Bondage and Dependency in Southeast Asia*, ed. Anthony Reid and Jennifer Brewster (New York: St. Martin's Press, 1983), 246–62.

37. Qtd. in Leonard Blussé, *Strange Company: Chinese Settlers, Mestizo Women and the Dutch in VOC Batavia* (Dordrecht: Foris, 1986), 162.

38. On the use of Portuguese captives for marriage purposes, see Pietro della Valle, *Viaggi di Pietro della Valle il pellegrino* (Rome, 1650), trans. George Havers as *The Travels of Pietro della Valle in India*, ed. Edward Grey (London, 1892), 1: 25; and Foster, *The English Factories in India*, vol. 2, *1622–1623* (1908), 155.

39. Leonard Blussé, *Bitter Bonds: A Colonial Divorce Drama of the Seventeenth Century*, trans. Diane Webb (Princeton, NJ: M. Wiener, 2002), 15.

40. The prohibition also applied to their husbands and children. See Jean G. Taylor, *The Social World of Batavia: European and Eurasian in Dutch Asia* (Madison: University of Wisconsin Press, 1983), 16–18; and Eric Jones, *Wives, Slaves, and Concubines: A History of the Female Underclass in Dutch Asia* (DeKalb: Northern Illinois University Press, 2010).

41. Thomas Mills and John Milward to the president at Surat, 14 Nov. 1622, British Library, IOR G/36/102, f. 10v. An abstract of this letter can be found in Foster, *The English Factories in India*, vol. 2, *1622–1623*, 145–47.

42. Beamont's plea for "a third part of the merchandise" is an explicit reference to the Anglo-Dutch agreement of 1619. The accord stipulated that the VOC and EIC would have an equal share of the pepper crop at Java; in the Moluccas, Bandas, and Amboina, the English portion would be limited to one-third.

43. My discussion of this scene is greatly indebted to Bridget Orr, *Empire on the English Stage* (Cambridge: Cambridge University Press, 2001), 158–59.

44. Valerie Traub, *Desire and Anxiety: Circulations of Sexuality in Shakespearean Drama* (New York: Routledge, 1996), 70.

45. Even Ysabinda's self-description as a "black Adulteress" may be taken as a reference to Jeremiah 13, where the stubborn blackness of the Moor's skin is analogized to the "adulteries" of the Jews: "I have seene thine adulteries, and thy neiings, the filthinesse of thy whoredome on the hils in the fieldes, and thine abominations. Wo unto thee, O Ierusalem: wilt thou not bee made cleane? When shal it once be?" (Jeremiah 13:27, Geneva Bible).

46. Karen Newman, "'And Wash the Ethiop White': Femininity and the Monstrous in *Othello*," in *Shakespeare Reproduced: The Text in History and Ideology*, ed. Jean E. Howard and Marion F. O'Connor (New York: Methuen, 1987), 143–62. See also Jean Michel Massing, "From Greek Proverb to Soap Advert: Washing the Ethiopian," *Journal of the Warburg and Courtauld Institutes* 58 (1995): 180–201; and Anu Korhonen, "Washing the Ethiopian White: Conceptualising Black Skin in Renaissance England," in *Black Africans in Renaissance Europe*, ed. Thomas F. Earle and Kate J. P. Lowe (Cambridge: Cambridge University Press, 2005), 94–112.

47. Shankar Raman, *Framing "India": The Colonial Imaginary in Early Modern Culture* (Stanford, CA: Stanford University Press, 2001), 233.

48. Raman, *Framing "India,"* 233.

49. "The Relation of the Priest of Poolaroone, touching the beginnings and occasions of quarrels betwixt the Dutch and Bandaneses. . . . ," in *Purchas his Pilgrimes*, comp. Samuel Purchas (London, 1625), 1: 722.

50. *A True Relation*, sigs. A2v, A3r.

51. The play's investment in obscuring the parallels (and collusions) between English a true relation, sig. A2v and Dutch VOC are insightfully explored in Markley, "Violence and Profits," 2–17. See also Raman, *Framing "India,"* 189–36.

52. As J. A. van der Welle points out in *Dryden and Holland* (Groningen: J. B. Wolters, 1962), 62, the final couplet is Dryden's own invention; the rest of the epithalamium is derived from Johannes Secundus's homonymous poem.

53. Johannes Secundus, "Epithalamium," in *An Anthology of Neo-Latin Poetry*, trans. and ed. Fred J. Nichols (New Haven, CT: Yale University Press, 1979), 515–23.

54. Paul Salzman, *English Prose Fiction, 1558–1700: A Critical History* (Oxford: Clarendon Press, 1985), 238; and Tim Thornton, *Prophecy, Politics and the People in Early Modern England* (Woodbridge: Boydell & Brewer, 2006), 84, n. 138.

55. Head, *The English Rogue* (1665), sig. B2v.

56. Some of Latroon's adventures in Asia are borrowed from Fernão Mendes Pinto's *Peregrinaçam de Fernam Mendez Pinto* (Lisbon, 1614), which had appeared in Henry Cogan's translation as *The Voyages and Adventures of Fernand Mendez Pinto. . . .* (London, 1653); most others are taken from Thomas Herbert's *A Relation of Some Yeares Travaile* (1634; enlarged editions published in 1638, 1665, and 1677).

57. Ron Harris, "The English East India Company and the History of Company Law," in *VOC, 1602–2002: 400 Years of Company Law*, ed. Ella Gepken-Jager, Gerard Van Solinge, and Levinus Timmerman (Deventer: Kluwer, 2005), 227, 240.

58. Foster, *The English Factories in India*, vol. 10, *1655–1660*, 47, 108; and Ian B. Watson, *Foundation for Empire: English Private Trade in India, 1659–1760* (New Delhi: Vikas, 1980), 107. In this respect, EIC merchants in Asia were merely following in the footsteps of the Portuguese casados, in whose hands private trade and royal monopoly often converged. Michael N. Pearson, *The Portuguese in India* (Cambridge: Cambridge University Press, 1987), 82.

59. An excellent example is the 1670 poem "The Queen's Ball," sometimes attributed to Andrew Marvell: "With a white vizard you may cheat our eyes; / You know a black one would be no disguise." George de Forest Lord, ed., *Poems on Affairs of State: Augustan Satirical Verse, 1660–1714* (New Haven, CT: Yale University Press, 1963), 1: 421.

60. On European stereotypes of Indian submissiveness, see Kate Teltscher, "'Maidenly and Well Nigh Effeminate': Constructions of Hindu Masculinity and Religion in Seventeenth-Century English Texts," *Postcolonial Studies* 3, no. 2 (2000): 159–70.

61. Arthur C. Sprague, *Beaumont and Fletcher on the Restoration Stage* (Cambridge, MA: Harvard University Press, 1926).

62. Ian Watt, *The Rise of the Novel: Studies in Defoe, Richardson and Fielding* (Berkeley: University of California Press, 1957), 10; and Howard Mancing, "The Protean Picaresque," in *The Picaresque: Tradition and Displacement*, ed. Giancarlo Maiorino (Minneapolis: University of Minnesota Press, 1996), 273–91.

63. Virginia M. Vaughan, *Performing Blackness on English Stages* (Cambridge: Cambridge University Press, 2005), 55.

64. On the seventeenth-century "fanchono," see Luiz R. B. Mott, *Escravidão, Homossexualidade e Demonologia* (São Paulo: Icone, 1988); and David Higgs, "Lisbon," in *Queer Sites: Gay Urban Histories Since 1600*, ed. David Higgs (New York: Routledge, 1999), 112–37. On the emergence of a "molly" subculture in England, see Randolph Trumbach, "The Birth of the Queen: Sodomy and the Emergence of Gender Equality in Modern Culture, 1660–1750," in *Hidden from History: Reclaiming the Gay and Lesbian Past*, ed. Martin B. Duberman, Martha Vicinus, and George Chauncey (New York: Penguin, 1990), 129–40. On the "puto" (an effeminate male who made himself available for anal penetration), see Rafaél Carrasco, *Inquisición y represión sexual en Valencia: Historia de los sodomitas, 1565–1785* (Barcelona: Laertes, 1985); and Zeb Tortorici, "'Heran Todos Putos': Sodomitical Subcultures and Disordered Desire in Early Colonial Mexico," *Ethnohistory* 54, no. 1 (2007): 35–67. On the "tribade" in early modern France, see Marie-Jo Bonnet, "Sappho, or the Importance of Culture in the Language of Love: *Tribade, Lesbienne, Homosexuelle*," in *Queerly Phrased: Language, Gender, and Sexuality*, ed. Anna Livia and Kira Hall (Oxford: Oxford University Press, 1997), 147–66.

65. Edward Ward, *The Secret History of Clubs. . . .* (London, 1709), 299.

66. Havelock Ellis, *Studies in the Psychology of Sex: Sexual Inversion* (Philadelphia: F. A. Davis, 1901), 13.

67. Robert Knox, *An historical relation of the island Ceylon, in the East-Indies. . . .* (London, 1681).

68. Vinton A. Dearing, "Commentary [to *Amboyna*]," in *The Works of John Dryden*, vol. 12 ed. Vinton A. Dearing (Berkeley: University of California Press, 1994), 317.

69. *A True Relation*, 13.

70. Qtd. in Margaret Healy, *Fictions of Disease in Early Modern England: Bodies, Plagues and Politics* (New York: Palgrave, 2001), 125; see also Richard Bunworth, *A New discovery of the French Disease and Running of the Reins* (London, 1662), 10.

71. Kim F. Hall, *Things of Darkness: Economies of Race and Gender in Early Modern England* (Ithaca, NY: Cornell University Press, 1995), 226–39. Although most of the sitters represented alongside black servants were women, there are several portraits in which the sitters are prominent male colonizers. On the origins of the genre, see Paul H. D. Kaplan, "Titian's Laura Dianti and the Origins of the Motif of the Black Page in Portraiture," *Antiquità viva* 21, no. 1 (1982): 11–18 and no. 4 (1982): 10–19.

72. Gary Taylor, *Buying Whiteness: Race, Culture, and Identity from Columbus to Hip Hop* (New York: Palgrave, 2005), esp. 184–85.

73. Benjamin Schmidt, *Innocence Abroad: The Dutch Imagination and the New World, 1570–1670* (Cambridge: Cambridge University Press, 2001), 81. For English propaganda on the subject, see Thomas Scott, *An Experimentall Discoverie of Spanish Practises* (London, 1623); and Stephen Ofwod, *A Relation of Sundry Particular Wicked plots and Cruel, Inhumaine, Perfidious; yea, Unnaturall Practises of the Spaniards.* . . . (London, 1624).

74. John Crouch, *Belgica Caracteristica; or, The Dutch Character* (London, 1665), 5. In *Buying Whiteness*, Taylor dates the earliest instance of "white" as a generic or racial noun to a 1661 manuscript source (263). To the best of my knowledge, John Crouch's *Belgica Caracteristica* is one of the earliest print sources to use "white" in the same sense.

BIBLIOGRAPHY

MANUSCRIPT SOURCES

Manoscritti Gesuitici, Biblioteca Nazionale, Rome

India Office Records (IOR), British Library, London

Boxer Codex, Boxer MSS II. Lilly Library at Indiana University, Bloomington, IN

PRIMARY PRINT SOURCES

Albuquerque, Afonso de. *Cartas de Affonso de Albuquerque, seguidas de documentos que as elucidam*. Ed. Raymundo A. de Bulhão Pato and Henrique Lopes de Mendonça. 7 vols. Lisbon: Academia das Ciências de Lisboa/Imprensa Nacional, 1884–1935.

Albuquerque, Brás de. *The Commentaries of the Great Afonso Dalbuquerque, Second Viceroy of India*, trans. and ed. Walter De Gray Birch. 4 vols. London, 1875–84.

Alcina, Francisco Ignacio. *La Historia de las islas e indios Visayas del Padre Alcina, 1668*. Ed. María Luisa Martin-Merás and María Dolores Higueras. Madrid: Instituto Histórico de Marina, 1974.

"Altitudo Divini Consilii" (1 Jun. 1537). In *Enchiridion Symbolorum: Definitionum et Declarationum de Rebus Fidei et Morum*, ed. Henry Denziger. Freiburg: Herder, 1965, 363.

An answere to the Hollanders Declaration, Concerning the Occurrents of the East-India. London, 1622.

The Answer unto the Dutch Pamphlet, Made in Defence of the Iniust and Barbarous Proceedings Against the English at Amboyna in the East Indies, by the Hollanders there. London, 1624

Aquinas, Thomas. *Summa Theologica*. Trans. Fathers of the English Dominican Province. 3 vols. New York: Benzinger, 1947.

Argensola, Bartolomé Leonardo de. See Leonardo de Argensola, Bartolomé.

Augustine. *Contra Faustum Manichaeum*. In *A Select Library of Nicene and Post-Nicene Fathers of the Christian Church*, vol. 4, ed. Philip Schaff. Buffalo, 1887.

"An Authentick Copy of the Confessions and Sentences against M. Towerson, and Complices, Concerning the Bloudy Conspiracy enterprised against the Castle of Amboyna." In *A Remonstrance of the Directors of the Netherlands East India Company presented to the Lords States Generall of the United Provinces. . . .* London, 1632.

Avity, Pierre d'. *Les Estats, empires et principautez du monde*. Paris, 1613. Trans. Edward Grimston as *The estates, empires, & principallities of the world*. London, 1615.

Baião, António, Artur de Magalhães Basto, and Damião Peres, eds. *Diário da viagem de Vasco da Gama*. 2 vols. Porto: Livraria Civilização, 1945.

Balbi, Gasparo. *Viaggio dell'Indie Orientali*. Venice, 1590. Partially trans. as "Gasparo Balbi his Voyage to Pegu, and Observations there." In *Purchas his Pilgrimes*, comp. Samuel Purchas. London, 1625, 2: 1722–29.

Barros, João de. *Ásia de João de Barros: Dos feitos que os portugueses fizeram no descobrimento e conquista dos mares e terras do Oriente [Década primeira-quarta]*. Ed. Hernâni Cidade and Manuel Múrias. 4 vols. Lisbon: Divisão de Publicações e Biblioteca, Agência Geral das Colónias, 1945–46.

Barzeu, Gaspar. "Carta ao Padre Inácio de Loiola." In *Documentação para a história das missões do padroado português do Oriente: Índia*, vol. 7, *1559*, ed. António da Silva Rêgo. Lisbon: Divisão de Publicações e Biblioteca, Agência Geral do Ultramar, 1952, 71–92.

Bellan, Louis Gédoyn de. "Histoire memorable de Dias Espagnol, et de Quixaire Princesse des Moluques." In *Nouvelles de Miguel de Cervantes Saavedra. Ou sont contenues plusiers rares adventures, memorables exemples d'amour, de fidelité, de force de sang, de jalousie, de mauvaise habitude, de charmes, & d'autres accidents non moins estranges que veritables. Traduictes d'espagnol en françois: Les six premieres par F. de Rosset. Et les autres six, par le Sr. d'Audiguier. Avec l'histoire de Ruis Dias, & de Quixaire princesse des Moluques, composee par le Sr. de Bellan*. Paris, 1615.

Béthune, Philippe de. *Le conseiller d'État; ou, Recueil des plus générales considérations servant au maniement des affaires publiques*. Paris, 1632. Trans. by Edward Grimston as *The Counsellor of Estate: contayning the Greatest and most Remarkable Considerations serving for the Managing of Publicke Affaires*. London, 1634.

Bluteau, Rafael. *Vocabulario Portuguez e Latino*. Vol. 2. Coimbra, 1712.

Bodin, Jean. *Les Six livres de la République*. Paris, 1576. Trans. by Richard Knolles as *The Six Books of a Commonweale*. London, 1606.

————. *Methodus ad facilem historiarum cognitionem*. Paris, 1566. Trans. Beatrice Reynolds as *Method for the Easy Comprehension of History*. New York: W. W. Norton, 1969.

Boemus, Johannes. *Omnium gentium mores, leges et ritus ex multis clarissimis rerum scriptoribus*. Augsburg, 1520. Trans. Edward Aston as *The Manners, Lawes and Customes of all Nations*. London, 1611.

Bohun, Edmund. *A geographical dictionary representing the present and ancient names of all the counties, provinces, remarkable cities, universities, ports, towns, mountains, seas, streights, fountains, and rivers of the whole world*. London, 1693.

Botero, Giovanni. *Della ragion di stato*. Venice, 1589. Trans. P. J. Waley and D. P. Waley as *The Reason of State*. New Haven, CT: Yale University Press, 1956.

————. *Le Relationi Universali*. Venice, 1596.

Boxhorn, Marcus Zuerius van. *Commentariolus de Statu Confoederatarum Provinciarum Belgii*. The Hague, 1649.

Brito, Bernardo de. *Primeyra parte da Chronica de Cister, onde se contam as cousas principais desta religiam com muytas antiguidades, assi do Reyno de Portugal como de outros muytos da Christandade*. Lisbon, 1602.

Bruce, John. *Annals of the Honourable East India Company*. 2 vols. London, 1810.

Bruno, Giordano. *Lo spaccio della bestia trionfante*. London, 1584. Trans. Arthur D. Imerti as *The Expulsion of the Triumphant Beast*. Lincoln: University of Nebraska Press, 2004.

Bry, Johann Theodor de, and Johann Israel de Bry. *Quinta pars Indiae Orientalis: Quâ continetur Vera & accurata descriptio universae navigationis illius, quam Hollandi cum octonis navibus in terras orientales, præcipuè vero in Iavanas & Moluccanas Insulas, Bantam, Bandam & Ternatem, &c. susceperunt*. Frankfurt, 1601.

Bulwer, John. *Anthropometamorphosis: Man Tranform'd; or, the Artificial Changeling. Historically Presented, In the mad and cruel Gallantry, Foolish Bravery, ridiculous Beauty, Filthy Finenesse, and loathsome Lovelinesse of most Nations, Fashioning & altering their Bodies from the Mould intended by Nature*. London, 1650.

————. *Anthropometamorphosis: Man Transform'd; or, The Artificiall Changling Historically presented, In the mad and cruell Gallantry, foolish Bravery, ridiculous Beauty, filthy Finenesse, and loathsome Loveliness of most Nations, fashioning and altering their bodies from the mould intended by Nature; with Figures of those Transfigurations*. London, 1653.

Bunworth, Richard. *A New discovery of the French Disease and Running of the Reins*. London, 1662.

Camões, Luís Vaz de. *Os Lusíadas*. Ed. Frank Pierce. Oxford: Clarendon Press, 1973. Trans. Landeg White as *The Lusíads*. Oxford: Oxford University Press, 1997.

Campanella, Tommaso. "De Matrimonio." In *I sacri segni*, ed. Romano Amerio. Vol. 6. Rome: Centro Internazionale di Studi Umanistici, 1968.

Capel, Richard. *Tentations: Their Nature, Danger, Cure*. London, 1633.

Carletti, Francesco. *Ragionamenti del mio viaggio attorno al mondo*. Ed. Paolo Collo. Torino: Giulio Einaudi Editore, 1989. Trans. Herbert Weinstock as *My Voyage Around the World: The Chronicles of a Sixteenth-Century Florentine Merchant*. London: Methuen, 1965.

Castanheda, Fernão Lopes de. *História do descobrimento e conquista da Índia pelos Portugueses*. 8 vols. Lisbon, 1833.

Chalmers, George, ed. *A Collection of Treaties Between Great Britain and Other Powers*. Vol. 2. London, 1790.

Chijs, Jacobus A. van der. *Nederlandsch-Indisch Plakaatboek, 1602–1811*. 17 vols. Batavia: Landsrukkerij, 1885–1900.

Chirino, Pedro. *Relacion de las islas Filipinas i de lo que en ellas an trabaiado los Padres de la Compañia de Iesus*. Rome, 1604. Trans. Frederic W. Morrison and Emma H. Blair as "Relation of the Filipinas Islands and of What Has There Been Accomplished by the Fathers of the Society of Jesus." In *The Philippine Islands, 1493–1803*, ed. Emma H. Blair and James A. Robertson. Cleveland: Arthur H. Clark, 1904, 12: 169–321 and 13: 27–217.

Colombo, Realdo. *De Re Anatomica Libri XV*. Venice, 1559.

Concepción, Juan de la. *Historia general de Philipinas. Conquistas espirituales y temporales de estos españoles dominios, establecimientos, progresos, y decadencias*. 14 vols. Manila, 1788–92.

Conti, Niccolò de', and Poggio Bracciolini. *India Recognita*. Milan, 1492. Trans. John W. Jones as part of *Travelers in Disguise: Narratives of Eastern Travel by Poggio Bracciolini and Ludovico de Varthema*, ed. Lincoln D. Hammond. Cambridge, MA: Harvard University Press, 1963.

Cooke, John. *Greenes Tu Quoque; or, The Cittie Gallant*. London, 1614.

Couto, Diogo do. *O Soldado Prático*. Ed. Manuel Rodrigues Lapa. Lisbon: Livraria Sá da Costa, 1937.

———. *Da Ásia de Diogo de Couto: Dos feitos, que os Portuguezes fizeram na conquista, e descubrimento das terras, e mares do Oriente. Década decima, parte segunda*. Vol. 21 of *Da Ásia de João de Barros e de Diogo de Couto*. Lisbon, 1788.

Coutre, Jacques de. "Vida de Iaques de Couttre natural de la ciudad de la Brugas." 1640. First pub. as *Andanzas asiáticas*, ed. Eddy Stols, Benjamin Teensma, and Johan Verberckmoes. Madrid: Historia 16, 1991.

Crouch, John. *Belgica Caracteristica; or, The Dutch Character.* London, 1665.

D'Anghiera, Pietro Martire. *Decadas de Orbe Novo.* Alcalá, 1530. Trans. Francis Augustus MacNutt as *De Orbe Novo: The Eight Decades of Peter Martyr D'Anghera.* 2 vols. New York: G. P. Putnam's Sons, 1912.

Darrell, John. *A True and Compendious Narration; or (The Second Part of Amboyna) of Sundry Notorious or Remarkable Injuries, Insolences, and Acts of Hostility which the Hollanders Have Exercised from time to time against the English Nation in the East Indies.* London, 1665.

Defoe, Daniel. *Conjugal Lewdness; or, Matrimonial Whoredom. A Treatise Concerning the Use and Abuse of the Marriage Bed.* London, 1727.

Della Valle, Pietro. *Viaggi di Pietro della Valle il pellegrino.* Rome, 1650. Trans. George Havers as *The Travels of Pietro della Valle in India.* Ed. Edward Grey. 2 vols. London, 1892.

De Rhodes, Alexandre. *Relazione de' felici successi della santa fede predicata da' padri della Compagnia di Giesu nel regno di Tunchino.* Rome, 1650.

Diodorus Siculus. *Bibliotheca Historica.* Trans. Charles H. Oldfather, Charles L. Sherman, C. Bradford Welles, Russel M. Geer, and Francis R. Walton as *Library of History,* ed. George P. Goold. 12 vols. Cambridge, MA: Harvard University Press, 1933–1967.

Dryden, John. *Amboyna; or, The Cruelties of the Dutch to the English Merchants,* ed. Vinton A. Dearing. In *The Works of John Dryden,* ed. Edward N. Hooker, Hugh, T. Swedenberg, and Vinton A. Dearing. 20 vols. Berkeley: University of California Press, 1956–2000, 12: 3–77.

Du Jarric, Pierre. *Histoire des choses plus memorables advenues tant ez Indes Orientales, que autres païs de la descouverte des Portugais, en l'establissement et progrez de la foy Chrestienne et Catholique: Et principalement de ce que les Religieux de la Compagnie de Iésus y ont faict, & endure pour la mesme fin; depuis quils y sont entrez jusques à l'an 1600.* Bourdeaux, 1608–14. Partially trans. C. H. Payne as *Akbar and the Jesuits: An Account of the Jesuit Missions to the Court of Akbar by Father Pierre du Jarric, S. J.* Ed. E. Denison Ross and Eileen Power. New Delhi: Tulsi, 1979.

Dumont, Jean, comp. *Corps universel diplomatique du droit des gens.* Vol. 5. Amsterdam, 1723.

Eden, Richard, comp. *The decades of the newe worlde or west India conteynyng the navigations and conquestes of the Spanyardes, with the particular description of the moste ryche and large landes and ilandes lately founde in the west ocean perteynyng to the inheritaunce of the kinges of Spayne.* London, 1555.

Eden, Richard, and Richard Willes, comps. *The History of Travayle in the West and East Indies, and other countreys lying eyther way, towardes the fruitfull and ryche Moluccaes.* London, 1577.

"The famous voyage of Sir Francis Drake into the South Sea, and there hence about the whole Globe of the Earth, begun the yeere of our Lord, 1577." In *The Principal Navigations. . . . ,* comp. Richard Hakluyt (London, 1600) 3: 730–42.

Faria e Sousa, Manuel de. *Asia portuguesa.* Lisbon, 1666–75. Trans. and abr. John Stevens as *The Portugues Asia; or, The History of the Discovery and Conquest of India by the Portugues; Containing All their Discoveries from the Coast of Africk, to the farthest Parts of China and Japan; all their Battels by Sea and Land, Sieges and other Memorable Actions; a Description of those Countries, and many Particulars of the Religion, Government and Customs of the Natives.* 3 vols. London, 1695.

———, trans. and ed., *Lusiadas de Luis de Camoens, principe de los poetas de España . . . Comentadas por Manuel de Faria i Sousa, Cavallero de la Orden de Christo, i de la Casa Real.* 2 vols. Madrid, 1639.

Felltham, Owen. *Resolves: Divine, Morall, Politicall.* London, 1623.

Fernández de Figueroa, Martín. *Conquista de las Indias de Persia & Arabia que fizo la armada del rey don Manuel de Portugal e delas muchas tierras, diversas gentes, extrañas riquezas & grandes batallas que allá ovo.* Salamanca, 1512. Trans. and ed. James McKenna as *A Spaniard in the Portuguese Indies: The Narrative of Martín Fernández de Figueroa.* Cambridge, MA: Harvard University Press, 1967.

Fernández de Oviedo y Valdés, Gonzalo. *Historia general y natural de las Indias, islas y tierra-firme del Mar Océano.* Ed. José Amador de los Rios. Vol. 2. Madrid, 1852.

Fernández Navarrete, Domingo. *Tratados historicos, politicos, ethicos, y religiosos de la monarchia de China.* Madrid, 1676. Partially trans. James S. Cummins in *The Travels and Controversies of Friar Domingo Navarrete, 1618–1686.* 2 vols. London: Hakluyt Society, 1962.

Fitch, Ralph. "The Voyage of Master Ralph Fitch, Merchant of London to Ormus, and so to Goa in the East India, to Cambaia, Ganges, Bengala; to Bacola, and Chonderi, to Pegu, to Iamahay in the Kingdome of Siam, and backe to Pegu, and from thence to Malacca, Zeilan, Cochin, and all the Coast of the East India: begun in the yeere of our Lord 1583 and ended 1591." In *Purchas his Pilgrimes,* comp. Samuel Purchas. London, 1625, 2: 1730–44.

Fletcher, John. *The Island Princess.* Ed. George W. Williams. In vol. 5 of *The Dramatic Works in the Beaumont and Fletcher Canon,* ed. Fredson Bowers. Cambridge: Cambridge University Press, 1982, 552–651.

Foster, William, ed. *A Calendar of the Court Minutes Etc. of the East India Company, 1644–1649.* Oxford: Clarendon Press, 1914.

————, ed. *Early Travels in India, 1583–1619*. New York: AMS Press, 1975.

————, ed. *The Embassy of Sir Thomas Roe to the Court of the Great Mogul, 1615–1619, As Narrated in His Journal and Correspondence*. 2 vols. London, 1899.

————, ed. *The English Factories in India*. 13 vols. Oxford: Clarendon Press, 1906–27.

————, ed. *The Voyage of Thomas Best to the East Indies, 1612–1614*. London: Hakluyt Society, 1934.

————, ed. *The Voyages of Sir James Lancaster to Brazil and the East Indies, 1591–1603*. London: Hakluyt Society, 1940.

Foster, William, and Frederick C. Danvers, eds. *Letters Received by the East India Company by Its Servants in the East*. 6 vols. London: Sampson, Low, Marston, 1896–1902.

Foxe, John. *Actes and Monuments of these latter and perillous dayes, touching matters of the Church, wherein ar comprehended and described the great persecutions & horrible troubles, that have bene wtought and practised by the Romishe Prelates, speciallye in this Realmes of England and Scotlande, from the yeare of our Lorde a thousande, unto the tyme nowe present*. London, 1563.

Galván Rivera, Mariano, ed. *Concilio III Provincial Mexicano, celebrado en México el año de 1585, confirmado en Roma por el Papa Sixto V, y mandado observar por el gobierno español en diversas reales órdenes*. Mexico City, 1859.

Gonçalves, Diogo. *História do Malavar*. Ed. Josef Wicki. Rome: IHSI, 1953.

Guarini, Giambattista. *Il pastor fido; or, The Faithfull Shepheard. Translated out of Italian into English*. London, 1602.

Guevara, Antonio de. *Relox de Príncipes*. Valladolid, 1529. In *Obras Completas de Fray Antonio de Guevara*, ed. Emilio Blanco. Vol. 2. Madrid: Fundación José Antonio de Castro, 1994.

Hakluyt, Richard, comp. *The Principal Navigations, Voyages, Traffiques, and Discoveries of the English Nation, Made by Sea or Overland, to the Remote and Farthest Distant Quarters of the Earth, at Any Time within the Compasse of these 1600 Yeres*. 3 vols. in 2. London, 1598–1600.

Hawkins, William. "Relations of the Occurents Which Happened in the Time of His Residence in India, in the County of the Great Mogoll, and of his departure from thence, written to the Company." In *Purchas his Pilgrimes*, comp. Samuel Purchas. London, 1625, 1 (bk. 3): 206–26.

Head, Richard. *The English Rogue. Described, In the Life of Meriton Latroon, a Witty Extravagant. Being a Compleat Discovery of the Most Eminent Cheats of both Sexes*. London, 1668.

———. *The English Rogue: Described, In the Life of Meriton Latroon, a Witty Extravagant. Being a compleat History of the most Eminent Cheats of both Sexes.* London, 1665.

Herbert, Thomas. *A relation of some yeares travaile, begunne anno 1626. Into Afrique and the greater Asia, especially the territories of the Persian monarchie: and some parts of the Orientall Indies, and iles adiacent. Of their religion, language, habit, discent, ceremonies, and other matters concerning them. Together with the proceedings and death of the three late ambassadours: Sir D. C. Sir R. S. and the Persian Nogdibeg: as also the two great monarchs, the king of Persia, and the great mogol.* London, 1634.

Hernáez, Francisco J., ed. *Colección de bulas, breves y otros documentos relativos a la Iglesia de América y Filipinas.* 2 vols. Vaduz: Kraus Reprint, 1964.

Huan, Ma. *Ying-Yai Sheng-Lan.* 1451. Trans. J. V. G. Mills as *Ying-Yai Sheng-Lan: The Overall Survey of the Ocean's Shores.* Cambridge: Hakluyt Society, 1970.

Jacobs, Hubert M., ed. *Documenta Malucensia.* 3 vols. Rome: IHSI, 1974–84.

Jonge, Johan Karel Jakob de, Marinus Lodewijk van Deventer, Leonard Wilhelm Gijsbert de Roo, Pieter Anton Tiele, Jan Ernst Heeres, Johannes Jacobus Meinsma, and J. W. G. van Haarst, eds. *De Opkomst van het Nederlandsch gezag in Oost-Indië: Verzameling van onuitgegeven stukken uit het Oud-Koloniaal Archief.* 18 vols. The Hague: Martinus Nijhoff, 1862–1909.

Justinian's Institutes. Trans. Peter Birks and Grant McLeod. Ithaca, NY: Cornell University Press, 1987.

Karant-Nunn, Susan C., and Merry E. Wiesner-Hanks, eds. *Luther on Women: A Sourcebook.* Cambridge: Cambridge University Press, 2003.

Knox, Robert. *An historical relation of the island Ceylon, in the East-Indies together, with an account of the detaining in captivity the author and divers other Englishmen now living there, and of the authors miraculous escape: Illustrated with figures, and a map of the island.* London, 1681.

Lancillotto, Nicola. "Carta ao Padre Inácio de Loiola." In *Documentacão para a história das missões do padroado português do Oriente: Índia* vol. 7, *1559*, ed. António da Silva Rêgo. Lisbon: Divisão de Publicações e Biblioteca, Agência Geral do Ultramar, 1952, 32–38.

Lara, Silvia Hunold, ed. *Ordenações Filipinas: Livro V.* São Paulo: Companhia das Letras, 1999.

Leonardo de Argensola, Bartolomé. *Conquista de las Islas Malucas al Rey Felipe III Nuestro Señor.* Madrid, 1609. Trans. John Stevens as *The Dis-*

covery and Conquest of the Molucco and Philippine Islands. Contain-
ing Their History, Ancient and Modern, Natural and Political: Their
Description, Product, Religion, Government, Manners, Habits, Shape,
and Inclinations of the Natives. . . . London, 1708.

Linschoten, Jan Huygen van. *Itinerario, voyage ofte schipvaert, van Ian*
Huygen van Linschoten naer Oost ofte Portugaels Indien inhoudende
een corte beschryvinghe der selver landen ende zee-custen. . . . Amsterdam, 1596. Trans. William Phillip as *The Voyage of John Huyghen van*
Linschoten to the East Indies: From the Old English Translation of 1598,
ed. Arthur Coke Burnell and Pieter Anton Tiele. 2 vols. London, 1885.

Lord, George de Forest, ed., *Poems on Affairs of State: Augustan Satirical*
Verse, 1660–1714. Vol. 1. New Haven, CT: Yale University Press, 1963.

Maffei, Giovanni Pietro. *Historiarum Indicarum libri XVI.* Florence, 1588.
Trans. Francesco Serdonati as *Le istorie delle Indie orientali.* 2 vols. Bergamo: Pietro Lancellotti, 1749.

Martínez, Juan. "Relación detallada de los sucesos ocurridos durante el viaje
de la nao San Jerónimo." In *Colección de documentos inéditos relativos*
al descubrimiento, conquista y organización de las antiguas posesiones
españolas de Ultramar. Madrid, 1887. 3: 371–475.

Medina, Juan de. *Historia de los sucesos de la Orden de N. Gran P. S. Agus-*
tin de estas Islas Filipinas. Manila, 1893.

A Memento for Holland; or, A True and Exact History of the most Villain-
ous and Barbarous Cruelties used on the English Merchants residing at
Amboyna in the East-Indies, by the Netherland Governor and Conncel
[sic] there. London, 1653.

"Memorial to the Council by Citizens of the Filipinas Islands, 26 July 1586."
In *The Philippine Islands, 1493–1803,* ed. Emma H. Blair and James A.
Robertson. Cleveland: Arthur H. Clark, 1903, 6: 157–233.

Méntrida, Alonso de. *Diccionario de la lengua bisaya, hiligueina y haraya*
de la Isla de Panay. [Manila], 1841.

Middleton, Thomas. *The Tryumphs of Honor and Industry.* London, 1617.

Milton, John. *The Complete Prose Works of John Milton.* Vol. 6, (*ca. 1658–*
ca. 1660). Trans. John Carey. Ed. Maurice Kelly. New Haven, CT: Yale
University Press, 1973.

Monserrate, António. "Mongolicae Legationis Commentarius." Ca. 1582. Pub.
as "Mongolicae Legationis Commentarius or the First Jesuit Mission to
Akbar by Fr. Anthony Monserrate S. J." Ed. H. Holsen. *Memoirs of the Asi-*
atic Society of Bengal 3, no. 9 (1914): 513–704. Trans. J. S. Hoyland and ann.
S. N. Banerjee as *The Commentary of Father Monserrate, S. J., on His Jour-*
ney to the Court of Akbar. London: Oxford University Press, 1922.

Montaigne, Michel de. *Les Essais de Michel, Seigneur de Montaigne.* Paris,

1595. Trans. John Florio as *Essayes Written in French by Michael Lord of Montaigne, Knight of the Order of S. Michael, Gentleman of the French Kings Chamber: Done into English, according to the last French edition, by Iohn Florio Reader of the Italian tongue unto the Soveraigne Maiestie of Anna, Queene of England, Scotland, France and Ireland, &c. And one of the Gentlemen of hir Royall Privie chamber.* London, 1613.

Morga, Antonio de. *Sucesos de las Islas Filipinas.* Mexico City, 1609. Trans. James S. Cummins as *Sucesos de las Islas Filipinas.* Cambridge: Hakluyt Society, 1971.

Neck, Jacob Corneliszoon van. *Het Tweede Boeck, Journael oft Dagh-register, inhoudende een warachtich verhael ende Historische vertellinghe vande reyse, gedaen door de acht schepen van Amstelredamme, gheseylt inden Maent Martij 1598. . . .* Amsterdam, 1601.

———. *Historiale beschrijvinghe inhoudende een waerachtich verhael vande reyse ghedaen met acht schepen van Amsterdam: onder 't beleydt van den kloeckmoedighen admirael Iacob Cornelisz. Neck, ende Wybrant van Warwijck vice-admirael van't ghene haer op de selfde reyse is bejeghent ende weder-varen.* Amsterdam, 1619.

———. *Journael ofte Dagh-register, inhoudende een waerachtigh verhael ende Historische vertellinghe van de reyse, ghedaen door de acht schepen van Amsterdamme, onder 'tbeleydt van Jacob Cornelisz. Neck, als Admirael, ende Wybrandt van Warwijck, als Vice-admirael, van Amsterdam gheseylt inden jare 1598 den eersten dag der Maent Martij.* [Amsterdam], 1600. Trans. William Walker as *The Iournall, or Dayly Register, Contayning a True manifestation, and Historicall declaration of the voyage, accomplished by eight shippes of Amsterdam, under the conduct of Iacob Corneliszen Neck Admirall, & Wybrandt van Warwick Vice-Admirall, which sayled from Amsterdam the first day of March, 1598.* London, 1601.

———. *Waerachtigh verhael van de schipvaert op Oost-Indien ghedaen bij de acht schepen in den jare 1598 van Amsterdam uyt-ghezeylt, onder 't beleyd van den admirael Jacob Cornelisson van Neck, ende vice-admirael Wybrand van Warwijck.* Amsterdam, 1646.

Ochino, Bernardino. *Dialogi XXX.* Basel, 1563. Partially trans. into English as *A Dialogue of Polygamy, Written Originally in Italian: Rendred into English by a Person of Quality; and Dedicated to the Author of that well known Treatise call'd Advice to a Son.* London, 1657.

Ofwood, Stephen. *A Relation of Sundry Particular Wicked plots and Cruel, Inhumaine, Perfidious; yea, Unnaturall Practises of the Spaniards Chiefly against the Seventeen Provinces of the Netherlands.* London, 1624.

Olearius, Adam, and Johann Albrecht von Mandelslo. *Morgenländische Reyse-Beschreibung.* Schleßwig, 1658. Trans. John Davies as *The Voyages & Travels of the Ambassadors sent by Frederick, Duke of Hol-*

stein . . . beginning M.DC.XXXIII and finished in M.DC.XXXIX containing a compleat history of Muscovy, Tartary, Persia, and other adjacent countries . . . whereto are added the Travels of John Albert de Mandelslo . . . into the East Indies. London, 1662

Orta, Garcia da. *Colóquios dos simples e drogas e cousas medicinais da India: Reprodução facsimilada da edição impressa em Goa em 10 de abril de 1563, comemorando o quarto centenário da edição original.* Lisbon: Academia das Ciências de Lisboa, 1963. Trans. Clements Markham as *Colloquies on the Simples and Drugs of India,* ed. Conde de Ficalho. London: Henry Sotheran, 1913.

Ovidius Naso, Publius. *Ovid in Six Volumes.* Vol. 2, *The Art of Love, and Other Poems.* Trans. John H. Mozley and ed. George P. Goold. Cambridge, MA: Harvard University Press, 1979.

Paracelsus. *Selected Writings.* Trans. Norbert Guterman. Ed. Jolande Székács Jacobi. New York: Pantheon, 1951.

Paré, Ambroise. *Des monstres et prodiges.* 1573. In *Les Oeuvres d'Ambroise Paré, conseiller et premier chirurgien du roy, divisées en vingt-sept livres.* Paris, 1579. Trans. Janis L. Pallister as *On Monsters and Marvels.* Chicago: University of Chicago Press, 1982.

Pato, Raymundo A. Bulhão, ed. *Documentos remettidos da Índia; ou, Livros das Monções.* Vol. 1. Lisbon, 1880.

Pelsaert, Francisco. "Remonstrantie." Ca. 1626. Trans. and ed. W. H. Moreland and Pieter Geyl as *Jahangir's India: The Remonstrantie of Francisco Pelsaert.* Cambridge: W. Heffer, 1925.

Pereira, Duarte Pacheco. *Esmeraldo de Situ Orbis.* Ed. Damião Peres. Lisbon: Academia portuguesa da história, 1954. Trans. George H. T. Kimble as *Esmeraldo de Situ Orbis.* London: Hakluyt Society, 1937.

Petty, William. "The Scale of Animals." In *The Petty Papers: Some Unpublished Writings of Sir William Petty,* ed. Marquis of Lansdowne. 2 vols. Boston: Houghton Mifflin, 1927, 2: 25–34.

Pigafetta, Antonio. *Relazione del primo viaggio attorno al mondo,* ed. Andrea Canova. Padua: Antenore, 1999. Trans. Theodore J. Cachey as *The First Voyage Around the World, 1519–1522: An Account of Magellan's Expedition.* Toronto: University of Toronto Press, 2007.

Pinto, Fernão Mendes. *Peregrinaçam de Fernam Mendez Pinto.* Lisbon, 1614. Trans. Rebecca D. Catz as *The Travels of Mendes Pinto.* Chicago: University of Chicago Press, 1989.

Pires, Tomé. *The Suma Oriental of Tomé Pires.* Trans. and ed. Armando Cortesão. 2 vols. London: Hakluyt Society, 1944.

Plutarchus, Mestrius. *Plutarch: Lives.* Trans. Bernadotte Perrin. 11 vols. Cambridge, MA: Harvard University Press, 1914–26.

Pretty, Francis. "The Admirable and Prosperous Voyage of the Worship-full Master Thomas Ca[ve]ndish of Trimley in the Countie of Suffolke Esquire, into the South sea, and from thence round about the circumference of the whole earth, begun in the yeere of our Lord 1586, and finished 1588." In *The Principal Navigations, Voyages, Traffiques, and Discoveries of the English Nation. . . .* Comp. Richard Hakluyt. London, 1600, 3: 803–25.

Purchas, Samuel. *Purchas his Pilgrimage: Or, Relations of the World and the Religions Observed in all Ages and places Discovered, from the Creation unto this Present.* London, 1626.

————, comp. *Purchas his Pilgrimes.* 4 vols. London, 1625.

Pyrard, François. *Voyage de François Pyrard, de Laval, contenant sa navigation aux Indes Orientales, Maldives, Moluques, Bresil: Les divers accidens, adventures & dangers qui luy sont arrivez en ce voyage, tant en allant & retournant, que pendant son sejour de dix ans en ce païs là.* 2 vols. Paris, 1619. Trans. Albert Gray and H. C. P. Bell as *The Voyage of François Pyrard of Laval to the East Indies, the Maldives, the Moluccas and Brazil.* 2 vols. in 3 parts. London, 1887–90.

Raithby, John, ed. *The Statutes at Large of England and Great Britain: From Magna Carta to the Union of the Kingdoms of Great Britain and Ireland.* 13 vols. London, 1804–35.

Ramsey, James. *Bloudy newes from the East-Indies: Being a true Relation, and perfect Abstract of the cruel, barbarous, and inhumane proceedings of the Dutch-men against the English at Amboyna.* London, 1651.

Ramusio, Giovan Battista. *Delle navigationi et viaggi.* 3 vols. Venice, 1550–65.

Ravenhill, William. *A Short Account of the Company of Grocers.* London, 1689.

Rebelo, Gabriel. "Historia das Ilhas de Maluco escripta no anno de 1561." In *Documentação para a história das missões do padroado português do Oriente: Insulíndia,* vol. 3, *1563–1567,* ed. Artur Basilio de Sá. Lisbon: Divisão de Publicações e Biblioteca, Agência Geral do Ultramar, 1955, 192–343.

————. "Informação das cousas do Maluco." In *Documentação para a história das missões do padroado português do Oriente: Insulíndia,* vol. 3, *1563–1567,* ed. Artur Basilio de Sá. Lisbon: Divisão de Publicações e Biblioteca, Agência Geral do Ultramar, 1955, 345–508.

"The Relation of the Priest of Poolaroone, touching the beginnings and occasions of the quarrels betwixt the Dutch and Bandaneses, written in the Malayan language with his owne hand, in a very faire Arabecke letter, and the sense rendred to me in English by M. Rob. Haies." In *Purchas his Pilgrimes,* comp. Samuel Purchas. London, 1625, 1: 720–23.

A *Remonstrance of the Directors of the Netherlands East India Company presented to the Lords States Generall of the United Provinces, in defence of the said Companie, touching the bloudy proceedings against the English merchants, executed at Amboyna.* London, 1632.

"A Reply to the Remonstrance of the Bewinthebbers or Directors of the Netherlands East-India Companie." In *A Remonstrance of the Directors of the Netherlands East India Company presented to the Lords States Generall of the United Provinces.* . . . London, 1632.

Riche, Barnabe. *The Excellency of Good Women.* London, 1613.

Rivara, Joaquim Heliodoro da Cunha, ed. *Archivo Portuguez-Oriental.* 6 fascicles in 10 parts. Nova-Goa, 1857–76.

Rowley, William. *A Tragedy Called Alls Lost by Lust.* London, 1633.

Sá, Artur Basilio de, ed. *Documentação para a história das missões do padroado português do Oriente: Insulíndia.* 6 vols. Lisbon: Divisão de Publicações e Biblioteca, Agência Geral do Ultramar, 1954–88.

Sadler, John. *The Sicke Womans Private Looking-Glasse.* London, 1636.

Sainsbury, Ethel B., ed. *A Calendar of the Court Minutes Etc. of the East India Company.* 11 vols. Oxford: Clarendon Press, 1907–38.

Sainsbury, William N., ed. *Calendar of State Papers.* Colonial Series. 9 vols. London, 1860–1893.

Sánchez, Alonso. "De la entrada de la China en particular." In *Labor Evangelica de los Obreros de la Compañía de Jesús en las Islas Filipinas,* ed. Francisco Colín and Pablo Pastells. Barcelona: Henrich, 1904, 1: 438–45.

Sanchez, Tomás. *De Sancto Matrimonii Sacramento.* 3 vols. Antwerp, 1607.

Sande, Francisco de. "Relación" (1577). Trans. José M. Ascencio as "Relation and Description of the Phelipinas Islands." In *The Philippine Islands, 1493–1803,* ed. Emma H. Blair and James A. Robertson. Cleveland: Arthur H. Clark, 1903, 4: 98–118.

San Pedro, Sebastião de. "Retrato da perdição que teve o Padre Frey Sebastião de S. Pedro, da Ordem de Sto. Agostinho, indo pera Ormus o anno de 1592 e dos trabalhos que nella passou e do mais que lhe aconteceo depois que chegou a India ate que veio a Ormus." *Analecta Augustiniana* 47 (1984): 48–73.

Sassetti, Filippo. *Lettere dall'India, 1583–1588.* Ed. Adele Dei. Rome: Salerno Editrice, 1995.

Scott, Edmund. *An Exact Discourse of the Subtilties, Fashishions [sic], Pollicies, Religion, and Ceremonies of the East Indians as well Chyneses as Iauans, there abyding and dweling.* London, 1606.

Scott, Thomas. *An Experimentall Discoverie of Spanish Practises.* London, 1623.

Secundus, Johannes. "Epithalamium." In *An Anthology of Neo-Latin Poetry*, trans. and ed. Fred J. Nichols. New Haven, CT: Yale University Press, 1979, 515–23.

Shadwell, Thomas. *Psyche: A Tragedy, Acted at the Duke's Theater*. London, 1675.

Silva Rêgo, António da, ed. *Documentos remetidos da Índia; ou, Livros das Monções*. Vol. 7. Lisbon: Imprensa Nacional, 1975.

Silveira, Francisco Rodrigues de. *Reformação da milícia e governo do Estado da Índia Oriental*. Ed. Benjamin Teensma, George Winius, and Luís Filipe Barreto. Lisbon: Fundação Oriente, 1996.

Tasso, Torquato. *Gerusalemme liberata: Poema heroico*. Ferrara, 1581. Trans. and ed. Anthony M. Esolen as *Jerusalem Delivered*. Baltimore: Johns Hopkins University Press, 2000.

Temple, Richard C., ed. *The Diaries of Streynsham Master, 1675–1680*. 2 vols. London: John Murray, 1911.

———, ed. *The Travels of Peter Mundy in Europe and Asia, 1608–1667*. 5 vols. in 6 parts. London: Hakluyt Society, 1907–36.

Torquemada, Antonio de. *Jardín de flores curiosas*. Salamanca, 1570. Trans. Lewis Lewkenor as *The Spanish Mandevile of Miracles*. London, 1600.

Tosi, Clemente. *Dell'india Orientale*. 2 vols. Rome, 1669.

Transylvanus, Maximilianus. *De Moluccis insulis itemque alijs pluribus mirandis, quae novissima Castellanorum navigatio Serenissimi Imperatoris Caroli V auspicio suscepta, nuper invenit*. Cologne, 1523.

"Tratado de las yslas de los Malucos." Trans. and ed. Hubert M. Jacobs as *A Treatise on the Moluccas (c. 1544): Probably the Preliminary Version of António Galvão's Lost* História das Molucas. Rome: IHSI, 1970.

A True Declaration of the News that Came out of the East-Indies, with the Pinace called the Hare, which arrived in Texel, in Iune, 1624. London, 1624.

A True Relation of the Late Uniust, Cruell and Barbarous Proceedings against the English at Amboyna. London, 1624.

Ussher, James. *The annals of the world deduced from the origin of time, and continued to the beginning of the Emperour Vespasians reign, and the totall destruction and abolition of the temple and common-wealth of the Jews*. London, 1658.

Valignano, Alessandro. "Sumario de las cosas que perteneçen a la provincia de la Yndia Oriental y al govierno della, compuesto per el Padre Alexando Valignano visitador della, y dirigido a nuestro Padre General Everardo Mercuriano en el año de 1579." In *Documentação para a história das missões do padroado português do Oriente: Índia*, vol. 12, *1572–1582*, ed. António da Silva Rêgo. Lisbon: Divisão de Publicações e Biblioteca, Agência Geral do Ultramar, 1958, 470–634.

Varen, Bernhard. *Geographia generalis, in qua affectiones generales telluris explicantur*. Amsterdam, 1650.

Vātsyāyana. *The Complete Kāma Sūtra: The First Unabridged Modern Translation of the Classic Indian Text by Vātsyāyana*. Trans. Alain Daniélou. Rochester, VT: Park Street Press, 1994.

Vives, Luis. *De institutione foeminae Christianae*. Antwerp, 1524. Trans. Charles Fantazzi as *The Education of a Christian Woman: A Sixteenth-Century Manual*. Chicago: University of Chicago Press, 2000.

Ward, Edward. *The Secret History of Clubs: Particularly the Kit-Cat, Beef-Stake, Vertuosos, Quacks, Knights of the Golden-Fleece, Florists, Beaus, &c. with their Original: And the Characters of the Most Noted Members thereof*. London, 1709.

Waterworth James, trans. *The Canons and Decrees of the Sacred and Oecumenical Council of Trent*. London, 1848.

Wicki, Josef, ed. *Documenta Indica*. 18 vols. Rome: IHSI, 1948–88.

Wolfe, John. "To the Reader." In Jan Huygen van Linschoten, *The Voyage of John Huyghen Van Linschoten to the East Indies. . . .*, ed. Arthur Coke Burnell and Pieter Anton Tiele. London, 1885, 1: xlvii-lii.

Wybarne, Joseph. *The New Age of Old Names*. London, 1609.

Zuck, Lowell H., ed. *Christianity and Revolution: Radical Christian Testimonies, 1520–1650*. Philadelphia: Temple University Press, 1975.

SECONDARY SOURCES

Abusharaf, Rogaia Mustafa. *Female Circumcision: Multicultural Perspectives*. Philadelphia: University of Philadelphia Press, 2006.

Aguiar e Silva, Vítor Manuel de. *Camões: Labirintos e Fascínios*. Lisbon: Cotovia, 1994.

Alloula, Malek. *The Colonial Harem*. Minneapolis: University of Minnesota Press, 1986.

Althusser, Louis. *Lenin and Philosophy and Other Essays*. New York: Monthly Review Press, 1971.

Andaya, Leonard Y. *The World of Maluku: Eastern Indonesia in the Early Modern Period*. Honolulu: University of Hawaii Press, 1993.

Andrea, Bernadette D. *Women and Islam in Early Modern English Literature*. Cambridge: Cambridge University Press, 2008.

Andrews, Kenneth. *Trade, Plunder, and Settlement: Maritime Enterprise and the Genesis of the British Empire, 1480–1630*. Cambridge: Cambridge University Press, 1984.

Appel, G. N. "The Penis Pin at Peabody Museum, Harvard University." *Journal of the Malaysian Branch, Royal Asiatic Society* 41 (1968): 202–5.

Appleton, William. *Beaumont and Fletcher: A Critical Study*. London: Allen and Unwin, 1956.

Ariès, Philippe. "Love in Married Life" In *Western Sexuality: Practice and Precept in Past and Present Times*, ed. Philippe Ariès and André Béjin. Oxford: Blackwell, 1985, 130–39.

Ariès, Philippe, and Andre Béjin, eds. *Western Sexuality: Practice and Precept in Past and Present Times*. Oxford: Blackwell, 1985.

Bacon, Leonard, trans. and ed. *The Lusiads of Camões*. New York: Hispanic Society of America, 1950.

Balibar, Etienne. "Is There a 'Neo-Racism'?" In Etienne Balibar and Immanuel Wallerstein, *Race, Nation, Class: Ambiguous Identities*. London: Verso, 1991, 17–28.

Ballhatchet, Kenneth. *Race, Sex and Class Under the Raj: Imperial Attitudes and Policies and Their Critics, 1793–1905*. New York: St. Martin's Press, 1980.

Barradas de Carvalho, Joaquim. *A la recherche de la spécificité de la Renaissance portugaise: L' "Esmeraldo de Situ Orbis" de Duarte Pacheco Pereira et la littérature portugaise de voyages à l'époque des grandes découvertes*. 2 vols. Paris: Fundação Calouste Gulbenkian, 1983.

Barroll, Leeds, ed. "Forum: Race and the Study of Shakespeare." *Shakespeare Studies* 26 (1998): 19–82.

Bartels, Emily C. *Speaking of the Moor: From Alcazar to Othello*. Philadelphia: University of Pennsylvania Press, 2008.

Bartlett, Robert. "Medieval and Modern Concepts of Race and Ethnicity." *Journal of Medieval and Early Modern Studies* 31, no. 1 (2001): 39–56.

Beard, Mary. "The Erotics of Rape: Livy, Ovid and the Sabine Women." In *Female Network and the Public Sphere in Roman Society*, ed. Päivi Setälä and Liisa Savunen. Rome: Institutum Romanum Finlandiae, 1999, 1–10.

Belardinelli, Renata Cusmai. "Discorso sopra il viaggio di Nicolò di Conti veneziano." *Accademie e biblioteche d'Italia* 53 (1985): 155–70.

Bellasis, Augustus Fortunatus. "Monumental Inscriptions in the English and Dutch Cemeteries at Surat." MS Add. 44948, British Library.

Belsey, Catherine. "Love as Trompe-l'oeil: Taxonomies of Desire in *Venus and Adonis*." *Shakespeare Quarterly* 46, no. 3 (1995): 257–76.

———. "The Serpent in the Garden: Shakespeare, Marriage, and Material Culture." *Seventeenth Century* 11, no. 1 (1996): 1–20

Bennassar, Bartolomé. "Le modèle sexuel: l'Inquisition d'Aragon et la répression des péchés 'abominables.'" In *L'Inquisition espagnole XVe–XIXe siècle*, ed. Bartolomé Bennassar. Paris: Hachette, 1979, 339–69.

Betzig, Laura. "Roman Polygyny." *Ethnology and Sociobiology* 13 (1992): 309–49.

Bingham, Caroline. "Seventeenth-Century Attitudes to Deviant Sex." *Journal of Interdisciplinary History* 1 (1971): 447–67.

Biolsi, Thomas. "Race Technologies." In *A Companion to the Anthropology of Politics*, ed. David Nugent and Joan Vincent. Oxford: Blackwell, 2004, 400–417.

Blair, Emma H., and James A. Robertson, eds. *The Philippine Islands, 1493–1803*. 55 vols. Cleveland: Arthur H. Clark, 1903–1909.

Blanc-Szanton, Cristina. "Collision of Cultures: Historical Reformulations of Gender in the Lowland Visayas, Philippines." In *Power and Difference: Gender in Island Southeast Asia*, ed. Jane Monnig Atkinson and Shelly Errington. Stanford, CA: Stanford University Press, 1990, 345–84.

Bleys, Rudi C. *The Geography of Perversion: Male-to-Male Sexual Behaviour Outside the West and the Ethnographic Imagination, 1750–1918*. New York: New York University Press, 1995.

Blussé, Leonard. *Bitter Bonds: A Colonial Divorce Drama of the Seventeenth Century*. Trans. Diane Webb. Princeton, NJ: M. Wiener, 2002.

———. *Strange Company: Chinese Settlers, Mestizo Women and the Dutch in VOC Batavia*. Dordrecht: Foris, 1986.

Bohigian, Gary W. "Life on the Rim of Spain's Pacific-American Empire." PhD diss., University of California, Los Angeles, 1994.

Bonnet, Marie-Jo. "Sappho, or the Importance of Culture in the Language of Love: *Tribade, Lesbienne, Homosexuelle*." In *Queerly Phrased: Language, Gender, and Sexuality*, ed. Anna Livia and Kira Hall. Oxford: Oxford University Press, 1997, 147–66.

Boon, James A. "'Extravagant Art' and Balinese Ritual." In *Recovering the Orient: Artists, Scholars, Appropriations*, ed. C. Andrew Gerstle and Anthony Crothers Milner. New York: Routledge, 1994, 339–56.

———, *Other Tribes Other Scribes: Symbolic Anthropology in the Comparative Study of Cultures, Histories, Religions, and Texts*. Cambridge: Cambridge University Press, 1982.

Borris, Kenneth, ed. *Same-Sex Desire in the English Renaissance: A Sourcebook of Texts, 1470–1650*. New York: Routledge, 2004.

Bosma, Ulbe, and Remco Raben. *Being "Dutch" in the Indies: A History of Creolisation and Empire, 1500–1920*. Trans. Wendie Shaffer. Athens: Ohio University Press, 2008.

Bovilsky, Laura. *Barbarous Play: Race on the English Stage*. Minneapolis: University of Minnesota Press, 2008.

Bowra, Cecil Maurice. *From Virgil to Milton*. London: Macmillan, 1948.

Boxer, Charles R. "Anglo-Portuguese Rivalry in the Persian Gulf, 1615–1635." In *Chapters in Anglo-Portuguese Relations*, ed. Edgar Prestage. London: Watford, 1935, 46–129.

————. "A Late Sixteenth Century Manila Manuscript." *Journal of the Royal Asiatic Society of Great Britain and Ireland* 87 (1950): 37–49.

————. *Portuguese Conquest and Commerce in Southern Asia, 1500–1750.* London: Variorum, 1985, 118–36.

————. *The Portuguese Seaborne Empire, 1415–1825.* London: Hutchinson, 1969.

————. *Race Relations in the Portuguese Colonial Empire, 1415–1825.* Oxford: Clarendon Press, 1963.

————, ed. *A True Description of the Mighty Kingdoms of Japan and Siam by François Caron and Joost Schouten.* London: Argonaut Press, 1935.

————. *Women in Iberian Expansion Overseas, 1415–1815.* Cambridge: Cambridge University Press, 1975.

Boyajian, James C. *Portuguese Trade in Asia Under the Habsburgs, 1580–1640.* Baltimore: Johns Hopkins University Press, 1993.

Bray, Alan. *Homosexuality in Renaissance England: With a New Afterword.* New York: Columbia University Press, 1995.

Breazeale, Kennon. "Editorial Introduction to Nicolò de' Conti's Account." *SOAS Bulletin of Burma Research* 2, no. 2 (2004): 100–109.

Brewer, Carolyn. *Shamanism, Catholicism and Gender Relations in Colonial Philippines, 1521–1685.* Burlington, VT: Ashgate, 2004.

Brockey, Liam M. *Journey to the East: The Jesuit Mission to China, 1579–1724.* Cambridge, MA: Harvard University Press, 2007.

Brown, Donald E. "The Penis Pin: An Unresolved Problem in the Relation Between the Sexes in Borneo." In *Borneo: Contributions to Gender Studies*, ed. Vinson H. Sutlive. Williamsburg: Borneo Research Council, 1991, 435–54.

Brown, Donald E., James W. Edwards, and Ruth P. Moore. *The Penis Inserts of Southeast Asia: An Annotated Bibliography with an Overview and Comparative Perspectives.* Berkeley: Center for South and Southeast Asia Studies, University of California, 1988.

Brown, Peter. *The Body and Society: Men, Women, and Sexual Renunciation in Early Christianity.* New York: Columbia University Press, 2008.

Brownmiller, Susan. *Against Our Will: Men, Women and Rape.* New York: Simon and Schuster, 1975.

Brundage, James A. *Law, Sex and Christian Society in Medieval Europe.* Chicago: University of Chicago Press, 1987.

Buell, Denise Kimber. *Why This New Race: Ethnic Reasoning in Early Christianity.* New York: Columbia University Press, 2005.

Bullough, Geoffrey. "Polygamy Among the Reformers." In *Renaissance and*

Modern Essays, ed. G. R. Hibbard. London: Routledge & Kegan Paul, 1966, 5–24.

Burns, Kathryn. "Unfixing Race." In *Rereading the Black Legend: The Discourses of Religious and Racal Difference in the Renaissance Empires*, ed. Margaret Greer, Walter D. Mignolo, and Maureen Quilligan. Chicago: University of Chicago Press, 2007, 188–202.

Burton, Jonathan. "English Anxiety and the Muslim Power of Conversion: Five Perspectives on 'Turning Turk' in Early Modern Texts." *Journal for Early Modern Cultural Studies* 2, no. 1 (2002): 35–67.

———. *Traffic and Turning: Islam and English Drama, 1579–1624*. Cranbury: University of Delaware Press, 2005.

Butler, Judith. *Bodies that Matter: On the Discursive Limits of "Sex."* New York: Routledge, 1993.

Cadden, Joan. *Meanings of Sex Difference in the Middle Ages: Medicine, Science, and Culture*. Cambridge: Cambridge University Press, 1993.

Cahoon, Leslie. "The Bed as Battlefield: Erotic Conquest and Military Metaphor in Ovid's *Amores*." *Transactions of the American Philological Association* 118 (1988): 293–307.

Cairncross, John. *After Polygamy Was Made a Sin: The Social History of Christian Polygamy*. London: Routledge & Kegan Paul, 1974.

Canova, Antonio. "Esperienza e letteratura nella *Relazione*." In Antonio Pigafetta, *Relazione del primo viaggio attorno al mondo*, ed. Andrea Canova. Padua: Antenore, 1999, 62–102.

Canova, Andrea. "Faraway Countries and Useful Books: Some Remarks on Antonio Pigafetta and Other Travellers in the Pacific at the Beginning of the Sixteenth Century." *Studies in Travel Writing* 5 (2001): 1–34.

Carrasco, Rafaél. *Inquisición y represión sexual en Valencia: Historia de los sodomitas, 1565–1785*. Barcelona: Laertes, 1985.

Carroll, Margaret D. "The Erotics of Absolutism: Rubens and the Mystification of Sexual Violence." In *The Expanding Discourse: Feminism and Art History*, ed. Norma Broude and Mary D. Garrard. New York: HarperCollins, 1992, 139–59.

Carton, Adrian. "Historicizing Hybridity and the Politics of Location: Three Early Colonial Indian Narratives." *Journal of Intercultural Studies*, 28, no. 1 (2007): 143–55.

Catz, Rebecca. "Camões and the Writers of the Discoveries." In *Camoniana Californiana*, ed. Maria de Lourdes Belchior and Enrique Martínez-López. Santa Barbara, CA: Jorge de Sena Center for Portuguese Studies, 1985, 147–53.

Chaudhuri, K. N. *The English East India Company: The Study of an Early Joint-Stock Company, 1600–1640*. New York: AMK, 1965.

————. *The Trading World of Asia and the English East India Company:
1660–1760*. Cambridge: Cambridge University Press, 2006.

Chew, Samuel C. *The Crescent and the Rose: Islam and England During the
Renaissance*. New York: Oxford University Press, 1937.

Clay, C. G. A. *Economic Expansion and Social Change: Industry, Trade,
and Government*. Cambridge: Cambridge University Press, 1984.

Coates, Timothy. *Convicts and Orphans: Forced and State-Sponsored Colonizers in the Portuguese Empire, 1550–1755*. Stanford, CA: Stanford University Press, 2001.

Cohen, Jeffrey J. *Medieval Identity Machines*. Minneapolis: University of
Minnesota Press, 2003.

————. "Monster Culture (Seven Theses)." In *Monster Theory: Reading
Culture*, ed. Jeffrey J. Cohen. Minneapolis: University of Minnesota
Press, 1996, 3–25.

Cohen, Shaye J. D. *Why Aren't Jewish Women Circumcised? Gender and
Covenant in Judaism*. Berkeley: University of California Press, 2005.

Comaroff, John, and Jean L. Comaroff. "Home-Made Hegemony: Modernity, Domesticity, and Colonialism in South Africa." In *African Encounters with Domesticity,* ed. Karen T. Hansen. New Brunswick, NJ: Rutgers University Press, 1992, 37–74.

Costa Ramalho, Américo da. *Estudos Camonianos*. Lisbon: Instituto Nacional de Investigação Científica, 1980.

Couto, Dejanirah. "Alguns dados para um estudo ulterior sobre a 'sociedade espontânea' no *Estado da Índia* na primeira metade do séc. XVI."
In *Metahistory: History questioning History*, ed. Teotónio R. de Souza,
Charles J. Borges, and Michael N. Pearson. Lisbon: Nova Vega, 2007,
283–301.

————. "Some Observations on Portuguese Renegades in Asia in the Sixteenth Century." In *Vasco da Gama and the Linking of Europe and Asia*,
ed. Anthony Disney and Emily Booth. New Delhi: Oxford University
Press, 2001, 178–201.

Crawford, Katherine. *European Sexualities, 1400–1800*. Cambridge: Cambridge University Press, 2007.

Crewe, Jonathan V. "Recalling Adamastor: Literature as Cultural Memory
in 'White' South Africa." In *Acts of Memory: Cultural Recall in the Present*, ed. Mieke Bal, Jonathan V. Crewe, and Leo Spitzer. Hanover, NH:
University Press of New England, 1999, 75–86.

Crivat-Vasile, Anca. "El viaje de Nicolo dei Conti en los relatos de Pero Tafur
y Poggio Bracciolini." *Revista de Filologia Románica* 13 (1996): 231–52.

Curtin, Philip D. *Cross-Cultural Trade in World History*. Cambridge: Cambridge University Press, 1984.

Dalgado, Sebastião R. *Glossário Luso-Asiático*. 2 vols. Coimbra: Imprensa da Universidade, 1919–1921.

Daniel, Norman. *Islam and the West: The Making of an Image*. Edinburgh: Edinburgh University Press, 1960.

Daston, Lorraine, and Katharine Park. "The Hermaphrodite and the Orders of Nature: Sexual Ambiguity in Early Modern France" In *Premodern Sexualities*, ed. Louise Fradenburg and Carla Freccero. New York: Routledge, 1996, 117–36.

———. *Wonders and the Order of Nature: 1150–1750*. New York: Zone Books, 1998.

Davidson, Arnold I. *The Emergence of Sexuality: Historical Epistemology and the Formation of Concepts*. Cambridge, MA: Harvard University Press, 2002.

Davidson, Nicholas. "Theology, Nature and the Law: Sexual Sin and Sexual Crime in Italy from the Fourteenth to the Seventeenth Century." In *Crime, Society and the Law in Renaissance Italy*, ed. Trevor Dean and K. J. P. Lowe. Cambridge: Cambridge University Press, 1994, 74–98.

Davies, Kathleen M. "Continuity and Change in Literary Advice on Marriage." In *Marriage and Society: Studies in the Social History of Marriage*, ed. R. B. Outhwaite. New York: St. Martin's Press, 1981, 58–80.

Dearing, Vinton A. "Commentary [to *Amboyna*]." In *The Works of John Dryden*, Vol. 12. Ed. Vinton A. Dearing. Berkeley: University of California Press, 1994, 252–319.

Denzinger, Henry, ed. *Enchiridion Symbolorum: Definitionum et Declarationum de Rebus Fidei et Morum*. Freiburg: Herder, 1965.

DiGangi, Mario. *The Homoerotics of Early Modern Drama*. Cambridge: Cambridge University Press, 1997.

During, Simon. "Postcolonialism and Globalisation: A Dialectical Relation After All?" *Postcolonial Studies* 1 (1998): 31–47.

Eccles, Audrey. *Obstetrics and Gynaecology in Tudor and Stuart England*. Kent, OH: Kent State University Press, 1982.

Ellis, Havelock. *Studies in the Psychology of Sex: Sexual Inversion*. Philadelphia: F. A. Davis, 1901.

Engels, Friedrich. *The Origin of the Family, Private Property, and the State*. Ed. Eleanor B. Leacock. New York: International, 1972.

Erickson, Peter. "The Moment of Race in Renaissance Studies." *Shakespeare Studies* 26 (1998): 27–36.

Fausto-Sterling, Anne. "Gender, Race, and Nation: The Comparative Anatomy of 'Hottentot' Women in Europe, 1815–1817." In *Deviant Bodies: Critical Perspectives on Difference in Science and Popular Culture*, ed. Jennifer Terry and Jacqueline Urla. Bloomington: Indiana University Press, 1995, 19–48.

Fawcett, Charles, ed. *The English Factories in India*. New series. 4 vols. Oxford: Clarendon Press, 1936–55.

Feerick, Jean. "'A Nation Now Degenerate': Shakespeare's *Cymbeline*, Nova Britannia, and the Role of Diet and Climate in Reproducing Races." *Early American Studies* 1, no. 2 (2003): 30–70.

———. *Strangers in Blood: Relocating Race in the Renaissance*. Toronto: University of Toronto Press, 2010.

———. "Tragicomic Transformations: Passion, Politics, and the 'Art to Turn' in Fletcher's *Island Princess*," *Early Modern Literary Studies* 19, no. 3 (2009): 1–24.

Fell, R. T. *Early Maps of South-East Asia*. Oxford: Oxford University Press, 1991.

Ferguson, Gary. *Queer (Re)readings in the French Renaissance: Homosexuality, Gender, Culture*. Burlington, VT: Ashgate, 2008.

Fernández-Armesto, Felipe. "Times and Tides." *History Today* 47, no.12 (1997): 9–11.

Figueira, Dorothy. "Civilization and the Problem of Race: Portuguese and Italian Travel Narratives to India." In *Imperialisms: Historical and Literary Investigations, 1500–1900*, ed. Anthony Pagden, Balachandra Rajan, and Elizabeth Sauer. New York: Macmillan, 2004, 75–92.

Filgueira Valverde, José. *Camões: Comemoração do Centenário de Os Lusíadas*. Coimbra: Almedina, 1981.

Finkelpearl, Philip J. "Fletcher as a Spenserian Playwright: *The Faithful Shepherdess* and *The Island Princess*." *Studies in English Literature* 27 (1987): 285–302.

Finucci, Valeria. "Maternal Imagination and Monstrous Birth: Tasso's *Gerusalemme Liberata*." In *Generation and Degeneration: Tropes of Reproduction in Literature and History from Antiquity Through Early Modern Europe*, ed. Valeria Finucci and Kevin Brownlee. Durham, NC: Duke University Press, 2001, 41–77.

Fischer, Kirsten. *Suspect Relations: Sex, Race, and Resistance in Colonial North Carolina*. Ithaca, NY: Cornell University Press, 2002.

Fisher, Michael H. *Counterflows to Colonialism: Indian Travellers and Settlers in Britain, 1600–1685*. Delhi: Permanent Black, 2004.

Flandrin, Jean-Louis. "Sex in Married Life in the Early Middle Ages: The Church's Teaching and Behavioural Reality." In *Western Sexuality: Practice and Precept in Past and Present Times*, ed. Philippe Ariès and Andre Béjin. Oxford: Blackwell, 1985, 114–29.

Floyd-Wilson, Mary. *English Ethnicity and Race in Early Modern Drama*. Cambridge: Cambridge University Press, 2003.

Forman, Valerie. *Tragicomic Redemptions: Global Economics and the Early*

Modern English Stage. Philadelphia: University of Pennsylvania Press, 2008.

Forrest, George W., ed. *Selections from the Letters, Despatches, and Other State Papers Preserved in the Bombay Secretariat*. Home Series, vol. 1. Bombay, 1887.

Foucault, Michel. *Abnormal: Lectures at the Collège de France, 1974–1975*. New York: Picador, 2003.

———. *Discipline and Punish: The Birth of the Prison*. New York: Vintage, 1995.

———. "The Eye of Power." In *Power/Knowledge: Selected Interviews and Other Writings, 1972–1977*, ed. Colin Gordon. New York: Pantheon, 1980, 146–65.

———. *The History of Sexuality*. Vol. 1, *An Introduction*. New York: Vintage, 1990.

———. *The History of Sexuality*. Vol. 2, *The Use of Pleasure*. New York: Vintage, 1990.

———. *Society Must Be Defended*. New York: Picador, 2003.

Fox, James. "'For Good and Sufficient Reasons': An Examination of Early Dutch East India Company Ordinances on Slaves and Slavery." In *Slavery, Bondage and Dependency in Southeast Asia*, ed. Anthony Reid and Jennifer Brewster. New York: St. Martin's Press, 1983, 246–62.

Freccero, Carla. "Acts, Identities, and Sexuality in (Pre)Modern Regimes." *Journal of Women's History* 11, no. 2 (1999): 186–92.

Freitas, William. *Camões and His Epic: A Historic, Geographic and Cultural Survey*. Stanford, CA: Institute of Hispanic and Luso-Brazilian Studies, 1963.

Friedl, Raimund. *Der Konkubinat im kaiserzeitlichen Rom: Von Augustus bis Septimius Severus*. Stuttgart: Steiner, 1996.

Friedman, Jerome. "Jewish Conversion, the Spanish Pure Blood Laws and Reformation: A Revisionist View of Racial and Religious Antisemitism." *Sixteenth Century Journal* 18, no. 1 (1987): 3–30.

Fuchs, Barbara. "Faithless Empires: Pirates, Renegadoes and the English Nation." *ELH* 67, no. 1 (2000): 45–69.

———. *Mimesis and Empire: The New World, Islam, and European Identity*. Cambridge: Cambridge University Press, 2001.

Garay, René P. "Camões, Luíz Vaz de (c. 1524–1580)." In *Literature of Travel and Exploration: An Encyclopedia*, ed. Jennifer Sparke. New York: Routledge, 2003, 1: 176–78.

Gardiner, Anne B. "Dating Dryden's *Amboyna*: Allusions in the Text to 1672–1673 Politics." *Restoration and Eighteenth Century Theatre Research* 1, no. 1 (1990): 18–27.

Ghosh, Durba. *Sex and the Family in Colonial India*. Cambridge: Cambridge University Press, 2006.

Giamatti, A. Bartlett. *The Earthly Paradise and the Renaissance Epic*. Princeton, NJ: Princeton University Press, 1996.

Giffert, Michael, ed. "Constructing Race: Differentiating Peoples in the Early Modern World." Spec. issue of *William and Mary Quarterly* 54, no. 1 (1997).

Gilman, Sander L. "Black Bodies, White Bodies: Toward an Iconography of Female Sexuality in Late Nineteenth-Century Art, Medicine, and Literature." *Critical Inquiry* 12, no. 1 (1985): 204–42.

———. *Difference and Pathology: Stereotypes of Sexuality, Race, and Madness*. Ithaca, NY: Cornell University Press, 1985.

Goldberg, Jonathan. *Sodometries: Renaissance Texts, Modern Sexualities*. Stanford, CA: Stanford University Press, 1992.

Gonçálvez Guimarãis, A. J., ed. *Os Lusíadas de Luis de Camões*. Coimbra: Universidade, 1919.

Goodman, Jennifer R. "Marriage and Conversion in Late Medieval Romance." In *Varieties of Religious Conversion in the Middle Ages*, ed. James Mouldon. Gainesville: University Press of Florida, 1997, 115–28.

Gorski, Philip S. "The Protestant Ethic Revisited: Disciplinary Revolution and State Formation in Holland and Prussia." *American Journal of Sociology* 99, no. 2 (1993): 265–316.

Gough, Melinda J. "'Her Filthy Feature Open Showne' in Ariosto, Spenser, and *Much Ado About Nothing*." *Studies in English Literature* 39, no. 1 (1999): 41–67.

Green, Mary Ann E., ed. *Calendar of State Papers, Domestic 1623–25*. London, 1859.

Greenberg, David F. *The Construction of Homosexuality*. Chicago: University of Chicago Press, 1988.

Greene, Roland. *Unrequited Conquests: Love and Empire in the Colonial Americas*. Chicago: University of Chicago Press, 1999.

Grewal, Inderpal. *Home and Harem: Nation, Gender, Empire and the Cultures of Travel*. Durham, NC: Duke University Press, 1996.

Grosrichard, Alain. *The Sultan's Court: European Fantasies of the East*. London: Verso, 1999.

Gutierrez, Ramón. *When Jesus Came, the Corn Mothers Went Away: Marriage, Sexuality, and Power in New Mexico, 1500–1846*. Stanford, CA: Stanford University Press, 1991.

Hadfield, Andrew. *Literature, Travel and Colonial Writing in the English Renaissance*. Oxford: Clarendon Press, 1998.

Hall, Kim F. "Object into Object? Some Thoughts on the Presence of Black Women in Early Modern Culture." In *Early Modern Visual Culture: Representation, Race, and Empire in Renaissance England*, ed. Peter Erickson and Clarke Hulse. Philadelphia: University of Pennsylvania Press, 2000, 346–79.

———. *Things of Darkness: Economies of Race and Gender in Early Modern England*. Ithaca: Cornell University Press, 1995.

Hallet, Judith, and Marilyn Skinner, eds. *Roman Sexualities*. Princeton, NJ: Princeton University Press, 1997.

Halperin, David M. *How to Do the History of Homosexuality*. Chicago: University of Chicago Press, 2002.

———. *A Hundred Years of Homosexuality and Other Essays on Greek Love*. New York: Routledge, 1990.

Hamer, Mary. *Signs of Cleopatra: History, Politics, Representation*. New York: Routledge, 1993.

Harden, Robert. "The Element of Love in the Chansons de Geste." *Annuale Mediaevale* 5 (1963): 65–80.

Harris, Ron. "The English East India Company and the History of Company Law." In *VOC, 1602–2002: 400 Years of Company Law*, ed. Ella Gepken-Jager, Gerard Van Solinge, and Levinus Timmerman. Deventer: Kluwer, 2005, 219–247.

Harrisson, Tom. "The 'Palang,' Its History and Proto-History in West Borneo and the Philippines." *Journal of the Malaysian Branch, Royal Asiatic Society* 37, no. 2 (1964): 162–74.

———. "Rhinoceros in Borneo: And Traded to China." *Sarawak Museum Journal* 7 (1956): 263–74.

Hazard, Paul. *The European Mind, 1680–1715*. Cleveland: Meridian, 1963.

Healy, Margaret. *Fictions of Disease in Early Modern England: Bodies, Plagues and Politics*. New York: Palgrave, 2001.

Helgerson, Richard. *Forms of Nationhood: The Elizabethan Writing of England*. Chicago: University of Chicago Press, 1992.

Hendricks, Margo. "Race: A Renaissance Category?" In *A Companion to English Renaissance Literature and Culture*, ed. Michael Hattaway. Malden, MA: Blackwell, 2001, 690–98.

Hendricks, Margo, and Patricia Parker, eds. *Women, "Race" and Writing in the Early Modern Period*. New York: Routledge, 1994.

Heng, Geraldine. "The Invention of Race in the European Middle Ages I: Race Studies, Modernity, and the Middle Ages." *Literature Compass* 8, no. 5 (2011): 315–31.

———. "The Invention of Race in the European Middle Ages II: Locations of Medieval Race." *Literature Compass* 8, no. 5 (2011): 332–50.

Higgs, David. "Lisbon." In *Queer Sites: Gay Urban Histories Since 1600*, ed. David Higgs. New York: Routledge, 1999, 112–37.

Hillman, Eugene. "Polygamy and the Council of Trent." *The Jurist* 33 (1973): 358–76.

Holden, Philip. "Rethinking Colonial Discourse Analysis and Queer Studies." In *Imperial Desire: Dissident Sexualities and Colonial Literature*, ed. Philip Holden and Richard J. Ruppel. Minneapolis: University of Minnesota Press, 2003, 291–321.

Howell, Martha. *Commerce Before Capitalism in Europe, 1300–1600*. Cambridge: Cambridge University Press, 2010.

Howell, Philip. *Geographies of Regulation: Policing Prostitution in Nineteenth-Century Britain and the Empire*. Cambridge: Cambridge University Press, 2009.

Hull, Isabel V. *Sexuality, State and Civil Society in Germany, 1700–1815*. Ithaca, NY: Cornell University Press, 1996.

Hulme, Peter. *Colonial Encounters: Europe and the Native Caribbean, 1492–1797*. London: Routledge, 1992.

Hutcheson, Gregory S. "The Sodomitic Moor: Queerness in the Narrative of Reconquista." In *Queering the Middle Ages,* ed. Glenn Burger and Steven F. Kruger. Minneapolis: University of Minnesota Press, 2001, 99–122.

Iyengar, Sujata. *Shades of Difference: Mythologies of Skin Color in Early Modern England*. Philadelphia: University of Pennsylvania Press, 2004.

JanMohamed, Abdul R. "Sexuality on/of the Racial Border: Foucault, Wright, and the Articulation of Racialized Sexuality." *Discourses of Sexuality: From Aristotle to AIDS*, ed. Domna C. Stanton. Ann Arbor: University of Michigan Press, 1992, 94–116.

Jasma, L. G. "Crime in the Netherlands in the Sixteenth Century: The Batenburg Bands After 1540." *Mennonite Quarterly Review* 62 (1988): 221–35.

Jones, Eric. *Wives, Slaves and Concubines: A History of the Female Underclass in Dutch Asia*. DeKalb: Northern Illinois University Press, 2010.

Jowitt, Claire. "*The Island Princess* and Race." In *Early Modern English Drama: A Critical Companion,* ed. Patrick Cheney, Andrew Hadfield, and Garrett A. Sullivan. Oxford: Oxford University Press, 2006, 287–97.

Kahf, Monja. *Western Representations of the Muslim Woman: From Termagant to Odalisque*. Austin: University of Texas Press, 1999.

Kamps, Ivo. "Colonizing the Colonizer: A Dutchman in Asia Portuguesa." In *Travel Knowledge: European "Discoveries" in the Early Modern Period*, ed. Ivo Kamps and Jyotsna C. Singh. New York: Palgrave, 2001, 160–81.

Kaplan, Caren. "'Getting to Know You': Travel, Gender, and the Politics of Representation in *Anna and the King of Siam* and *The King and I*."

In *Late Imperial Culture*, ed. Román de la Campa, E. Ann Kaplan, and Michael Sprink. New York: Verso, 1995, 33–52.

Kaplan, Paul H. D. "Titian's Laura Dianti and the Origins of the Motif of the Black Page in Portraiture," *Antiquità viva* 21, no. 1 (1982): 11–18 and no. 4 (1982): 10–19.

Karras, Ruth M. "Response: Identity, Sexuality, and History." *Journal of Women's History* 11, no. 2 (1999): 193–98.

———. *Sexuality in Medieval Europe: Doing onto Others*. New York: Routledge, 2005.

———. "Theoretical Issues: Prostitution and the Question of Sexual Identity in Medieval Europe." *Journal of Women's History* 11, no. 2 (1999): 159–77.

Katzew, Ilona. *Casta Painting: Images of Race in Eighteenth-Century Mexico*. New Haven, CT: Yale University Press, 2005.

Keay, John. *The Honourable Company: A History of the English East India Company*. London: HarperCollins, 1991.

Kingsley-Smith, Jane. *Cupid in Early Modern Literature and Culture*. Cambridge: Cambridge University Press, 2010.

Kinoshita, Sharon. *Medieval Boundaries: Rethinking Difference in Old French Literature*. Philadelphia: University of Pennsylvania Press, 2006.

Klobucka, Anna. "Lusotropical Romance: Camões, Gilberto Freyre, and the Isle of Love." *Portuguese Literary and Cultural Studies* 9 (2002): 121–38.

Knott, John R. *Discourses of Martyrdom in English Literature, 1563–1694*. Cambridge: Cambridge University Press, 1993.

Knowles, James "Sexuality: A Renaissance Category?" In *A Companion to English Renaissance Literature and Culture*, ed. Michael Hattaway. Malden, MA: Blackwell, 2000, 674–89.

Kochuthara, Shaji George. *The Concept of Sexual Pleasure in the Catholic Moral Tradition*. Rome: Editrice Pontificia Università Gregoriana, 2007.

Koloski-Ostrow, Ann Olga. "Violent Stages in Two Pompeian Houses: Imperial Taste, Aristocratic Response, and Messages of Male Control." In *Naked Truths: Women, Sexuality, and Gender in Classical Art and Archaeology*, ed. Olga Koloski-Ostrow and Claire L. Lyons. New York: Routledge, 1997, 243–66.

Korhonen, Anu. "Washing the Ethiopian White: Conceptualising Black Skin in Renaissance England." In *Black Africans in Renaissance Europe*, ed. T. F. Earle and K. J. P. Lowe. Cambridge: Cambridge University Press, 2005, 94–112.

Kuznesof, Elizabeth. "Ethnic and Gender Influences on 'Spanish' Creole Society." *Colonial Latin American Review* 4, no. 1 (1995): 153–76.

Lach, Donald F. *Asia in the Making of Europe*. Vol. 2 in 3 bks., *A Century of Wonder*. Chicago: University of Chicago Press, 1970–77.

Lach, Donald F., and Edwin J. van Kley. *Asia in the Making of Europe.* Vol. 3 in 4 bks., *A Century of Advance.* Chicago: University of Chicago Press, 1993.

Laichen, Sun. "Burmese Bells and Chinese Eroticism: Southeast Asia's Cultural Influence on China." *Journal of Southeast Asian Studies* 38, no. 2 (2007): 247–73.

Lal, Ruby. *Domesticity and Power in the Early Mughal World.* Cambridge: Cambridge University Press, 2005.

Laqueur, Thomas. *Making Sex: Body and Gender from the Greeks to Freud.* Cambridge, MA: Harvard University Press, 1990.

———. "Orgasm, Generation, and the Politics of Reproductive Biology." *Representations* 14 (1986): 1–41.

Leupp, Gary P. *Interracial Intimacy in Japan: Western Men and Japanese Women, 1543–1900.* London: Continuum, 2003.

Levine, Philippa. *Prostitution, Race, and Politics: Policing Venereal Disease in the British Empire.* New York: Routledge, 2003.

Lewis, Reina. *Rethinking Orientalism: Women, Travel and the Ottoman Harem.* New Brunswick, NJ: Rutgers University Press, 2004.

Longhena, Mario. "I manoscritti del IV libro del *De Varietate Fortunae* di Poggio Bracciolini." *Bollettino della Società Geografica Italiana* 6, no. 1 (1925): 191–215.

———. *Viaggi in Persia, India e Giava di Nicolò de' Conti, Girolamo Adorno e Girolamo di Santo Stefano.* Milan: Istituto Editoriale Italiano, 1960.

Loomba, Ania. "'Break Her Will, and Bruise No Bone Sir': Colonial and Sexual Mastery in Fletcher's *The Island Princess.*" *Journal for Early Modern Cultural Studies* 2, no. 1 (2002): 68–108.

———. "'Delicious Traffick': Alterity and Exchange on Early Modern Stages." *Shakespeare Survey* 52 (1999): 201–14.

———. *Gender, Race, Renaissance Drama.* Manchester: Manchester University Press, 1989.

———. *Shakespeare, Race, and Colonialism.* Oxford: Oxford University Press, 2002.

Loomba, Ania, and Jonathan Burton. *Race in Early Modern England: A Documentary Companion.* New York: Palgrave, 2007.

Love, Henry D. *Vestiges of Old Madras, 1640–1800.* Vol. 1. London: John Murray, 1913.

Lynch, John. *Spain Under the Habsburgs.* Vol. 2, *Spain and America 1598–1700.* Oxford: Basil Blackwell, 1981.

Macedo, Helder. *Camões e a viagem iniciática.* Lisbon: Moraes, 1980.

———. "*The Lusiads*: Epic Celebration and Pastoral Regret." *Portuguese Studies* 6 (1990): 32–37.

Macfarlane, Alan J. "Love and Capitalism." *Cambridge Anthropology* 11 (1987): 22–39.

MacGregor, Ian A. "Notes on the Portuguese in Malaya." *Journal of the Malayan Branch of the Royal Asiatic Society* 28, no. 2 (1955): 5–47.

MacLean, Gerald. "On Turning Turk, or Trying To: National Identity in Robert Daborne's *A Christian Turn'd Turk*." *Explorations in Renaissance Culture* 29 (2003): 225–52.

Maclean, Ian. *The Renaissance Notion of Woman*. Cambridge: Cambridge University Press, 1980.

Mancing, Howard. "The Protean Picaresque." In *The Picaresque: Tradition and Displacement*, ed. Giancarlo Maiorino. Minneapolis: University of Minnesota Press, 1996, 273–91.

Manderson, Lenore. "Colonial Desires: Sexuality, Race, and Gender in British Malaya." *Journal of the History of Sexuality* 7, no. 2 (1997): 372–88.

Margolf, Diane C. "Wonders of Nature, Diversity of Events: The *Voyage de François Pyrard de Laval*." In *Distant Lands and Diverse Cultures: The French Experience in Asia, 1600–1700*, ed. Glenn J. Ames and Ronald S. Love. Westport, CT: Praeger, 2003, 111–33.

Mariscal, George. "The Role of Spain in Contemporary Race Theory." *Arizona Journal of Hispanic Cultural Studies* 2 (1988): 7–22.

Markley, Robert. "Violence and Profits on the Restoration Stage: Trade, Nationalism, and Insecurity in Dryden's *Amboyna*." *Eighteenth-Century Life* 22, no. 1 (1998): 2–17.

Marshall, P. J. "The English in Asia to 1700." In *The Origins of Empire: British Overseas Enterprise to the Close of the Seventeenth Century*, ed. Nicholas Canny. Oxford: Oxford University Press, 1998, 264–85.

Massarella, Derek. *A World Elsewhere: Europe's Encounter with Japan in the Sixteenth and Seventeenth Centuries*. New Haven, CT: Yale University Press, 1990.

Massing, Jean Michel. "From Greek Proverb to Soap Advert: Washing the Ethiopian." *Journal of the Warburg and Courtauld Institutes* 58 (1995): 180–201.

Matar, Nabil. *Islam in Britain, 1558–1685*. Cambridge: Cambridge University Press, 1998.

———. *Turks, Moors, and Englishmen in the Age of Discovery*. New York: Columbia University Press, 1999.

Mattoso, José, ed. *Narrativas dos livros de linhagens*. Lisbon: Imprensa Nacional, 1983.

McClintock, Anne. *Imperial Leather: Race, Gender and Sexuality in the Colonial Context*. New York: Routledge, 1995.

McClintock, Anne, Aamir Muft, and Ella Shohat, eds. *Dangerous Liaisons: Gender, Nation, and Postcolonial Perspectives*. Minneapolis: University of Minnesota Press, 1997.

McCrindle John W., ed. *Ancient India as Described in Classical Literature*. Vol. 6. Westminster, UK: Archibald Constable, 1901.

McDougall, Sara. "The Punishment of Bigamy in Late-Medieval Troyes." *Imago Temporis: Medium Aevum* 3 (2009): 189–204.

McLaren, Anne. "Monogamy, Polygamy and the True State: James I's Rhetoric of Empire." *History of Political Thought* 25, no. 3 (2004): 446–80.

McMullan, Gordon. *The Politics of Unease in the Plays of John Fletcher*. Amherst: University of Massachusetts Press, 1994.

McWhorter, Ladelle. "Sex, Race, and Biopower: A Foucauldian Genealogy." *Hypatia* 19, no. 3 (2004): 38–62.

Meer, Theo van der. "Medieval Prostitution and the Case of a (Mistaken?) Sexual Identity." *Journal of Women's History* 11, no. 2 (1999): 178–85.

———. "Sodom's Seed in the Netherlands: The Emergence of Homosexuality in the Early Modern Period." *Journal of Homosexuality* 34, no. 1 (1997): 1–16.

Melman, Billie. *Women's Orients: English Women and the Middle East, 1718–1918*. Ann Arbor: University of Michigan Press, 1992.

Mercer, Kobena, and Isaac Julien. "Race, Sexual Politics and Black Masculinity: A Dossier." In *Male Order: Unwrapping Masculinity*, ed. Rowena Chapman and Jonathan Rutherford. London: Lawrence & Wishart, 1988, 97–164.

Metlitzki, Dorothee. *The Matter of Araby in Medieval England*. New Haven, CT: Yale University Press, 1977.

Mickle, William J., trans. *The Lusiad; or, The Discovery of India. An Epic Poem. Translated from the Portuguese of Luis de Camoëns*. London, 1877.

Miller, Charles. *Black Borneo*. New York: Modern Age Books, 1942.

Miller, Leo. *Milton Among the Poligamophiles*. New York: Loewenthal Press, 1974.

Milton, Giles. *Nathaniel's Nutmeg or, The True and Incredible Adventures of the Spice Trader Who Changed the Course of History*. New York: Farrar, Straus and Giroux, 1999.

Mir, Miguel. "Estudio literario sobre el doctor Bartolomé Leonardo de Argensola." In Bartolomé Leonardo de Argensola, *Conquista de las Islas Malucas al Rey Felipe Tercero Nuestro Señor*. Zaragoza, 1891, xvii–cl.

Monta, Susannah B. *Martyrdom and Literature in Early Modern England.* Cambridge: Cambridge University Press, 2005.

Monter, E. William. "Sodomy and Heresy in Early Modern Switzerland." *Journal of Homosexuality* 6, nos. 1–2 (1980): 41–55.

Montrose, Louis. "The Work of Gender in the Discourse of Discovery." *Representations* 33 (1991): 1–41.

Mott, Luiz R. B. *Escravidão, Homossexualidade e Demonologia.* São Paulo: Icone, 1988.

———. "Justitia et misericordia: A Inquisição portuguesa e a repressão ao nefando pecado de sodomia." In *Inquisição: Ensaios sobre mentalidade, heresias e arte,* ed. Anita Novinsky and Maria Luiza Tucci Carneiro. São Paulo: EDUSP, 1992, 703–38.

———. *O sexo proibido: Virgens, gays e escravos nas garras da Inquisição.* Campina: Papirus, 1988.

Moulton, Ian F. *Before Pornography: Erotic Writing in Early Modern England.* Oxford: Oxford University Press, 2000.

Nabuco, Joaquim. *Camões: Discurso pronunciado a 10 de Junho de 1880.* Rio de Janeiro: Biblioteca Nacional, 1980.

Neill, Michael. "'Mulattos,' 'Blacks,' and 'Indian Moors': *Othello* and Early Modern Constructions of Human Difference." *Shakespeare Quarterly* 49, no. 4 (1998): 361–74.

———. *Putting History to the Question: Power, Politics, and Society in English Renaissance Drama.* New York: Columbia University Press, 2002.

Neill, Stephen. *A History of Christianity in India: The Beginnings to* AD *1707.* Cambridge: Cambridge University Press, 1984.

Newman, Karen. "'And Wash the Ethiop White': Femininity and the Monstrous in *Othello.*" In *Shakespeare Reproduced: The Text in History and Ideology,* ed. Jean E. Howard and Marion F. O'Connor. New York: Methuen, 1987, 143–62.

Nirenberg, David. "Mass Conversion and Genealogical Mentalities: Jews and Christians in Fifteenth-Century Spain." *Past and Present* 174 (2002): 3–41.

Nocentelli, Carmen. "The Erotics of Mercantile Imperialism: Cross-cultural Requitedness in the Early Modern Period." *Journal for Early Modern Cultural Studies* 8, no. 1 (2008): 134–52.

———. "Spice Race: *The Island Princess* and the Politics of Transnational Appropriation." *PMLA* 125, no. 3 (2010): 572–88.

Noordam, Dirk Jaap. "Sodomy in the Dutch Republic, 1600–1725." In *The Pursuit of Sodomy: Male Homosexuality in Renaissance and Enlightenment Europe,* ed. Kent Gerard and Gert Hekma. New York: Harrington Park Press, 1989, 207–28.

Onishi, Yoichi. "In Quest of National Solidarity: Gender and Empire in John Dryden's *Amboyna*." *Shiron* 35 (1996): 1–18.

Orr, Bridget. *Empire on the English Stage*. Cambridge: Cambridge University Press, 2001.

Pagden, Anthony. *Lords of All the World: Ideologies of Empire in Spain, Britain and France c. 1500–c. 1800*. New Haven, CT: Yale University Press, 1995.

Parker, Geoffrey. "Europe and the Wider World, 1500–1750: The Military Balance." In *The Political Economy of Merchant Empires: State Power and World Trade, 1350–1750*, ed. James D. Tracy. Cambridge: Cambridge University Press, 1991, 161–95.

Parker, Grant. "*Ex Oriente Luxuria*: Indian Commodities and Roman Experience." *Journal of Economic and Social History of the Orient* 45, no. 1 (2002): 40–95.

Parker, Patricia. "Preposterous Conversions: Turning Turk and Its Pauline Righting." *Journal for Early Modern Cultural Studies* 2, no. 1 (2002): 1–34.

Parr, Charles McKew. *Jan van Linschoten: The Dutch Marco Polo*. New York: Thomas Y. Crowell, 1964.

Pearson, Michael N. *The Portuguese in India*. Cambridge: Cambridge University Press, 1987.

Penny, Frank. *The Church in Madras: Being the History of the Ecclesiastical and Missionary Action of the East India Company in the Presidency of Madras in the Seventeenth and Eighteenth Centuries*. Vol. 1. London: Smith and Elder, 1904.

Perry, Mary E. *Gender and Disorder in Early Modern Seville*. Princeton, NJ: Princeton University Press, 1990.

———. "The 'Nefarious Sin' in Early Modern Seville." In *The Pursuit of Sodomy: Male Homosexuality in Renaissance and Enlightenment Europe*, ed. Kent Gerard and Gert Hekma. New York: Harrington Park Press, 1989, 67–89.

Phang, Sara E. *The Marriage of Roman Soldiers, 13 B.C.–A.D. 235: Law and Family in the Imperial Army*. Leiden: Brill, 2001.

Phelan, John L. *The Hispanization of the Philippines: Spanish Aims and Filipino Responses, 1565–1700*. Madison: University of Wisconsin Press, 1959.

Phillips, Richard. *Sex, Politics and Empire: A Postcolonial Geography*. Manchester: University of Manchester Press, 2006.

Pierce, Frank. "The Place of Mythology in the *Lusiads*." *Comparative Literature* 6 (1954): 97–122.

Pissurlencar, Panduronga, ed. *Roteiro dos Arquivos da Índia Portuguesa*. Bastorá: Rangel, 1955.

Plane, Ann Marie. *Colonial Intimacies: Indian Marriage in Early New England*. Ithaca, NY: Cornell University Press, 2000.

Poska, Allyson M. "When Bigamy Is the Charge: Gallegan Women in the Holy Office." In *Women in the Inquisition: Spain and the New World*, ed. Mary E. Giles. Baltimore: Johns Hopkins University Press, 1999, 189–205.

Potter, Lois. "Pirates and Turning Turk in Renaissance Drama." In *Travel and Drama in Shakespeare's Time*, ed. Jean-Pierre Maquerlot and Michèle Williams. Cambridge: Cambridge University Press, 1996, 124–40.

Povinelli, Elizabeth A. *The Empire of Love: Toward a Theory of Intimacy, Genealogy, and Carnality*. Durham, NC: Duke University Press, 2006.

Prakash, Om. *The Dutch East India Company and the Economy of Bengal, 1630–1720*. Princeton, NJ: Princeton University Press, 1984.

Price, Curtis, and Robert D. Hume, eds. *The Island Princess: A Semi-Opera*. Tunbridge Wells: Richard Macnutt, 1985.

Puff, Helmut. *Sodomy in Reformation Germany and Switzerland, 1400–1600*. Chicago: University of Chicago Press, 2003.

Quint, David. *Epic and Empire: Politics and Generic Form from Virgil to Milton*. Princeton, NJ: Princeton University Press, 1993.

Quirino, Carlos, and Mauro Garcia, trans. and eds. "The Manners, Customs and Beliefs of the Philippine Inhabitants of Long Ago." *Philippines Journal of Science* 87, no. 4 (1958): 324–449.

Rabinow, Paul. *French Modern: Norms and Forms of the Social Environment*. Cambridge, MA: Massachusetts Institute of Technology Press, 1989.

Radding, Cynthia. "The Común, Local Governance, and Defiance in Colonial Sonora." In *Choice, Persuasion, and Coercion: Social Control on Spain's North American Frontiers*, ed. Jesús F. de la Teja and Ross Frank. Albuquerque: University of New Mexico Press, 2005, 179–200.

Raman, Shankar. *Framing "India": The Colonial Imaginary in Early Modern Culture*. Stanford, CA: Stanford University Press, 2001.

Rawlings, Helen. *The Spanish Inquisition*. Malden, MA: Blackwell, 2006.

Reeser, Todd. *Moderating Masculinity in Early Modern Culture*. Chapel Hill: University of North Carolina Press, 2006.

Reid, Anthony. *Charting the Shape of Early Modern Southeast Asia*. Bangkok: Silkworm, 1999.

———. "Islamization and Christianization in Southeast Asia: The Critical Phase, 1550–1650." In *Southeast Asia in the Early Modern Era: Trade, Power, and Belief*, ed. Anthony Reid. Ithaca, NY: Cornell University Press, 1993, 151–79.

———. *Southeast Asia in the Age of Commerce, 1450–1680*. New Haven, CT: Yale University Press, 1992.

Rice, Warner G. "To Turn Turk." *Modern Language Notes* 46, no. 3 (1931): 153–54.

Rocke, Michael. *Forbidden Friendships: Homosexuality and Male Culture in Renaissance Florence.* Oxford: Oxford University Press, 1996.

———. "Gender and Sexual Culture in Renaissance Italy." In *Gender and Society in Renaissance Italy,* ed. Judith C. Brown and Robert C. Davis. New York: Longman, 1998, 150–70.

Roper, Lyndal. "Sexual Utopianism in the German Reformation." *Journal of Ecclesiastical History* 42, no. 3 (1991): 394–418.

Rosenthal, Laura J. *Infamous Commerce: Prostitution in Eighteenth-Century British Literature and Culture.* Ithaca, NY: Cornell University Press, 2006.

Rowenchilde, Raven. "Male Genital Modification." *Human Nature* 7, no. 2 (1996): 189–215.

Rubiés, Joan-Pau "New Worlds and Renaissance Ethnology." *History and Anthropology* 6, nos. 2–3 (1993): 157–97.

———. "Oriental Despotism and European Orientalism: Botero to Montesquieu." *Journal of Early Modern History* 9, nos. 1–2 (2005): 109–80.

———. "The Spanish Contribution to the Ethnology of Asia in the Sixteenth and Seventeenth Centuries." *Renaissance Studies* 17, no. 3 (2003): 418–48.

Ruggiero, Guido. *The Boundaries of Eros: Sex Crime and Sexuality in Renaissance Venice.* Oxford: Oxford University Press, 1985.

Salomon, Andrea R. "'A Wild Shambles of Strange Gods': The Conversion of Quisara in Fletcher's *The Island Princess.*" In *Christian Encounters with the Other,* ed. John C. Hawley. New York: New York University Press, 1998, 17–32.

Salzman, Paul. *English Prose Fiction, 1558–1700: A Critical History.* Oxford: Clarendon Press, 1985.

Scheidel, Walter. "A Peculiar Institution? Greco–Roman Monogamy in Global Context." *History of the Family* 14, no. 3 (2009): 280–91.

Schelling, Felix E. *Elizabethan Drama.* Vol. 2. Boston: Houghton Mifflin, 1908.

Schmidt, Benjamin. *Innocence Abroad: The Dutch Imagination and the New World, 1570–1670.* Cambridge: Cambridge University Press, 2001.

Sedgwick, Eve K. *Epistemology of the Closet.* Berkeley: University of California Press, 1990.

Seed, Patricia. *To Love, Honor, and Obey in Colonial Mexico: Conflicts over Marriage Choice, 1574–1821.* Stanford, CA: Stanford University Press, 1988.

Seltmann, Friedrich. "Palang and Pûjâ: An Analysis of Studies of the Use of Penis-Pins and Related Paraphernalia in Certain South east Asian Countries and an Initial Treatment of Their Former Ritualistic Use in Java." *Tribus: Jahrbuch des Linden-Museums* 24 (1975): 67–78.

Shapiro, James. *Shakespeare and the Jews.* New York: Columbia University Press, 1996.

Sibalis, Michael. "Homosexuality in Early Modern France." In *Queer Masculinities, 1550–1800: Siting Same-Sex Desire in the Early Modern World,* ed. Michael O' Rourke and Katherine O'Donnell. London: Palgrave, 2006, 211–31.

Sigal, Pete, ed. *Infamous Desire: Male Homosexuality in Colonial Latin America.* Chicago: University of Chicago Press, 2003.

Silva Gracias, Fátima da. *Kaleidoscope of Women in Goa, 1510–1961.* New Delhi: Concept, 1996.

Silva Rêgo, António da, ed. *Documentação para a história das missões do padroado português do Oriente: Índia.* 12 vols. Lisbon: Divisão de Publicações e Biblioteca, Agência Geral das Colónias/ do Ultramar, 1947–58.

———. *História das missões do padroado português do Oriente: Índia, 1500-1542.* Lisbon: Divisão de Publicações e Biblioteca, Agência Geral das Colónias, 1949.

———. *Portuguese Colonization in the Sixteenth Century: A Study of the Royal Ordinances.* Johannesburg: Witwaresrand University Press, 1965.

Silverblatt, Irene. "Honor, Sex, and Civilizing Missions in the Making of Seventeenth Century Peru." *Journal of the Steward Anthropological Society* 25, nos. 1–2 (1997): 181–98.

Smith, Bruce R. *Homosexual Desire in Shakespeare's England: A Cultural Poetics.* Chicago: University of Chicago Press, 1991.

Smith, Ian. *Race and Rhetoric in the Renaissance: Barbarian Errors.* New York: Palgrave Macmillan, 2009.

Soman, Alfred. "The Parliament of Paris and the Great Witch-Hunt." *Sixteenth Century Journal* 9, no. 2 (1978): 31–44.

Somerville, Siobhan. *Queering the Color Line.* Durham, NC: Duke University Press, 2000.

Spivak, Gayatri. "Three Women's Texts and a Critique of Imperialism." *Critical Inquiry* 12 (1985): 243–61.

Sprague, Arthur C. *Beaumont and Fletcher on the Restoration Stage.* Cambridge, MA: Harvard University Press, 1926.

Steenbrink, Karel. *Dutch Colonialism and Indonesian Islam: Contacts and Conflicts, 1596–1950.* Amsterdam: Rodopi, 1993.

Steensgaard, Niels. *The Asian Trade Revolution of the Seventeenth Century:*

The East India Companies and the Decline of the Caravan Trade. Chicago: University of Chicago Press, 1973.

Stephens, Henry Morse. *Albuquerque.* London, 1897.

Stevenson, Laura C. *Praise and Paradox: Merchants and Craftsmen in Elizabethan Popular Literature.* Cambridge: Cambridge University Press, 1984.

Stiefel, A. L. "Uber die Quelle von J. Fletcher's *Island Princess.*" *Archiv für das Studium der neueren Sprachen* 103 (1899): 277–308.

Stoler, Ann Laura. *Carnal Knowledge and Imperial Power: Race and the Intimate in Colonial Rule.* Berkeley: University of California Press, 2002.

———. "Making Empire Respectable: The Politics of Race and Sexual Morality in 20th-Century Colonial Cultures." *American Ethnologist* 16, no. 4 (1989): 634–60.

———. *Race and the Education of Desire: Foucault's* History of Sexuality *and the Colonial Order of Things.* Durham, NC: Duke University Press, 1995.

———. "Rethinking Colonial Categories: European Communities and the Boundaries of Rule," *Comparative Studies in Society and History* 31, no.1 (1989): 134–61.

Stone, Lawrence. *Family, Sex, and Marriage in England, 1500–1800.* New York: Harper and Row, 1977.

———. *The Past and Present Revisited.* London: Routledge and Kegan Paul, 1987.

Strachey, Ray, and Oliver Strachey. *Keigwin's Rebellion, (1683–4): An Episode in the History of Bombay.* Oxford: Clarendon Press, 1916.

Subrahmanyam, Sanjay. *The Portuguese Empire in Asia, 1500–1700: A Political and Economic History.* New York: Longman, 1993.

Taylor, Gary. *Buying Whiteness: Race, Culture, and Identity from Columbus to Hip Hop.* New York: Palgrave, 2005.

Taylor, Jean G. *The Social World of Batavia: European and Eurasian in Dutch Asia.* Madison: University of Wisconsin Press, 1983.

Teltscher, Kate. "'Maidenly and Well Nigh Effeminate': Constructions of Hindu Masculinity and Religion in Seventeenth-Century English Texts." *Postcolonial Studies* 3, no. 2 (2000): 159–70.

Terwiel, Barend Jan. "The Body and Sexuality in Siam: A First Exploration in Early Sources." *Manusya: Journal of Humanities* 14 (2007): 42–52.

Thomas, Keith. *Man and the Natural World: A History of Modern Sensibility.* New York: Pantheon, 1983.

Thompson, Ayanna. *Performing Race and Torture on the Early Modern Stage.* New York: Routledge, 2007.

Thompson, John L. "Patriarchs, Polygamy, and Private Resistance: John Calvin and Others on Breaking God's Rules." *Sixteenth Century Journal* 25, no. 1 (1994): 3–27.

Thornton, Tim. *Prophecy, Politics and the People in Early Modern England.* Woodbridge: Boydell & Brewer, 2006.

Tiele, Pieter Anton. Introduction to *The Voyage of John Juyghen van Linschoten to the East Indies: From the Old English Translation of 1598.* London, 1885, 1: xxiii–xlii.

Todd, Margo. *Christian Humanism and the Puritan Social Order.* Cambridge: Cambridge University Press, 1987.

Torrance, Robert M. "Se fantasticas são, se verdadeiras: The Gods of the *Lusiads* in the Isle of Love." *Modern Language Notes* 80, no. 2 (1965): 210–34.

Tortorici, Zeb. "'Heran Todos Putos': Sodomitical Subcultures and Disordered Desire in Early Colonial Mexico." *Ethnohistory* 54, no. 1 (2007): 35–67.

Traub, Valerie. *Desire and Anxiety: Circulations of Sexuality in Shakespearean Drama.* New York: Routledge, 1996.

———. "Mapping the Global Body." In *Early Modern Visual Culture: Representation, Race, and Empire in Renaissance England,* ed. Peter Erickson and Clark Hulse. Philadelphia: University of Pennsylvania Press, 2000, 44–97.

———. *The Renaissance of Lesbianism in Early Modern England.* Cambridge: Cambridge University Press, 2002.

Trexler, Richard. *Sex and Conquest: Gendered Violence, Political Order, and the European Conquest of the Americas.* Ithaca, NY: Cornell University Press, 1995.

Truman, James C. W. "John Foxe and the Desires of Reformation Martyrology." *ELH* 70, no.1 (2003): 35–66.

Trumbach, Randolph. "The Birth of the Queen: Sodomy and the Emergence of Gender Equality in Modern Culture, 1660–1750." In *Hidden from History: Reclaiming the Gay and Lesbian Past,* ed. Martin B. Duberman, Martha Vicinus, and George Chauncey. New York: Penguin, 1990, 129–40.

Van den Boogaart, Ernst. *Civil and Corrupt Asia: Image and Text in the* Itinerario *and the* Icones *of Jan Huygen van Linschoten.* Chicago: University of Chicago Press, 2003.

———, ed. *Jan Huygen van Linschoten and the Moral Map of Asia: The Plates and Text of the* Itinerario *and* Icones, habitus gestusque indorum ac lusitanorum per Indiam viventium. London: Roxburghe Club, 1999.

Vasvári, Louise O. *The Heterotextual Body of the Mora Morilla.* London: Queen Mary and Westfield College, 1999.

Vaughan, Virginia M. *Performing Blackness on English Stages.* Cambridge: Cambridge University Press, 2005.

Villiers, John. "The Estado da Índia in Southeast Asia." In *The First Portuguese Colonial Empire,* ed. Malyn Newitt. Exeter: University of Exeter Press, 1986, 37–67.

———. "'A Truthful Pen and an Impartial Spirit': Bartolomé Leonardo de Argensola and the *Conquista de las Islas Malucas.*" *Renaissance Studies* 17, no. 3 (2003): 449–73.

Visser, Colin. "John Dryden's *Amboyna* at Lincoln's Inn Fields, 1673." *Restoration and Eighteenth Century Theatre Research* 15, no. 1 (1976): 1–11.

Vitkus, Daniel J. "Early Modern Orientalism: Representations of Islam in Sixteenth- and Seventeenth-Century Europe." In *Western Views of Islam in Medieval and Early Modern Europe,* ed. D. Blanks and M. Frassetto. New York: St. Martin's Press, 1999, 207–30.

———. *Turning Turk: English Theater and the Multicultural Mediterranean, 1570-1630.* New York: Palgrave, 2003.

Vogel, Ursula. "Political Philosophers and the Trouble with Polygamy: Patriarchal Reasoning in Modern Natural Law." *History of Political Thought* 12, no. 2 (1991): 229–51.

Voltaire, François-Marie Arouet de. "Essai sur la poésie épique." In *Oeuvres complètes de Voltaire.* Paris, 1828, 13: 429–533.

Warren, F. M. "The Enamoured Moslem Princess in Orderic Vital and the French Epic." *PMLA* 29, no. 3 (1914): 341–58.

Watson, Ian B. *Foundation for Empire: English Private Trade in India, 1659–1760.* New Delhi: Vikas, 1980.

Watt, Ian. *The Rise of the Novel: Studies in Defoe, Richardson and Fielding.* Berkeley: University of California Press, 1957.

Weever, Jacqueline de. *Sheba's Daughters: Whitening and Demonizing the Saracen Woman in Medieval French Epic.* New York: Garland, 1998.

Welle, J. A. van der. *Dryden and Holland.* Groningen: J. B. Wolters, 1962.

Wheeler, J. Talboys. *Madras in the Olden Time: Being a History of the Presidency from the First Foundation of Fort St. George to the French Occupation of Madras.* Madras, 1862.

White, Helen C. *Tudor Books of Martyrs.* Madison: University of Wisconsin Press, 1963.

White, Landeg. "Explanatory Notes." In Luis Vaz de Camões, *The Lusíads,* trans. Landeg White. Oxford: Oxford University Press, 1997, 229–58.

Whitehead, Neil L., Peter Sigal, and John F. Chuchiak, eds. "Sexual Encounters/Sexual Collisions: Alternative Sexualities in Colonial Mesoamerica." Special issue of *Ethnohistory* 54, no. 1 (2007).

Wicki, Josef. "Duas cartas oficiais de Vice-Reis da Índia, escritas em 1561 e 1564." *Studia* 3 (1959): 36–89.

Wiesner-Hanks, Merry E. *Christianity and Sexuality in the Early Modern World: Regulating Desire, Reforming Practice.* London: Routledge, 2000.

Williams, Raymond. *The Country and the City.* New York: Oxford University Press, 1973.

Wilson, Edward M. "Did Fletcher Read Spanish?" *Philological Quarterly* 27, no. 2 (1948): 187–90.

Winius, George D. *The Black Legend of Portuguese India: Diogo do Couto, His Contemporaries and the 'Soldado Prático.'* New Delhi: Concept, 1985.

———. "The Portuguese Asian 'Decadência' Revisited." In *Empire in Transition: The Portuguese World in the Time of Camões,* ed. Alfred Hower and Richard A. Preto-Rodas. Gainesville: University of Florida Press, 1985, 106–17.

Winn, James A. *John Dryden and His World.* New Haven, CT: Yale University Press, 1987.

Wolfthal, Diane. *Images of Rape: The "Heroic Tradition" and Its Alternatives.* Cambridge: Cambridge University Press, 1999.

Yeazell, Ruth B. *Harems of the Mind: Passages of Western Art and Literature.* New Haven, CT: Yale University Press, 2000.

Yule, Henry. *Hobson-Jobson: A Glossary of Colloquial Anglo-Indian Words and Phrases, and of Kindred Terms, Etymological, Historical, Geographical and Discursive.* Ed. William Crooke. Delhi: Munshiram Manoharlal, 1968.

Zahorca, Herwig. "The Palang Phenomenon and Its Historic and Socio-Cultural Background in Southeast Asia." *Tribus: Jahrbuch des Linden-Museums* 53 (2004): 185–202.

Županov, Ines G. "Lust, Marriage and Free Will: Jesuit Critique of Paganism in South India (Seventeenth Century)," *Studies in History* 16, no. 2 (2000): 199–220.

INDEX

Page numbers in italics refer to images.

ACKNOWLEDGMENTS

This book could not have been written without the help and encouragement of many smart people. First among them are my Stanford mentors, colleagues, and friends, who helped me venture into uncharted waters and trusted me to know where I was going. Stephen Orgel has been a pillar of support and a constant source of inspiration. The depth of his insights and the elegance of his prose are the stars by which I have set my course. Sepp Gumbrecht, whose encyclopedic knowledge is matched only by his generosity, showed me what it means to navigate multiple languages and cultures with aplomb. Roland Greene and Paula Findlen were the most attentive and astute of readers. Ania Loomba first emboldened me to look east; Patricia Parker offered wisdom and encouragement at different junctures. Courtney Quaintance read almost every word I wrote, tracked down phantom sources, and generously indulged my weakness for Southeast Asian maps. Barbara Fuchs pointed me to key critical sources, Anston Bosman verified my translations from Dutch, and Edmund Campos was a patient listener and the most sympathetic of respondents.

Many other readers and audiences provided welcome critique and advice. A Renaissance seminar at the University of Chicago and a symposium at Stanford University were especially helpful in revising Chapters 1 and 2. I thank Richard Strier, Suzanne Gossett, and Michael Wyatt for inviting me, and audience members Valerie Traub, David Nirenberg, Steven Mullaney, and Bradin Cormack for their thoughtful and thought-provoking responses. Several generous interlocutors offered opportunities for public conversation and engagement: Anita Obermeier (Feminist Research Institute, 2006), William J. Kennedy (Renaissance Society of America, 2008), Walter Cohen (Group for Early Modern Cultural Studies, 2008), Carla Zecher and

Megan Moore (Newberry Library, 2009), and Lisa Voigt and Pedro Pereira (Ohio State University, 2012). It is with immense gratitude that I acknowledge them here.

At the University of New Mexico, I have enjoyed the active interest and support of colleagues from across departments: Walter Putnam, Gail Houston, Raji Vallury, Gary Harrison, Aeron Hunt, Susanne Baackmann, Marissa Greenberg, Monica Cyrino, Helen Damico, Natasha Kolchevska, Jesse Alemán, Osman Umurhan, Rebecca Schreiber, Jennifer Denetdale, Alyosha Goldstein, and Patricia Risso. I am particularly thankful for the sustaining friendships of Carolyn Woodward, whose enthusiasm for this project kept mine stoked, and of Pamela Cheek, whose acuity and advice inform more than one chapter.

Several grants and fellowships enabled me to do research and gave me time for writing. I am especially grateful to the Huntington Library for the summer I spent in its idyllic surroundings, and to the University of New Mexico for three generous grants that supported research at the British Library (London), the Archivum Romanum Societatis Iesu (Rome), and the Biblioteca Apostolica Vaticana (Vatican City). A substantial portion of the book was written at the Newberry Library, where I had the good fortune to be an Audrey Lumsden-Kouvel Fellow in 2006 and a National Endowment for the Humanities Fellow in 2008–2009. The manuscript has benefited greatly from the dedication of the Special Collections Library staff, the generosity of Paul F. Gehl and John S. Aubrey, and the critical engagement of Newberry fellows Rita Costa-Gomes, Sarah Burns, Natalie Rothman, Holly Pickett, Renzo Baldasso, Barry D. Sell, David Karmon, and Barbara Naddeo. Special thanks go to Jim Grossman, for his interest and encouragement, to Ed Muir, for his guidance and friendship, and to Diana Robin, whose warmth and energy made my year in Chicago one of the happiest ever.

Heartfelt thanks also go to Jerry Singerman, who championed this book from the beginning, and to the anonymous press readers, whose good suggestions helped clarify and strengthen parts of the argument. The editorial staffs at the University of Pennsylvania Press and the Modern Language Initiative have been unfailingly patient, helpful, and efficient. For all their work, I am truly grateful.

Small sections of Chapters 5 and 6 have appeared in *PMLA*, *The Journal of Early Modern Cultural Studies*, and *Indography: Writing the "Indian" in Early Modern England*, ed. Jonathan Gil Harris.

An early version of Chapter 3 was published as part of *Rereading the Black Legend: The Discourses of Religious and Racial Difference in the Renaissance Empires*, ed. Margaret R. Greer, Walter D. Mignolo, and Maureen Quilligan. © 2007 by the University of Chicago Press. All rights reserved.

My parents, Franca Prestia and Alberico Nocentelli, and my siblings, Emanuele and Serena, always remind me that life is not only about work while respecting the time needed for work. My debts to them are too deep and numerous to detail here, but they are always present in my thoughts. My deepest and greatest debt, however, is to Sam Truett, partner in crime and publicist extraordinaire, whose intellectual curiosity, practical wisdom, and passion for life are the winds that carry me forward.